AF228254

ADDISON MIZNER

ADDISON MIZNER

The Architect Whose Genius Defined Palm Beach

STEPHEN PERKINS
JAMES CAUGHMAN
Photography by Craig Kuhner

LYONS PRESS
GUILFORD, CONNECTICUT

For Martha and Dede

An imprint of Globe Pequot

Distributed by NATIONAL BOOK NETWORK

Copyright © 2018 by Stephen Perkins and James Caughman

British Library Cataloguing in Publication Information Available

Library of Congress Cataloging-in-Publication Data

Names: Perkins, Stephen, 1950- author. | Caughman, James, 1947- author.
Title: Addison Mizner : the architect whose genius defined Palm Beach /
   Stephen Perkins and James Caughman.
Description: Guilford, Connecticut: Lyons Press, 2018. | Includes
   bibliographical references and index.
Identifiers: LCCN 2017047411 (print) | LCCN 2017047833 (ebook) | ISBN
   9781493026562 (e-book) | ISBN 9781493026555 (hardback : alk. paper)
Subjects: LCSH: Mizner, Addison, 1872-1933. | Architects—United
   States—Biography.
Classification: LCC NA737.M59 (ebook) | LCC NA737.M59 P47 2018 (print) | DDC
   720.92 [B]—dc23
LC record available at https://lccn.loc.gov/2017047411

♾™ The paper used in this publication meets the minimum requirements of American National Standard for Information Sciences—Permanence of Paper for Printed Library Materials, ANSI/NISO Z39.48-1992.

Printed in India

CONTENTS

CHAPTER ONE: "I Josh and I Paint" 1

CHAPTER TWO: California Pioneers 19

CHAPTER THREE: "The Greatest Day of My Life" 27

CHAPTER FOUR: Path to Architecture 45

CHAPTER FIVE: Miner, Painter, Writer, Fighter 63

CHAPTER SIX: Extravagance and Display 79

CHAPTER SEVEN: "Friends in High Places" 89

CHAPTER EIGHT: Ambition and Architecture 101

CHAPTER NINE: The Perfect Setting 125

CHAPTER TEN: A Moorish Tower 145

CHAPTER ELEVEN: Society Architect 161

CHAPTER TWELVE: An Entrepreneur 221

CHAPTER THIRTEEN: The Greatest Resort in the World 239

CHAPTER FOURTEEN: Rebirth and Recognition 269

CHAPTER FIFTEEN: Master Builder 307

ENDNOTES 323

BIBLIOGRAPHY 333

INDEX 342

ACKNOWLEDGMENTS 352

"I JOSH AND I PAINT"

On a gray day, late in the afternoon of February 9, 1933, hundreds of people were making their way to Worth Avenue in Palm Beach to honor the life of a dear friend who had passed away only four days earlier. The rain that washed over the resort city would generally be interpreted as an appropriate symbol for a day of mourning; however, this memorial service that attracted so many people could only be a celebration. Unacquainted with sentimentality, Addison Mizner had specified in his will that there be no funeral service, that his ashes be buried without fanfare in California. Aware of Addison Mizner's wishes, his friends still insisted on a secular service to honor their special companion, always an indefatigable source of warmth and wit and forever the inimitable author of architectural beauty.

Addison Mizner was known as a society architect who adapted the Mediterranean Revival style to the climate and topography of South Florida. By designing houses to accommodate the social requirements of his clientele, he transformed the Palm Beach lifestyle from one of regulated activity centered around Henry Flagler's hotels to a more relaxed, informal manner of living focused on personal entertaining. His architecture still defines Palm Beach.
Courtesy of Historical Society of Palm Beach County.

Many visitors that day were already familiar with their destination; those who had never been inside the Villa Mizner would happily find a home that reflected with absolute fidelity the nature and interests of the man they had come to commemorate. The living room, although very large, was insufficient to accommodate the throng of guests, necessitating many to gather in the vaulted foyer and on the tiled steps leading to the main floor. The remarkable feature of this congregation was its diversity, from friends and clients of high social station to laborers and artisans of the working class. Addison Mizner knew well the difference between the two but possessed the gift of sincerely liking both. His attraction to a person was governed less by social position and more by individual character and skill, a point of view that created disparate associations throughout his colorful life. In this setting, people who would ordinarily not share the same space were united in admiration and appreciation for a remarkable friend.

Addison's living room was a window into his capacious mind. Spanish furniture and carvings from the sixteenth and seventeenth centuries, large tapestries, and a collection of crucifixes that had been displayed at the Boston Museum of Fine Arts blended with terra cotta floor tiles, wrought iron chandeliers, and a dramatic beamed ceiling to reflect his powerful affinity for the noble charm of Old Spain and its colonies. These personal objects were outlined on the rainy afternoon by a soft, pale light diffused through the stained glass of three Moorish windows. The dim glow that washed over the room created an effect redolent of the Old World, of a distant time that was so familiar to Addison Mizner. The guests were witnessing the material biography of the home's owner.

The living room and foyer were also filled with the fragrance of hundreds of flowers, gifts from tradesmen as well as the social elite. One leader of Palm Beach sending flowers was his friend and client Mrs. Edward "Eva" Stotesbury. So congested was Villa Mizner that "Queen Eva," as Addison playfully called her as a result of her social prominence, had to stand with her husband in the foyer outside the crowded living room. She recognized early Addison's towering talent and was the first to offer him a residential commission in Palm Beach in 1919. Excusing herself to push into the great room, she wanted to verify that her orange blossoms were resting on Addison's favorite chair.

Although the service was devotional and not religious, Addison's good friend, the Reverend Nathaniel Seymour Thomas, opened with a prayer. He then read passages of poetry from

Living Room, Villa Mizner, 1924. The gathering place for Addison's memorial service, the large living room featured the Spanish furniture, tapestries, and antiquities that so captivated the architect. The stained glass, wrought iron chandeliers, terra cotta floor tiles, and architectural stonework were all made in the workshops of Mizner Industries, a collection of artisanal manufactories begun by Mizner.
Photograph by Frank E. Geisler reproduced by Craig Kuhner.

the Romantics who, like Addison himself, created expressive works through richness of imagery and description. Each selection of verse spoke to a prominent attribute of the architect. In reading from Percy Bysshe Shelley's *Adonaïs*, the poignant lament composed for the dead John Keats, Thomas suggested the timelessness of Addison's architectural legacy:

> Forget the Past, his fate and fame shall be
> An echo and a light unto eternity![1]

He also read from Shelley's *Prometheus Unbound*, likening the creative architect to the mythical figure who gave humanity fire, the symbol representing the imaginative powers of thought. Finally, he read from Alfred Lord Tennyson's *Crossing the Bar* in which the poet reminds friends to have a placid attitude toward death and not to lament his passing. This was a reminder to all present that Addison Mizner reveled in life, even in its darkest moments, and wished his friends to celebrate him, not to mourn his passing.

While the literary references employed to memorialize Addison would have been familiar to him, it was the simple story that he considered the most powerful form of expression. Addison Mizner had always possessed the capacity to tell a story that allowed him to captivate and enchant. Mizner was an alchemist for whom words, reality, and imagination were transmuted into fascinating mixtures. It would have pleased Mizner greatly to know that, at his memorial service, many people told funny anecdotes about him while others read aloud complimentary telegrams and letters.

If relating stories of individuals prolongs their life, Mizner survives today, for he enjoyed an adventurous, creative, and picaresque life. His was an unconfined existence that gave birth to unforgettable tales, some authentic and some apocryphal. What is unmistakable and unambiguous is his astonishing architectural vision that transformed Palm Beach into a vaunted, picturesque resort community. For this raconteur, each villa that he designed told a personal story about its owner and, in a broader sense, conveyed a vivid sense of history. Just like the stories he loved to tell, his architectural narratives are rich, evocative, and timeless.

❖ ❖ ❖

Posterity remembers Addison Mizner as an architect. Like most simple attributions, "architect" fails to convey the nuanced contours of a complex man who was the rare synthesis of pioneer stock, ancient taste, and innovative vision. Addison Mizner was a bold and robust character, the descendent of pioneer families who, in their pursuit of a better life, consistently overcame challenge and adversity to settle in California before

1850. The personal qualities that allowed Mizner to thrive and persevere in his adventurous life were a by-product of this frontier spirit. The itinerant, unpredictable journey of becoming one of America's most innovative architects in the early twentieth century would have been impossible for an individual deficient in enterprise and courage. Unfamiliar with idleness and uncomfortable in repose, Mizner was a spirited seeker.

As a young man, Mizner roamed the world. His early years were filled with the kind of exotic escapades that could only be found in adventure novels. He was born in 1872 and grew up in a pioneer family in Benicia, California, a small town just north of San Francisco. As the second youngest of eight children, he quickly learned the art of survival and developed the ability to think quickly, well, and creatively. At the age of sixteen, he traveled all over Central America during the time his father held an ambassadorial post in Guatemala and, three years later, went to Spain with the intention of pursuing university studies. In the last five years of the century, he practiced architecture in San Francisco, contributed to an avant-garde periodical, and successfully prospected for gold in the Yukon. Before turning thirty-one in 1903, he had traveled throughout Hawaii, Samoa, Australia, and China cleverly supporting himself variously as an art restorer, writer of epigrams, boxer, and artist, none of which he could have claimed to practice professionally before the voyage.

Drawing by Addison Mizner. At the age of fifteen, Mizner moved to Guatemala after his father had been appointed ambassador by President Benjamin Harrison. There, he lived an adventurous life, became fluent in Spanish, and cultivated a love of Hispanic architecture. Throughout his life, he drew interesting details of furniture and architecture that he would later incorporate into his designs. Of interest to him here was the pairing of a low roof line with a carved stone entrance facade of important scale.
Drawing courtesy of the Society of the Four Arts. Photograph by Craig Kuhner.

Just as America had defined its continental frontiers during the forty years between the Mizners' arrival in California and Addison's travels in the Pacific, the future architect had clearly developed his own boundaries that enclosed a wellspring of qualities essential to his future success. Frontiersmen, continuously challenged by harsh conditions and deprivation, were forced to sharpen their wits and instincts merely to survive. Like his forebears, Mizner consistently used an elastic mind to devise solutions through tenacity and resourcefulness, characteristics that largely defined his life.

Addison Mizner was indefatigable and happiest when in motion. Setting out in late 1897 to join three of his brothers in a quest for gold, Mizner continually bore the brunt of physical labor that exhausted his siblings, causing them to retire from the demanding venture. Finding other partners, he led them in a sustained effort in harsh conditions that resulted in a discovery of the precious metal. In the course of this undertaking, he single-handedly put down a rebellion of his partners, designed and built a cabin, and handled the lion's share of the mining work. In 1925, while in the process of developing his grand vision for the "perfect city" of Boca Raton, he suddenly found himself in severe financial difficulty due to a real estate bubble. While other developers in similar circumstances had ceased fulfilling their construction obligations, Mizner persevered. Ignoring declining market conditions, he not only designed complete plans for a city of sixteen hundred acres but also completed construction of various buildings including a luxury hotel, two administration buildings, a city hall, and many smaller houses, all in a little more than a year.[2] It was Mizner's lifelong habit to follow conception with furious, focused activity.

Another feature of the pioneer spirit that greatly benefitted Addison Mizner was his resourcefulness. He simply refused to allow challenges to stand in his way. This outlook animated a protean individual, one who was able to identify possibilities and to re-invent himself to conform to whatever mold was required. This is aptly illustrated by his manifold vocations. Among the occupations attributed to him in his early adult life were traveler, wit, bon vivant, bohemian, prospector, capitalist, and promoter; later, he was professionally recognized as an architect, artist, landscape architect, builder, interior designer, and connoisseur. Within his great frame resided the wherewithal to do many things well, not because he had received formal training in them but because his agile mind provided ready analysis and comprehension.

While Addison Mizner is remembered primarily as a creator, he was also an entrepreneur and skilled developer of artisans. Creativity and logic do not usually reside in equal measure in the same individual, but their coexistence in Mizner allowed him to conceive grand architectural schemes

Arthur D. Claflin House, 1923. Addison Mizner designed large architectural projects and simultaneously managed every facet of the construction and installation process, from creating building materials to furnishing the interiors and landscaping the grounds. Mizner was also highly skilled in his use of color. The blues and greens of nature contrast well with the subtle pastels of the exterior and the variegated reds of the roof tiles.
Photograph by Craig Kuhner.

and simultaneously manage the myriad business processes necessary to realize them: creating materials and finishes, overseeing construction, furnishing the interiors, and landscaping the grounds. Efficiency was essential considering that there were many projects of grand scale underway at the same time and each project had to be completed within the condensed period of time between Palm Beach winter seasons. Beyond the exigencies of design, construction, and logistics, Mizner also had to manage client relations and develop new business.

Due to national and regional circumstances when he began his Palm Beach career in 1918, Mizner was forced to overcome a dearth of human and material resources in the construction business. With the United States still involved in World War I, construction materials were restricted and residential building materials were virtually nonexistent. South Florida was also deficient in skilled labor because of the sparse population, the absence of regional residential construction, and the military necessity for able men to serve in the armed forces. To meet the phenomenal demands of his architectural practice, Mizner was forced to develop his own skilled artisans and to start various businesses to produce sophisticated building materials and furnishings. Considering the conditions, all of this would have been a daunting task for anyone, much less for a novice entrepreneur whose primary business was his architectural practice.

Among Addison Mizner's greatest gifts that fed into his success as an innovative architect were a burning curiosity, highly refined visual acuity, and generative imagination. This trinity of attributes was especially useful for an individual who, by temperament and circumstance, was not meant to have a conventional education. Mizner experienced a varied and disjointed brush with formal education that produced little satisfaction; however, he thrived outside the groves of academe as a result of a mind that was highly receptive to artistic conception. Enraptured by Hispanic culture, he benefitted from passion and curiosity to attain a high level of expertise and connoisseurship.

Mizner's spirit of inquiry was catholic. Not confining himself solely to the pursuit of artistic ideas, he also developed a profound appreciation for materials and an expert comprehension of the building trades. At the age of twenty-one, he began an almost three-year association with Willis Jefferson Polk, a noted San Francisco architect, first serving as an apprentice and then as a partner. Not only did Mizner learn the principles and practice of architecture but, due to Polk's comprehensive understanding of all facets of building, he became a master who could lay brick, pour concrete, and glaze windows. As a result of this artisanal knowledge, Mizner was more than an architect; he became a master builder, a designation used in the Middle Ages to describe the immensely talented individual charged with the responsibility of both designing and building imposing cathedrals and palaces.

Reinforcing his intellectual curiosity was a keen ability to perceive and analyze aesthetic ideas and concepts. Many become technically proficient in the arts through patient study; however, few possess the capacity to see. Such a remarkable keenness was an innate gift that readily allowed him to apprehend with clarity what remained obscure to others. With a photographic memory that absorbed everything from fine detail to spatial relationships, he was able to process logically both the concrete and abstract. While appreciating the beauty of a building, he could naturally perceive the relationship between various parts and the whole as well as the correlation between the whole and its surroundings. Not surprisingly, he was captivated not only by architecture but by the attendant disciplines of interior design and landscape architecture. These three specialties, harmoniously aligned, informed the holistic approach to design that characterized his work.

Throughout his professional life, he collected postcards and photographs of the places he saw—castles, palaces, churches, fountains, furniture, sculpture, moldings, gardens, landscapes, and cityscapes—and glued them into scrapbooks. This trove of visual reference filled twenty-five volumes that served as a personal canon of architecture, landscape, and decorative arts. Over the years, colleagues were continuously amazed at his power of recall: a detail on a Spanish building long ago discovered or a piece of furniture fleetingly appreciated on a buying trip. All of these ideas in his mind were appropriately synthesized and projected through a rich imagination to produce dramatic architectural statements for his clients.

Addison Mizner had always possessed a strong imagination, a quality that more than compensated for a dearth of formal schooling. It was this creative innovation that Mizner brilliantly utilized in his Palm Beach houses, projects that, because of their sheer size, demanded creative solutions. His first commission after completing the Everglades Club in 1919 was from Mr. and Mrs. Edward T. Stotesbury, whose home in the Philadelphia suburbs was Whitemarsh Hall, a palatial residence with 147 rooms designed by Horace Trumbauer. For a couple accustomed to grandeur, Mizner designed El Mirasol, a villa situated on forty acres of land that stretched from the Atlantic Ocean to Lake Worth and one of the grandest homes ever built in Palm Beach. The ground floor alone was approximately thirty-five thousand square feet and its features included an auditorium, a forty-car garage, a teahouse, and a private zoo. Remarkably, this house was not the largest of Mizner's commissions.

Mizner's houses were imagined as stories. Rather than copying prevailing styles, the architect sought to "make a building look traditional and as though it had fought its way from a

El Mirasol, 1928. Prominent Philadelphians Ned and Eva Stotesbury gave Addison Mizner one of his first residential commissions in Palm Beach after the opening of the Everglades Club in February 1919. "Queen Eva" was recognized as the social leader of Palm Beach, a position that was emphasized with the grandeur of El Mirasol, one of the largest projects ever undertaken by Addison Mizner.

Courtesy of Historical Society of Palm Beach County.

small, unimportant structure to a great, rambling house." He elaborated: "I sometimes start a house with a Romanesque corner, pretend that it has fallen into disrepair and been added to in the Gothic spirit, when suddenly the great wealth of the New World has poured in and the owner had added a very rich Renaissance addition."[3] Also informing his creative approach was the sensibility of the female clients who would occupy the houses. Each of his creations was effectively a stage setting appropriate for the role that he thought each wife should play. Bearing in mind that he completed over thirty-five houses in Palm Beach between 1919 and 1925, such imagining was necessary to avoid duplication.

Addison Mizner was one of the global leaders in Mediterranean and Spanish Revival architecture, the latter a style that was related to the Spanish missions of his native California. The Spanish period in California lasted from 1769 to 1821, succeeded by the Mexican period from 1821 to 1848. The customs and architecture of Mizner's California youth were certainly more Hispanic than American, so it is not surprising that he began to take notice of the Mission style as a young man and came to a fuller appreciation of it in the architectural office of Polk, who was fascinated by the Hispanic period as well. Certainly, the unpretentious and welcoming style resonated early, as it was sympathetic to the land and culture of California that he loved and a material reflection of his own distinctive character. This restrained and quietly noble architecture, such a familiar and meaningful part of his early life, would contribute to his affinity for the Spanish culture that would inform the dominant expression of the architect's mature years in Palm Beach.

Beginning at the age of fifteen, Addison Mizner developed an abiding passion for Hispanic culture at roughly the same time that he began to cultivate his artistic abilities. As a result of an accident to his leg that left him bedridden for a year at the age of fifteen, he began to draw and paint. Before his leg had fully healed, he departed for Guatemala where his father was to assume a diplomatic post. While living in Central America, he not only became fluent in the Spanish language but coincidentally discovered the beauty of Spanish Colonial architecture, an awakening that motivated him forever after. This revelation later inspired him to spend several months studying at the University of Salamanca, one of Europe's oldest universities and the site of majestic Renaissance and baroque plazas, palaces, and churches. The profound Moorish influence in Granada and other southern Spanish cities would inform his mature architecture. This cultural understanding, developed over a period of many years, would eventually make possible his great architectural achievement. He had identified his aesthetic archetypes and, in Palm Beach, he would discover how to employ them.

Addison Mizner in Guatemala. Mizner was a large man and, with his wit and personality, was a recognizable presence wherever he went. His knowledge of Spanish, developed in formal classes as well as on the streets of Guatemala, was so extensive that he could tell bawdy jokes to workers or listen to academic lectures. In 1893, three years after having returned from living in Guatemala, he attended the University of Salamanca, one of Spain's oldest and most respected universities.
Courtesy of The Oakland Museum of California.

Addison Mizner was a colossal figure whose imposing presence was keenly felt wherever he happened to be. Physically large at 6'2" and 250 pounds, his personality and capacity for friendship were more than the equal of his bodily magnitude. His friend, the author Arthur Somers Roche, described him aptly: "He is large, of brain and heart as well of body, and every ounce of him is concocted of roguery and gayety and mischief and laughter. It needs a great frame to contain tremendous mirth."[4] Early exposure to extreme wealth and power and, importantly, poverty and powerlessness, provided Mizner the confidence and empathy to move among people of every level of society and to understand what resonated with each. Earthy and ebullient, he had friendships that reflected the gamut of society: from royals and industrialists to hustlers and tradesmen. He truly enjoyed the various threads that made up the broad tapestry of humanity.

Addison Mizner's easy and familiar relationship with the elite prompted his professional ascent to society architect. In fact, his life was a crescendo of creating important relationships that began in childhood as a result of parents who were well positioned in California society. Arriving in New York in 1904, he found an ambitious city whose society was ruled at the apex by Caroline Astor and her elite coterie of friends. Provided entree by socially prominent San Francisco friends then living in New York, he was able to be accepted into the world of Fifth Avenue, Newport, and Long Island. Addison's new friends in many cases became clients for his newly established architectural practice.

On arriving in Palm Beach in 1918, Addison Mizner quickly befriended the leading figures in society and established a very successful architectural office catering to them. By 1925, he had charmed and delighted all with his personality, humor, and imaginative brilliance. After having decided to develop the ideal city of Boca Raton in 1925, he formed a corporation for the purpose and counted among the syndicate of investors such prominent names as Rodman Wanamaker, Paris Singer, Irving Berlin, William Kissam Vanderbilt II, Elizabeth Arden, and T. Coleman du Pont. It was in Palm Beach that his relentless ascendance to the summit of society reached its peak.

Although Addison Mizner was widely known as a society architect, he held other meaningful and perhaps more important distinctions for those who knew him. In the many obituaries and articles that appeared after his death, he was universally recognized for his humanity and loyalty. These are prominent among the reasons why such a varied throng turned out on an unpleasant day to attend his memorial service. An anonymous reviewer of his autobiography stated that Addison was "the kindest of men, a splendid son, a good brother, a loyal and generous friend, and a hard worker. Addison Mizner

Stair and cloister at Villa Flora, 1923. One of Mizner's six major houses of 1923, the Venetian fantasy of Villa Flora faces the Atlantic Ocean on North Ocean Boulevard. The interior stair connecting the cloister with the bedrooms above illustrates Mizner's effective board-form concrete, freestanding stair that he employed in many of his houses. Many cloisters in surviving Mizner houses have been glazed for year-round use. This photograph illustrates Mizner's original airy intent.

Photograph by Frank E. Geisler reproduced by Craig Kuhner.

was one of those simple souls who believed it best to trust all and be deceived than to doubt one worthy soul."[5] There are numerous additional sentiments expressing the same generosity of spirit from a broad range of the social spectrum.

Another reason that Mizner was admired by so many was his utter lack of pretense. He detested falseness, especially hypocrisy and self-inflation. At his memorial service, Bishop Thomas said, "He hated sham, hypocrisy, unreality, untruth."[6] Rather than inflate his accomplishments, he was known for jocular self-deprecation. Architecture is a cerebral discipline and is generally treated as such by it practitioners. Frank Lloyd Wright referred to architecture as "sublimated mathematics" and Le Corbusier said it was "intellectual speculation".[7] When asked what his profession was, Mizner responded offhandedly "I josh and I paint."[8] It was not that Mizner was demeaning either the practice of architecture or his own abilities; he simply never felt the need for pomposity or intellectual posturing. Perhaps an awareness of his large size or absence of formal education might have shaded the human inclination for self-promotion. Most likely, his behavior, influenced by a youth on the frontier and an adolescence of adventurous travel, produced a natural self-deprecation that disdained bombast.

Known for his humanity, Addison Mizner was also human. He was composed of contrary elements that concurrently furnished the potential for strength and accomplishment as well

Sketch of proposed Addison Station, 1925. Addison Mizner planned an entire community in Boca Raton that was to include the new railway terminal seen here. With its tall tower, this depot would have had a commanding presence in a landscape that was conceived to be "The First Tailor-Made City in All The World." This concept had its origin in the City Beautiful Movement greatly influenced by the Chicago World's Fair that Mizner visited in 1893.
Courtesy of Boca Raton Historical Society.

as weakness and failure. Throughout the Palm Beach years, he had consistently demonstrated a high level of competence and a flair for innovation; at the height of his creative powers in 1925, he embarked on a venture that would illustrate the capacity for folly. It is a natural human instinct to want to soar, especially for an artistic temperament who had already tasted inordinate success. Inspired by the well-conceived urban design that he had closely studied in various European cities and in Chicago at the World's Columbian Exposition, he yearned for the opportunity not just to build individual houses but to design an entire community of his own. Based on his knowledge of the luxury market, it was a sound idea; however, what he did not foresee was the ever-changing nature of the Florida real estate market. It was timing, not necessarily the idea, that cast a long shadow on his life.

The grand scheme for the development of Boca Raton would exercise an inexorable force that pulled the architect down to a level of disgrace and financial ruin that he never fathomed possible. The harmonious convergence of positive conditions that greeted Mizner in 1918 had surreptitiously changed seven years later. The appeal of Florida as a resort destination and the subsequent demand for property created a real estate bubble that ultimately sabotaged the architect's dream and consumed his personal investment funds. Always a man of boundless energy and ingenuity, Mizner struggled mightily to avert the calamity, but ultimately to no avail. The harmful effects of speculators, easy credit, and depreciating property values were insuperable forces. This fall represented the nadir of his life.

At this point, Mizner appears to have been the victim of bad timing due to an unforeseeable shift in market conditions. There have been many critics who have produced a more severe assessment of the architect and his actions. Historian George B. Tindall refers to Mizner as "one of the great charlatan-geniuses of the 20th century."[9] Other authors have detailed the intricate web that connected the architect and his development company with Florida banks and identified the banks' owners and directors as stockholders of Mizner's business. This opaque network resulted in a situation in which conservative depositors became unwitting investors in speculative real estate ventures, subsequently losing their savings. To what degree Addison was actually driven by dishonesty is impossible to assess; to what extent he was involved in actual business operations is impossible to know. What is unmistakable is that he was guilty of bad judgment. By placing irresponsible people in the critical positions of sales, promotion, and finance, he made decisions that would have detrimental consequences. Although responsible for operations, Addison Mizner was consumed, for the most part, by the ardent passion of an artist to realize what he considered to be his crowning achievement.

While such criticism speaks to his ethics, there are other detractors who questioned his credentials to practice architecture. After Mizner's death in 1933, there was a tendency to deprecate both his architectural style and his qualifications as an architect. Because he lived such a fascinating life, it was tempting for writers to publish myths and exaggerations to embellish their stories. Over time, legend became fact. Tales abound about plans hastily drawn in sand on the beach, staircases forgotten and belatedly added to the exterior of a house, and commissions received as a result of charm instead of professional competence. Such oversights would have been highly unusual in an office that employed at least twenty architects and draftsmen in the 1920s. Moreover, Mizner was very well qualified by the standards of the time and was actually licensed to practice architecture.

Charm was certainly part of Mizner's nature, and it constituted a necessary and discernible component in developing commissions for his practice. His great personal appeal was a combination of knowledge and bawdiness. Although by nature a casual man, he understood the necessity of attending parties where he could step "with all my might on the charm peddle" to cultivate business.[10] One evening, dressed in a tuxedo, Mizner was confronted by one of his contractors who asked why he was dressed so elegantly. Mizner replied that he was in his "fishing clothes," intending to land a commission at a party he was attending.[11] Regardless of circumstances, earthy words and phrases were part of his lexicon. A salutation preceded by "you son of a bitch" or "you old bastard" was not unusual. Remarkably, his language never offended, and the only effect of such unconventional behavior was to make him more enticing.

Deemed attractive by so many, Mizner never married but enjoyed the romantic company of both men and women. There were various women that he found attractive and professed to have loved, and there was even one to whom he considered himself informally engaged. In his later years, Mizner was known to have had brief relationships with men; however, from what is known of his private life, it appears that his sexual needs were not consuming. What can be reliably stated is that he was emotionally private and, until his later years, mostly discreet. The animating force in his life seemed to derive from the overarching desire to conceive beauty and from the satisfaction of bringing his ideas to fruition. In the end, it is not known what effect the lack of a satisfying personal relationship might have had on Mizner.

Throughout his life, when confronted with disappointment, Addison Mizner was able to rely on humor as an antidote. Humor and wit, greatly prized and highly refined by all Mizners, were necessary weapons employed during Addison's youth to triumph over older and more experienced siblings and to sustain himself with a more mature audience during family dinners. Also present at the Mizner dining table was a younger sibling who dedicated himself to the art of conversation and consequently became a master of repartee and a virtuoso hustler. Wilson Mizner, four years Addison's junior, was closely and, by many accounts, inextricably connected to Addison

Wilson Mizner, February 6, 1926. In contrast to Addison's genial countenance, his younger brother Wilson projected a more calculating, appraising look. Wilson made a living by identifying and hoodwinking the gullible, those he referred to as "platinum suckers." A conversationalist, Wilson has been remembered by posterity more for what he said than anything he wrote. Although Wilson complicated the life of his brother, Addison looked after his younger brother his entire life.

Courtesy of Historical Society of Palm Beach County.

his entire life. Wilson spent his life chasing opportunity after opportunity and, since Addison's adult life was spent in the company of the wealthy and notable, Wilson frequently sought out his brother for ready access to financial enhancement.

Described as a man who "sparkled with larceny," Wilson Mizner was clever, louche, and trenchantly witty.[12] Referring to his success as a playwright and con man in New York, Damon Runyon called him "the greatest man-about-town that any town ever had."[13] For Wilson, anything that remotely glittered invited temptation. Just as Addison's humanity was democratic, so too was Wilson's venality. His victims constituted a spectrum of society: from *grandes dames* and captains of industry to hookers and less gifted swindlers. For Addison, a scheme was an artistic composition in which constituent parts were aligned; for Wilson, it was an artful deception in which the unsuspecting were fleeced. Wilson, both a source of entertainment and embarrassment to his brother, appeared episodically yet at critical times in the life of Addison Mizner. Each the other's best friend, the brothers died within two months of one another in 1933; Wilson in Hollywood and Addison in Palm Beach.

Addison Mizner spent his last days at his beloved Villa Mizner where he fittingly enjoyed a panoramic view of Palm Beach, the city that he worked heroically to beautify. The cityscape he surveyed in his last days told a story of the architect's extraordinary life. His existence and achievement were a reflection of ancestors who persevered as a result of boldness and cleverness. Like Addison, they were intrepid pathfinders who faced incalculable risk in the quest of realizing their dreams. It was this inheritance that gave Addison Mizner the wherewithal to walk alone on an unconventional road to realize a level of accomplishment known to few.

CHAPTER TWO

CALIFORNIA PIONEERS

Like so many American families, Addison Mizner's antecedents turned their backs on old Europe for a continent of new cities and vast, unexplored wilderness. If there was to be advantage and privilege in this new land, it would derive not from birthright but from achievement. Addison Mizner's forebears proved to be men and women of adventure and accomplishment. From them, Mizner inherited courage, tenacity, and resourcefulness, characteristics that would serve him well in his remarkable and animated life. Just as he consistently embraced challenge and welcomed innovation, his ancestors were pioneers not easily daunted nor reluctant to explore opportunity.

The Mizners, distinguished and well connected, were among the first families of California. Lansing Bond Mizner, Addison's father, arrived in 1849 and was a member of the Society of California Pioneers, an organization established by settlers who arrived in the state before 1850.[1] Like other pioneer families in California, the Mizners came from somewhere else. The family originated in Germany, went to England in the sixteenth century, and finally immigrated to New Jersey in the eighteenth century before settling in Illinois. Charles Mizner served as a tax collector in the reign of Henry VIII and his descendants became very prosperous.[2] At the time of their arrival in America, the Mizners appeared to be financially comfortable as Addison relates in his memoirs that his great-grandfather, Lawrence Mizner, left his grandfather an estate worth $300,000.[3]

Lansing Mizner's father was Henry Caldwell Mizner, a prominent lawyer whose two brothers were generals in the US Army.[4] Lansing's mother was Mary Stevenson Cairns, daughter of Dr. Caldwell Cairns, a member of the first Continental Convention of Illinois and the niece of Shadrack Bond, a congressional representative from the Illinois Territory who later became the first governor of the State of Illinois in 1818.[5] Although there is no substantiation, Mizner lore claimed that a family member gave Abraham Lincoln his first political appointment. This information comes from an autobiography by Alex Waugh, an employee and good friend of Addison and his family, who would have heard this story several times

Lawrence Mizner by an unknown artist, circa 1790. Mizner settled in New Jersey and became prosperous as a merchant and financier. When Mizner died in 1795, he left an estate worth $300,000 according to Addison's biography. When Addison's father died in 1893, he left the family an estate valued only at $25,000, mostly in small lots of real estate. This lack of inheritance contributed to Addison's pursuit of architecture as a profession.
Courtesy of The Oakland Museum of California.

during his association with the family in the early 1920s. If this is not true, there was a certain connection between Lincoln and Addison Mizner's step-grandfather.

Lansing Mizner, born in 1825, had the misfortune of losing his father at the age of four. Four years later, his mother married James Semple, a general in the Illinois militia who later became a US senator from Illinois.[6] In 1834, Semple became speaker of the Illinois House of Representatives where he became a personal friend of Abraham Lincoln and, eight years later, served as an Illinois Supreme Court judge where he heard seven cases argued by Lincoln.[7] In 1837, he was appointed by President Martin Van Buren as *chargé d'affaires* to the Republic of New Grenada, at that time a Central American state consisting of Colombia and Panama. With this appointment, General Semple moved his new family to Bogota, Colombia, where they lived for three years. When Lansing Mizner returned to Illinois in 1843, he was fluent in Spanish, a skill that would have significant implications for him, his family, and especially for his son, Addison.

After the US annexation of Texas in 1845, war broke out between the United States and Mexico. At this point, Lansing Mizner left Shurtleff College in Alton, Illinois, and joined the Illinois volunteers regiment in which he carried messages through enemy territory and eventually rose to the rank of captain.[8] Due to his knowledge of Spanish, he served as an interpreter and may have been involved in translating documents relating the Mexican surrender at the end of the battle of Buena Vista in February 1847.[9] When the Treaty of Guadalupe Hidalgo was signed in 1848, the United States was granted control not only of Texas but also the territory that today represents the American Southwest.

After returning to Illinois, Lansing Mizner received a letter from his stepfather's brother, Robert Baylor Semple, imploring him to come to California. As a lieutenant in the California Battalion, Semple befriended influential Mexican general Mariano Vallejo, who helped bring about the transition of California from a province of Mexico to a state of the United States. In 1846, the two men agreed to found a town on the Strait of Carquinez, thirty miles north of what would soon become San Francisco. Semple was given a half-interest from Vallejo in return for agreeing to name the town after Vallejo's wife. The town became Benicia, the birthplace of Addison Mizner.

In the letter, Semple told Lansing Mizner about his connections with wealthy and influential Californians and elaborated on his friendship with General Vallejo. He made an enticing proposal that induced Lansing to move west: "Now, my dear boy, if you have finished your studies and can get to this country, with a small library and your knowledge of the Spanish language, and my influence, you can make ten thousand dollars a year at the practice of law."[10] Semple's fortunate circumstances, confirmed in the letter, were proof of the bounty that northern California offered: "My property is worth two hundred thousand dollars, and popularity enough to get into any office in the gift of the people."[11]

Portrait in oil of Lansing Bond Mizner by Cyrus Pease, 1853. Addison Mizner's father sat for this painting before his marriage to Ella Watson in 1856. Mizner was a lawyer and distinguished figure in California politics before being appointed ambassador to Costa Rica, El Salvador, Guatemala, Honduras, and Nicaragua by President Benjamin Harrison in 1889. As a result, Addison spent a year in Guatemala and became fluent in Spanish and enamored of Spanish Colonial architecture.
Courtesy of The Oakland Museum of California.

In May 1849, Lansing arrived in California by way of New Orleans and Panama and immediately found a destination of opportunity. Gold had been discovered just the year before in Sutter's Mill, and many men in Benicia had departed to prospect for gold. Having completed his law studies, Mizner was admitted to the California bar in 1850 and then served admirably as private secretary for Governor John Bigler from 1852 to 1855.[12] During this time, Mizner began to create a financial interest in various enterprises. He invested in a general merchandise company, bought land in partnership with his prominent uncle, and, recognizing the need for transportation in a rapidly growing region, started a stage line operating between Benicia and Sacramento.[13] His growing importance and stature were confirmed when he was appointed collector of customs for Northern California and subsequently elected to the State Senate in 1855.[14]

Addison Mizner's mother was born Elmira Watson in 1836 in Armstrong County, Pennsylvania, and was known as Ella. Her forebears arrived from the ports of a troubled Ireland and settled in Pennsylvania in the middle of the eighteenth century.

Left: *Addison Mizner circa 1925.*

Right: *Oil portrait of John Smiley Watson by William J. Wilgus, circa 1850. John Watson, the maternal grandfather of Addison Mizner, shared a remarkable physical resemblance with his grandson including the fair complexion and sandy hair.*

Courtesy of Historical Society of Palm Beach County (photo); courtesy of The Oakland Museum of California (painting).

Her parents, Mary Reynolds and John Watson, produced eight children, three of whom died in infancy. The family history included a distant relationship through Ella's mother to Sir Joshua Reynolds, one of England's greatest painters as well as the first president of the Royal Academy of Arts in 1768.

The pioneer spirit, evident in the family of Addison Mizner's father, was present in equal measure in that of his mother. According to Addison, one of his mother's earliest memories was of gunfire directed at Indians near the Mississippi River. She also vividly recalled traveling down the Mississippi in a boat, accompanied only by her mother, brother and sisters, all of whom were trying to join her father who had preceded the family to establish a new home in St. Louis in 1838.[15] Seeking the economic opportunities offered by a growing and prosperous northern California, John Watson decided to move his family there in January 1853.

As transcontinental trains were not completed until 1869, the journey from the East Coast of America to the West was fraught with inconvenience and peril. One option was an ocean voyage of fifteen thousand nautical miles from the East Coast around the southern tip of South America to San Francisco, a voyage that took from five to eight months. Alternatively, John Watson chose the shorter "isthmus" route that took his family by ship to Central America, where they then traversed Nicaragua to San Juan del Sur on the Pacific coast. There they boarded the steamship *Independence*, a vessel belonging to the Accessory Trading Company, owned in part by Cornelius Vanderbilt, whose destination was San Francisco.[16] The shorter route chosen by John Watson was intended to save valuable time but, ultimately, it would prove physically difficult and heartrending in personal terms.

Early in the morning of February 16, 1853, the captain of the *Independence* mistook huge rocks just south of Margarita Island in Baja California for whales. The ship struck a rock in very rough seas and began taking on water.[17] Although Ella managed to escape, she was left with searing images of suffering and pain. Not only was she forced to endure the gruesome sight of watching one of her friends burn to death while hanging from the side of the ship, she also tragically learned that her only brother, Asa, was among the 150 casualties of the disaster.[18]

The sinking of the *Independence* was a harrowing and tragic experience, borne out in a grieving letter from Mary Watson to her brother: "I was on shore and knew that my husband and child were struggling for life and I could give them no assistance. Oh! How I screamed and begged and prayed for the sailors to take back the boat, but they would not do it."[19] These words were the lamentation of a heartbroken and suffering mother, powerless to offer assistance to those she loved. The impact on seventeen-year-old Ella had to have been no less affecting.

Wreck and burning of the steamer Independence *near Margarita Island off the coast of Baja California, February 16, 1853. The* Independence *was transporting the family of Ella Watson from San Juan del Sur, Nicaragua, to San Francisco when it struck rocks, burned, and sank. Among the 150 killed in this accident was Ella's little brother, Asa. This was a tragic prelude to Ella's arrival in San Francisco where she met Lansing Bond Mizner.* Courtesy of the Library of Congress.

After being stranded for three days, the remaining 250 passengers were taken to San Francisco on the whaling ship *Meteor,* another arduous voyage that lasted an additional four weeks.[20] Beset by personal tragedy, the family stayed in San Francisco until the death of John Watson four years later in 1857. Seeking a land of promise and the prospect of happiness, the Watsons encountered misfortune, an emotional loss for which there was no compensation. Without her husband and devoid of opportunity, Mary Watson returned with two daughters to Armstrong County, Pennsylvania. Only Ella remained.

After arriving in San Francisco, Ella Watson met Lansing Mizner. Lansing was smitten with Ella as evidenced by a letter he wrote after she had given him encouragement about their relationship: "I am getting to be a perfect child about you, can't stay 3 or 4 days without getting into a stew and neglecting important business."[21] In another letter, he had become much more demonstrative: "The first night here, I dreamed, of you; oh, that it may not be all a dream."[22] On May 26, 1856, they were married at Grace Church in San Francisco. Although no record of his reaction exists, one could imagine that the marriage of his daughter to a prosperous and well-established Lansing Mizner would have brought pleasure to John Watson, a small recompense for the tragedy that befell his family only three years earlier.

Newly married, Ella and Lansing Mizner settled in Benicia. At the time of its founding, Benicia appeared destined to become a city of consequence. Although San Francisco was important, it was lawless and rowdy as a result of the influx of fortune seekers. Following the discovery of gold in 1848,

Ella Watson Mizner, circa 1866. Known as "Mama" Mizner, Ella married Lansing Bond Mizner in 1856 and had eight children, only one of whom was a girl. Possessed of a good sense of humor and a strong constitution, she was able to raise a group of mischievous and rowdy sons. The children loved her very much for her understanding and playful temperament. Courtesy of Oakland Museum of California.

northern California was growing rapidly and, two years later, California became the thirty-first state in the Union. Benicia, the first city in California to be incorporated, became the seat of Solano County. In 1853, it received the crowning accolade of being named the state capital; however, this exalted designation proved transitory as Sacramento was selected only a year later.

Despite the reversal of political fortune, Benicia was an active town. It benefitted from the presence of the Pacific Mail Steamship Company, which had been awarded a contract to transport mail from the United States to the Isthmus of Panama. With a large workforce, it established a major shipyard that included a foundry, machine shops, and docks. Industrial activity was complemented by the arrival of many schools so that Benicia became known as "The Athens of California."[23] In 1851 the US Army established the Benicia Arsenal, the first ordnance supply depot in the West. From 1860 until 1886 the arsenal was commanded by Julian McAllister, the son of Matthew Hall McAllister, a distinguished lawyer and judge in San Francisco, and the brother of Ward McAllister, a prominent New York social arbiter and intimate friend of Mrs. William B. Astor Jr.[24] Among the soldiers stationed there were future generals Joseph Hooker and Ulysses S. Grant. The sight of young soldiers, magnificently attired in dress uniforms with badges and ribbons, had to be an exciting and inspiring spectacle to the youthful eyes of the Mizner children.

Later in life, Addison Mizner would humorously belittle his place of birth. Commenting on his father's decision to raise the family in Benicia, he said, "Papa Mizner was the best wrong guesser the world had probably ever produced, and when he moved from San Francisco to Benicia, he crowned his misjudgment with mud to the ears."[25] After listening to Addison's response to the question "Where were you born?" a friend uncomprehendingly replied, "For God's sake, where was your mother going?"[26] Although already insignificant in the mind of Addison's friend, Benicia was a more than satisfactory place for Ella and Lansing Mizner to raise eight children, all but one very active and mischievous boys.

CHAPTER THREE

"THE GREATEST DAY OF MY LIFE"

Addison Mizner grew up in a family of seven boys. This was an aggressive and sometimes combative environment that demanded keen survival skills to avoid being overwhelmed by siblings. Such a competitive existence either diminishes self-confidence or engenders boldness and resourcefulness. Owing to his childhood experience, Addison Mizner was well armed with confidence. He also had a caring spirit that made him a wonderful friend to many. Compassion was an inheritance from his mother, whose well-being he sought to ensure his entire life.

Ella Mizner would play a central role in the life of her son Addison. By all accounts, she was a beautiful young lady and a kind, loving, and understanding mother. After marriage, her husband recognized that a growing family would need a larger home than the one it currently occupied. Lansing Mizner bought three prefabricated houses in Boston and had them shipped around Cape Horn to Benicia, where they were reassembled. One of these was sited in the center of town and became the Mizner home. As the family grew, Lansing Mizner would enlarge the home by adding rooms in such a manner that would later inspire Addison to observe, "from the

The Mizner family, circa 1884. Top Row: Edgar Mizner; Second Row: Ella Watson "Mama" Mizner, Lansing Mizner Jr., William Mizner; Third Row: Lansing Bond "Papa" Mizner, Wilson Mizner, Mary Isabella "Minnie" Mizner, Henry Mizner; Bottom Row: Addison Mizner. Addison and Wilson were the youngest children in the family and, to the distress of Addison, spent much of their lives together.
Courtesy of the Library of Congress.

The Mizner home in Benicia, California, circa 1878. Lansing Mizner shipped the core of this prefabricated house from Boston to Benicia around Cape Horn. As the family grew, the house was continually enlarged. This was a rather modest house for one of the city's most prominent citizens, but it did have the city's first flush toilet.
Courtesy of Benicia Historical Museum.

air it must have looked like a telescope, with the smaller end toward the street."[1]

The Mizner home, considering it belonged to one of the town's most prominent citizens, was relatively modest, although it was the first home in Benicia to have a flush toilet. By contrast, there was Daniel Hastings's spectacular home which had three and a half stories, forty rooms including a billiard room, marble floors, and onyx and marble mantels. Immensely expensive at the time, it cost over $85,000 to construct and another $265,000 to furnish.[2] Hastings's apparent reason for building such a home was to upstage Lansing Mizner, with whom he had had a dispute. The castle became known as "Hastings' Folly," a luxury that had consumed his fortune. This compulsion on the part of an obsessed Hastings to eclipse Lansing Mizner spoke indirectly to the importance and distinction Mizner enjoyed in Benicia. The local press confirmed the Mizners' prominence, commenting on "their antiquity and elegant ways, particularly their habit of taking tea in the afternoon."[3]

Lansing and Ella Mizner had their first child in 1857. Addison Cairns Mizner was born fifteen years later on December 12, 1872, the seventh child in a family that, at that point, included six boys and a girl. One last son, Wilson, would be born four years later. This meant that there was a span of nineteen years that separated the oldest Mizner from the youngest. With such a large household, those children close in age naturally tended to form bonds and play together. Since Addison and Wilson were the youngest, they would be connected not only in childhood but throughout their entire lives.

Lansing Mizner's many business interests and political responsibilities frequently required him to be separated from his family. His absence meant that Ella Mizner, known as "Mama" Mizner, had the loving yet onerous task of raising a very active and frequently misbehaving brood of children. Both by temperament and experience she was suited to manage her challenging household. Mama Mizner's good nature and sense of humor served her well in dealing with troublesome and naughty sons. At the age of sixteen, Wilson decided to run away from home and, in need of funds, sent a telegram to his mother requesting $50. She replied, "Sorry did not receive your telegram."[4] Ella surely inherited cleverness and composure from her own mother. While visiting her daughter in Benicia, Mary Watson caught a pair of burglars in the Mizner house and, armed with a rifle, turned them in. In congratulating her, the sheriff said it was fortunate that she did not have to shoot them. She replied, "I could not—the gun wasn't loaded."[5]

By the time their last child was born, Lansing Mizner was forty-seven years old and Ella Mizner thirty-six. As Addison and Wilson grew up, the discipline familiar to the other children not surprisingly became less rigorous. As Wilson was her last child, Mama Mizner assumed a more protective attitude toward him. Addison was aware of this sentiment early and always did his best to support his younger brother and to protect Wilson's image in the eyes of their mother. Throughout his life, Addison had witnessed this maternal dispensation and, though it might have been frustrating at times, he endured it without acrimony or animosity. Until her death, his mother remained the most important person in Addison's life. It was her unexcitable and adoring attitude, maintained even in the

St. Mary's of the Pacific, Benicia, California, circa 1878. This was where several of the Mizner children went to school in Benicia. St. Mary's, a school that primarily served girls, was the sister school of St. Augustine College that taught boys. Interestingly, the Mizner children attended St. Mary's as their father, a prominent member of the community, was on the board of the school. The mischievous and rambunctious Mizner boys must have been a bracing addition to a mostly female student body.
Courtesy of Benicia Historical Museum.

face of perpetual calamity, that Addison adored: "Her placidity was never ruffled for long, for behind it was the most divine sense of humor that I have ever known."[6]

Childhood for Addison Mizner and his siblings was at once rough-and-tumble and cultivated. Many influential and distinguished individuals spent time at the Mizner home. In such a prominent household, it was expected that the children would enter appropriate professions. Lansing would become a lawyer, William a physician, Henry an Episcopal clergyman, and Edgar a mining engineer. The eldest son, Murray, died at the age of seventeen and the only daughter, Minnie, married Horace Chase, the founder and owner of Stag's Leap Vineyard. This left the youngest, Addison and Wilson.

Mama Mizner naturally held grand expectations for Addison and Wilson, hoping that they might become "bishops or ambassadors"; however, confronted with unfolding reality, she lightheartedly concluded by stating that "the only ambition I have for you is to keep you out of State prison."[7] Addison took a long, circuitous path to architecture and Wilson, the most pampered of the brood, succeeded in avoiding regular work for most of his life. He was an artful rogue whose embarrassing antics constantly interfered with the life of his brother Addison. Reminiscing in his memoirs about the troubled life of Wilson, Addison humorously remarked: "When Wilson was born the doctor congratulated Papa Mizner. I wondered then, and we have wondered ever since, why he congratulated my father."[8]

While the Mizner children came to occupy respectable positions, none of the boys, with the exception of Wilson and Addison, distinguished themselves. All of the boys were highly competitive, energetic, and pugnacious in youth. The only sibling to defy such categorization was Henry, whose piety guided him to the ministry. The words of Lansing Jr. describe his odd brother and also provide revealing commentary on the other boys: "Poor Henry, from the beginning, seemed to be one apart. He was serious, studious, and kind, to a fault. These three qualities made him the question mark in the family, and laid him open to all the annoyances that could be applied to one we did not understand."[9] Apart from the two youngest Mizners, none was galvanized by a strong desire to succeed. Addison and Wilson, the exceptions, would both excel: one as a transformative architect, the other as an unapologetic grifter.

The Mizner boys were not only spirited, but creative and enterprising. Based on the behavior of both Addison and Wilson, it is not surprising to find that there was a thespian inclination in these early years. All of the boys enjoyed performing and created an "opera house" in a neighbor's barn where they staged theatricals and circuses and actually charged for admission. Their creativity was not always directed toward productive ends. As a gesture of gratitude, a house guest of the Mizners presented the family with a silver tureen for their generous hospitality. The clever boys, oblivious to the fact that this fine object was intended to magnify the importance of their mother's dining room table, filled it with gunpowder and managed to blow it up.

The inventiveness of the Mizner boys also extended to martial skills. All of the boys became proficient with their fists, a competence that would later serve Addison and Wilson well, the two brothers who frequently made a living from their wits. With seven potential combatants in the household and many more in the neighborhood, the probability of fisticuffs was high. When altercations turned into fights, the boys involved were sent by Mama Mizner to an outbuilding called "the tank house" to settle their disputes. Addison noted that he fought a lot as a boy and, during the two or three years spent at public school, he had a black eye the entire time. Although the mischievous and spirited boys were frequently in trouble, they were exempt for the most part from severe punishment. Wilson stated that his father never administered anything more than a verbal rebuke and that his kind mother was incapable of inflicting harsh penalty.[10] Any leniency displayed by the boys appeared to be directed to their attractive sister, Min, who had begun to attract the attention of young men.

It was in the family dining room that the children received a significant part of their education. Not just a relaxed place of daily congregation, the dining table provided an important focus for development. Lansing Mizner was a sophisticated man of affairs and presided over a meal like a skilled master guiding apprentices. Betraying great respect for his father, Addison said he "was considered one of the greatest

Mary Isabella Mizner by Henry Raschen, circa 1900. Known as "Minnie" or "Min" and born in 1860, she was Addison's only sister. As Wilson and Addison were much younger, they would bribe Minnie's boyfriends by agreeing to disappear when the suitors called on their sister. She married Horace Blanchard Chase in 1888 who started Stag's Leap Winery in 1893. Courtesy of The Oakland Museum of California.

extemporaneous speakers of the day. He taught us the value of words of one syllable; the colorfulness of similes."[11] Having so many children at one table created a very competitive atmosphere where inserting oneself into a dialogue to make a point was a formidable challenge. It was in this environment that Addison sharpened his mind, refined his conversational skills, and cultivated a keen wit. He would later comment that "these gatherings did more to make or break character and destiny than I can explain."[12]

The years 1888 and 1889 would have a profound effect on the ultimate direction of Addison Mizner's life. Two events would serve to awaken in Addison an appreciation of beauty and to animate his artistic sensibility, both prerequisites for the successful practice of architecture. The first event occurred two weeks before his sister's marriage. On July 18, 1888, Addison Mizner's only sister, Minnie, married Horace Chase, the founder of Stag's Leap Vineyard and a descendent of a prominent Chicago family involved in real estate. On July 4, Addison's parents hosted a holiday party for fifty neighborhood children. Everyone ate holiday food and then enjoyed a display of fireworks. The traditional conclusion to this celebration was for the children to jump over the fire. In the process of leaping, Addison caught his foot in a rut and fell down with a twisted ankle. All the boys who followed fell on top of him, causing a sprain. When the injury failed to heal and became infected three weeks later, a San Francisco doctor advised amputation. At this point, his older brother William, a medical student in San Francisco, intervened and introduced Addison to his teacher, who performed an operation that saved the leg.

Very happy to have retained his leg, Addison was now upset at having to remain bedridden, an ordeal that would last almost a year. For an active young man of fifteen, this

Addison Mizner and friends, circa 1888. Addison Mizner (third from the left, back row) is seen on a picnic with friends of his sister, Minnie (second from left, front row), and her fiancé, Horace Chase (fourth from the left, back row). Importantly, "Tessie" Fair, the daughter of Silver King, James Graham Fair, is along (far left, front row). She would become very prominent in New York society and facilitate Addison's entry among the elite when he moved there in 1904. Courtesy of The Oakland Museum of California.

was the devastating equivalent of incarceration. The sedentary and solitary existence forced him to find entertainment in activities that had previously been completely foreign to him. It was at this time that Addison acquired the lifelong habit of reading. For an individual whose gifts included a vivid imagination, books introduced him to spectacular experiences and images that stirred his creativity. Speaking about a book by Charles Dickens that refined his power of observation and study of character, he remarked, "I think what I learned from that book has been more of value to me, and more fun, than anything in my life."[13]

Another benefit of his enforced immobility was the cultivation of the ability to draw and paint. It was during convalescence that his brother Henry gave him a set of watercolors and, with nothing but time on his hands, Addison painted everything. This represented an informal first step in training his eye to appreciate the compositional components of proportion, balance, and the harmony of parts. In a practical sense, he would always sketch furniture and buildings during his travels and frequently did watercolors to present architectural ideas to clients. In an artistic sense, he benefitted from the ability to analyze and synthesize component parts. After finally dedicating himself to architecture, he would design not just buildings, but coherent compositions of structure, landscape, and environment.

The second event that had a pronounced impact on his life occurred the next year. On March 30, 1889, the Senate of the United States confirmed Lansing Mizner as envoy extraordinary and minister plenipotentiary to Central America. The purview of this appointment included five Central American nations: Guatemala, El Salvador, Honduras, Nicaragua, and Costa Rica. Lansing Mizner had been involved in Republican politics for quite some time and had been an ardent supporter in California of Benjamin Harrison, the newly elected president. When Harrison was inaugurated, Ella and Lansing Mizner attended the festivities in Washington. Acknowledging his political support, legal competence, and fluency in Spanish, the new president made Mizner America's highest-ranking diplomat in Central America.

On May 12, 1889, ten months after Addison's accident, the family departed for Guatemala City where they would live. As the older children were either married, studying, or practicing vocations, the parents chose to be accompanied by three sons: Addison, Wilson, and Edgar. Edgar at this time was twenty-six years old and would serve as his father's secretary. At sixteen years of age, Addison probably would have stayed in San Francisco to attend school; however, due to the fact that his injury had not yet healed, it was thought prudent that he should remain with his parents. This fortuitous circumstance resulted in an epiphany for the young man: He would be introduced to the Spanish culture that would later define his perspective on architecture. Befitting a respected family, the Mizner departure from San Francisco was accompanied by speeches and a marching band.

Addison Mizner spent over a year in Central America before returning to San Francisco. His aesthetic stimulation began immediately. On the steamship that took the family to Mexico, he met Ellen "Bay" Emmet, a young lady two years his junior who taught him about watercolor and drawing. At the time Addison met her, she had already been studying art formally at the Cowels Art School in Boston. Known today as Ellen Rand, she later became a successful portrait artist who studied with William Merritt Chase and completed many important commissions during her career, including ones for President Franklin D. Roosevelt and her cousin, Henry James.[14] It was not only the art lessons that stimulated Addison: "I fell desperately in love with her."[15]

Later in the voyage, the ship docked at Mazatlan, Mexico, where the beautiful city presented a vision that moved Addison to comment, "It was probably the greatest day of my life, for there lying white in the sun was my first Spanish town."[16] After arriving in Guatemala, he accompanied his father on a trip to Escuintla, a small town on the Pacific coastal plain. He was clearly enchanted with the beauty and exoticism: "chattering monkeys gave way to squirrels; and squawking parrots and macaws to mocking birds. Nothing I've ever seen since is more astonishingly beautiful than this trip. We climbed over five thousand feet and just before sunset got our first glimpse of Guatamala City, lying like an opal, with its great expanse of colored houses and churches."[17] This vivid and emotive language reflects indelible impressions that would have crucial and enduring consequences.

Antigua, Guatemala, circa 1890. Addison Mizner was immediately enthralled with the culture and architecture of Guatemala when he moved there with his parents in 1889. His initial impressions of Mexico and Guatemala were an epiphany that immediately inspired his imagination and later served to inform his architectural ideas. The silhouettes of noble buildings such as this and their details would be recorded in the many drawings he did during subsequent visits. Courtesy of the Library of Congress.

One of the first things Addison and Wilson did after settling in Guatemala City was to take classes at the Instituto Nacional to learn Spanish. As Addison noted succinctly, "It was one time that we worked at our studies, for without the language we could make no friends."[18] He was able to travel widely with his father and observe closely the culture that so resonated with him. Both Addison and Wilson had a wide range of memorable experiences during this time. As Wilson told his biographer, "things in Guatemala were just about perfect for a young fellow, with box seats for every thing of interest in the country."[19] At a time when the lives of most young men their age were defined by a structured environment centered on formal schooling, Addison and Wilson enjoyed an exciting existence of relative freedom and privilege. Not surprisingly, they would spend much of the rest of their lives in pursuit of adventure and discovery.

It was during this time that Addison developed a love of monkeys, an attraction that would last the rest of his life. During a visit to Managua, Nicaragua, he was presented with a pet spider monkey named "Deuteronomy," which he simplified to "Duty." Unfortunately, during a chaotic and confusing welcoming ceremony in Limon, Costa Rica, Duty was hit on the head with a trombone, a blow that caused him to fall into the water and drown. Duty must have greatly impressed his owner in their abbreviated time together because Addison would use the same name for future pet monkeys.

It was not only Spanish culture that had a profound effect on Addison. His father had a strong affinity for the pre-Spanish Mayan civilization and introduced his son to the ruins at Copan, located in western Honduras. Copan, abandoned in the tenth century and excavated in the nineteenth century, was one of the most important sites of a magnificent culture. "It has left an indelible picture on my mind of what was once the glory of a great and vanished civilization—a city that must have housed a half million souls, with all its pomp of royalty, and priesthood."[20] This comment from his memoirs indicates that Addison's mind was becoming very sensitive to a broad range of aesthetic perceptions.

Although things were going well for Addison, this was not the case for his father. Prior to his departure, Lansing Mizner's diplomatic objectives had been set forth in written instructions by Secretary of State James Blaine. Beyond creating goodwill between the governments of the individual republics and the United States, the most pressing issue was to settle the border dispute between Nicaragua and Costa Rica, an impasse he was able to resolve in three months. He also managed to facilitate a settlement between Guatemala and El Salvador in 1890 after they had gone to war with one another.

These successes notwithstanding, the balance of his diplomatic tenure would be fraught with problems. By encouraging the five Central American republics under his aegis to unify against menacing neighbors, Mizner offended the republics' southern neighbor, Colombia. Mizner's proposal was at variance with the official American policy of impartiality and resulted in a reprimand from the State Department: "it would be especially unfortunate if your words should be construed as the authoritative expression of the [United States] government."[21]

What determined Lansing Mizner's fate as a diplomat was an incident during the war between Guatemala and El Salvador. A former Guatemalan general, thought to be aiding El Salvador, was apprehended by Guatemalan officials with Mizner's permission and, unbeknownst to the ambassador, subsequently killed. This was an embarrassment that the United States could not countenance and resulted in another rebuke, citing that the ambassador had exceeded his authority.[22] Lansing Mizner was dismissed by Secretary of State Blaine on November 18, 1890. A State Department historian later described Mizner as unfortunately having an unerring propensity for making the wrong decision at the wrong time. Devastated, Lansing Mizner returned to San Francisco where he would live only three more years.

Before his father's disgrace in November, Addison Mizner had already returned to San Francisco during the summer of 1890. His sojourn in Central America was a salutary and profitable time for various reasons. At the end of his stay, a healthy Addison commented on his linguistic facility: "We now spoke Spanish more often and with greater ease than we did English."[23] He had also developed a heartfelt appreciation for Spanish culture, art, and architecture. For a young man who had always lacked an academic focus, the growing curiosity for this captivating civilization was a profound revelation. His experience in Guatemala demonstrated that his most

Mizner family at the American Legation, Guatemala, 1889. When Lansing Mizner was appointed ambassador and moved to Guatemala, the only children who accompanied Mama and Papa Mizner were Addison, Wilson, and Edgar, who served as first secretary of his father's ministry. Addison and Wilson led an exciting life and came home a year later fluent in Spanish. In this photograph, William and Minnie visit the legation with friends. (Above are Minnie and Addison; below is Wilson; in the middle left to right are Mama and Papa Mizner, two friends, Edgar, and William).
Courtesy of The Oakland Museum of California.

meaningful academic experiences in life would be extracurricular. Lastly, there is evidence from his memoirs that there is a growing maturity and sense of confidence emerging during this time. At the end of his year in Guatemala, it was becoming clear what kind of adult Mizner would become.

When Addison Mizner returned to San Francisco at the age of seventeen, he wanted to attend the University of California, an objective that would require academic preparation. San Francisco, bustling and burgeoning, was becoming a cosmopolitan city recognized for its extravagance and luxury. The city that Addison would soon know very well had all the trappings of prosperity: theater, an opera house, music halls, saloons, luxury hotels, and restaurants, many of them French. In contrast to New York, San Francisco's urban park, Golden Gate Park, was larger than the venerable Central Park and its Palace Hotel was "the largest, most modern, and most luxurious hotel in the world" before the Waldorf and Astoria Hotels were even built.[24] The Palace's splendor motivated Andrew Carnegie to proclaim, "There is no other hotel building in the world equal to this."[25]

The population of San Francisco had grown from under one thousand in 1848 to approximately three hundred thousand in 1890.[26] It was a dynamic center of transformation, a place where bartenders had become silver barons, where the rowdy and undisciplined were now civic leaders. It was a city with one of the highest number of millionaires per capita.[27] By 1871, the year before the birth of Addison Mizner, the newspapers actually carried stories describing the wealth of its leading citizens. Naturally, this thriving activity attracted many visitors, among them Oscar Wilde, who arrived in late March 1882 during his US lecture tour. His impressions of the city were summarized in 1890 when he published *The Picture of Dorian Gray*. While discussing the disappearance of artist Basil Hallward with a friend, Dorian speculated: "It's an odd thing, but anyone who disappears is said to be seen in San Francisco. It must be a delightful city and possess all the attractions of the next world."[28]

One of the principal reasons for the meteoric transformation of San Francisco in the last decades of the nineteenth century was the discovery of the Comstock Lode, the richest deposit of silver in American history. With this discovery, many miners flocked to the boomtown of Virginia City in the western Utah Territory. Among them were four Irish Americans who organized the Consolidated Virginia Silver Mine and became known as the Silver Kings. Beginning in 1873, their mines began producing what became known as the Big Bonanza, a yield of $105 million in gold and silver that would make the owners very wealthy.[29] One of the Silver Kings was James Graham Fair, who would establish his family in San Francisco, a move that would have implications for Addison Mizner.

James Graham Fair, portrait by Mathew Brady, circa 1885. Fair was one of the Silver Kings who made a fortune in silver mining in Nevada with the Comstock Lode. He later became a US senator from Nevada. His two daughters, Tessie and Birdie, married prominent New Yorkers and introduced Addison Mizner to their friends who formed the basis of polite society in New York, Newport, and Long Island.
Courtesy of the Library of Congress.

Difficult, selfish, and deceitful, James Fair became known as "Slippery Jim" and often used deception and duplicity not only against enemies but his own family as well.[30] Divorced by his wife, he left an immense fortune to his two daughters, Teresa and Virginia, known respectively as Tessie and Birdie. In contrast to other members of the Fair family, the daughters found happiness and enjoyed brilliant lives at the apex of American social life. Their enduring relationship with the Mizners and specifically with Addison would propel him to a privileged social position when he moved to New York in 1904. Familiarity with the Fairs and other affluent San Francisco families helped to cultivate Mizner's adroit social skills and to expose him to the lifestyle and material manifestations of wealth.

The city of San Francisco, a playground of prosperity and indulgence, was certainly found seductive by a gregarious and exuberant young man just months shy of his eighteenth birthday. Addison Mizner, perfectly capable of navigating his own way through San Francisco, enjoyed the additional benefit of being aided by the presence of older brothers, all well connected. At this time, Edgar Mizner, in partnership selling Mumm's champagne with social arbiter Ned Greenway, had fallen in love with Tessie Fair. Disappointing Edgar and especially Mama Mizner, Tessie later became engaged to Hermann Oelrichs, a wealthy New York businessman and shipping agent. She obviously remained very fond of Edgar as he served as an usher in her wedding, one of the most spectacular and extravagant social affairs in San Francisco. It was during his brother's courtship of Tessie that Addison would get to know her well, a friendship that would intensify with time.

Addison's sister, Min, had arranged for him to attend the Bates School in San Raphael, "a school for young gentlemen," a claim Addison found amusing because the school administrators had not yet met him.[31] Although dedicated to renewing his education, Addison Mizner spent significant time pursuing a social life in San Francisco. Genial and humorous, he easily made friends, many from San Francisco's finest families. Among his intimate companions were Paul Delmas, whose father was noted defense attorney and civic leader Delphin Delmas, and Peter Martin, whose mother was the city's preeminent hostess and whose uncle had been the governor of California. He also befriended Richard Harding Davis, who would soon become a journalist, writer, and war correspondent of significance. As he would do for the rest of his life, Addison liberally attracted sophisticated and important people.

This sociability, along with his artistic vision, would later make his successful architectural practice possible. Biographer Donald Curl rightly categorized Mizner as a society architect and conflated the importance of his social life and the success of his professional career. Curl elaborated: "During the first thirty-two years of Addison Cairns Mizner's life, he prepared for the career of a society architect. The son of prominent California pioneers, he spent his youth among the best families of San Francisco. From his earliest days, knowing 'the right people' became one of the important ambitions of his life."[32] Premeditated or not, Mizner's easy familiarity with the grand opened a door that eventually permitted cosmopolitan clients to experience his architectural virtuosity.

With the return of the family from Guatemala, Addison was unfortunately joined at Bates by his younger brother Wilson, who had been quickly dismissed from three other schools. The traits that would make them the most illustrious bearers of the Mizner name were well evident. Both were tall, adventurous, witty, and gregarious. While Wilson was thin and Addison stout, both were strong and willing to fight. In appearance, Addison's bright blue eyes and fair complexion projected a baby face and an air of amiable innocence. Although Wilson still had a look of innocence at this time, it was not long before he developed a more appraising and calculating aspect. Addison captured the contrast in his memoirs when he wrote that Wilson "could start more trouble (and get caught at it) than anyone in the world; whereas, I could look blue-eyed and innocent, he had a criminal look that convicted him at once."[33]

For two young men emboldened by exotic adventures in Guatemala, returning to a traditional classroom would prove

Photograph of Wilson Mizner, 1891. Having just returned from Guatemala at the age of fifteen, Wilson was attempting to resume his formal education. Before joining Addison at Bates, Wilson had been thrown out of three schools within a period of four weeks. After the thrilling adventure of living in Guatemala and traveling throughout Central America, neither Addison nor Wilson was able to readjust to the sedentary existence of a traditional education.
Courtesy of The Oakland Museum of California.

tedious. Addison and Wilson had spent their young lives in the presence of important people. Around the dinner table in Benicia, the boys were exposed to politicians, businessmen, and civic leaders and, with the move to Guatemala, they interacted regularly with generals, politicians, and diplomats. Not only were they confident in the presence of powerful people, they might also have developed an exaggerated sense of importance due to the deference consistently extended to them as a result of having an influential father. After all, each had his own valet. For young men who filled their time with bullfights, horse races, revolutions, and opera, conventional education could only pale in comparison.

The pursuit of education was just another adventure for the brothers. Wilson's unruly behavior, always a problem in structured environments, provided entertainment to his peers; however, it worked to the detriment of his brother. After four months, Wilson was expelled from Bates and, in his wake, Addison followed at the command of Mama Mizner. During the next nine months, they together attended various schools without finding success. Recognizing Wilson's inordinate capacity for trouble-making, his parents finally identified an institution believed to be capable of corralling their misguided son. Santa Clara College was known for its high walls and its vigilant bulldogs; however, none of its battlements proved an impediment to Wilson. With his distinguished record for disturbance unblemished, he was expelled. In his memoirs, Addison feigned incredulity: "Imagine being expelled from a penitentiary."[34]

With Wilson on his own at this point, Addison began taking classes at Boone's College in Berkeley in hopes of passing the entrance exam for the University of California. His peripatetic and fragmented academic career proved inadequate for the purpose and he predictably failed his examination. Although largely deprived of a formal education, he had nonetheless amassed a significant cultural and practical education during his life of travel. Even at this age, he was aware of his strengths, recognizing that he would do well "had they examined me in observation, history, the joy of things beautiful, my delight in color as well as form."[35]

After almost two years of academic struggle in San Francisco, Addison traveled to Spain and enrolled in the University of Salamanca, founded in 1134, the oldest university in Spain. Most probably, Addison took classes in Spanish humanities, a discipline in which art and architecture would have been included. Since there was only brief reference to his time in Salamanca in his memoirs and no mention in his journal, biographer Carolyn Seebohm concluded that "the experience made no lasting impression upon him."[36] Even if this was a stay of only a few months, it is difficult to dismiss his time in Salamanca as inconsequential. This majestic culture and its grand architecture would have greatly impressed a sensibility

In Salamanca, Mizner saw, for the first time, buildings of great age and fine architecture. His impressions of the ways that changing fortune are evident in the colliding massing and detail of centuries of architectural change left a durable impression.
Courtesy of the Library of Congress.

so receptive to aesthetic impressions in general and to Hispanic expressions in particular.

Salamanca is the capital of the province of Salamanca and has significant university and religious buildings, imposing palaces, and magnificent public squares, all illustrative of its exalted status. This experience would have supplemented and amplified all that he had experienced in Central America. Donald Curl summarized this moment: "If the Salamanca experience produced no degrees, it did help mold the artist's sense of beauty and fitness. Like many before him, he began studying architecture by seeing and sketching great examples of the art."[37] According to historian Christina Orr, the evidence of the impact of Salamanca resides in his voluminous scrapbooks and commentary.[38]

After returning from Salamanca in 1893, Addison resumed a social life that revolved around his many friends. Conspicuous among this group were Andy and Peter Martin, whose family was socially prominent in San Francisco. They managed to get into a lot of trouble at this time and, according to Addison's memoirs, were sexually promiscuous. Addison's parents feared that he was leaning toward a life in the arts and, hoping to derail this tendency, sent him on a foreign trip with his brother Henry. In his memoirs, Addison describes an artist as "the lowest form of long-haired, flowing-cravat ass extant," a description that was humorous but no doubt a reflection of his parents' commentary on the profession.[39]

William Mizner, a practicing physician since 1890, accepted a position as a doctor on a ship traveling to China and agreed to have his younger brother accompany him. If this voyage was intended to dissuade Addison's artistic proclivities, it only further provoked an imagination that readily responded to exotic stimuli. Addison was attracted to the mystery of the Orient and returned home with chow dogs and other oddities. He also developed an affinity for eastern architecture and landscape design, ideas that were recorded in his sketchbook and that would later appear in his architectural commissions.

In August 1893, Addison traveled with Peter Martin and others to Chicago to visit the World's Columbian Exposition, a world's fair that celebrated Christopher Columbus's trip to the New World in 1492. This episode would prove valuable to the development of his architectural thinking. Although most structures were in the neoclassical style, the uniformity was subordinated to the stunning effect created by white buildings that were illuminated by the ubiquitous use of streetlights. This not only had the practical effect of rendering the streets and buildings useable at night, but it created the optical effect of dramatically highlighting an idealized cityscape. This was known as the White City, and it inspired the City Beautiful movement across America. This campaign advocated the idea that the city was more than just an economic unit providing the means for industrial activity. The new city should also be a representation of beauty, contributing to the spiritual well-being and visual delight of its denizens.

Among the distinguished architects who contributed to the White City were Richard Morris Hunt, Daniel Burnham, and

Grand Basin and Court of Honor at the Chicago World's Fair, 1893. Before beginning the practice of architecture in 1894 in the office of Willis Polk, Addison Mizner visited the Chicago World's Fair, also known as the World's Columbian Exposition, which commemorated Christopher Columbus's arrival in the New World in 1492. Mizner was greatly impressed with the architecture and urban planning. The ideas he saw there would influence his development and work in New York and Palm Beach.

Courtesy of Wikipedia. Photograph by C. D. Arnold.

Louis Sullivan; however, it was the buildings of two dissenters that would have an impact on Addison's career. One was the Agricultural Building by McKim, Mead & White. Stanford White would, in a few years, come to play a meaningful role in the life of Addison Mizner. The second was the California State Building by A. Page Brown from San Francisco. In stark contrast to the neoclassical principles of symmetry, balance, and order, Brown's building was designed in the California Mission style that betrayed its Spanish influence with bell towers, exterior arcades, arched windows, tiled roofs, and stuccoed walls. As this was a style that Addison had already seen in California and Central America, he innately understood it. Standing in high relief against the profusion of Beaux-Arts buildings, the Spanish architectural influence resonated strongly.

Finally, the White City represented a stunning example of urban planning, a consistent and comprehensive point of view extended to all components of the whole: the site, the arrangement of buildings, and the surrounding landscape. This perspective of compositional harmony was reawakened in Europeans during the Renaissance and was manifest in the planning of all great cities of the western world in the late 1890s. Throughout his architectural career, Addison Mizner would have an eye for coherence even in his smallest projects. In the mature years of his architectural practice, he would have the opportunity to design a monumental urban planning project, a conception that no doubt returned him to the indelible effects of the White City. He later remarked that "Nothing for a moment could describe the sublime grace of the buildings, [or] the artistic and clever way in which the grounds are laid out."[40] The impact of the White City was considerable, for he spent three months there.

Addison Mizner returned to San Francisco on December 1, 1893, after visits to New York and St. Louis. His homecoming was a sad one. Suffering from ill health since his return from Guatemala, Lansing Mizner passed away on December 10. Two days later, on his twenty-first birthday, Addison attended the burial of his father. Since his return from Guatemala, Lansing Mizner, always a respected and distinguished gentleman, had only been able to view himself in diminished terms. This self-perception derived from the memory of his disgraceful dismissal as a minister of the US government and from a feeling of inadequacy owing to the significantly reduced state of his investment portfolio. As a result of bad decisions, he left to his family an inheritance of approximately $25,000. This knowledge would have been devastating to a proud man whose paramount concern was to provide adequately for his family. For many reasons, this was a dark moment for the Mizners. Without prospects and inheritance, Addison Mizner at this moment decided to pursue architecture as a profession.

CHAPTER FOUR

PATH TO ARCHITECTURE

When Addison Mizner finally made the decision to remain in San Francisco, he was taking a path less out of clarity and conviction than frustration and ambivalence. Confronted with the reality of a lack of inheritance, Addison was in search of a vocation. Not to be overlooked in his development was the role played by San Francisco. It was a prosperous and alluring city at this time, especially for a young man of twenty-one years of age and for one whose family enjoyed relationships with San Francisco's leading citizens. Establishing a pattern that continued in New York and Palm Beach, Addison combined work with pleasure, reestablishing long-held personal relationships and cultivating friendships with people who would need the services of a sophisticated architect. His growing familiarity with wealth and power during this period engendered a level of confidence and ease that paved the way to become a society architect. The next two and a half years of his life provided the professional and social tools that served as the building blocks of Addison Mizner's architectural education.

With an affinity for the arts and a maturing sensibility, Mizner clearly enjoyed a profound attraction to both writing and architecture. Although he had been writing short stories at this time, he had no reason to believe that taking this path professionally could produce adequate compensation. Before returning to San Francisco, Addison had taken three trips that had a profound impact on his interest in and eventual commitment to architecture: his educational sojourn to Salamanca and Spain, his travels to China with his brother, William, and his extended summer visit to Chicago at the height of the 1893 World's Columbian Exhibition.

In Salamanca, Mizner no doubt connected his childhood memories of the sixteenth-century Guatemalan architecture of Antigua with its antecedents in Spain, and therein lay his first intellectual architectural experience and the imaginary framework within which he would approach architectural creativity. Mizner learned that Spain's architecture derived from many influences from the Romans, Visigoths, and Moors. The cosmopolitan architecture of Spain clearly drew order

During Mizner's tenure at the University of Salamanca, his impressions of the accretive architecture of several hundred years of transformation would become among his most indelible sources of inspiration. The Patio del Palacio de la Salinas, built in 1546, illustrates those characteristics that Mizner cherished, primarily the evidence that cycles of growth and change produce a rich architectural record.
Courtesy of Wikimedia Commons. Photograph by Tamorlan.

from the Romans and an orientalism from the Moors, the exotic combination of which fascinated Mizner in his youth and later as a highly successful explicator of its essence in his most important Palm Beach residences and public buildings.

In China, Mizner witnessed a wholly new approach to architecture, planning, and the cultural determinants of authentic orientalism. And, in the 1893 Chicago summer, Mizner repeatedly visited the World's Columbian Exposition, fascinated by its scale, complexity, innovation, and, most importantly, by its planning and architecture. Little did Mizner

know that, by later that same year, he would be in league with Willis J. Polk, a San Francisco architect known by his family and tied, by employment and personal friendship, to the planners and most important architects of the exposition: Daniel Burnham, Stanford White, and Page Brown, all critically involved in the most important movements in architecture at this time.

Mizner's summer of 1893 was spent in Chicago and repeated trips to the "White City." He would have certainly visited the California Building, A. Page Brown's clear move toward regional expression. A contemporary critic, Montgomery Schuyler, declared that the California Building "was one of the noteworthy ornaments of the fair."

In the autumn of 1893, Mizner would join Willis Polk in San Francisco, an architect with deep experience with many of the leading architects responsible for the exposition including Brown. For the first time, Mizner experienced a 686-acre, planned and built "city." The "fair" experience would be among his strongest memories as Mizner dreamed of his own city in Boca Raton thirty-two years later.
Courtesy of Wikimedia Commons. Chicago Gravure Company.

The importance of the historical context of architectural education and practice in the late nineteenth century cannot be overstated. The turbulent period between 1885 and 1914 is still resonating in architecture and is responsible for much of the way that we think about architecture's role in civilization. The ferment of the period was profound, and into this maelstrom stepped Addison Mizner without formal education, but with a general historical and cultural framework within which to understand the intellectual discussions that surrounded him. He was, at twenty-one, exceptionally bright, affable, hardworking, clever, and well traveled. These traits along with his personality, artistic sensibility, and high social connections, enabled him to navigate the highest levels of society and the bohemian worlds of art and architecture.

The systems of architectural education established in early nineteenth century Europe had only begun to attract American interest in the third quarter of the century, most prominently, to the Ecole des Beaux Arts in Paris. The first American graduate of the Ecole was Richard Morris Hunt, with Henry Hobson Richardson the second. Many of the Ecole's architecture students also worked in the Paris ateliers of leading architects to learn the practical aspects of business, construction, and technological development, subjects largely ignored by the Ecole. Richardson certainly gathered as much technical knowledge in Labrouste's atelier as he learned about composition in the Ecole.

Following Hunt's return to New York in 1855, he founded the first American school of architecture in the Tenth Street Studio Building with four students, one of whom, William Robert Ware, later founded the architectural programs at MIT in 1866 and Columbia in 1881. As with most aspiring architects, the means and methods of designing and constructing buildings were handed down through apprenticeships, generation to generation. And, as importantly, the pure construction aspect of practice was heavily dependent on a complex building community. Successful building required collaboration between the apprenticeship and guild structures of the building trades, which provided craftsmen, tradesmen, and artists to construct the many extraordinary built structures that improved cities and American civilization over the last 150 years.

And so it was in American architecture in the nineteenth century: many of the greatest architects in American history were educated in the studios and ateliers of older architects who had been trained in the same manner. Some, and arguably some of the best, were educated at the Ecole des Beaux Arts. Many others were merely "educated" and produced a large body of mediocre work that was distinguished only by its slavish embrace of conventional patterns of accepted academic models, widely published by a growing architectural media. By the 1880s, the architectural embrace of academic models was undergoing change as architects broadened their sources of inspiration. Seeking and accepting a broader range of historical architectural precedents, architects borrowed liberally and in ways that created juxtapositions that suited new and innovative architectural applications. This tendency toward Academic Eclecticism was abetted by the rapidly increasing availability of historic architectural media, including photographs depicting architecture from around the globe. The movement succeeded in responding to the need for creative freedom within a system of principles that many architects believed would enable a clearer evaluation of the success of the architect's aesthetic goals. Great importance was attached to the rationalization of the design process by the establishment of principles and order so as to avoid pastiche, that grave error of incongruously or inconsistently employing architectural principles or subjective style with cacophonous result.

In Richard Longstreth's excellent book, *On the Edge of the World: Four Architects in San Francisco at the Turn of the Century*, he states regarding "Academic Eclecticism" that: "Obtaining a comprehensive view of the past supposedly could increase the architect's faculty for critical analysis of abstract qualities, which could then be applied to new work regardless of changes in requirements and taste. The aim of the movement was academic in the liberal sense of the term: developing a broad base of knowledge founded on precedent in order to formulate solutions for contemporary problems in a rational manner. Far from constituting a theory of design, these principles were a series of loosely defined attributes, based on interpretations of the past that could lend authority to architecture without inhibiting its growth and change." By example, the principle of "unity" is one that enables the Gothic or Romanesque styles to be understood by professional or layman to be internally consistent across all aspects of its architecture. By the adoption of these principles, the schism between Classicism and Gothicism was reconciled and architects began to embrace a broader view that, while still subjective, led to a belief that "all elements should act in concert to form a logical and coherent statement."[1]

No place in the world was more attuned to the theories of Academic Eclecticism than New York. As the leading North American center of capital and industry, the work of architecture, in all of its guises, was put to work imagining what the next global center could become. With several schools of architecture and substantial practices supported by wealthy clients, architecture and architects blossomed to lead design thinking in the last quarter of the nineteenth century. In New York, no firm was more prominent or powerful than McKim, Mead & White, whose office at 57 Broadway was more important as a nursery for American architects and architectural firms than any other.

Most of these architects traced their lineage to Henry Hobson Richardson, the second graduate of the Ecole des Beaux Arts. Richardson continues to be a pivotal figure in American architecture and his students and critics are widely varied in their view of the reasons for his importance. Some embrace the success of his picturesque approach, which is characterized by asymmetry and the use of informal romantic features. Others embrace the clear three-dimensional massing that derived from his rigorous Ecole-derived planning. Most agree that Richardson's true genius derived from his ability to manage picturesqueness within a strong framework of confident personal principle. Richardson presented architects in the second half of the nineteenth century a one-man sourcebook for many seemingly disparate approaches to architecture. Unique in Richardson's beginning as an architect was his embrace of Byzantine, Medieval, and Norman architectural forms in direct opposition to antecedents that would have been the daily subject of his Ecole des Beaux Arts education.

Richardson was open to many influences, demonstrating his embrace of beauty in all of its forms including the Japanese vogue incited by Edward S. Morse by his book, *Japanese Homes and Their Surroundings*, not published until 1886, but presented frequently to the public as a series of lantern slides as early as

Manoir d'Ango, Varengeville, Normandy, France
    In the early 1890s, a sixteenth-century complex of buildings in Varengeville-sur-mer, known as Manoir d'Ango, became the inspiration for Joseph Wells, an important architect at McKim, Mead & White, and Stanford White. In this Norman farm complex, White and others saw the potential of an historical architecture that could displace Anglo-American precedents as models for resort and seaside architectural exterior finishes: uniform stone textures rendered as wood shingles.
Courtesy of Creative Commons. Photograph by Paul Hermans.

1878 as part of Morse's Lowell lectures at MIT.[2] Clearly, the Japanese drawings and pictures in the Morse lectures influenced Richardson's work as evidenced by Japanese motifs in the Ames Gate Lodge and many of the small railway stations such as the Boston and Albany Railroad Station in Brighton, Massachusetts.[3]

Richardson's broad embrace of beauty took him to the north coast of France and the small villages of Japan. His use of allusions served to produce "the ultimate creative synthesis of eclecticism, projecting his age into the next." Richardson was influenced by Norman architecture particularly the Manoir d'Ango, south of Dieppe in Normandy.[4] The Manoir d'Ango also finds its way into the work of many of Richardson's disciples such as Stanford White of McKim, Mead & White in the Newport Casino of 1879 and A. W. Longfellow's design approach over thirty years.[5]

As Richardson wrote little about his work, and little is reported of interviews in the contemporaneous architectural press, it is useful to understand his influence by the evidence of those architects who rose to individual success following their work in Richardson's firms, particularly those with whom Addison Mizner worked or enjoyed influential social relationships. Longstreth points to McKim, Mead & White as having owed an enormous debt to Richardson. As both McKim and White worked for Richardson at a critical period in his developing approach to architecture, they would have been keenly aware of the disparate influences leading Richardson to his novel approach to architecture and its pivot from the Victorian to the academic period. In 1892, Mariana Griswold Van Rensselaer, a contemporary critic of Richardson, noted: "We thought that he had shown us the virtue of the Romanesque style when what he had really shown us was the difference between weak, confused, commonplace, trivial buildings and buildings with instinct and vigor, individuality, and beauty. We are not likely to forget his teaching with regard to the essentials of good architecture: in a greater degree than any one can estimate it has affected and will affect the work of the whole profession."[6]

Longstreth concludes that, "in contrast to the narrow scope of historical references used by Richardson, the firm of McKim, Mead & White turned to a multitude of sources, encompassing buildings of numerous periods, regions and types. It interpreted and combined these sources in a variety of ways. The result was a design vocabulary of unusual breadth that became a major influence in establishing the parameters of expression over the next several decades."[7]

The history of McKim, Mead & White may be best understood when divided into two periods: pre-1879 and post-1879. During the 1870s, Charles McKim had, with others, synthesized many English and American domestic architectural forms into what Vincent Scully described in his classic study as "The Shingle Style."[8] In 1879, upon returning from a fifteen-month tour of Europe following his departure from Richardson's office, Stanford White joined McKim and Mead to form McKim, Mead & White. White had spent his time in Europe studying the vernacular architecture of northern Europe and primarily in the coastal regions of Normandy and Brittany. White had concluded from his tour that emerging American architectural needs could be met by the scale and size of Norman manor houses and that the large masonry expanses of walls could, instead, be sheathed with wooden shingles. The effect of changing the architectural language and synthesizing the architectural references would be to create buildings that were "styleless."[9]

These houses—both the established European structures and the American structures to come—were primarily for use as summer cottages. As such, and in support of the social nature of these "cottages," multiple bedrooms were required and cross ventilation would require an open plan which in turn encouraged architects to develop new formal approaches that would incorporate picturesque flourishes to manage the scale.

Longstreth notes that: "By the early 1890s, eclectic diversity had become a widespread phenomenon, and McKim, Mead & White were regarded as being both its leading exponents and among the country's foremost architects. Their example had great influence on established firms, as well as on a younger generation just beginning independent practice."[10]

In the 1890s diverse expression remained a significant characteristic, but a new movement toward regional expression took hold and began a new chapter in eclecticism and the approach to regional architecture that challenged McKim, Mead & White. The vastness of the United States and the variety of historic architectural expression across the continent suggested that local and regional character were as valid in references as European examples. Leland Stanford's wish for a "distinctly Californian" campus sought to recognize the state's unique Spanish heritage and landscape. Richardson's successor firm, Shepley, Rutan & Coolidge, and Frederick Law Olmsted favored this approach, but the resulting master plan and initial architecture of the Stanford campus largely reflect Richardsonian forms.

More interesting are the two Carrère & Hastings hotels, The Ponce de Leon and The Alcazar Hotel, both designed for Henry Flagler in St. Augustine, Florida, and completed in 1887. Both Carrère and Hastings had worked for McKim, Mead & White at 57 Broadway in New York and had left the firm to design this very important project while establishing their office in the very same building. The Ponce de Leon Hotel (1885–1887) draws from Italian, Moorish, Romanesque, and French Renaissance architecture, all ordered within a rigorous Beaux-Arts plan. These highly successful projects recognized the Spanish Colonial history of northeast Florida, though without recognizing that the scale, form, and detail of these buildings were completely foreign to the region.

Bernard Maybeck, an Ecole-trained architect who had emigrated from Germany, worked in the Carrère & Hastings office during the construction period on the Ponce de Leon

Hotel and is credited for the interiors. Maybeck eventually was among those architects who migrated to San Francisco and was a contemporary of Willis Polk during the period of Mizner's employment with Polk. Maybeck is, undoubtedly, the most successful of a group of important Bay Area architects who represented a scholarly and unique approach to architecture.

Since the discoveries of gold and silver, and statehood in 1850, San Francisco had grown largely as a wooden town with all of the risk and spectacular damage that fires and earthquakes could summon. The architecture that followed the early booms of the 1860s and 1870s was not sophisticated and had been produced by architects who were chiefly the result of technical education. Two 1870s arrivals began to shift the San Francisco cultural landscape for architecture: Albert Pissis, trained at the Ecole des Beaux Arts, and F. F. Hamilton, who had worked in the important office of Peabody & Stearns. Both men were accomplished before their arrival and brought a level of worldly sophistication and architectural ability that would respond to the dreams of newly wealthy San Franciscans. Pissis and Hamilton would be followed to San Francisco by many architects who, in concert, led to the creation of a city that still looms large as a place of aspiration for many around the world.[11]

The 1890s in San Francisco were a time of maturation in the real estate industry and the architectural profession.

The enormous wealth of the city driven by mining, shipping, manufacturing, and related interests provided the impetus for building in new and more permanent ways. Architects, never far behind a boom, were attracted to the Bay Area's beauty, climate, and vitality. As the new century approached, wealth desired permanence in its residential and commercial architecture and sought out architects from the Midwest and East. In 1887, *San Francisco Chronicle* newspaperman Michael de Young engaged the Chicago firm of Burnham & Root as architects for his Chronicle Building. Burnham & Root were also engaged by de Young's chief rival, William Randolph Hearst, to develop the design of the headquarters of the *San Francisco Examiner* in 1890. Darius Ogden Mills secured the firm for the design of a new office building larger than Hearst's.[12]

The arrival of A. Page Brown in San Francisco, however, may have caused the biggest cultural impact. Brown had attended Cornell's School of Architecture for one year before joining McKim, Mead & White's New York office in 1879 as an apprentice in its drafting department. Brown started his own New York firm in 1884 under the patronage of Mrs. Cyrus McCormick designing institutional and architectural projects related to her philanthropic pursuits. The majority of Brown's other early work came directly or indirectly from Mrs. McCormick's East Coast friends.[13] In 1889, Brown was commissioned by Mary Ann Crocker to design a mausoleum for her husband, Charles Crocker, the California industrialist.[14] With this commission and another from her to design an Old People's Home, Brown decided to move to San Francisco in 1889, bringing with him Willis Polk, who was working in New York at the same time. Polk was hired from his position with Charles Atwood, who would become chief designer for D. H. Burnham & Company (the firm which would become Burnham & Root, a future Willis Polk relationship). After establishing his San Francisco office, Brown also hired Albert Schweinfurth, who had worked for McKim, Mead & White and Bernard Maybeck, who had graduated from the Ecole des Beaux Arts and had worked in the offices of Carrère & Hastings.[15]

Brown understood the principles and view of McKim, Mead & White's work and was a fine interpreter of their urbane approach. Only a few architects working in San Francisco could match Brown's experience and capabilities. Working generously and closely with his very talented architects, each member of the firm enjoyed great freedom in their respective approaches to design and supervision. All of these architects took advantage of that latitude and succeeded in creating the impression that Brown's firm could design across a broad range of styles. Many of these architects, Polk, Maybeck, and Schweinfurth chief among them, would soon become the most important architects working in San Francisco and would retain that status for the next thirty years.

As with a large number of architects formerly working with McKim, Mead & White, Page Brown's first office was also located in the legendary 57 Broadway building in New York. Many of these architects and firms would become leading American firms in their own right. McKim, Mead & White's office was more than an office, serving as the salon of the academic movement and "a council chamber where men could meet and discuss the renaissance of American Art." Carrère, Hastings, Brown, and many leading painters and sculptors—Millet, LaFarge, Saint-Gaudens, Chase, Sargent—gathered to discuss art and architecture on a regular basis.[16]

In establishing his new firm in San Francisco, Brown modeled his studio from his experience in New York and with McKim, Mead & White. He surrounded himself with very talented architects and encouraged them to express their architectural imaginations. By this time, the Mission Revival architectural period which had found its footing in the mid-1880s had become the inspiration for Page Brown's highly successful California Building at the Chicago World's Columbian Exposition of 1893, and Brown's interest in Mission prompted his attraction to Willis Polk. Polk had explored many design approaches, among them Colonial Revival, Richardsonian, the Shingle Style, and, of course, Mission Revival and contributed to many of Brown's most important commissions, including the Crocker Bank building designed on a thin wedge-shaped lot on Market and Montgomery Streets in San Francisco's financial district and completed in 1891.[17]

Willis Polk left Page Brown to open his own office in 1890 and designed the Avery House in Sausalito, a long box, covered by cedar shingles and waxed redwood paneling, returning for inspiration to Richardson's Atlantic coast cottages. Polk, described by Kirker as an *enfant terrible*, was becoming a leader of the design community in San Francisco, and in November of 1890 created the first number of the *Architectural News*, a magazine that lasted for three issues before "Polk skipped to Carmel with the subscription money."[18] Kirker credits Polk with having "prepared the way for the Mission Revival and set[ting] the tone for sophisticated building in California for a quarter century" and notes that Polk's intent, through the pages of the *Architectural News* and his bohemian set, was to "start a number of young men upon 'the civilized adventure'."[19]

At age eight, Willis Polk began work with a local building contractor in Jacksonville, Illinois, and proceeded from there to small architectural firms, a family design-build practice, and an itinerant practice with many of the leading New York architects of the day including Page Brown, who had left McKim, Mead & White to establish his own practice at 57 Broadway.

Brown's move to San Francisco, accompanied by Polk, and shortly joined by Maybeck and Schweinfurth, was the pivotal event in the Bay Area's architectural renaissance. Yet, Polk yearned to lead his own firm and when his larger family moved to San Francisco, Polk and his father established Polk & Polk in 1892, and employed a young Addison Mizner. Polk's ebullience and recklessness caused Mizner to recall that Polk was "a genius, only spoiled by having read Whistler's 'Gentle Art of Making Enemies'. . . . [and] became a genius at this as well." Nonetheless, Mizner's experience with Polk was the true beginnings of Mizner's architectural education and aspiration.

Courtesy of The Library of Congress.

As the architectural disruptor of late nineteenth century San Francisco, Polk understood and embraced the principles of Academic Eclecticism and saw in the Colonial Revival, popularized by Stanford White in the wake of the influential Philadelphia Centennial of 1876, an opportunity to create its analog, Mission Revival, in California. While California was briefly affected by the enthusiasm for Colonial Revival, its architects saw in this movement an opportunity to create a mission-inspired revival from its Spanish Colonial past. "The first architect to become seriously aware of the possibilities that the missions offered contemporary builders was Willis Polk."[20]

Polk's *Architectural News* was devoted to the architecture and building scene in San Francisco, and in each issue he dedicated a section to articles on the Franciscan establishments, which he illustrated with drawings of mission details. It is uncertain at what date Polk realized the architectural possibilities of the missions, but "as early as 1887 he made a sketch for an imaginary 'Mission Church of Southern California Type' and it is claimed that the architect's greatest pride was his role in rehabilitating Mission Dolores, in the course of which he studied Spanish tile-making and Franciscan methods of construction."[21] Willis Polk, a purely self-taught and apprenticed architect, had worked since age eight with a local contractor in St. Louis, and within five years had accepted a job as an office boy in the architectural firm of Jerome B. Legg. Shortly after, Polk joined his father, who was an accomplished carpenter, and by 1885, the family had moved to Kansas City, Missouri, where his father, W. W. Polk, created the partnership of W. W. Polk and Son. Young Willis Polk designed many of the projects built by him and his father, and as was the practice of the time, probably had access to pattern books, journals, and catalogues.[22]

In 1887, an ambitious Willis Polk departed his father's partnership and went to work as a draftsman with Van Brunt & Howe, a well-known Boston firm that had moved its office to Kansas City.[23] Van Brunt was an important architect, a prolific writer and lecturer who ran his office as an atelier in the fashion of Richard Morris Hunt, his mentor. Longstreth notes that Polk did not necessarily embrace Van Brunt's intellectual interests but that he was "strongly committed to the academic movement." A strong admirer of Richardson, Van Brunt placed him at the pinnacle of the architectural profession. Polk's scheme for the City Hall in Washington, DC, in 1887 and other projects in the office were inspired by Richardson and Van Brunt. Restless, Polk left Van Brunt after six months and crossed the country repeatedly for five different architects until his move to New York where he would join other architects eager to learn more about and from the academic movement.[24]

Willis Polk drawing of his proposed design for the Washington, DC, City Hall

In 1887, Polk decided to leave his partnership with his father and took a drafting position with Van Brunt & Howe, important Boston architects that had established an office in Kansas City. Van Brunt was a leading American educator and practitioner, and was, at that time, changing his own views of art and architecture. Polk could not have found a more edifying position and it changed the course of his life.

Polk's sketch for a new DC City Hall reflects the strength of H. H. Richardson's influence in the country at that time. Although Polk's design was not built, the Old Post Office is an actual DC building that reflects Richardson's influence. Completed in 1899, it was designed by Willoughby J. Edbrooke, the supervising architect of the Treasury Department.

Polk was intellectually curious and arranged during his period in New York to take classes from William Robert Ware, Van Brunt's former partner. Polk remembered these lectures as pivotal in his architectural experience.[25]

From Atwood's office, Polk joined A. Page Brown in New York. As Brown's office was at 57 Broadway, he introduced Polk to the partners and senior staff at McKim, Mead & White. In a few years, Polk had been exposed to the leading architects and artists in New York and had demonstrated a clear ability to understand the principles and techniques of the modern movements that were transforming the design and practice of architecture.

Given his prominence in San Francisco cultural circles, Polk had come to know many of San Francisco's leading social families. Addison Mizner's sister, Minnie Mizner Chase, had become close friends with Polk and had entertained Polk at her home, Stag's Leap. Mindful of Addison's interest in both writing and architecture, Minnie would introduce Polk to Mizner, who was only six years older. With an affinity for the arts and a maturing sensibility, Mizner was drawn to an irreverent group of kindred spirits who were avant-garde writers and thinkers, a leader of which was Polk. Described by Addison as "a young architect of great taste and little work," Polk hired him as an apprentice draftsman. It was with Polk that he learned the practice of architecture and became skilled in all of the building trades. Importantly, he also participated in the literary salon from which Polk had published the *Architectural News* and would publish *The Lark* and contribute to *The Wave*, a magazine that had been founded in 1890 to "drum up interest in the snazzy Hotel del Monte near Monterey, a property of Samuel Huntington's Southern Pacific Railroad."[26] *The Wave* had changed over the years and had begun to combine, as noted by Kevin Starr, "the high spirits of an undergraduate humor magazine with the chatty nonchalance of a town-and-topics review."[27] Addison Mizner would be profoundly attracted to this collection of bohemians.

Mizner's diary assertion regarding the low levels of work at Polk & Polk was, like many of Mizner's observations, more for humorous effect. The Polk firm during Mizner's employment was small and was not ever larger than Willis Polk, his father, brother Dan (until 1896), and Addison and Wilson Mizner,

who was employed as an "artist." Notwithstanding the size of the firm, a number of important commissions were completed during Mizner's tenure, chief among them the W. B. Bourn residence on Webster Street in Pacific Heights. Bourn was a member of a mining family that was also instrumental in designing and operating private water companies in San

The Bourn Residence, 2550 Webster Street, San Francisco, California, 1895

Despite Mizner's having recorded that Willis Polk had little work during the period of his employment, Polk was busy at that time with several projects that are among his best work.

Over many decades, Polk's relationship with William Bourn, the owner of the Spring Valley Water Company in San Francisco, resulted in several built projects. Bourn's personal city residence on Webster Street in the Pacific Heights neighborhood of San Francisco is notable.

Polk's approach to the development of the Bourn residence façades was evidence of his intellectual growth from his New York days. For the facades, Polk created a very flat façade that was sharply incised for fenestration and other apertures, and he employed clinker brick, a waste product of the brick-making process, for all of the planar surfaces. In employing this radical approach, he relied upon the uneven, misshapen, and wildly varying color of the bricks to perform in the same ways that wood shingles replaced stone for Stanford White. The contradiction of sharp incision in a highly irregular surface was a conscious and successful effort to create a new way of thinking about the treatment of façades.

Photograph by author.

Francisco. Bourn would later commission Polk for the design of Filoli, his country house south of San Francisco.

The Bourn residence is interesting for many reasons: it is a spare Georgian-Italian structure with a low, heavily-rusticated base and a wall surface that is a highly creative adaptation of one of the original techniques of the Shingle Style. The front door occurs in a deep recess in the base marked by alternating quoins of brick and dressed brown stone. Above this aperture is a balcony of dressed stone fronting a large pair of French doors surrounded by a mannered, vaulted, and segmented pediment supported by single pilasters on either side of the doors.

The brick surface is made of clinker bricks, a vitrified brick that results from very high heat, typically unused due to their individual inconsistencies: purplish, with uneven texture and, sometimes, highly reflective surface. Polk's use of this material is interesting for two reasons: First, the building is a highly formal and ordered composition, the tautness of the skin reinforcing this approach. Second, the use of such irregular material, mottled purple with reflective, misshapen bricks randomly distributed, relaxes the tension conferred by the composition but also creates the appearance of natural material in a small masonry format, a complete visual contradiction that restores the tension. This is a lesson that Stanford White learned at Manoir d'Ango and that is at the core of the Shingle Style's genius.

Polk's very modern approach to surface was the mark of his genius and it would be repeated later in his career in the creation of San Francisco's Hallidie Building, one of the first glass curtain wall buildings in the world. For Mizner to be in the close presence of this kind of innovation must have given him creative confidence and instilled pride in having been a member of a firm associated with such design excellence. Mizner did think of himself as an architect, and there is evidence in Polk's (Langley's) *Directory to San Francisco, 1890–1898* of his presence in the Polk & Polk and Willis J. Polk firms, but there is no evidence of Mizner's presence in San Francisco past 1896. In the city directory, Mizner was listed as "Mizner, Addison C., Architect, r[esidence] 1520 Clay Street."[28] By the fall of 1895, Mizner was sharing a house in Russian Hill with Polk as reported in his diary.[29]

But to Mizner's point about little work, commissions were uneven and infrequent at best and Polk, in maintaining his *enfant terrible* reputation, balanced architecture with his coterie of San Francisco writers and critics. As Willis Polk was a leader of the salon, Les Jeunes, Addison's association with the architect not only satisfied his desire to learn architecture but it also allowed him to nurture his literary impulses. Polk and his bohemian friends began to publish *The Lark*, a monthly periodical that satirized the conservative nature of *fin-de-siècle* San Francisco. The first volume appeared on

Cover art for The Lark *by Florence Lundborg, August 1896. This artwork was featured on the cover of the September 1, 1896 issue, number 17. When Addison began working for the architect Willis Polk, he was introduced to a group of bohemian artists and thinkers who published* The Lark, *a periodical that satirized conservative values. The iconoclastic tone of the magazine aligned with his own irreverent point of view.*
Courtesy of the Library of Congress.

May 1, 1895, and its last was published exactly two years later in April 1897. Although begun as a literary amusement, its circulation grew and its content managed to attract the notice of the *New York Times*.[30] Involved in the preparation of the periodical literally on Willis Polk's kitchen table, Addison associated with a collection of well-known artists and writers as well as editors Gillette Burgess, Bruce Porter, and Frank Norris, a close friend of the muckraker Ambrose "Bitter" Bierce. The iconoclastic tone of the publication exposed Addison to cynical and sarcastic observations consistent with his irreverent sense of humor and it certainly informed the color and voice of his subsequent witty writing.

The troubling part of Addison's culturally rich relationship with Polk was the complete absence of income. Polk was famously derelict in his financial responsibilities and eventually declared bankruptcy in 1897. Mizner's lack of pay was no doubt assuaged by Polk's offer of partnership and shared housing during this period. His social ambitions did not appear to be particularly hampered as he continued to see his wealthy San Francisco friends and attend horse shows, the theater, and other cultural gatherings; however, he must have been somewhat embarrassed by his inability to reciprocate socially. Identified in the news and cartoons as "Addie," Mizner was well known and generally portrayed as rotund and foppish.

Mizner is pictured in a Jimmy Swinnerton cartoon in the San Francisco Examiner. *Mizner is depicted as a man of society whose charm, wit, and learning provided entrée to the elite. The cartoon is signed "Swin," as Swinnerton was known during the years that he lived in San Francisco as a contemporary of Addison Mizner. The artist was a favorite of William Randolph Hearst, who moved him to New York for a brief period at the turn of the century.* Courtesy of The Oakland Museum of California.

Having grown up with so many of the young women who were now prominent in San Francisco society, it is not surprising that Mizner would fall in love, a condition complicated by his pennilessness. Since 1891 and his Bates School days, Mizner had been in love with Aileen Goad, the daughter of a wealthy family and the sister of Genevieve Goad, known as the "California Venus."[31] By the fall of 1893, Goad had become seriously interested in someone else and Mizner glumly faced the truth of his loss, salved somewhat by his interest in Ella Hobart and Mary Belle Gwin, both wealthy and beautiful daughters of socially prominent families.

Now approaching twenty-five years of age, he was faced with the dispiriting contrast of his friends' apparent comfort with his own limiting poverty. His tenure with Polk, while exciting and culturally rewarding, provided no acceptable future. Realizing that his financial status was a durable barrier to gaining the serious interest of suitable women, Mizner began expressing his frustration in a diary with various stories that reflected the amorous disappointments he experienced at the time. Mizner's three-year commitment to a journal revealed not only his romantic feelings during these years but also his capacity for imagination. His journals provided evidence of his thoughtfulness, sensitivity, and commitment to story and they importantly revealed much about the ways that Mizner's future architecture would be bound by story and imagination.

Despite the beneficial time spent in Polk's office, Mizner had no evidence yet that the practice of architecture could be a financially sustainable vocation. At this moment of doubt came an invitation from an old acquaintance that seemed to dispel this negative perception. Reyna Barrios, the president of Guatemala since 1892, offered Mizner a commission to design and oversee construction of a $2 million presidential palace to be built in Guatemala City.[32] This would not be the only time in Mizner's life that opportunity arose from a past relationship.

José María Reyna Barrios, the nephew of a former Guatemalan president, was elected to office and replaced General Manuel Barillas Bercian, who had managed to occupy the presidency for seven years without ever having won an election. Throughout Barillas's presidency, Reyna Barrios was politically active in Guatemala and was considered a threat to the government. In 1889, the year of the Mizners' arrival, Barillas had his opponent imprisoned and, according to Mizner's memoirs, intended to have him executed.

Upon incarceration, Algeria Barrios, the American wife of Reyna Barrios, went to the US ministry in Guatemala City desperately seeking help in gaining the freedom of her spouse. Since his father was away on embassy business, Addison listened to the plea and immediately accompanied Señora Barrios to the presidential palace to seek the release of her husband. Unable to refuse the request of the American embassy, President Barillas granted Addison the pardon but, in reality, had no intention of allowing Barrios to leave prison. Mizner knew that the president intended to have Barrios shot at daybreak

Portrait of José María Reyna Barrios, the president of Guatemala from 1892 to 1898. Mizner claimed to have received a commission from Barrios for a $2 million presidential palace as repayment for having saved his life prior to becoming president. With a promised retainer of $25,000 in gold, Mizner quit his position in the firm of Willis Polk in 1897 only to learn subsequently of Barrios's assassination. The architect never received the retainer nor the commission and left San Francisco to mine for gold with his brothers.
Courtesy of Wikipedia and the Museo Nacional de Historia de Guatemala.

on charges of insurrection, so he had his coach driver race to the prison where he was able to free the prisoner just before the president's messenger reached the guard to countermand the order. The couple ultimately managed to escape to Mexico before assuming the presidency three years later.

Remembering Mizner's interest in architecture, Barrios wanted to repay him in 1897 for saving his life eight years earlier. The president's contract stipulated that Addison was to receive a retainer of $25,000 in gold, a lavish sum of money at the time, especially for an individual accustomed to indigence.[33] A stunned Addison indulged in expenditures that his forced frugality never permitted: "I went drunk with excitement. I ordered a tropic trousseau, gave dinners, and sent flowers—all charged, of course."[34] Addison must have enjoyed communicating his new prominence and wealth to those who had only been familiar with his relative poverty.

Nothing is known of Mizner's ideas for the presidential palace. With such a large commission, he might have considered the possibility of bringing this project into Polk's office. Although he had absorbed a great deal of knowledge with Polk, he nonetheless lacked sufficient knowledge of what would have been required to design, build, furnish, decorate, and landscape such a significant palace. In the end, he did not need to worry about any perceived shortcomings because his patron died. Anticipating the arrival of his retainer by ship, Addison went to the docks to greet the boat from Guatemala, whereupon he was made aware of the news of Barrios's assassination.

Struck with another misfortune, Mizner now confronted a burden of debt and an intensified disillusionment with the profession of architecture. In spite of having learned a substantial amount about architecture and of having gratified his literary impulses with an avant-garde group of friends, Addison still had no more clarity about his future than he did when he began with Polk almost three years earlier. Neither architecture nor writing would support the lifestyle to which he aspired. Frustrated at this point with life in San Francisco, Mizner became animated by adventure. Embracing the pioneer spirit of their ancestors, Addison Mizner and his brothers decided to pursue the greatest get-rich-quick scheme of the late nineteenth century.

MINER, PAINTER, WRITER, FIGHTER

Never fearful of risking everything, Addison Mizner was willing to dare, to experiment, to fail. In the next seven years of his life, Mizner sometimes struggled and frequently lived by his wits. He sustained himself with audacity, determination, and, true to his spirit, with good humor. Filled with exploration and adventure, this period of Addison's life represented a journey of self-discovery that engendered confidence. It ultimately led to a decision to forsake a life of desultory variety in favor of one of purposeful focus. Addison Mizner needed to experience life's many offerings before he could dedicate himself to a singular pursuit.

Seeking an opportunity in 1898 beyond the world of architecture, Addison accepted the invitation of his brother William to join him in the Sierras to work his gold mine. Not long after his arrival, Addison received a letter from his brother Edgar reporting a large gold strike in the Klondike. Edgar was then head of the Alaska Commercial Company for the Yukon district and was aware of new discoveries being made. Addison was instructed by his older brothers to close down the

Sierra mine and to travel to Seattle to meet brother Wilson for the journey to northwest Canada. Addison and three of his brothers would partner to mine for gold, a prospect that

The steamer Excelsior *is shown leaving San Francisco for the Klondike in July 1897 with 350 passengers and eight hundred tons of supplies. Newspapers in San Francisco later reported that the* Excelsior *was returning from the Klondike with prospectors loaded with huge amounts of gold. With such news, flocks of prospectors departed for northwest Canada. A year later, the Mizner brothers would follow.*
Courtesy of Wikipedia. Photograph by Sam C. Partridge.

thrilled him: "The old pioneer blood of the tribe rose in my brain, and I was panting to go."[1]

All of the Mizners were optimistic for good reason. Gold had been discovered in the Klondike region on August 15, 1896. A year later, it was reported in San Francisco and Portland newspapers that the ships *Excelsior* and *Portland* were transporting returning prospectors with huge amounts of this precious metal. When the *Portland* arrived in Seattle, it was found to be carrying almost two tons of gold.[2] With these discoveries, one hundred thousand prospectors flocked to northwest Canada, most of whom knew nothing about mining. Their destination was Dawson City, a boom town located on the Yukon River that saw its population swell from five hundred in 1896 to approximately thirty-five thousand by the time the Mizners arrived in the spring of 1898.[3]

The dream of treasure was seductive to these four Mizners, especially in light of the fact that none had yet been able to settle on a suitable or remunerative profession. The enticement of fortune was nonetheless insufficient to engender the perseverance required to succeed. All of the Mizners were strong and tough, but none had been exposed to such demanding conditions. After a grueling day, Addison would remark "Thank God, the worst is over," when in reality, the worst was yet to come.[4] During the six months required to travel to Dawson, it was Addison who bore the heaviest burden of the unending work, a fact that had caused dissension among the brothers. He remarked: "Finally, William and Wilson decided on a week's rest; though I never could find out what had made them tired."[5] Indicating that he was unlikely to stay in the Klondike very long, William remarked, "This is a country for the young, strong, and stupid."[6] His brothers, unable to cope with the harsh and rigorous demands, had become discouraged and disheartened. Edgar and William decided to return home at the end of June and Wilson, more inclined to self-indulgence, opened a gambling hall in the Dominion Hotel.

Upon arrival in Dawson, Addison initially chose to work in a grocery store of the Alaska Commercial Company. It was here that he received a tip from a friend about a discovery at Dominion Creek, a tributary of the Indian River about forty-five miles away. He was able to stake a two-hundred-foot claim but, due to the exodus of his brothers, he had no one to work it with him. This abandonment did not pose immediate problems for Addison. As gold could only be mined in winter when the water was frozen, he had a few months before he needed to proceed to Dominion Creek. He occupied himself by laying out the city of Dawson and by constructing an office building. He had already learned something of the demands of gold mining during his weeks in the Sierra so, aware of the physical requirements necessary to work his stake, he put together a team of three strong Swedes who would accompany

Grocery store in Dawson City, Yukon Territory, Canada, 1899. After arriving in Dawson City in 1899, Addison Mizner went to work in a grocery store like this. Not only a place that sold provisions and weighed gold, the grocery was a crossroads where information about discoveries could be gained. Addison impressed the tough characters who hung around the grocery by holding a solid wood chair with one hand at arm's length.
Courtesy of Wikipedia. Photograph by Per Edward Larss and Joseph Duclos.

him. Addison had exhibited his credentials to lead such men by frequently holding a substantial chair with one hand at arm's length to demonstrate his strength.[7]

After arriving at Dominion Creek on September 22, 1898, the four men spent the first three weeks constructing a cabin. Even in these trying conditions, Addison was attuned not only to the utilitarian but also to the aesthetic effects of his design. He was pleased with the outcome: "the luck and pull I had exerted in getting two windows with four panes of glass in them made the cabin an outstanding and architectural triumph."[8] It was at this time that Addison, utilizing skills developed with animals during his youth, midwifed the baby of neighboring prospectors in their tent. The baby was christened Addison Mizner Olson.[9]

Then began the laborious process of mining, a punishing undertaking in mostly solitary, difficult conditions. For the next six months, they would dig holes and endlessly hoist gravel and residue to the surface for examination. Addison wrote about this to his mother, stating that the average man would hoist about one hundred buckets of gravel in a day while he was averaging 175. He later recorded: "Today I hoisted two hundred and fifty-six buckets and am just alive to tell the tale."[10] Mining for gold demanded a Herculean effort in exacting conditions over a period of many months.

Like some prospectors around them, they were eventually successful in finding gold. While the prospect of discovery sustained the miners, discovery itself tempted. In January, Addison happened to overhear the Swedes' plan to kill him to increase their take. Devoid of alternatives, he had the wherewithal to confront them, commencing with the verbal assault "Sit down, you Lice!"[11] Standing six feet two inches and weighing approximately 250 pounds, Addison commanded attention. He then set forth his own ideas about why they could not possibly get away with this murder before throwing out his audacious coda: "As to killing me—none of you have got guts enough for that."[12] For the next week, he ordered them about relentlessly and worked them excessively hard. At this point, suspecting another betrayal by his untrustworthy colleagues, Addison began hiding gold in an old boot in the cabin.

When spring arrived in 1899, it was time to pack and go home. The profit Addison made from his claim was diminished by the assertion by the Canadian government that he had mined beyond his original claim and that, therefore, this gold did not legally belong to him. Rather than pursuing the unattainable victory, he ceded the reported gold to the Canadian officials, contenting himself with taking home only the gold that he had been hiding in his boot. The value of his cache would be approximately $27,000.[13]

With the arrival of summer, Wilson Mizner had made the decision to leave Dawson and move to Nome, where gold discoveries had just been reported the previous winter. Nome was "a town that bloomed from the tundra overnight."[14] Formerly a deserted stretch of coastline, it was now "so white with tents set peg-to-peg that the landscape appeared to be snow-covered."[15] By the time of Wilson's arrival, there were approximately two thousand inhabitants, a figure that would grow tenfold within a year.[16] The more tolerant atmosphere of this embryonic town offered greater opportunity to Wilson, who felt circumscribed by the rules and laws of a mature and much larger Dawson.

Addison, William, and Wilson Mizner, 1898. It took the brothers six months of grueling travel to reach Dawson City, a period of time that tested their mettle. When Addison began to prospect his claim, his brothers had found the conditions too harsh and decided to return to California. Wilson remained but dedicated himself to disreputable activities that kept him safely in town. The experience in the Klondike revealed Addison to be clever, brave, and tenacious. Courtesy of Kim Mizner Hollins.

Before returning home, Addison visited Wilson in his new home at the request of his mother to verify that her youngest son was all right. Addison did not need to remain long for he quickly found that "the town was agog with Wilson's prowess."[17] According to Addison's memoirs, the inhabitants of Nome considered Wilson "the bravest man in town," a reputation no doubt constructed on artifice. A biographer more realistically regarded him as "one of the founding fathers of its underworld."[18] On July 24, 1899, after just over one year in the Pacific Northwest, Addison Mizner began his journey home.

The year Addison spent in the Northwest represented a quest for riches, yet it was to be a defining period that yielded treasure far greater in value than the assayed gold dust. As a result of his age, Addison had always occupied a lower rung in the family hierarchy and had predictably looked up to his older brothers. Embarking on this odyssey, he expected to be guided by his more experienced siblings. When the arduous journey ended, only Addison remained. The others had been vanquished by the demanding and boring drudgery. Finding great reserves of strength and courage, Addison alone was able to persevere.

The physical demands were considerable. In making his way to Dominion Creek, he traveled by foot hauling hundreds of pounds of supplies along the way. As wood was a necessity for construction and fires, he not only felled trees but found himself on the strenuous bottom position in the saw pit to cut planks necessary for the cabin. He had the raw strength to hoist more gravel buckets than his partners. There was also solitude, threats, and injury. On the initial overland trip from Dyea to Dawson, Addison was slicing frozen bread and accidentally cut off part of his index finger. Brother William sewed stitches in the injured finger without giving the patient an anesthetic. This journey proved to be far more demanding than Addison could ever have fathomed.

Wilson Mizner, circa 1895. Addison's younger brother by four years, Wilson was very talented but ill-suited to traditional vocations. Having spent a desultory life moving from one scheme to another, he is remembered as a playwright and screenwriter. A master of repartee, he spewed witticisms that others recorded and repeated. He and Addison spent much of their lives together, not always to the benefit of the older brother.
Courtesy of The Oakland Museum of California.

The revelation at the end of the year was not just that he had endured and triumphed physically; it was that he had grown psychologically. Exposed to a broader swath of humanity than he had previously known, most ethically flexible and many absolutely corrupt, he had become more perceptive in assessing people. Whether or not he realized it at this point in his life, Addison had crossed another threshold. Behind the hardy carapace of confidence and strength was a swelling sense of responsibility. He was distressed to see Wilson leading a life that would have greatly disappointed his mother. His sense of decency would never permit him to do the same and would induce him always to conceal his brother's antics from Mama Mizner.

Wilson Mizner was a different story. He had become a colorful character, facile in the arts of gambling, fighting, and quipping. Addison remarked that his brother knew women "from the best homes and houses" and a biographer said that Wilson had "a vast first-hand criminal erudition."[19] Even Wilson acknowledged his strength: "I know more about crime than any other man who still owns controlling interest in his own liberty."[20] In short, Wilson Mizner was an entertaining rascal who had already cultivated a gimlet eye for the next caper. These two brothers, with disparate yet sympathetic sensibilities, would frequently converge in the next thirty years to the constant frustration and recurring detriment of Addison.

Despite the inimical effects of this association on him, Addison never begrudged it and never excluded his brother from his life. Addison's return to San Francisco in the summer of 1899 was without Wilson; it was also without professional prospects.

Upon his return Addison Mizner enjoyed the luxury of being once again in a civilized city and experienced the novelty of having in his possession a considerable amount of money. He found an investment for his funds that would mature in two years. Addison had just been informed by his friend Andrew Martin of his intention to marry and of his desire to have Addison be one of his ushers. On September 26, 1899, Andrew married Genevieve Goad in her parents' San Francisco home. This was a spectacular wedding that represented the union of two venerable and wealthy California families. Addison had to have been pleased to be again among good friends in familiar surroundings.

This happiness was unfortunately brief. Prior to the wedding, Andrew had become sick and, at the advice of doctors, the newly married couple moved south to Palm Springs where the climate would be more salubrious for his lung condition. Andrew had asked Addison to help them with their new house, a plan that included redesigning the interior and exterior of the existing structure as well as constructing two other buildings on the property. Addison remained engaged in his friends' project through early November when, sadly and only seven weeks after the wedding, Andrew passed away. Addison, along with Genevieve and her brother, were at Andrew's bedside. Devastated by this personal loss, Addison also had to be eminently disappointed to be unable to complete the architectural plans for his dear friend. The exposure and publicity from a project for so prominent a couple could have successfully launched his architectural career.

The dawn of a new century is a time of optimism and this was particularly the case with the twentieth century, a transition characterized by progress and prosperity. In assessing his life at the age of twenty-seven, Addison Mizner could hardly have identified any semblance of professional progress or personal prosperity. Even his social life was suddenly jeopardized. He had locked horns with social arbiter Ned Greenway, who presided over the prestigious Mardi Gras Ball and had Addison's name omitted from the invitation list. Greenway sold Mumm's Extra Dry champagne and was very fond of his product. It was reported that he consumed prodigious amounts of Mumm's every night, a feat that caused him to remark: "No gentleman ever feels well in the morning."[21] Addison had caused a rift in their relationship apparently by making disparaging remarks about Ned's brand of champagne, a slight that caused Greenway to seek retribution. Never one to shrink from provocation, Addison confronted Greenway in a cafe and challenged him to a fight, an invitation that was smartly refused. The

Addison Mizner in Honolulu, 1900. When Addison found himself in Honolulu without a job, he managed to secure a position restoring paintings from the royal collection at the Iolani Palace. He is conserving a portrait of Emperor Napoleon III, most probably a copy of a work by Franz Xaver Winterhalter in 1855.
Courtesy of The Oakland Museum of California.

satisfaction he took from embarrassing Greenway did nothing to alter Addison's Mardi Gras status.

At this point there was nothing substantial to keep Mizner in San Francisco. While his aimless status was in contrast to the promise offered by the new century, his confident outlook prevailed and banished any thought of self-pity. With architecture still on his mind, he met an artful man from Hawaii who purported to lead a syndicate that wanted to build a hotel and who also needed an architect for additional projects, including a house for himself. Addison accepted the offer to accompany him to Honolulu but, upon arrival, he immediately realized his gullibility, stating, "I found he had about as much influence as a Protestant in the Vatican."[22]

While touring the island, Addison visited the former royal palace. On January 17, 1893, the Hawaiian monarchy of Queen Liliuokalani was overthrown and replaced by a republic led by Sanford Dole. While surveying the royal collection of paintings, he found canvases "flapping on their shrunken stretchers."[23] Addison met President Dole and lamented the deplorable condition of the art and, in the ensuing conversation, Dole offered Addison the job of restoring the paintings. He certainly had no experience in art restoration, yet through enterprise and talent, he quickly became proficient and successfully worked at this project for the next year.

His genial nature and witty charm produced the same results in Hawaii as they did elsewhere. Among the people Addison befriended was the former Queen Liliuokalani, who had met his parents when they attended an anniversary party in 1892 to celebrate her accession the previous year. She was grateful to learn that he had been able to restore her family's patrimony. In rummaging through the attic of the former palace, Addison found a trunk of medals and decorations that belonged to the ex-queen's family and managed to return them to her surreptitiously. The retrieval of this trove was especially meaningful to Liliuokalani, and she repaid this magnanimous gesture by knighting him. "I knelt and she struck me three gentle taps on the shoulder and said, in the most serious tone, 'Arise, Sir Addison.'"[24] After arising, the former queen pinned on Addison's chest the Star of Kalakaua, a medal that acknowledges special service to the monarch and kingdom.

Since Hawaii was a popular vacation destination for Americans, he was able to meet many visitors from the mainland. One he particularly enjoyed was Ethel Watts Mumford, a young divorcee from New York who shared his wit and sense of humor. Mumford was sophisticated, educated, well traveled, and possessed of an artistic temperament. She would become the author of plays, novels, short stories, and poems and, having studied art at the Julian Academy of Paris, a painter and illustrator. Beyond shared interests, they possessed similar powers of observation and expression.

As their coterie of like-minded wits grew, they "gathered together all the amusing and witty ones, so that it became the first outdoor salon the Island had ever known."[25] As diversion, they would exchange jokes and witticisms, humorously altering words to resonate with their tastes. They thought a compilation of such thoughts would make an appropriate Christmas present called *The Cynic's Calendar*. When their San Francisco printer read the manuscript, he suggested that they publish it commercially. The first *Calendar*, written in 1902 and published in 1903, earned Addison Mizner $1,500 in royalties, an unanticipated gift that the author must have found astonishing considering his impecunious circumstances. New editions of *The Calendar* would appear annually through 1910. Among his many contributions were: "Many are called, but few get up."; "Where there's a will, there's a law suit."; and "People who live in glass houses should pull down the blinds." The ready wit that had been sharpened around the dining table with his family as a young man in Benicia was paying dividends.

Addison never designed buildings during his stay in Hawaii, but he did fall back on his creative skills to earn money. He did miniature ivory portraits and made charcoal drawings from photographs of popular island scenes for tourists' consumption. None of this was satisfying so, after two years in Hawaii,

Queen Liliuokalani, 1891. By the time of Addison's arrival in Honolulu in 1898, the monarchy had been overthrown and replaced with a provisional republican government. Addison met Queen Liliuokalani, the deposed monarch, and secretly managed to return many medals and decorations that had belonged to the royal family. In gratitude of Addison's actions, the former queen knighted Addison and bestowed the Star of Kalakaua, a medal that acknowledged special service to the monarch.
Courtesy of Wikipedia. Photograph by James J. Williams.

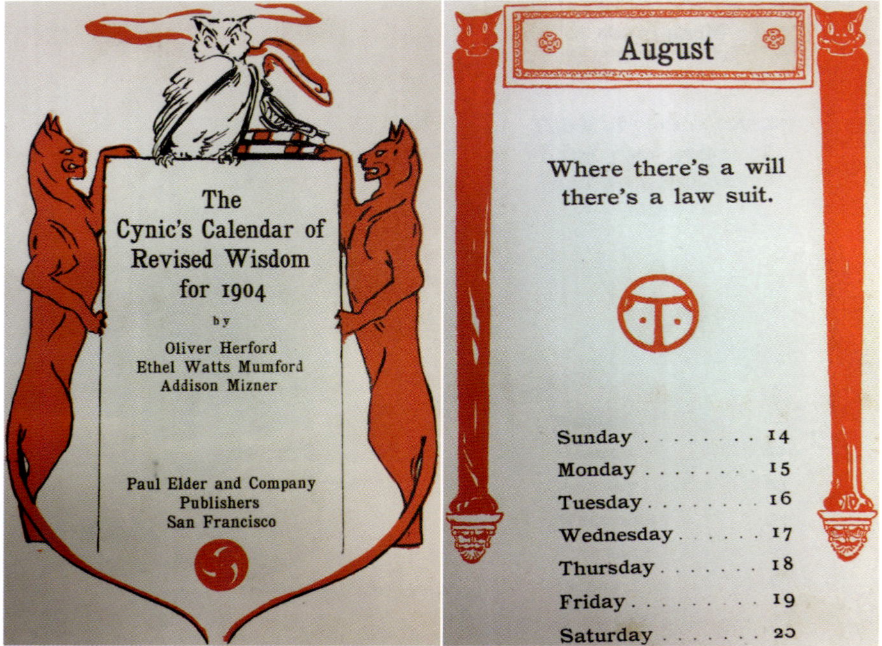

The Cynic's Calendar of Revised Wisdom *for 1904.*
While Addison Mizner was in Honolulu in 1900, he met Ethel Watts Mumford with whom he formed
a salon of witty friends. They began twisting and distorting aphorisms in a humorous way and decided
to publish them. Entitled the Cynic's Calendar, *the books appeared annually between 1903 and 1910*
with a revised edition in 1917. The royalties from this publication enhanced Addison's meager earnings
during these years.
Courtesy of Historical Society of Palm Beach County.

he decided to move on. As one of his investments was maturing, he requested $2,000 be sent to Apia, Samoa. Addison Mizner, the pioneer, had decided to go to the South Pacific.

Upon arrival in Apia, Addison received bad news. To his great distress, he learned that there would be no dividends as his investment was now worthless. Discouraged certainly, he

remained optimistic. His genial nature brought him in touch with an English professor who sold lantern slides described as "colored accurately by a great artist."[26] Professor Collins was losing his "great artist" and needed a replacement. With less than five dollars in his pocket, a strapped Addison discussed Japanese art glibly and convinced the professor that he was highly skilled in this specialty.[27] A partnership was born and success was immediate. Belying the fact that Addison had never colored slides before, he quickly figured out the technique and produced prodigiously. Desiring a larger market for their product, they decided to proceed to Melbourne, Australia; however, after ten days in Melbourne, the partnership was dissolved over a dispute.

Once again without employment, Mizner was presented with another opportunity. Sufficiently comfortable with the pugilistic skills developed during childhood in Benicia, he agreed to a boxing match. While in Murphy's, a Melbourne saloon familiar to fighters, Addison witnessed the great excitement surrounding the impending bout that would feature the "Pride of Australia," the regional boxing champion. The manager of the fight related that the Pride's opponent had thought better of taking on the champion and decided to back out. With a sold-out crowd of over eight thousand expecting to see a rousing fight the next day, the manager thought Addison a suitable opponent since he was big. More importantly, certain of the

Pride's ability to win, the manager thought it would be particularly satisfying for the local crowd to witness the knock-out of an American. Mindful of his maternal grandfather, Addison called himself "Whirlwind Watson from 'Frisco.'" To the great dismay of the Pride and the crowd, Addison fought the champion to a draw after twenty rounds, earning a meager $150. Needless to say, the locals were mystified and bewildered that their man had not knocked out this unknown itinerant.

A rematch was demanded and agreed to. This time, aware of his leverage, Addison told "the old bone head that I would do it if the winner got one third of the gate and the loser one hundred and fifty dollars."[28] They fought to a draw in the first three rounds but, in the fourth, Addison's opponent landed a hit to the nose. Addison said that "It had always annoyed me to be hit on the end of my nose that way, so I reached out and picked one up off the floor and slammed him one on the chin. He dropped like a felled ox."[29] In knocking out the "Pride of Australia," Addison stirred the wrath of the incredulous spectators. After collecting his pay, Addison hustled to the docks to avoid the seething crowd and jumped on a ship, thinking its destination was San Francisco. Safely on board, he enquired where the steamer was going. To his surprise, he was heading to Shanghai.

Now underway, he was happy to find that the proceeds from winning the fight had yielded $2,000. The next day, the ship stopped in Sydney where the steward went ashore and bought newspapers at Addison's request. He was worried to read that the Pride was out for a full three hours. Realizing that he could have killed his opponent, he later wrote, "I may have nicked most of the other Commandments, but I don't think I have ever committed a murder."[30] En route to Shanghai, Addison stopped over in Manila, Siam, and finally India. In Shanghai, he made an acquaintance who encouraged him to buy at blind auction a box whose contents would only be revealed after his bid was accepted. Addison's purchase turned out to be seventy-two coffin handles that, with his friendly and easy manner, he was able to sell for a small profit.

In the summer of 1902, having satisfied his appetite for exotic travel, Addison returned to San Francisco. Though none of his experiences fed directly into his future profession of architecture, he was exposed to a multiplicity of cultures and assimilated many visual ideas that were incorporated into his artistic vocabulary. In that two-and-a-half-year period he repeatedly demonstrated an amazing capacity to survive. His optimistic spirit and mental agility combined to fashion opportunity in even the most grim and unpropitious circumstances. This cast of mind would work to his benefit later in his architectural practice when he would frequently be called upon to satisfy a vain, imperious, and highly demanding clientele through subtlety and finesse. Throughout his career, with only a couple of

Bertha Dolbeer, circa 1900. With the death of her entrepreneurial father, Bertha inherited a fortune that made her, along with her beauty and charm, a very attractive prospect for marriage. Addison Mizner was smitten with Bertha and was optimistic that she would accept his proposal for marriage. On July 9, 1904, Bertha ended her life by jumping from a window at the Waldorf Astoria hotel. Sadly, her mother committed suicide when Bertha was two years old. This loss was one of the factors that caused Addison to move from San Francisco to New York in 1904.

Photograph by Arnold Genthe.

exceptions, Mizner deftly guided his clients through the maze of problems and vexing issues with skill and humor.

Back in San Francisco, Addison Mizner was cognizant of his growing maturity: "I had arrived in San Francisco a much more thoughtful fellow than when I had left there nearly two years before."[31] Perhaps wishing to bring stability to his life and to fill an emotional void, he fell in love with Bertha Dolbeer. He had always enjoyed an abundance of female friends and had several infatuations during his life, but this was more than boyish fascination: "I fell desperately in love."[32] Addison even admitted being "insanely jealous" if any other man paid attention to her.[33] Bertha was the daughter of John Dolbeer, who had just passed away in August 1902. He left to his only surviving child a significant inheritance derived from huge redwood lumber operations and from various patents, one of which was the "steam donkey," a steam-powered winch that revolutionized nineteenth-century logging.

Bertha was not only wealthy but, in Addison's eyes, alluringly different: "She was a new type for me; tall, straight, and dark, with a great deal of dignity, and a quiet humor, and a certain 'hands off' attitude."[34] His new maturity and focus did not mean that he was immune to an entertaining romp. After spending "two heavenly days with my beloved," Addison spirited himself off to an illegal prizefight that resulted in all spectators being thrown in jail.[35] In the confusion, Addison managed to hide in the back of a hearse to avoid detection. In addition to incarceration, the names of all culprits were listed in the newspaper the next day, publicity that was consumed by all of his friends. When Addison next saw Bertha, she congratulated him on having the good sense not to have attended "anything so vulgar and vile."[36] Aware of the harmful effect that could easily have befallen him in his relationship, Addison must have taken sheepish pride in his felicitous escape.

He was not always successful in avoiding Bertha's vigilant gaze. In early 1904, Addison traveled to Santa Barbara by automobile with a good friend, Jack Baird. Surrounded by friends around the swimming pool at the Delmar Plaza Hotel, Jack made a bet that, if Addison would slide fully clothed into the pool, he would reward him with a new suit. Never one to retreat from a challenge, Addison took the plunge. He surfaced and triumphantly strolled through the cheering crowd. As he passed Jack, he uttered his only words: "I think I win."[37] This shenanigan was reported in various newspapers and the news was met with annoyance and reproof by Bertha.

Though drawn to his affability and good nature, Bertha was more concerned about responsibility and stability. She told Addison that, to consider his proposal of marriage, he would have to find a responsible position with an appropriate salary. Although he was employed as a draftsman at this time, he knew that it would not generate a sufficient income to be able to support Bertha, so he decided to become an importer of coffee from Guatemala. He appreciated Guatemalan coffee and knew that there was no coffee in America that compared favorably. Bertha had decided to travel to Europe so, during her absence, Addison planned to leave in April 1904 for Guatemala to develop relationships with growers and sign contracts. Assessing his romance with Bertha at this time, he noted in his memoirs: "We soon came to a better understanding."[38] As he departed San Francisco, he must have been optimistic.

Beginning his trip in Guatemala City, Addison soon made a visit to Antigua, the former capital located approximately thirty miles away. Antigua was founded in the sixteenth century and was the economic, religious, political, and cultural center of the region. In 1773, the Santa Marta earthquakes destroyed much of the town and resulted in the capital being moved to a less precarious location, now known as Guatemala City. Addison would have been captivated by Antigua, even in its dilapidated condition. Since much of Antigua was constructed in the seventeenth and eighteenth centuries, it had very sophisticated civic and religious architecture in the baroque style. The muscular presence of churches like El Carmen and La Merced projected grand, theatrical, and dynamic façades that Addison would have found majestic. Later, as an adult, he continued to be fascinated with the city. Another

Iglesia de la Merced, Antigua, Guatemala. In 1904 Addison Mizner traveled again to Guatemala to develop a coffee importing business and went to Antigua, a city founded in the sixteenth century that possessed wonderful examples of architecture. He found these buildings captivating and drew them throughout his life. In this pen and ink sketch capturing the magnificent dome of the church of the Merced, Mizner illustrates his early artistic facility.
Photograph by Zack Clark, courtesy of Wikipedia. Drawing courtesy of the Society of the Four Arts, photographed by Craig Kuhner.

feature of Antigua that greatly appealed to Mizner was the excellent example of town planning inspired by Renaissance ideas. Evidence of the appeal of Antigua could be found in the many sketches and photographs assembled in his scrapbooks entitled "Spain and Its Colonies."

After the capital moved to Guatemala City, Antigua was diminished in importance and size. Later, when the government reduced the role of the Roman Catholic Church and seized its property, many churches, including those in Antigua,

were vacated. Addison remarked that "there was only one priest to every two churches, and they were very poor…. They had vast treasures in old velvet, damask, and embroideries, together with silver and furniture."[39] He decided to purchase these exquisite objects. If this sounds like desecration, Addison explained the situation: "I mean no disrespect to the church, and it should be understood that it was legitimate at this time for the priests to sell, as they were near starvation."[40] Addison bought a huge quantity of objects.

The prospect of dealing in antiquarian objects must have been much more enticing and exciting than selling coffee. He quickly found that it could also be rewarding. Prominent among his purchases were eight side chapels from a monastery, each having enormous carved and gilded altars. Addison bought the altars for $600 and sold them for $6,000 to a client who did not like gilding.[41] Addison had the gilding removed and, upon calling the smelter to enquire about the gold, was informed that it had a value of $11,000. Such buying trips would become part of his business model for the rest of his architectural career.

Addison's good fortune was interrupted that summer when he opened a telegram from a friend informing him of the death of Bertha Dolbeer on July 9, 1904. The pain was accentuated by the fact that, for three weeks following the receipt of this shocking news, he continued to receive long letters that Bertha had written from New York, where she had arrived from her European trip. She reported that she had had a wonderful time and that she had missed Addison very much and looked forward to seeing him soon. Bertha had jumped from a window in her room at the Waldorf-Astoria Hotel. The exact circumstances surrounding the death were never determined, but it was known that she had been despondent after the death of her father and that she had been treated in Paris for emotional disturbance.

Devastated, Addison Mizner made two decisions: to leave San Francisco for New York and to give up the coffee business for architecture. If he had been considering the merits of a change in residence and profession before, this tragedy might have convinced him to start anew. San Francisco at this moment was a reminder of personal misfortune and professional frustration, while New York was a city that was the epicenter of the Gilded Age, a dynamic metropolis that presented unlimited opportunity to the ambitious and enterprising. For an architect seeking commissions, it offered not only wealth but, as Donald Curl pointed out, "the right people."[42] Addison Mizner's charm and sophistication made him an ideal companion for East Coast plutocrats and his confidence and pioneer spirit provided the necessary ingredients to establish himself successfully in a profession that had never gratified him financially. Little did he know but his nomadic existence and casual professional choices were at an end.

CHAPTER SIX

EXTRAVAGANCE AND DISPLAY

When Addison Mizner decided to leave California for New York in 1904, it was a time of unprecedented confidence and expansion in America. By the turn of the century, the population had reached seventy-five million, a remarkable increase of 50 percent in just twenty years.[1] In the last decade of the century, America ceased looking inward and began to develop a more aggressive foreign policy that would quickly establish it as a world power. In the span of six years just before Mizner's arrival in New York, America had annexed Hawaii and gained control of the territories of Guam, Puerto Rico, and the Philippines. It had also assumed responsibility for the Panama Canal project from the French, a move that included not only authority for its construction but also ownership of the actual canal property. A thriving America was beginning to look beyond its borders.

This expanded horizon had implications not just for American culture and society but especially for Addison Mizner. Shifting attitudes among the elite created an ethos that facilitated his acceptance into polite society and paved the way for him to become a society architect. Growing prosperity created a leisure class that began to enjoy its wealth and took gratification in displaying it. The social customs of English and French aristocrats informed the tastes and habits of the newly affluent Americans and induced them to demand sophisticated symbols of prosperity to publicize their grandeur. These trends began in New York and continued, despite the interruption of World War I, in Palm Beach, and each city played an integral role in the development of the young architect.

The ramifications of an expanded perspective were profound for society, especially in America's largest city at the upper echelon. After the Civil War, New York society was composed of the Knickerbockers, the original English and Dutch settlers, for whom intellect, propriety, and courtesy were important touchstones.[2] Into this static Knickerbocker culture soon came individuals, emboldened with new fortunes and brazen aspirations, whose conflicting values posed a challenge to the existing social structure. As the Gilded Age was concerned with achievement and mobility, its greatest representatives

avidly sought inclusion into the upper reaches of New York society.

The newly created fortunes that invaded New York's Knickerbocker aristocracy in the Gilded Age were derived through industry and pluck as well as cunning and deceit. Mark Twain spoke of the greed and corruption of the times in 1871, "What is the chief end of man?—to get rich. In what way?—dishonestly if we can; honestly if we must."[3] The nouveaux riches attempted to penetrate existing society through extravagance and display, practices condemned by old New York aristocracy. Until the younger generation of Knickerbockers, led by Caroline Astor, began to include families of new money in its world in the 1880s, the only way to permeate the aristocratic caste was by marriage into one of the venerable families.

Economist Thorstein Veblen commented on the importance of "conspicuous consumption" as a means of elevating one's social status. In his view, the mere presence of consumption and leisure was not sufficient. What was more important was the recognition of their presence by others: "In order to gain and to hold the esteem of men it is not sufficient merely to

This portrait of Caroline Astor by the French painter Carolus-Duran shows the confidence of a wealthy woman who was the social arbiter of New York society after the Civil War. Known simply as "Mrs. Astor," she codified appropriate behavior and worked to integrate the traditional Knickerbocker society with wealthy arrivistes who represented "new money." As a result, many ladies who would befriend Addison Mizner became acceptable in polite society. Courtesy of Wikipedia. Portrait by Carolus-Duran.

possess wealth or power. The wealth or power must be put in evidence, for esteem is awarded only on evidence."[4] Veblen also observed that anyone striving to advance one's position emulated the characteristics of his superiors. The *arrivistes* understood the effective use of emblems of status and sought not just to emulate the magnificence of their superiors but to surpass them. The new conception of culture then developing in New York was constructed not so much on an appreciation of the arts but on an outward manifestation of wealth through architecture and the arts.[5]

The resolution of this struggle between old and new money fell to the redoubtable and capable Caroline Webster Schermerhorn Astor, the wife of William Backhouse Astor Jr., known later in life simply as *Mrs. Astor*. Recognizing the need to accommodate a changing society, she created new standards that united the old guard with the most worthy of the nouveaux riches. Beyond creating a powerful coalition between a static aristocracy and the more dynamic entrepreneurs, Astor wanted to create an identity for American society that would redound to the credit of the young nation. The late nineteenth century was a period of nationalism, and all countries were involved in establishing traditions that reinforced and enhanced perceptions of national identity. The more aristocratic cultural standards that Mrs. Astor was endeavoring to establish were to serve as a calibration against which America could be measured favorably against any nation.

With a codification of behavior that became the social catechism of the elite, New York society arrived at a satisfying synthesis in the 1880s. It was then infused with new blood but still anchored to the existing tenets of propriety and good taste. This remained a burnished, privileged world generally inimical to foreigners and arrivistes, a microcosm that grew "from within rather than from without."[6] Mrs. Astor was the unchallenged arbiter who had presided over a personally anointed collection of socialites called *The 400*.[7] She was aided in regulating the *beau monde* by her acolyte Ward McAllister and, together, they represented a barrier to those regarded as inferior or unworthy. According to many, Mrs. Astor had transformed society into a "secular religion."[8]

One of the factors that prompted a shift in the perceptions of New York society was a growing familiarity and fascination with Old World aristocracy. In the fall of 1860, New Yorkers thronged along Broadway to glimpse Albert Edward, Prince of Wales, in his open carriage. The occasion was special as this was the first time a member of the British royal family had visited North America. He was feted everywhere and was the guest of President James Buchanan in the White House. On the evening of October 12, approximately five thousand people squeezed into the Academy of Music to attend an exclusive ball given in

This illustration from Harper's Weekly *depicts the grand ball at the Academy of Music in New York on October 12, 1860 to honor the visit of the Prince of Wales to the United States. The prince, who would become King Edward VII in 1901, was greeted by large crowds everywhere. After the civil war, wealthy Americans began to emulate English social customs and many had their daughters married into the English aristocracy. These changes brought about a demand for grand architectural statements, some of which served to educate Addison Mizner.* Courtesy of the Library of Congress.

his honor.[9] This constituted the prince's first exposure to American women, an attraction that was warmly reciprocated. Despite marriage to a Danish princess in 1863, the prince led a lusty life until his death in 1910. The lavish attention he bestowed on women would have implications for young Americans.

Young ladies from many of America's richest families became a focal point in English society beginning in the 1870s. British aristocrats had historically derived their wealth from landed estates and typically shunned involvement in industrial ventures. Due to a depression in agriculture in the 1870s and a shift in wealth creation from farming to industry, many peers of the realm found themselves impoverished and saw their wealth eclipsed by industrial entrepreneurs. Many needed an infusion of cash to preserve family estates that required enormous upkeep. This coincided with the desire of many American nouveaux riches, some excluded from Mrs. Astor's tight circle, to have their daughters married to Old World nobility. This begat a spate of convenient alliances that prevailed during the Gilded Age when the glamorous and rich daughters of America became known as *Dollar Princesses*.[10]

The Prince of Wales and his fashionable set, finding these American young ladies more independent than English girls, welcomed them to London society. The prince introduced Jennie Jerome, the daughter of financier Leonard Jerome, to Lord Randolph Churchill, the third son of the 7th Duke of Marlborough, and their subsequent marriage became one of the best known of the Anglo-American alliances. Consuelo Yznaga, descended from Cuban and Natchez families who were plantation owners, was an important member of the prince's intimate circle and became through marriage Lady Mandeville, later the Duchess of Manchester. This trend would continue in the 1890s with many other unions, two of which involved Mary Goelet becoming the Duchess of Roxburghe and Consuelo Vanderbilt the Duchess of Marlborough. As duchesses, these daughters of the young American republic were now positioned at the very summit of the venerable British aristocracy.

The marriage of Consuelo Vanderbilt to the 9th Duke of Marlborough was engineered by the bride's socially ambitious mother, Mrs. William Kissam Vanderbilt, born Alva Erskine Smith in Mobile, Alabama. Introduced to her husband by her best friend Consuelo Yznaga, Alva recognized in Vanderbilt a convenient way to escape the devastation of the post–Civil War South.[11] Not only did Alva name her sole daughter after her childhood friend but identified in Consuelo Yznaga's ducal rise a model of social elevation for her own daughter. Such an advantageous transatlantic union would not only guarantee a prominent position in society for the daughter but would greatly enhance that of the mother as well, a circumstance that held great appeal to Alva.

Alva Vanderbilt was an important catalyst of social change during the Gilded Age. The shifts she initiated would have significant implications for Addison Mizner when he moved to New York in 1904. Not only did she finagle admittance to the impermeable world of Mrs. Astor's 400 but, at the turn of the century, she brought about a more relaxed style of entertaining to society. Like other members of the elite who had begun to adopt English and Continental habits, she was a pioneer in cultivating a lifestyle that embraced a country house as the natural complement to a city residence. An important patron of architects, she built several iconic homes that also precipitated shifts in style and design.

Alva Vanderbilt possessed the financial means and cleverness to confront New York's nobs in order to have her family elevated to the social firmament of New York. In 1875 Alva married William Kissim Vanderbilt, the grandson of Commodore Cornelius Vanderbilt and son of William Henry Vanderbilt. Following the death of Commodore Vanderbilt two years later, William Henry Vanderbilt and both of his sons filed plans to build new houses on Fifth Avenue. Alva's and William's splendid new French chateau at 660 Fifth Avenue was unlike the new homes of other Vanderbilts and contrasted significantly with existing New York brownstone mansions.[12] To celebrate the completion of the house in the winter of 1883 as well as to commemorate the visit of her childhood friend, Lady Mandeville, Alva scheduled a party for March 26, the Monday after Easter. This would be the first important social event following six weeks of Lent.[13] More aggressively, Alva chose to give a costume ball, an entertainment that invited the derision of proper Knickerbocker society as it was thought to encourage disreputable behavior. Finally, as Monday nights were traditionally reserved for Mrs. Astor's reception of guests in her home, Alva

had thrown down the gauntlet to the arbiter whose rule of social New York at this time was absolutely unassailable.

Excitement built for the ball as all wanted to see the splendid house that cost a fortune and to experience the luxurious entertainment promised by the hostess. To her great consternation, Mrs. Astor found that neither she nor her daughter Caroline were among the one thousand who were invited. This was not an oversight by Alva Vanderbilt but a conscious omission owing to social protocol. It was also a brilliant stratagem. Because Mrs. Astor considered the railroad fortune of the Vanderbilts distasteful, she had never introduced herself to them, an acknowledgement that would have signaled social acceptance. Without this overture, etiquette prevented Alva from extending an invitation to someone who had not formally recognized her. Aware of the prospect of an inconceivable snub to her daughter, Mrs. Astor immediately dispatched a calling card to Alva at 660 Fifth Avenue, whereupon an invitation was delivered to the Astor residence farther south at 350 Fifth Avenue. Alva's glorious ball had the effect of finally bringing the powerful women and their important families together.

The residence of William K. Vanderbilt at 660 Fifth Avenue, circa 1883. Alva Vanderbilt worked with her favorite architect, Richard Morris Hunt, to design the "Petit Chateau," a limestone house in the French Renaissance style. It was distinctly different from the brownstone houses that surrounded it. Alva conspired with Hunt to build imposing houses in New York, Newport, and on Long Island. Addison Mizner would have experienced them all. Courtesy of the Library of Congress.

At the end of the ball, Alva Vanderbilt, dressed as a Venetian princess by Charles Frederick Worth in Paris, took great satisfaction in the success of the evening, and triumphant pleasure in engineering Vanderbilt acceptance into the highest echelon of society.[14] This event had the effect of highlighting a transformation in New York society. Alva Vanderbilt and Lady Mandeville, childhood friends from the South and formerly Knickerbocker outsiders, stood this evening as social equals of the most formidable representative of New York society. These new initiates had pursued different paths to the pinnacle of acceptability: Alva Smith moved to New York and managed to penetrate the social inner sanctum with cleverness and wealth while Consuelo Yznaga went to London and achieved the same with charm and a title.

The Petit Chateau, the imposing new house where the Vanderbilt ball took place, represented a departure from the conventions of Gilded Age New York. The chateau's architectural style was designed by Richard Morris Hunt, the first American graduate of the Ecole des Beaux Arts in Paris, and its façade and elaborate interiors were a reflection of Alva's affinity for French design.[15] Clad in dressed limestone and capped by a steeply pitched, copper-crested roof, the asymmetrical structure had a slender tourelle that reached high above a façade of four floors. The interiors were sumptuously decorated with period French furnishings such as Gobelin tapestries and

Alva Vanderbilt, the wife of William K. Vanderbilt, is dressed in an evening dress by Charles Frederick Worth for the stunning masquerade ball she hosted to introduce New York society to her new townhouse on Fifth Avenue in 1883. Alva well understood the importance of architecture in the quest to advance her social position among the elite and collaborated with Richard Morris Hunt to do so.

Courtesy of Wikipedia. Photograph by Jose Maria Mora.

distinctive furniture by renowned ébénistes. This curated approach encouraged a taste for French design and decorative art in the Gilded Age.

As Alva Vanderbilt had astutely recognized, the most conspicuous and effective advertisement of wealth and taste was a grand mansion, a traditional architectural statement that, by its magnificence and scale, suggested lineage and tradition like the great ancestral homes and chateaux of England and France. That such houses could present compelling evidence of a family's worthiness to be accepted into the highest ranks of society created a demand for the services of the city's most sophisticated architects: Richard Morris Hunt; McKim, Mead & White; Carrère and Hastings; and others. As the neighborhood of the wealthy extended beyond the Knickerbockers' Washington Square, it moved northward on Fifth Avenue, a long boulevard offering unrestrained possibilities for grand statements like Alva Vanderbilt's Petit Chateau.

Comfortable yet unhappy, Alva Vanderbilt took an unusual step. In an age when divorce was unthinkable and scandalous, she astounded New York society in 1894 by separating from her husband, William K. Vanderbilt, and divorcing him a year later.[16] With a generous divorce settlement, she subsequently married Oliver Hazard Perry Belmont, a socialite and good friend of her former spouse. Continuing to demonstrate her fascination for architecture, she began to redecorate the interiors of Belmont's Newport mansion, Belcourt, and commissioned Hunt & Hunt to design a neoclassical townhouse at 477 Madison Avenue in New York. In 1897, she had the same architect design and build Brookholt, a neoclassical mansion in East Meadow, Long Island. Finally, after the death of her husband, Alva Belmont had Hunt's sons build Beacon Towers, a new Gothic country house completed in 1918 in the village of Sands Point on Long Island.

Attuned to the social significance and symbolism that accompanied grand architectural statements, others were also familiar with the traditional custom in England where aristocrats simultaneously maintained country houses and London townhouses. Eager to emulate English and European tastes, Americans at this time began to build magnificent country houses on Long Island where Addison Mizner would spend much of his time. Creating great estates by consolidating Long Island farms, the newly wealthy New Yorkers began to hire the best architects to design large houses with all manner of stables, garages, workshops, and agricultural buildings. These families also were expected to have a house in Newport, a camp in the Adirondacks, a place for a few weeks in Saratoga, and a winter hideaway in the South.

One of the early examples of a country house on Long Island was Idle Hour, a house in the Queen Anne style set on nine hundred acres in Oakdale, a privileged hamlet in the town of Islip. Built in 1878, this was the first of many collaborations between Alva Vanderbilt and William Morris Hunt, whom she befriended just after her marriage in 1875. When Alva Vanderbilt wanted a "summer cottage" in fashionable Newport, Rhode Island, she turned once more to her favorite architect. Again, the result of Vanderbilt's and Hunt's collaboration represented innovation. The elegant and elaborate Marble House, a Beaux-Arts structure completed in 1888, heralded a shift in attitude from the simple clapboard and shingle houses to the large stone mansions that define much of Bellevue Avenue today.

The material result of America's prosperity and social ambition was an array of magnificent mansions and country houses that provided Mizner with a cosmopolitan supplement to his extracurricular education. Through old friends and their superb connections, the architect was able to experience many of the best examples firsthand. Into the peak of this enormous pre-war expansion of domestic architecture stepped Addison Mizner, aspiring to become a society architect and eagerly anticipating life in America's greatest city. Shifting attitudes in society conveniently created a receptive environment for a bohemian, unconventional outsider that put him on a path to realize this dream.

CHAPTER SEVEN

"FRIENDS IN HIGH PLACES"

With the benefit of an optimistic temperament, Addison Mizner was starting over in New York. It would be in this ambitious city that the first ray of optimism would nurture his professional aspirations. At the turn of the century, New York had a clearly delineated social structure but, rather than being consigned to the margins like most newcomers, Addison was accepted among the elite through the connections of well-established friends from San Francisco. Although New Yorkers generally viewed West Coast behavior as crude and unrefined, they found Addison's authenticity and erudition greatly appealing. Through his remarkable capacity for cultivating friendships, he received commissions for country houses on Long Island that would foreshadow the style of his Florida work. While it would be in

Theresa "Tessie" Fair Oelrichs, circa 1905. Tessie was the older daughter of James Graham Fair, one of the Silver Kings who made a fortune in silver mining. She married sportsman Hermann Oelrichs in 1890 and was well entrenched in New York society when Addison arrived there in 1904. She introduced Addison to her many friends and provided entrée to the elite.

Courtesy of the Library of Congress.

Palm Beach that Addison's vision and talent would reach its fullest dimensions, it was in New York where his interests first converged with opportunity.

The New York that Addison Mizner encountered in 1904 was the second most populous city in the world after London, a city it would surpass by 1925.[1] It was a dynamic metropolis that was the centerpiece of the Gilded Age, the period of rapid economic growth in America that had, by 1890, created a plutocracy of four thousand millionaires who controlled nearly three-quarters of America's wealth.[2] For many of them, New York was a city of aspiration. As it was the only American city that could be compared to the great capital cities of Europe, there was a desire among the wealthy from the Midwest and West to settle there. As Thomas Beer stated in *The Mauve Decade*: "The goal was New York. Boston and Philadelphia civilly refused to be interested in western money, but New York was less coy. . . . It was assumed that all rich Westerners came wooing Eastern favour and since the Western cities were so crude and ugly it was not worthwhile to inspect them."[3]

Among this new aristocracy when Addison arrived in New York were his close childhood friends from San Francisco, Tessie Fair and her sister Virginia, known as Birdie. In 1890, Tessie became the wife of Hermann Oelrichs, a popular society figure and athlete known for polo and marathon swimming. Upon her marriage to Oelrichs, Tessie received a check

Virginia Fair Vanderbilt. Known as "Birdie," the younger daughter of James Graham Fair married William K. Vanderbilt II in 1899 and, like her older sister, facilitated Addison's entry into New York and Newport society. When her father died in 1894, Birdie and Tessie inherited a fortune. Together, the sisters and Tessie's husband, Hermann Oelrichs, bought land in Newport for the eventual construction of Rosecliff, a mansion in the Beaux-Arts style. Courtesy of the Library of Congress.

for $1 million as a wedding gift from her father, James Fair.[4] The Oelrichs emphasized their prominence in society with the construction of Rosecliff, a palatial Newport mansion designed by Stanford White. In 1899, Birdie married William K. Vanderbilt II, the great grandson of Commodore Cornelius Vanderbilt and the son of William K. Vanderbilt who had commissioned the building of Marble House in Newport. Even Addison's dear friend from San Francisco, Peter Martin, had married the niece of Tessie Oelrichs and had a home in Newport. Tessie and Birdie in turn introduced Addison to many of their friends, among them Mrs. Stuyvesant Fish and Mrs. Oliver Belmont, known respectively as Mamie and Alva. Just after his arrival in New York, Addison met Tessie and some of her friends at the horse show at Madison Square Garden and, overwhelmed by their opulent dress, remarked, "For the first time I learned the difference between jewelry and jewels."[5]

Before Mrs. Astor's death in 1908, her solid position as unchallenged leader of the social elite had begun to diminish both in New York and Newport. By the turn of the century, Alva Belmont, Mamie Fish, and Tessie Oelrichs had become so influential that they were known as the "Great Triumvirate."[6] In New York, these same ladies also challenged Mrs. Astor's primacy by hosting parties that deviated from the unimaginative tradition of very long dinners. Mrs. Astor's custom was to lavish her guests with three-hour dinners composed of interminable courses and a copious flow of different wines. Others thought it much more amusing to abbreviate the dinner to create time for dancing and entertainment. Mrs. Fish went so far as to reduce the dinner to a mere fifty minutes, offering only champagne instead of a different wine paired to each course. According to her, "You have to liven these people up. Wine only makes them sleepy."[7]

As the younger hostesses were much more adventurous and daring, dinner parties were now enlivened with exotic entertainments that would have been considered indecorous by Mrs. Astor. As the waltz was becoming very popular in 1907, Addison collaborated with Alva Belmont to spice up one of her dinner parties by teaching everyone the dance. As the instructor, he brought in Donald Brian, the "King of Broadway" and the male lead of the Broadway hit *The Merry Widow*.[8] Having been taught dancing by his mother, Addison began his own dancing class for six ladies in his apartment; however, as more women wanted to join, the class was forced to move to the larger ballrooms of the Vanderbilts and Whitneys to accommodate newcomers. Addison said, "it was only a short time before Birdie Vanderbilt and others were learning the 'bunny hug.'"[9]

Part of Addison Mizner's allure was his familiarity and intimacy with both the *beau monde* and the shadowy world of entertainment, a duality that made him very attractive in the more relaxed society emerging in New York at the time. He explained: "Through a lot of old family friends, I met many of the 'right people' and through Broadway acquaintances I met a great many who were not."[10] He introduced Mrs. Fish to Marie Dressler who, accompanied by Jerome Kern, performed in the socialite's home. He had joined The Lambs, a club devoted to the arts, and had connections to actors, singers, dancers, and amusing bohemians. After returning from a house party in Newport, Addison reported: "I was a success, for I was considered a curiosity."[11]

To suggest that Addison's acceptance and popularity owed solely to the entree provided by Tessie Oelrichs would be wrong. He was socially adept and skilled in his own right. The nimble mind and rapier wit cultivated around the family dining table in Benicia were great assets as he came in contact with the very formidable grandes dames now residing at the apex of society. Mrs. Stuyvesant Fish, known to be clever, overbearing, and intimidating, once remarked to an arriving guest: "Make yourselves perfectly at home, and believe me, there is no one who wishes you were there more heartily than I do."[12] She had no cultural interests and could have been the inspiration for Edith Wharton's biting comment in *The Age of Innocence* about America's ambivalent relationship with culture: "Americans want to get away from amusement even more quickly than they want to get to it."[13] Upon meeting Addison Mizner, the imperious Mrs. Fish challenged some of his assertions, verbal thrusts that he successfully parried. In private, he rejoiced in his triumph: "I had crossed swords with the greatest wit in society and had gotten away with it."[14] This commanding authority told Addison "you are the only person I know who's not afraid of me" and permitted him to call her "Miss Mamie," a familiarity reserved for friends.[15]

Another friend who entered Addison's life through Tessie Oelrichs was the redoubtable architect, Stanford White. Like Addison, White had no formal architectural training and began his career as an apprentice to a leading architect. Unlike Addison, he had become a titan in the world of architecture and was the most innovative partner in McKim, Mead & White. Among White's commissions were Madison Square Garden, the *New York Herald* Building, the triumphal arch at Washington Square, and Rosecliff, the magnificent Newport "cottage" of Tessie Oelrichs. Addison idolized White: "I worshipped, for he was my God."[16] At the suggestion of Tessie, White also provided Addison with a few small

Pennsylvania Station, circa 1915. Designed by McKim, Mead & White and completed in 1910, Pennsylvania Station was a superb example of the Beaux-Arts style and a symbol of the importance of New York, the second largest city in the world at the time. It was a dynamic city with an entrenched elite that Addison Mizner was able to penetrate as a result of San Francisco friends. Here, he began to practice architecture on his own and eventually received commissions from important people for houses on Long Island.
Courtesy of the Library of Congress.

projects that were too insignificant to be handled through his office.

Addison knew White well enough to be invited to several of his parties. Flamboyant and promiscuous, White maintained a splendid apartment on 24th Street in Manhattan designed for pleasure and gratification. At one of his soirées, White stopped Addison to point out a beautiful young lady. Knowing from the tone of the conversation that White had an amorous interest in her, Addison was curious to see who she was. It was someone he already knew: "I … almost dropped dead when I came face to face with Evelyn Nesbit."[17] Nesbit, a young chorus girl and model, was the object of desire that induced a jealous and unstable Harry Thaw to murder Stanford White in 1906. Like Mizner, Stanford White lived at the intersection of polite society and Bohemia. With the posthumous dissemination of White's scandalous life that damaged his professional reputation, Addison might have learned the virtue of discretion and the need to be careful in his own personal life.

More germane to the development of Addison Mizner was the fact that Stanford White was a creative genius who was willing to share part of himself with an avid and admiring young architect. The men were united by unconventional inclinations and a passionate interest in architecture. It was White's willingness to discuss architecture and to suggest books for study that fed Addison's curiosity and contributed to his education. By looking at the many photographs of White's work in Mizner's scrapbook, *Architecture of the United States*, the impact of the architect on Mizner becomes evident.

It is reasonable to suggest, even in the absence of any recorded visit, that Mizner would have visited Box Hill, Stanford White's summer house in St. James in Suffolk County, New York. It was begun in 1884 and was under constant renovation until the architect's death in 1906. As Mizner knew White in only the last two years of his life, the house would have been much as it is today: a ramble of unused details from other McKim, Mead & White buildings and flourishes composed from architectural artifacts. White was well known for raiding European buildings, frequently returning to New York with troves of architectural paneling, garden ornament, stones, doors, and windows, all skillfully used in his projects to create a new taste for the American upper class.

Mizner also would have been reminded of Stanford White every time the younger architect visited Newport, as he was a regular guest at Rosecliff. Following the settlement of her father's estate, Tessie Oelrichs had become one of the wealthiest women in America and she wanted to fulfill a desire to build the most splendid house in Newport, a masterpiece in both aesthetic and practical terms. Tessie had originally awarded the design commission for her Newport mansion to A. Page Brown, a family friend and noted San Francisco architect who had begun with McKim, Mead & White; however, considering Brown's Spanish Colonial villa insufficiently ambitious, she ultimately gave the commission to Stanford White in 1898.[18]

Rosecliff was inspired by the Grand Trianon, a retreat designed for Louis XIV by Jules Hardouin Mansart. Like its inspiration, Rosecliff is defined by a horizontal rhythm of recurring arches separated by paired Ionic pilasters and columns. At this point, however, the resemblance ends. White took the one-story Grand Trianon and exploded it "into a four-story machine for entertaining, inserting a full floor of bedrooms between the orders of double pilasters and the continuous balustrade. The Trianon's pink marble was replaced by white, glazed terra cotta, a building material that particularly interested Stanford White."[19] Mizner would have examined all aspects of White's design and, aware of the house's provenance, would also have explored the French classicism of Mansart.

While Addison Mizner had access to the grand ballrooms of New York and Newport, he lived in a more modest manner. Upon moving to New York, he rented a series of apartments that were beautifully furnished with the antiquarian objects purchased in Guatemala. Wherever he lived, Addison preferred to have a spacious reception room to be able to entertain his friends graciously. The gratifying effect achieved

One of the Gilded Age's most extravagant mansions, Rosecliff was commissioned by Tessie and Hermann Oelrichs. Designed by Stanford White and inspired by the architect's admiration for the Grand Trianon at Versailles, Rosecliff was a summer home appropriate for entertaining on a grand scale. Addison Mizner would have visited often and studied all aspects of the design of White, one of his architectural reference points.
Courtesy of the Library of Congress.

with tastefully arranged objects and luxurious fabrics not only reminded visitors that he offered design services but also sold antique furniture and decorative art as well. After moving to New York, Addison was able to sell a large quantity of textiles, priest robes, and "oddments" for over $25,000, after which he still had three-quarters of his stock.[20] Income derived from these sales and from investment income from his mining proceeds left Addison in a temporary position of being able to live comfortably.

Initially, Addison was busy cultivating the social contacts that would later feed his architectural practice. He did receive some small projects that he described as "a few old brownstone fronts … made over into apartments" and some decorating jobs that were stages for his antiquities.[21]

Although Addison's life in New York had begun promisingly, it was beclouded by the appearance of his younger brother Wilson. When later describing the arrival of Wilson in New York, Addison remarked: "I had never been happy in my life that a fly did not light in the ointment."[22] In 1904, Wilson had decided to leave the gold fields of Nome to become a theatrical agent in New York. Appearing one night at Madison Square Garden when Addison was the guest of Tessie Oelrichs, Wilson was considered, to Addison's distress, a dashing character by his new acquaintances. Quickly Wilson managed to catch the eyes of Addison's other female companions and, as was his wont, became engaged in shady activities that would complicate his brother's life.

In early 1905, Addison was invited by Tessie to accompany her on a trip to France and Italy and, on March 1, they sailed for Paris. This trip was stimulating and inspiring for Addison because each country had a rich architectural heritage and each was a prominent leader in the development of Western art. Having never been to Italy, he absorbed its wonderful culture in the company of someone he truly enjoyed and, owing to the connections of Tessie, managed to have an audience with Pope Pius X. After visiting Rome, they went to Venice before returning to Paris. At this point, Tessie returned to America while Addison remained behind to travel to Spain and Morocco with Frank Goad, an old friend from San Francisco. This would begin a tradition of traveling to Europe every year in his quest for knowledge and for fine and decorative art.

Also in 1905, Addison began the practice of keeping scrapbooks of architecture, furniture, and objects that would serve as a vast reference library in his architectural practice. On this trip, he discovered a lot of material: "I spent half of my time in shops buying photographs of palaces and cathedrals that I wasn't to use for many years."[23] That these many images truly fascinated Addison is confirmed by the fact that there are personal annotations, observations, measurements, and sketches that reflect his judgment and discernment. He was very observant and turned his critical eye on a variety of details, including the alluring colors and patinated finishes he encountered. By studying and sketching the form and ornament of great buildings, Mizner was continuing a venerable tradition of architectural education practiced for centuries.

Mizner returned home in the late summer of 1905 and fell right into a newly acquired social rhythm: "I got home again;

This drawing details the interior architecture of Marble House, the Newport home of William Kissam Vanderbilt II and his wife Birdie and another Newport mansion regularly visited by Addison Mizner. This magnificent house was designed by Richard Morris Hunt, the first American to attend the Ecole des Beaux Arts in Paris. Recognized as a society architect, Hunt was someone whose career Mizner certainly would have followed closely. The ability to observe great architecture firsthand was a significant part of Mizner's extracurricular education.
Courtesy of the Library of Congress.

so Newport and smart house parties were in order."[24] In the fall, he was pleased to have his mother visit from California. A solicitous and doting host always, and especially to the mother he adored, Addison treated her to dinners and plays and even updated one of her dresses with some of his Guatemalan lace. After two months in New York, his brother, Edgar, escorted her back to California. Early in 1906, Addison was invited to go to Mardi Gras in the private railroad car of a friend. After

the festivities in New Orleans, Addison and others in the group decided to make their way back to New York after first visiting Palm Beach, the Florida resort developed by industrialist Henry Morrison Flagler. Addison stayed a week and appeared to be underwhelmed, remarking, "There was nothing but two old wooden Flagler hotels," an observation that mirrored that of Henry James who called Palm Beach a "hotel civilization."[25] Mizner would eventually devote the most creative years of his life to building Palm Beach in such a manner as to prevent anyone else from ever making a similar comment.

The year 1906 would provide Addison with two disconcerting events: the first, an embarrassment that he was forced to endure; the second, a disaster whose devastation he worked to diminish. The first event occurred just after his return from Palm Beach when he learned that his brother, Wilson, had married. To Addison's astonishment, the bride was Myra Yerkes, an acquaintance he had met just after moving to New York in 1904. Charles Yerkes, Myra's husband and a successful entrepreneur, had moved his family into a New York mansion overlooking Central Park in 1899 and, almost simultaneously, established a young mistress in a flat only two blocks away. This arrangement had naturally resulted in conjugal disharmony and in the understandable need for Myra Yerkes to seek solace elsewhere. Unfortunately, Myra Yerkes coped with her husband's philandering with the liberal consumption of

ROYAL

alcohol, a habit that produced loutish behavior and spoiled an otherwise attractive countenance.

At Myra's invitation, Addison agreed to be her guest at the theater. Upon arrival, Addison noted that Myra looked "like a red velvet sofa" but, having disposed of her velvet coat trimmed in fur, she "was very lovely all in white, very slender and tall" and further distinguished by two enormous strings of pearls that resembled "mothballs."[26] When Addison subsequently received an invitation from Myra to attend a dinner party at her sumptuous mansion, he used the arrival of his brother as an excuse to decline. Insisting on Addison's presence at her party, Myra told Addison to bring along his brother. That evening, Myra Yerkes became infatuated with the charming, roguish Wilson Mizner. When Charles Yerkes died of kidney disease on December 29, 1905, Wilson saw an irresistible opportunity to fill his empty purse. Charles Yerkes, an extravagant voluptuary, had made a fortune investing in the tram business in Chicago and in the underground system in London.

On January 30, Myra Yerkes and Wilson Mizner were married at the Yerkes' palatial mansion at 864 Fifth Avenue.[27] The union stunned many because the bride, widowed only four weeks, was forty-eight years old and the groom but twenty-nine, a disparity in age of nineteen years that suggested a questionable motive on Wilson's part. As Myra Yerkes was not only an attractive woman but also heiress to a large sum of money, she was pursued by many eligible men. Her choice of a husband was baffling to those who knew her. Adding further to the operatic nature of the wedding was the account provided to reporters by the Reverend Andrew Gillies of Saint Andrew's Episcopal Church, who officiated and, when asked by reporters if the bride had been drinking, would only state that Mrs. Yerkes was "conscious at the time."[28] Myra Yerkes' emotional instability was also reflected in a comment made by Wilson just after the wedding. When asked what prompted his decision to marry, Wilson answered, "the most efficient waterpower in the world—women's tears."[29] Her friends were incredulous.

Wilson Mizner was now married to the owner of a remarkable mansion that contained a conservatory of rare birds, a penthouse theater, and nine bathrooms, one of which was done in onyx at a cost of $30,000.[30] Wilson's new home had an art gallery whose contents, featuring works by Rembrandt, Franz Hals, Anthony van Dyck, and Sir Joshua Reynolds, was valued at $2 million.[31] When Addison paid a visit, his brother commented "things are very comfortable here and the service is excellent."[32] Unawed by splendor, Wilson saw in the

Royal Poinciana Hotel 1900. When Addison Mizner visited Palm Beach in 1906, he was generally unimpressed, considering the town nothing but a community that revolved around Henry Flagler's two hotels, the Royal Poinciana and the Breakers. With Mizner's affinity for Mediterranean Revival architecture, he thought the clapboard hotels designed in a colonial Georgian style inappropriate for the semi-tropical climate of South Florida. Courtesy of the Library of Congress.

immensity of his opulent new home possibilities beyond the world of luxurious living. With a practiced affinity for promotion, Wilson turned one wing of his new home into a lavish training camp for prizefighters.

Wilson's behavior and Myra's drinking combined to create an antagonistic relationship that resulted in conflict and quarreling. The contentious couple was divorced after only one year of marriage, a fleeting union that, according to Addison, left Wilson with nothing "but his freedom."[33] One marriage appeared to be enough for Wilson: "I had never considered marriage, but I had an open mind, and I was to learn after a brief try at it that most open minds should be closed for repairs."[34] When Myra died five years later, the various treasures and splendid mansion that were a brief part of Wilson's life were sold.

The theater associated with this marriage and its protagonists was irresistible fodder for a ravenous press. With Wilson's colorful past, there were many ribald and earthy adventures begging to be excavated for the purpose of entertaining readers. For Wilson, this was just another amusing episode in his Rabelaisian life; however, for Addison, this very public display unfolded right in front of his new friends, the affluent audience he was trying to attract to his practice. Addison Mizner, an ardent fan of the raucous and the bawdy, was always tolerant of his younger brother's antics as long as they were not proximate; however, he could only have endured this latest display with chagrin and displeasure. Even Addison's secretary could foresee the consequences: "That will just about ruin your social career, Mr. Addison."[35]

The second event that affected Addison's life more profoundly than his brother's marriage was the San Francisco earthquake that occurred on April 18, 1906. This catastrophe caused disastrous fires that lasted several days and destroyed the greater part of the city, including the financial and retail districts, the libraries, and many of its schools and churches.[36] Among those affected was his family. An anxious Addison finally received news two days later from his brother, William, that all members of the family were all right but that William's own residence had been destroyed. Addison then received a letter from his mother stating that she had been at the Hotel Pleasanton when fire erupted early in the morning. His brother, Lansing, was eventually able to reach her and take her to Stag's Leap to be with her daughter, Min Chase. Addison sent money to his family and also worked with Marie Dressler, the Broadway actress who had organized a New York relief effort for the San Francisco earthquake victims, to raise $75,000 for the beleaguered city.[37] With the family in distress, Addison now focused on going to the aid of his mother, now seventy years old.

CHAPTER EIGHT

AMBITION AND ARCHITECTURE

Residing in New York at this time on 24th Street in an apartment with only one bedroom, Addison had begun to consider something larger in order that Mama Mizner could stay with him. In the spring of 1907, he was invited to spend the weekend at Port Washington, a small community on the North Shore of Long Island where many affluent families had country homes. Addison's host during this weekend was Bourke Cockran, a former congressman from New York and a friend of young Winston Churchill. With many grand mansions, the North Shore area near Port Washington is thought to have been the inspiration for F. Scott Fitzgerald's fictional East Egg in *The Great Gatsby*.[1]

With European settlements dating to the seventeenth century, Long Island had been a popular hunting and fishing destination for wealthy New Yorkers including Henry Longfellow and Washington Irving. Its bountiful natural advantages and relative ease of access by boat meant that wealthy families came to consider its protected bays ideal for the creation of summer cottages. The establishment of the Long Island Railroad in 1834 and the subsequent extension of its network with new rail and additional stations provided the means to escape the city quickly to this beautiful rural area.[2] The railroads displaced the seasonal steamship traffic that served the Sound and provided the means by which labor, food and drink, and other services could be made available to the cottagers. The construction of the Queensboro Bridge, spanning the East River to connect the boroughs of Manhattan and Queens, was begun in 1903, providing another option for a family to reach its country seat.

The completion of the bridge was still two years away when Addison Mizner visited the Cockrans. In the course of the weekend, he visited the Baxter Homestead, the earliest part of which dated from 1673. Situated at Whitestone Landing and known as the "Old Bay Manor House," it was built by John Betts and Robert Hutchings, members of the *Cow Neck* homestead settlement in Port Washington. The house had been purchased by Oliver Baxter around 1741 and was used to quarter Hessian soldiers during the Revolutionary War.[3] Despite the

CENTRAL DR.

fact that it had neither heating nor plumbing, Addison still found it charming, especially the "beautifully proportioned neo-classical rooms" from the late eighteenth century.[4] Addison arranged to purchase the house and then began renovations that included building three new bathrooms, installing heating, and planting a garden. Just after the purchase was arranged, his mother was able to visit for a couple of weeks. Later, by knocking out a wall, he joined two rooms that resulted in a spacious area for entertaining. Also, he switched the entrance of the house to the rear and created an eighteen-foot-wide terrace that provided an expansive view of the bay. The planning idea of rising to a terrace to set the entry would grow to prominence as a Mizner signature element.

Being careful to preserve its colonial character, Mizner continued to make alterations to his home and decided to name it Chateau Myscene. The name appears to be a reference to Mycenae, a cultural and military bastion of southern Greece during the late Bronze Age. Any reason for his choice of the name is undocumented. The palace of Mycenae was located on a hill that looked onto the Saronic Gulf, so it could have been the shared geography offering a view of water that inspired the name. Alternatively, it could have been a self-deprecating reference to the modesty of his house compared to the grandeur and importance of the country houses that surrounded him. Quite possibly, the clever Mizner might have been making a play on words, using the important classical name to refer to the unpretentious home as "my scene." Regardless, it was a home that was comfortable and inviting.

Despite the fact that the house was filled with fine antiquarian objects acquired during his travels, Addison created a welcoming refuge for his growing stable of friends and pets. Nurturing his affinity for animals, he kept dogs, monkeys, chickens, and a rabbit and ran a dog kennel, selling forty or fifty puppies per year. He also had the luxury of sufficient household help that at one time included an Italian butler, a French maid, an Irish parlor maid, and a Spanish cook.

To this menagerie, he added teenaged boys. In 1907, the New York Stock Exchange lost significant value and caused a panic that affected many, including one of his neighbors. When he learned that the despondent family would be forced to move, Addison offered to allow the eldest two boys to live with him so that they could continue in the same school and

Chateau Myscene, Mizner's home in Port Washington, Long Island, faced directly on Manhasset Bay just north of Baxter Pond. Known as the Baxter Homestead, portions of the house dated from the 1670s and had housed Hessian troops during the Revolutionary War.

Mizner had long dreamed of a place where Mama Mizner could live with him, and his purchase of this house finally made it possible.

In 1917, an eight-page article was published in the Architectural Record *detailing Mizner's restoration and remodeling, largely to the interiors of the house. Mizner's joining of two parlors to create a large living room enabled larger social gatherings that were the beginnings of Mizner's combination of architecture and social life and led to larger collections of antiques and pets.*

Photograph by Craig Kuhner.

maintain their friendships. His offer to the father was to "let the boys come down and stay with mother and me for a week or two. . . ."[5] The boys stayed eight years. This gesture was typical of the charitable and unselfish Mizner.

As his new property was very well situated, Addison found himself in a propitious location for cultivating friendships that were in need of sophisticated architectural services. Port Washington was part of the North Shore known as the Gold Coast, the location of one of the greatest concentrations of wealth in the early decades of the twentieth century and the site of a profusion of impressive country homes belonging to names such as Vanderbilt, Field, Phipps, Roosevelt, and Whitney. This huge cluster of affluence brought the most distinguished names in American architecture to design homes appropriate to the exalted station of their patrons. Richard Morris Hunt, John Russell Pope, McKim, Mead & White, and Carrère & Hastings built magnificent mansions that would serve as an inspiration to a young architect just beginning his practice.

Among the many splendid homes that would have greatly interested Addison during his residence on Long Island was Harbor Hill, completed for Clarence Mackay in 1902 by McKim, Mead & White. Mackay was the son of John William Mackay, one of the Silver Kings and a partner of the father of Tessie Oelrichs and Birdie Vanderbilt, all of whom made a fortune with the Comstock Lode. Overseen by Stanford White,

Harbor Hill, Stanford White's last great house, was designed for Mr. and Mrs. Clarence McKay, whose vast second-generation wealth was founded on the discovery of the Comstock Lode by Clarence's father, John William Mackay, with his partners, including James Fair, the father of Tessie Fair Oelrichs.

Under the strict direction of Katherine Duer Mackay, White employed a severe Loire Valley style largely copied from Mansart's Chateau de Maisons. White, by this time and perhaps worn down by Mrs. Mackay, was less concerned by the architecture and intently focused on the interiors and the accoutrements, the battles over which resulted in a mansion second only to Biltmore, the Vanderbilt estate in Asheville, North Carolina, designed by Richard Morris Hunt. Courtesy of the Library of Congress.

Harbor Hill was the largest house he ever designed and was inspired by Francois Mansart's 1642 masterpiece, the Château de Maisons-sur-Seine. The choice of a seventeenth-century French precedent was unusual for McKim, Mead & White, but may have resulted from Clarence and Katherine MacKay's explicit instructions to White, as a result of their knowledge of books in their library such as Claude Sauvageot's *Palais, Chateaux, Hotels, et Maisons du France de XVe au XVIIIe Siecles* (1867).[6]

Another house in which he would have shown a keen interest was The Eagle's Nest, a mansion built for William K. Vanderbilt II, the husband of his friend Birdie. This mansion was begun in 1910 and designed in the Spanish Revival style by the architects Warren and Wetmore, who had already participated with the firm of Reed and Stern to design the Grand Central Terminal for the Vanderbilts.[7] Whitney Warren was a cousin of the Vanderbilts and had studied at the Ecole des Beaux Arts in Paris. Knowing Birdie well and being sympathetic to Spanish architecture, Addison would have frequently visited, avidly absorbed every detail of its design and construction, and learned from the academic approach to the Spanish Colonial style that so resonated with him.

For his architectural practice, Addison would commute by train on weekdays to New York where he had an office on Fifth Avenue between 39th and 40th Streets. On weekends, Addison would entertain friends like Tessie Oelrichs and Birdie Vanderbilt who were happy to come to such a congenial and familiar location. His easy charm and warm hospitality made many friends and won him access to an ever expanding circle of influential friends, a group that Donald Curl described as "the smart set of New York," those now seeking his services for their country houses. That Addison had successfully infiltrated the social elite was confirmed when the local paper reported that the Chateau was the scene of raucous nocturnal festivities and provided a list of attendees, "most of them were from the higher echelons of the social register."[8] He had become such a character in Port Washington that the local paper even printed "interviews" with his monkey, chow, and Maltese cat. It would have been difficult not to notice Addison as he frequently shopped in his bathrobe or pajamas.[9]

That Mizner was making inroads among the elite was also evidenced by his association with Mrs. Stephen Brown, who gave him his first important commission. Stephen Brown, having gone into the brokerage business with his brother in 1895, was a governor of the New York Stock Exchange. In 1907, the Browns were unhappy with the work on their townhouse on 70th Street and, after firing their architect, hired Addison Mizner on the recommendation of Emma Eames. Eames, an accomplished soprano at the Metropolitan Opera who had also successfully performed at the Opera Garnier in Paris and the Royal Opera House in London, was a friend made through artistic circles. Addison assumed control immediately, completing the construction and subsequently overseeing all interior design. Brown was a serious collector of medieval art and certainly would not have been satisfied with design work that did not meet the high standards demanded of such a refined sensibility.[10]

In the same year, Mizner received a project for the redecoration of the Hotel Rand. Located on West 49th Street, the hotel became known for its magnificent central fountain in the lobby and fancy bar, reputed to be one of the best in town. The Rand, managed at this time by the penniless Wilson, tended to attract disreputable patrons that Addison described as "85% 'keptees.'"[11] One evening, Wilson apparently threw two guests into the lobby fountain for challenging their bills. They retaliated by bringing charges against the assailant. When a friend later complimented Wilson for being exonerated by cleverly convincing the judge that only one person could possibly fit in the fountain, Wilson immediately replied, "But I'm going to enlarge it."[12]

As Mizner's popularity grew, he began to attract other clients met through his expanding social circle and by word of mouth. In 1910, his Long Island work included gardens with a baroque stairway to the shore for the famous Broadway actor, Raymond Hitchcock, on Sands Point Road. While Hitchcock's long career from 1905 to 1927 was composed of leading or major support roles in dramatic and comedic plays, he also made several recordings, appeared in a movie by John Ford, and wrote a play, the music for which was composed by Cole Porter.

As mountain camps, particularly the Adirondack camps, were an important part of social life in the pre-war period, Mizner was commissioned in 1910 to design the expansion of a camp near Paul Smiths, New York, for Archibald S. White, president of Columbia Gas Company. Mizner planned a row of houses opposite an existing group of buildings along the ridge overlooking Osgood Lake, creating a street much like those that he remembered from his mining days in the Yukon Territory. The added buildings contained a grocery and munitions store, blacksmith shop, and post office. Mizner also added a teahouse with an oriental roof projecting over the lake, the only unique building in the whole assemblage and evidence of Mizner's sense of irony. As completed, the camp consisted of thirty buildings accommodating twenty-four guests.[13]

In 1911 and 1912, Mizner's geographic reach was expanded when he became actively involved in projects on the south shore of Connecticut and the North Shore of Long Island, particularly around Huntington and Port Washington. An important aspect of Mizner's approach that was to characterize his Palm Beach work was the blending of architecture with the landscape. Mizner's residential commissions were frequently on important sites with topographic interest or vistas that dictated the orientation and planning of the house or its addition. Mizner's background in California and his work with Polk in San Francisco enabled a keen eye for landscape and the possibilities for effect, especially when a view of water was available.

Port Washington, a northern peninsula on the Long Island Sound, offers lush landscape and dramatic topography. In 1911, William Bourke Cockran retained Mizner to make changes to the grounds of his Port Washington home, The Cedars. Cockran was a Democratic member of the US House of Representatives as well as the future nominator of presidential candidate Alfred E. Smith in 1920. Descended from Irish stock and educated in France, Cockran enjoyed a strong relationship with the Churchill family through his friendship with Lady Randolph Churchill, the former Jennie Jerome of New York. When her son, Winston, first visited the United States in 1895, Cockran introduced him to New York society.

Presented with a dramatic site, Mizner was determined to put his approach to landscape design on full display. The architect stated that "the day of gardens planted helter-skelter, without any preconcerted idea of the ultimate result, is over. . . . Things that have merit must also have a reason."[14] What the architect saw of merit was a beautiful view of the landscape that he intended to feature. To provide this vista from Cockran's home, Mizner removed a hedge and built thirty turf steps to a dry lake bed, which he converted to a miniature theater. By planting two new hedges to flank the stage, he created the opening allowing the guests to glimpse distant hills and trees.[15] From this impressive amphitheater, Cockran launched his 1912 campaign for reelection to Congress as a Progressive. The amphitheater was also the setting of the wedding of Cockran's sister-in-law to Shane Leslie, the nephew of Lady Randolph Churchill.

In 1911, Mizner also combined landscape and architecture in the creation of a Japanese house and garden for Sarah Cowen Monson, in Huntington, Long Island. Mizner's interest in the possibilities for miniaturization and shifts in scale in Japanese architecture and landscape led him to consider new thoughts of landscape conception for small one-acre lots. By creating a garden in miniature, Mizner could create seeming vistas at short distances, an approach that was becoming popular at that time. Mizner also began to experiment with the blurring of interior and exterior space by creating thinner walls that broadly opened to terraces and the landscape.

As has been noted, interest in Japanese architecture and landscape was prevalent at this time. After a period of isolation, Japanese ports were reopened to Western trade in 1853 and the importation of Japanese ideas had begun to influence European artists, including many American expatriates. Edward S. Morse, a lecturer at Harvard, had begun to travel to Japan as early as 1877 and his book, *Japanese Homes and Their Surroundings*, published nine years later, quickly became influential. By the turn of the century, the influence of his thought was widely spread.[16]

Sarah Monson's site overlooked Huntington Bay and enjoyed vistas over the treetops to the bay in the distance. Mizner oriented his planning to these views and landscaped the immediate grounds with small plants, stone lanterns, fountains, and stone slab paths through the lawns to a miniature lake. Mizner's inspiration was a Japanese nobleman's house in seventeenth-century Nikko, an ancient city eighty miles west of Tokyo. Mizner's approach strung pavilions approximately 150 feet apart along the top of a hill. Each building had a green glazed tile roof with upturned ends and the composition gave the appearance of a small village.

The brick entrance court led to a thirty-foot-square central hall, the seventeen-foot ceiling of which was built from exposed wooden rafters.[17] A gallery overlooking the hall provided access to Mrs. Monson's private rooms, which were above the dining room and butler's pantry. Also on the second floor, directly across the large hall, were guest quarters. As Mrs. Monson had traveled extensively in Japan and the Far East, the house was furnished with her large collection of Japanese furniture, screens, and other decorative items. Mizner westernized his design with glass windows and installed modern heating systems, bathrooms, and lighting fixtures. In striving to detail the home and gardens by using authentic Japanese motifs, building methods, furniture, and art, the effect must have been spectacular. Unfortunately, several pavilions of the Monson house were destroyed by fire in the 1950s.[18]

While overseeing the Monson construction, Mizner received another commission at the tip of Sands Point, Long Island, from Mr. and Mrs. Ralph Thomas. The estate, at 235 Middle Neck Road, was south of the lighthouse grounds at Sands Point and situated on a long, narrow, and hilly lot. The Thomases wished to build a home and, as Mrs. Thomas was an amateur tennis champion, a tennis court.

Middle Neck Road ran through the property in such a manner that, once the house was placed west of the road, there was scant space for the tennis court. Mizner solved the problem by locating the court east of the road, but the distance from the house had the effect of complicating service. To overcome this problem, he added a tennis pavilion just over the road closer to the house and fitted it with large doors that opened onto the court that enjoyed an excellent view of Long Island Sound. The pavilion included changing rooms, showers, and a large lounge with a seven-foot-wide fireplace that allowed the players to stay warm during cold weather. Based on an old inn, the Norman-style cottage was made of brick, stucco, and rough-hewn timber and featured lead-filled casement windows with diamond-shaped panes and uneven wooden shingles on the roof.

By this time, Addison Mizner had developed a wide architectural vocabulary, and there was evidence of a conscious

development in his approach to organizing a home for social use. As Mizner's
work matured, certain planning patterns
began to emerge. Most important among
them was the creation of a large, two-and-
a-half-story room at the center of the house
that served as the reception hall or living
room and that was connected to the dining
room, a porch or terrace, and the library.

In October of 1911, *Plain Talk*, a local
Port Washington biweekly magazine,
reported Mizner's trip to Winsted, Connecticut, to superintend the building of a
new $150,000 country home for Jerome
Alexandre of New York. The planning
and massing of this house, known as
"Rock Hall," exhibit early evidence of his
maturing architectural approach and even
express an interest in a "stripped-down"
aesthetic.

The H-shaped plan has a primary center section of two-and-a-half stories and
two wings of three-and-a-half stories. The
exterior of the house is Connecticut stone
at the ground floor and smooth stucco for

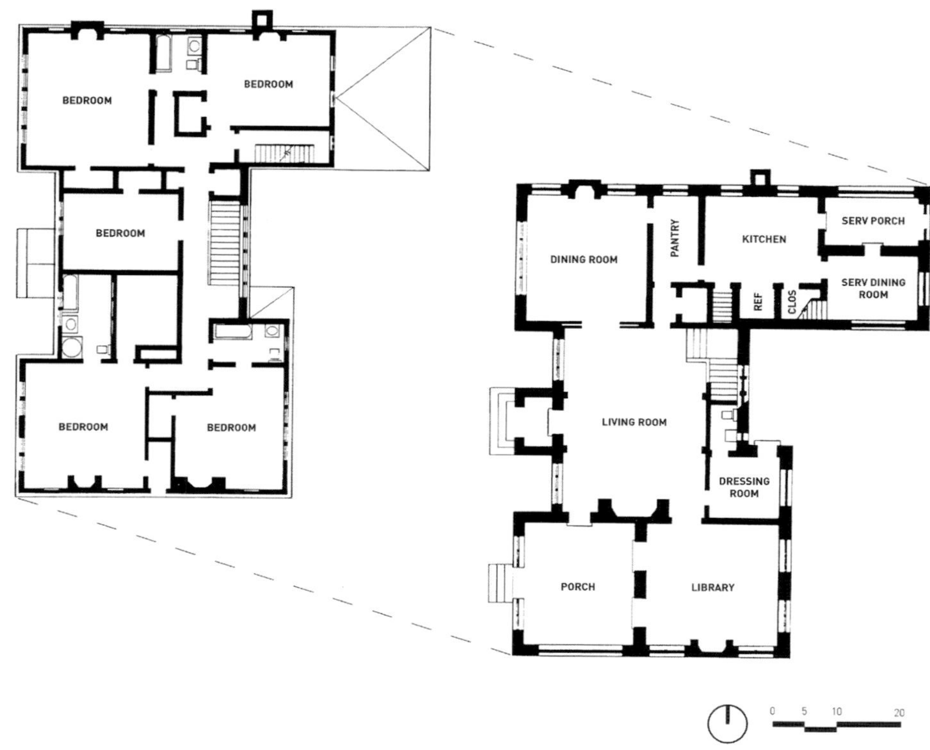

Jerome Alexandre's Residence, 1911, Winsted, Connecticut. This house was described, perhaps by Mizner, as Spanish-influenced. But in plans, massing, and elevations, the house had very little in common with what was then conventionally understood to be the Spanish style, except for the red barrel-tiled roof.

Notably, and unique in this Mizner house, the façades were flat with little or no detail around the windows, which were long, unbroken rows or single casements. The tripartite main elevation was composed of a two-and-one-half story central section recessed between three-story wings. At the lowest level of the right wing, a southwestern porch served the living room and the library, and could easily have been in southern California.
Plan reproduced by Chase R. Cothran.

the upper two floors of the wings. The large horizontal, leaded windows reside in punched openings and are untrimmed in natural or dressed stone, by this time a standard Mizner feature. Though the roof is covered in red barrel tile, the house could in no way be construed as having Spanish influence. The main west entry opens into a thirty-two-foot-long, two-story reception hall. Situated on the east façade across from the entry is a monumental stair with a stepped window allowing bright daylight into the reception hall. The porch and library are on the west and south facades. On the second floor are five spartan bedrooms and, on the third floor, a warren of servants' quarters.

The Alexandre house may be unique among Mizner's houses in that there is no imagined or recorded story and no perceptible style. The Alexandre house appears to be a brief

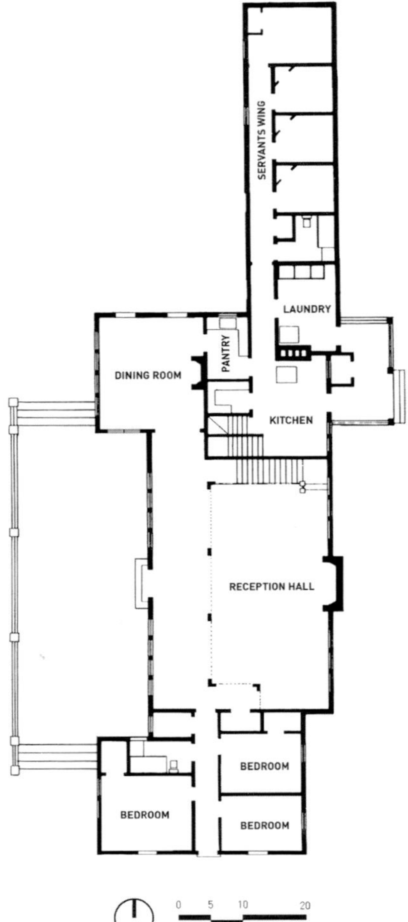

William Prime Residence, 1911, Brookville, New York. The William Prime house was set on a twenty-acre parcel at the crest of a hill in Brookville, New York. Mizner stretched out the plan and employed a device that would be repeated in New York, and to much greater effect in Palm Beach: an elevated terrace, accessed by flanking steps that enabled a procession across the broad western terrace to the front door.

The front door opened immediately into an impressive forty- by twenty-seven foot reception hall and was centered on a seven-foot-wide fireplace. Large windows on both long elevations allowed the great hall to be bathed in light.

In the early 1920s, the Primes sold the house to Edward F. Hutton and Marjorie Meriweather Post. The great hall survives today as the central interior feature of the mansion, which is located on the C. W. Post campus, created in 1954 by Long Island University in honor of Post's father.

Plan reproduced by Chase R. Cothran.

William Prime Residence, 1911, Brookville, New York. The Great Hall has been preserved by LIU/Post as the central feature of the facility.

Photograph by Craig Kuhner.

moment of architectural experimentation in which the role or influence of the owner is not recorded. Mizner's interest in simplicity and abstraction was short-lived; in his next houses he returned to his Spanish architectural roots in form and decoration, suggesting that this was an aberration at best.

In 1911, Mizner also began design and construction of the William A. Prime house on one hundred acres along Northern Boulevard in Brookville, New York. Planning the house for primarily western views, Mizner placed the house on the crest of a hill. Lawns and grounds consumed twenty acres and the balance was designed with swimming pools and other features. One approached the front door across a broad terrace, entering at the center of the reception hall that measured forty feet by twenty-seven feet and facing a seven-foot-wide fireplace at the opposite end. It was an exceptionally handsome, excellently proportioned and detailed room. As the two-story room was windowed on both long walls, daylight enveloped the room and served to enliven the wood paneling, stairs, balustrade, and beamed trusswork that grandly defined the room. The monumental stair connected the reception room to the gallery and the guest rooms.

The Prime residence was bought in 1921 in an estate sale by Edward F. Hutton and his wife, Marjorie Merriweather Post. They collaborated with the architecture firm of Hart & Shape to design Hillwood, a seventy-room Tudor Revival–style mansion that incorporated the original Prime house into its plan. The central feature of Hillwood was Mizner's reception hall, a grand room that survived intact despite a decade of renovations and many changes in planning. The retention of this principal room was evidence that Addison Mizner was very successful working on a grand scale, one of the defining characteristics of his mature houses.

With the Prime residence, Mizner began to consider seriously the role of procession in adding a sense of theater to a guest's entry into the residence. Mizner's deep experience in Spanish Colonial in California had taught him the value of the intermediate space, the outdoor "room" that set the tone for a guest's arrival. To enter the Prime residence, the guest climbed four steps at either end of a raised plaza and then walked across the plaza to the front door.

In his 1912 house for investment banker John Alley Parker, Mizner went further still. Parker spoke to Mizner of his intention to build a new six-thousand-square-foot house on thirty acres on Sands Point Road. He requested a Spanish-style house and Mizner designed a large U-shaped house around a ninety- by seventy-five-foot courtyard. However, the hilltop was relatively small, requiring that Mizner create a retaining wall on the west side so that the courtyard effectively concealed the servants' quarters below its edge, enabling the house to appear L-shaped when it is really U-shaped with the missing

John Alley Parker Residence, 1912, Sands Point, New York. Having purchased thirty acres on Sands Point Road, Parker requested that Mizner plan a "handsome villa . . . after the Spanish style of architecture." For the first time Mizner, with enough combined building program and site, designed a large U-shaped house which, with low walls, used a single-room depth to enclose a ninety- by seventy-five foot elevated courtyard. The Parker house is the earliest example of this manner of spatial enclosure that Mizner would repeat to great success a few more times in New York before replicating successfully in Palm Beach. Plan reproduced by Chase R. Cothran.

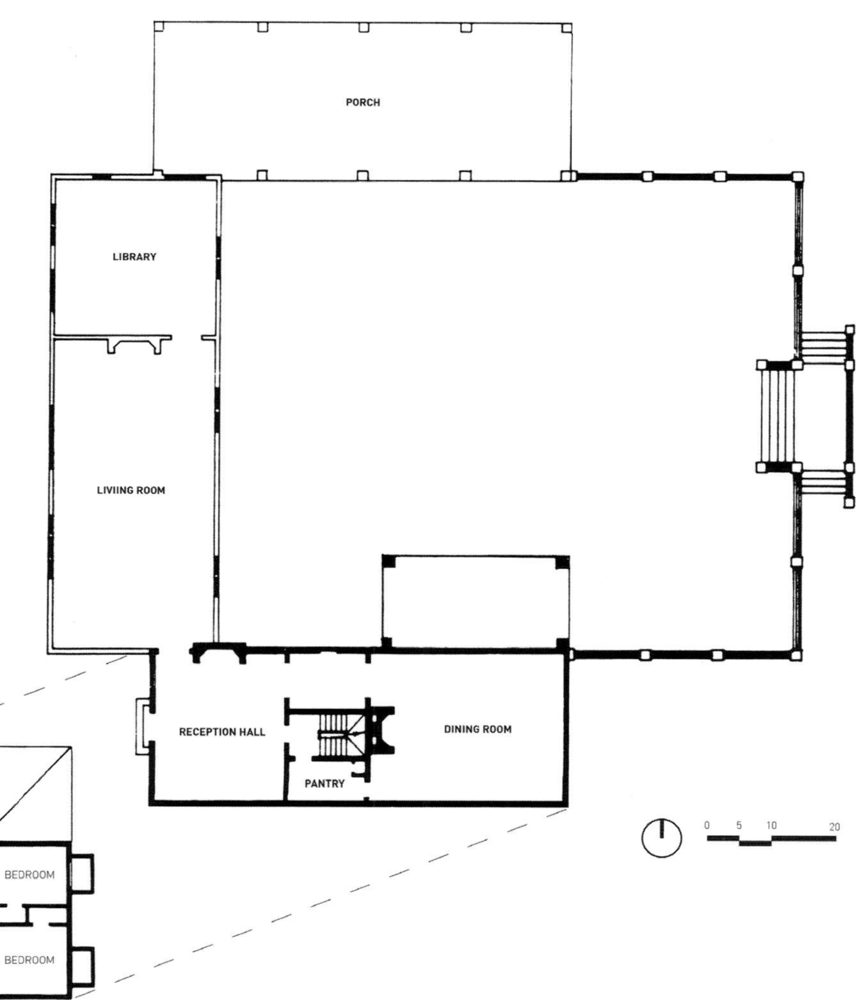

The John Alley Parker house as it appears today.
Photograph by Craig Kuhner.

leg being located below grade. Among the details ornamenting the house are a doorway of Spanish influence as well as a roof line defined by Spanish brackets. The asymmetrical massing more closely resembles conventional understandings of the Spanish Colonial style than Mizner's later adventuresome massing in Palm Beach.

Mizner, for the first time, took a complex site and managed to satisfy all of the functional requirements while enabling views through the courtyard to the east and of Hempstead Bay to the west, evidence of his ability to think in three-dimensional terms. By developing a plan using only a single room depth at the courtyard perimeter, Mizner again developed planning and massing patterns that would support his future residential planning in Palm Beach. However, from an environmental standpoint, Mizner largely ignored the harsh winter weather of the Long Island Sound in favor of a plan that would be better suited to his future work in Florida.

Mizner designed an important house for Alfred E. Dieterich, the only child of Charles F. Dieterich, who made a fortune in gas manufacturing and power plants. In the late 1880s, the elder Dieterich had combined five farms to create a 2,300-acre estate in Millbrook, a village in Dutchess County, New York, and in 1912 Alfred gave Mizner a commission for a new home to be situated on a hilltop. That Mizner now had a project in the Hudson Valley suggests that his reputation had grown and his market was beginning to expand beyond Long Island.

The very formal, long, low, and compact plan for the central pavilion allowed for symmetrical wings of sixty-nine feet each. Mizner employed a stone, groined vault loggia to shelter the entrance to a forty-five-foot-long living room with a heavy beamed wooden ceiling and a massive stone fireplace. Not only were all details consistently used in Mizner's later New York years, but they also became defining elements of

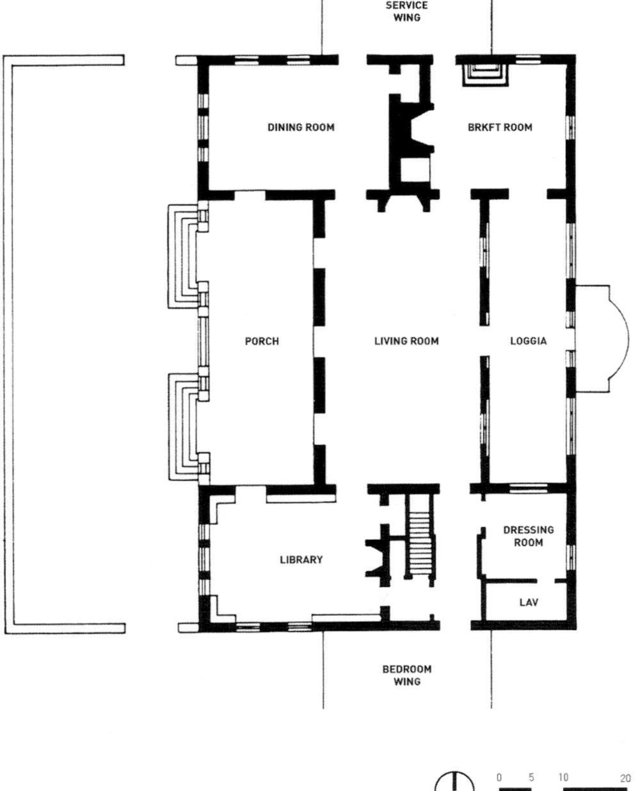

his Palm Beach work. The Dieterich house was Mizner's first, and most elegant, Spanish-style house of the New York period and was his first Spanish-style house that enjoyed a truly significant budget.

In 1914, I. Townsend Burden Jr. engaged Mizner to design a large Spanish-style house along Northern Boulevard in Greenvale, a hamlet west of the William Prime estate. Once again, Mizner was presented a challenging site that contained buildings that the owner wished to incorporate in the new house. With the existing stable unfortunately sited on the crest of a hill with good views to the north, Mizner decided to place the U-shaped house downhill

Alfred Elliot Dieterich Residence, 1912, Duchess County, New York. The son of Charles F. Dieterich, the founder of Union Carbide, Alfred commissioned Mizner to design a four-story, thirty-eight-room mansion on a parcel within his father's 2,300-acre estate. Named Daheim ("The Home Place"), the estate, complete with a gatehouse, stables, and other outbuildings, was Mizner's first experience with a budget that enabled features such as high, heavily beamed ceilings and massive cut stone fireplaces of the forty-five-foot-long living room. A twenty-foot square room off of the loggia and living room contained a stone fountain and a groined stone ceiling. This room was frequently used by Mrs. Dieterich for hunt breakfasts.

From 1963 to 1968, Daheim's successor ownership gave the estate to Timothy Leary for his exploration of the therapeutic potential of psychedelic drugs under controlled conditions.

Plan reproduced by Chase R. Cothran.

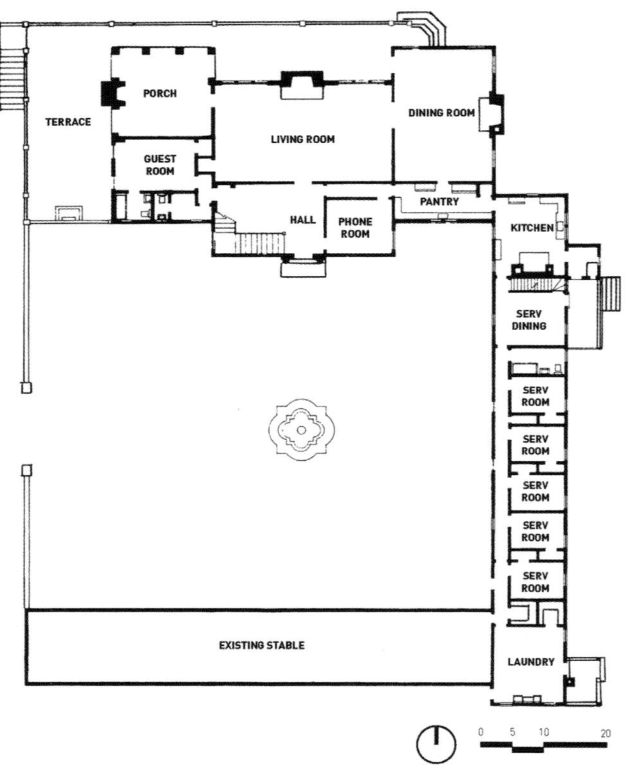

from the stable and connected the two with the servants' wing and related service areas. However, the design scheme remained highly formal with a centered entry into a symmetrically massed block. The house is successful on many levels but, even with its stucco walls, tiled roof, terraced patio, courtyard with fountain, and heavily cased door openings, it is not remarkable as a fine example of Spanish Revival architecture as compared to houses that would be designed over the next three years. Notably, Mizner for the first time used large expanses of windows that serve to illuminate the house against its northern exposure.

In 1915, Alva Belmont, America's premier society client, having been widowed in 1908, became the owner of substantial waterfront property acquired from the government in Sands Point. The site, composed of land south of the lighthouse and extending to the tip of the point, was among the most beautiful sites on Long Island. There she had Hunt &

I. Townsend Burden Residence, 1914, Greenvale, Long Island, New York. With a growing reputation, Mizner began to attract wealthy clients committed to his vision of Mediterranean architecture. In 1914, I. Townsend Burden, whose grandfather had founded a Troy, New York, steel company and amassed a great fortune, engaged Mizner to design a new estate on land alongside Northern Boulevard in Greenvale, Long Island. Again, Mizner devised a U-shaped house that enclosed a large entry courtyard.

Burden requested that Mizner utilize an existing stable and carriage house in his plan, which Mizner accomplished by linking the main house with the stable by the creation of a service wing and in so doing, creating a large entry court.

Plan reproduced by Chase R. Cothran.

I. Townsend Burden Residence, 1914, Greenvale, Long Island, New York. Burden's estate was perhaps "Spanish" in plan, but its elevations were "Spanish" only in their stucco walls, shallow, barrel-tiled roof, and elaborate main entry door. The fenestration was symmetrical and the center entry was formally organized against the "Spanish" idea.

Photograph by Craig Kuhner.

Hunt design and build Beacon Towers, a monumental French chateau that was completed in 1916. Originally, Mizner was asked to provide a sketch for this project but, given Belmont's lifelong and exclusive relationship with the Hunts, it is almost unimaginable that she would have awarded the chateau to

Beacon Towers, 1915, Sands Point, Long Island, New York. Mizner was introduced to Alva Belmont, the builder of Beacon Towers, by his childhood friend Tessie Fair Oehlrichs. So frequent and numerous were Alva Belmont's large architectural projects that she was made an honorary member of the American Institute of Architects. Beginning with Richard Morris Hunt on the design of her first mansion, the Petit Chateau on Fifth Avenue in New York, she built a series of large mansions including the Marble House in Newport, incidentally, a thirty-ninth birthday present.

Mizner hoped to attract Alva Belmont as a client and made a proposal for the design of Beacon Towers. Though Mizner's design was grand, it was no match for the sons of Richard Morris Hunt. The 1916 chateau was stunning and typical of Belmont's collaboration with the Hunts.

Courtesy of the Library of Congress.

Mizner, considering his limited experience with houses of this size, scale, and complexity.

Although Alva Belmont did not offer the commission for the chateau to her good friend, she did ask him to design a less conspicuous building on the property. Belmont drawings in Mizner's files, mislabeled as "Great Neck, New York," illustrate a small, one-room house placed at the top of the cliff that Mizner connected with the beach by an elaborate stair. As there are no changing rooms or other beach-related functions, one can only surmise that the structure was to have been a teahouse. Raised on a base and surrounded by a fretwork gallery, the rectangular polychrome pavilion has a pagoda-shaped roof with upturned ends.

Mizner's last New York house is, not surprisingly, his most successful of this period and one that serves as a clear prelude for his work in Palm Beach. In January of 1917, Mizner's former clients, the Stephen H. Browns, purchased a fifteen-acre estate in Matinecock, a village adjoining the Piping Rock Club in the town of Oyster Bay, and asked him to design a large Spanish-style house that they planned to furnish from their extensive antiques collection.

At the center of the house plan, Mizner planned a three-story tower from which three wings would emanate. The grouping of tower and emanating wings would figure prominently in many future Palm Beach houses as the tower served

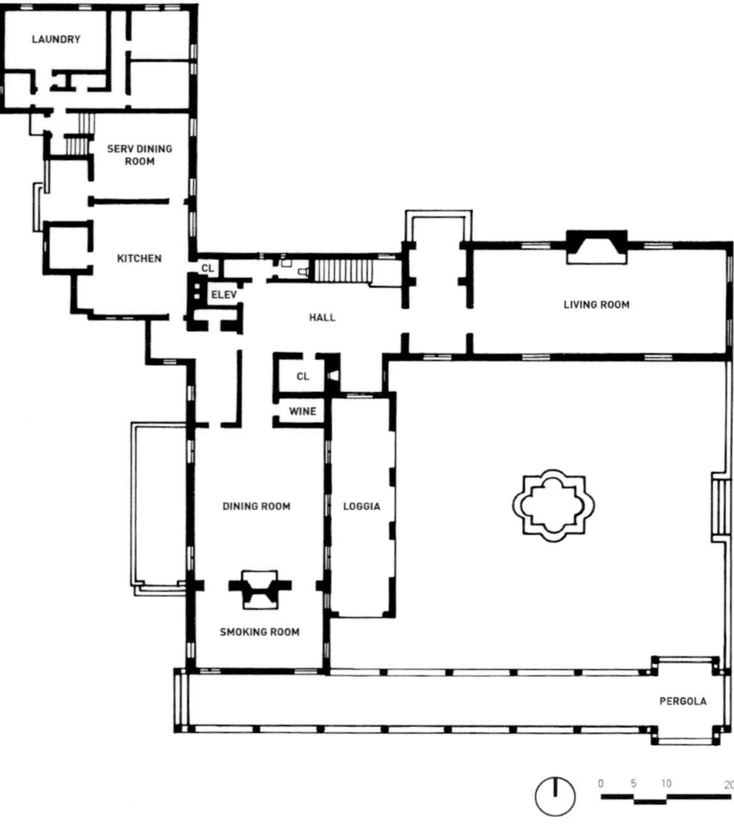

Stephen H. Brown Residence, 1917, Locust Valley, Long Island, New York. Brown purchased a fifteen-acre parcel adjoining the Piping Rock Club in Locust Valley, Long Island, and asked Mizner to design a large Spanish-style house. The Brown collection of sophisticated antiques would become the fine interiors of Mizner's last New York house.

In a plan that would more accurately predict Mizner's next Florida work, the plan and massing were irregular and appear to have been built and modified over time, one of the signature effects that Mizner would bring to fruition in his large Palm Beach houses and estates. Plan reproduced by Chase R. Cothran.

to organize the public circulation for the house. The freedom of the plan enabled Mizner to create surprise when, through the entry vestibule, one encounters the single room-thickness that surrounds a concealed courtyard bounded by the glass-walled living room, a loggia, and long pergola, at the center of which is a dripping fountain. Many of the features of the Brown residence would become hallmarks of Mizner's Florida work: interior stone walls, plain unarticulated facades, strongly articulated roof lines, beamed and paneled ceilings, tiled floors, vaulted stair halls, and loggias.

The Brown house also served as a transition between Mizner's northern, Spanish design and his future Florida work. The elements of surprise that captivated Mizner from his days in Guatemala and Spain were now a fixed part of his vocabulary. During his New York years, he gravitated from a Beaux-Arts orientation to a more personal style in which academic regularity yielded to random massing, classical ornament gave way to Spanish motives, and human scale organically moved to heroic scale. Mizner had clearly established himself as an architect: knowledgeable, creative, tasteful, and equipped with the business acumen to grow his practice.

While his architectural perspective was maturing, Addison Mizner continued to enjoy the life of a bohemian that had always defined his life in New York. By the end of the first decade of the twentieth century, his friend Alva Belmont had begun supporting the Suffragette movement in various ways. In 1916, she wrote a feminist operetta, *Melinda and Her Sisters*, that premiered at the Waldorf-Astoria. The music was composed by Elsa Maxwell, and a box seat commanded the astronomical price of $125. With "a $10 million cast," the operetta featured well-known actresses such as Marie Dressler and Marie Doro as well as Metropolitan opera star Frances Alda. In a supporting role with such luminaries was Addison Mizner.[19] *Melinda and Her Sisters* proved to be a success and earned over $8,000 for Belmont's Women's Party.[20]

Although Addison Mizner was enjoying social popularity and a measure of professional success, events would conspire to bring his stay in New York to an end. For different reasons, the same would be true for his brother. Wilson Mizner considered regular employment a repugnant task, something he vowed never to repeat after managing the Rand. If a job was a boring nuisance to Wilson, a hustle was much more natural and exciting to ferret out. Writer and journalist Djuna Barnes remarked that "Wilson at street level could hear a ten-dollar bill fall on a plush carpet ten stories up."[21] Before leaving New York, Wilson was convicted of running a gambling operation on Long Island. This was another misdeed that embarrassed Addison because, although Wilson was given a suspended sentence, reports circulated that he had been in prison.

Wilson's roguish ways did enable him to realize success as a playwright. From 1909 to 1911, he co-wrote *The Only Law* with George Bronson Howard and three plays with noted dramatist Paul Armstrong that were remarkable for popularizing criminal language and glamorizing underworld figures. One of their collaborations was *The Deep Purple,* a play that became very popular. Wilson's new vocation, described by him as "telling lies for two dollars a head," created such a reputation that he became known as "the night key of Broadway."[22] After an operation resulting from an attack of appendicitis in 1912, Wilson was motivated to draw up a will that commanded the executor to "have my coffin fit well around the shoulders."[23] That his operation was reported in various New York newspapers provided evidence of his notoriety at the time. In the end, Wilson's dissolute life led him to drug addiction and, once more, the loyal Addison would come to his rescue.

On April 6, 1915, Addison experienced a profound loss, the death of his beloved mother, Ella Watson Mizner. Mama Mizner, the survivor of two of California's most harrowing

Wilson Mizner and Paul Armstrong, circa 1910. Armstrong was already a successful playwright when he collaborated with Wilson to write The Deep Purple *in 1910 and* The Greyhound *in 1911. A man of various occupations, Wilson resorted to writing several times in his life to support himself. He co-wrote a play,* The Only Law, *with George Bronson Howard in 1909 and received writing credit for several screenplays at Warner Brothers in the early 1930s.*
Courtesy of the Library of Congress.

catastrophes, the sinking of the *Independence* and the 1906 earthquake, had been the central, cohesive figure of a large family of characters. Addison had always been solicitous of his mother and brought her to live with him permanently on Long Island in 1912. He lovingly remembered her in his memoirs: "she was a woman of the world and although she had a few old set rules for herself, she never expected the world to stop still for her and she loved every minute of the parade."[24] This generous woman, endowed with an abundance of spirit and affection, was faithfully preserved by Addison in a pastel portrait that he had commissioned in 1914. As Camille Showalter remarked in *The Many Mizners*, her "dignity and strength, her warmth and humor are all conveyed in this representation."[25]

This personal loss prefigured other distressing events that contributed to Addison's eventual departure from New York. A month after the loss of his mother, a German submarine sank the *Lusitania*, a British luxury ocean liner that had departed New York for Liverpool with almost two thousand passengers and crew on board. Almost twelve hundred perished, including 123 Americans, a catastrophe that outraged Americans.[26] In spite of the preference of a majority of Americans to avoid being drawn into a European war, the dark presentiment of engagement lurked in everyone's mind. With Europe already involved in a devastating war, international trade predictably subsided. As both the national mood and domestic economy

Pastel portrait of Ella Watson Mizner probably by William Thoma Lilburn Armstrong, circa 1914. This pastel was commissioned in New York by Addison Mizner the year before his mother died. The portrait depicts the humor and sweetness that made Addison a devoted, solicitous son. Mama Mizner lived with Addison in Port Washington at the end of her life. Courtesy of Oakland Museum of California.

were adversely affected, the tendency among the rich for display and ostentation was significantly diminished. The resulting dearth of building materials also led to a decline in construction. As a consequence, the demand for architectural services was all but extinguished.

Lastly, Addison was again plagued by an injury to the same leg that was originally disabled in an accident during adolescence. In the spring of 1917, he was mugged while giving three men a ride in his car. In the ensuing fight, one of the men kicked Addison hard in the leg, exactly at the location of his earlier wound. Speaking of a "terrible agony in my left leg that ran clear to the hip," Addison was in pain and immobilized.[27] Limited by world war and personal misfortune, the architect's prospects were dismal. During this challenging and dispiriting time, he was emotionally and financially sustained by many dear friends. One, Phelan Beale, married to the aunt of the future Jacqueline Bouvier Kennedy, was a wealthy attorney and sportsman who protected Addison from creditors by organizing a corporation that assumed ownership of his home.[28] Another, in particular, played a prominent role in his rescue and, unexpectedly, in his future.

Among his loyalists during this time was a well-connected English aristocrat with a grandfather who was the Marquis of Anglesey, a father who was chief equerry to Queen Victoria, and a husband who was a baron and member of the Privy

Lady Colebrooke by Frederick John Jenkins, 1900. Alexandra Harriet Paget was the granddaughter of the 1st Marquess of Anglesey and the wife of the 1st Baron Colebrooke. She was responsible for caring for Addison after an accident and for introducing him to Paris Singer, making their collaboration in Palm Beach possible. With her pedigree, she was another example of "the right people" that Mizner made a habit of befriending, a talent that allowed him to become known as a society architect.

Courtesy of National Portrait Gallery, London.

Council advising King George V. Lady Alexandra Cole-brooke, a noted international hostess and good friend of King Edward VII, was widely recognized not solely for her social standing but also for her generosity of spirit and unstinting public service.

While her husband was serving the governments of Henry Herbert Asquith and David Lloyd George as chief whip in the House of Lords during World War I, Lady Colebrooke was involved with many charities in both England and America. When war was declared, she worked at the Vickers munitions factory in Kent and turned a lathe that produced England's first wartime shell for the British Army.[29] She used her extensive social connections not only to support war relief organizations but to advance the careers of friends. Although she arranged a distinguished guest list for a Parisian dinner at the Hotel Ritz in 1919 honoring Arthur Balfour, then serving as British foreign secretary, she unselfishly gave credit to Elsa Maxwell. This celebrated event, also financed by Lady Colebrooke, launched Maxwell's career as a professional hostess for royalty and figures of high society.[30]

In 1916, Lady Colebrooke met Addison after moving to New York to play a significant role in organizing the Allied Bazaar, whose objective was to provide relief for the victims of the war in Belgium, Britain, France, and Russia. Insisting that Addison move back to New York to recuperate from his leg injury, Lady Alexandra Colebrooke installed Addison in an apartment in her own building at Madison Avenue and 48th Street. Convalescing in the city, he was able to see friends more readily and was frequently visited by other residents in his building. Among them were Syrie Maugham, the English decorator known for bringing a modern sensibility to early twentieth century interior design, and Elsa Maxwell, also a songwriter and entertaining pianist. Elsa, physically distinguished by her ample girth, arranged to have a grand piano delivered to Addison's apartment to provide the opportunity for entertainment. When she arrived with the piano, the pained Addison was still able to summon his sense of humor: "For a moment I couldn't tell which was which."[31]

Without business prospects, Addison's architectural practice waned and his financial situation deteriorated to the point where he could no longer afford to keep his cherished chateau. Incapacitated and impoverished, he once again was forced to contemplate what appeared to be a diminished future veiled in uncertainty. At this point, Lady Colebrooke serendipitously introduced Addison to someone who would profoundly change the trajectory of his life. No one could have possibly foreseen the astonishing, spectacular consequences that would eventuate from the new friendship of Addison Mizner and Paris Singer.

CHAPTER NINE

THE PERFECT SETTING

It was in Palm Beach that Addison Mizner would gain widespread recognition and considerable financial reward. With an introduction provided by his new friend Paris Singer, Mizner found this tropical island an ideal place where climate and topography were consonant with the artistic and architectural ideas long fermenting in his mind. For Mizner, the cultural history of Spain was not simply a forgotten, irrelevant story but a prism through which he filtered his own distinctive ideas. That he was eminently successful in articulating his vision is evident from surveying the Mizner architectural legacy in Palm Beach.

In examining the celebrated accomplishments of many achievers, it is not unusual to discover that they benefitted not solely from outsized personal gifts but also from a convergence

Paris Singer, circa 1920. Singer was a cultivated man who inherited a fortune from his father, Isaac, the founder of the Singer Sewing Machine Company. Singer met Addison Mizner in New York when he was convalescing from an injury to his leg and brought him to Palm Beach to recover. With Singer's vision and money and Mizner's architectural ideas, Palm Beach was transformed into one of the most beautiful resorts in the world.
Courtesy of Historical Society of Palm Beach County.

of favorable circumstances. In the case of Addison Mizner, he had the good fortune to be introduced to Paris Singer who, by leading him to Palm Beach, opened the door to an unforeseen creative journey with immense consequences. This small town, at this particular moment, uniquely offered a set of conditions that fostered the full expression of Mizner's defining inventiveness and made his remarkable triumph possible.

When Addison Mizner arrived in Palm Beach in 1918, many Americans were experiencing a period of growing prosperity and a fortunate few enjoyed vast wealth through personal industry or family inheritance. When World War I began in 1914, the American economy was in recession, but by the time the war ended in November 1918, the United States had experienced forty-four months of growth.[1] By 1919, the year after Mizner's arrival in Palm Beach, the economy had grown sixfold since 1870 and was much greater than the combined economies of Britain, France, and Germany.[2] The transition to an enormous war economy naturally enhanced the affluence of the great industrialists who could indulge in the world of leisure and luxury.

Not only was there the presence of enormous wealth in America after the war but there existed among the wealthy a renewed desire to display their wealth publicly. Just as colossal Fifth Avenue mansions by distinguished architects were deemed appropriate symbols of achievement and good taste in New York at the turn of the century, towering Palm Beach villas commissioned from Addison Mizner and others effectively served the same purpose in Palm Beach in the early 1920s. The architect thus benefitted from the interrupted financial and attitudinal legacy of the Gilded Age.

Another effect of World War I that benefitted Palm Beach was the provisional elimination of France as a resort destination. Four years of hostilities made it impossible for royalty and the wealthy to spend winter months in the familiar Mediterranean resorts to which they had become accustomed. Furthermore, the war brought down many European royal houses and left many of its members destitute. The temporary demise of the French Riviera, popularized by the English in the nineteenth century and recognized in the early twentieth century as the most prominent of aristocratic winter playgrounds, allowed Palm Beach to grow in stature. The *New York Times* quoted "The Uncrowned King of Nice" speaking about the popularity of Florida, citing its wonderful climate as the main attraction but predicting that Florida's high real estate prices would soon drive the Europeans back to the Riviera.[3]

Villa Vizcaya, Biscayne Bay. James Deering, whose family owned Deering Harvester Company, collaborated with Paul Chalfin, an aesthete trained as a painter and decorator, and Francis Burrall Hoffman, a young and inexperienced but well trained architect, to create Villa Vizcaya. Although begun in 1914 and not completed until 1922, it was structurally complete when Paris Singer and Addison Mizner visited in early April 1918. The successful realization of the Renaissance Revival style and the incorporation of sophisticated fine and decorative art would have impressed Singer and Mizner.
Courtesy of Florida Photographic Collection, State Archives of Florida.

Although Palm Beach had already been identified by Henry Flagler as a resort destination, it was still a relatively undeveloped part of Florida mostly served by two hotels built by Flagler before the turn of the century. This was a fact that did not elude Paris Singer. What Mizner quickly recognized in 1918 was that the small town possessed a tone, personality, and physical features that lent themselves to the Mediterranean Revival style that he intuitively understood. What also struck Addison was the incongruity of building material and style of Flagler's hotels. Both hotels were surprisingly constructed of wood. The Royal Poinciana Hotel was in the Georgian style and The Breakers, formerly the Palm Beach Inn, was Italianate, a distinct nineteenth-century phase of Classical architecture that referenced neoclassicism but used picturesque elements such as heavy brackets, belvedere towers, ground floor loggias, and a central fountain. Having been popularized by Andrew Jackson Downing and his subaltern Alexander Jackson Davis in the 1840s, the Italianate style was waning in popularity at the time of Mizner's arrival.

Considering the hot, humid climate and lush, abundant vegetation, Mizner imagined the architecture of Central America remembered so fondly from his adolescence and fervently believed that this expression would be particularly well suited to his new environment. His confidence would be reinforced after visiting the Villa Vizcaya on Biscayne Bay in March of 1918. Paris Singer and Mizner were guests of Charles and James Deering in South Miami, where they saw the villa designed by the aesthete Paul Chalfin and the young architect F. Burrall Hoffman. Vizcaya was inspired by Villa Rezzonico Borella, a seventeenth-century baroque villa in the Veneto near Vicenza.

In 1911, Deering and Chalfin had toured the Veneto, where wealthy Venetians had built their summer retreats since the sixteenth century. Although Andrea Palladio was the greatest architect in this region during the sixteenth century, his buildings were surprisingly not held in high esteem among some late nineteenth century cognoscenti and tastemakers such as Edith Wharton.[4] Villa Rezzonico, with its severe exterior and sumptuous interiors, attracted Deering and Chalfin and inspired in Florida a house that was intended to display the extraordinarily fine collection of art and antiques that Deering was collecting under Chalfin's guiding eye. Although a point of reference, Rezzonico differed in many respects from Deering's villa in Key Biscayne: Rezzonico was inland away from any water and was an architectural block without interior courtyard; its gardens were unimpressive; and its plan, with all rooms of the same size and shape, unrefined. The Romans and, indeed, the Renaissance Italians, with the exception of the Venetians, did not build directly on the water, but Deering used Biscayne Bay to great advantage in this original composition.

When Mizner visited Vizcaya, not yet having seen Venice or the Veneto, he must have felt both ecstatic and impressed. He understood what Deering, Chalfin, and Hoffman had accomplished and most probably was inspired by the drama, high level of craftsmanship, and exceedingly fine collection of art and antiques. But, he also knew that, as this extraordinary estate was only two hours away from Palm Beach, its grandeur and sophistication would lead others of Deering's caste to desire a similar level of antique splendor in Palm Beach. Although not recorded, the reaction of the aesthetically sensitive Singer would have been the same.

In Paris Singer, Addison Mizner now had a friend and patron who had lifted him out of his recumbent, destitute circumstances and fortuitously placed him in the right place to be able to realize unfulfilled aspirations. Paris Singer not only oversaw Mizner's rehabilitation but allowed him to see Palm Beach in a completely different light. Mizner had already passed through Palm Beach earlier in his life and had not been impressed. On his return in 1918 with Singer, he was of course older and more mature but, more importantly, he enjoyed the advantage of having a collaborator who was not only interested in architecture but open to the novel, sometimes exotic, concepts held by the architect. In Singer, Mizner also had a confederate who was willing to dedicate substantial financial resources to the realization of his and the architect's ideas.

Into the inspiring environment of Palm Beach entered Singer and Mizner, two enterprising men with the inventive capacity to conceive on a large scale. Not only would Addison Mizner prove to be an imaginative architect who could fulfill the dreams of the most socially ambitious, but he also possessed an abundance of energy and tenacity required to meet the unforgiving deadlines imposed by the short construction season in the summer and fall. All of the necessary conditions for the defining transformation of Palm Beach into one of the world's premier resort destinations were in place.

Paris Singer and Addison Mizner were two large individuals seeking solace and recuperation. Each man was tall with unmistakable presence, and both were informed, skilled conversationalists. They shared a passion for art, architecture, and travel. United less by temperament than by interest, Paris Singer, the developer, and Addison Mizner, the architect, would come to share a vision for the transformation of Palm Beach. The immediate need, however, was to allow Addison to recover from the debilitating injury to his leg suffered in New York. Providing refuge, Singer ultimately led Mizner to Palm Beach where he had recently purchased a small bungalow on Peruvian Avenue.

The penultimate of Isaac Singer's known progeny of twenty-four, Paris Singer was born into very fortunate circumstances. Named for the city of his birth, he moved with his family to

London with the outbreak of the Franco-Prussian War in 1870. According to Alice DeLamar, Singer had "a towering stature and impressive appearance. He looked the way a monarch ought to look and seldom does."[5] He had cultivated a taste for the finest of everything and was able to indulge on a scale unknown to most. He owned an English country house in Devonshire, a Mediterranean villa at St.-Jean-Cap-Ferrat, a Paris apartment on the Place des Vosges, a London townhouse on Sloane Street, and a four-hundred-ton yacht. He also held the distinction of being the owner of the first motorcar produced under the Rolls-Royce marque.[6] When his father died in 1875, Paris inherited an estate that produced a weekly investment income of $15,000.[7] In addition, there was his share of the significant profits from business operations of the Singer Manufacturing Company, a business begun in 1851 by his father.

Isaac Singer had been a self-made man with a passion for two things: business and women. He was a machinist and inventor whose wealth derived from creating the first domestic sewing machine and from developing a global business built on mass production. The Singer Manufacturing Company became a colossus, claiming to have had a market share of 80 percent in 1890 and to have produced a million sewing machines annually by the turn of the century.[8] In 1908 the company opened new corporate headquarters at 149 Broadway in New York, making the Singer Building for a brief time the tallest

Portrait of Isaac Meritt Singer, 1868. Having developed the first sewing machine adapted for domestic use, the flamboyant Singer created a global business that made him very wealthy. Singer had six children with his second wife, one of whom was Paris Singer, who benefitted significantly from his father's estate after his death in 1875. This inheritance allowed the son to indulge his passion for real estate development and architecture.
Courtesy of Wikipedia. Portrait by Edward Harrison May.

building in the world.[9] No less prodigious in his personal life, he was only twice married but had a number of mistresses. With his second wife, a French woman named Isabelle Boyer, he had six children, one of whom was Paris Singer. The eldest son from this union, Mortimer, would be knighted by King George V and two daughters would marry into the French nobility: Winaretta became Princesse Edmond de Polignac and Isabelle-Blanche became the Duchesse Decazes.[10]

Unlike his brother, Mortimer, whose lifestyle revolved around his English country estate, Paris enjoyed a more peripatetic existence, a fact evidenced by his real estate holdings. Raised in England, he attended Caius College, Cambridge University, where he studied medicine, chemistry, and engineering and he eventually held several engineering patents.[11] He might have studied architecture at the Ecole des Beaux Arts in Paris and, true or not, he certainly considered himself an architect as both his calling card and the plaque on his London residence identified him as such.[12] While certainly drawn to architecture, his temperament probably did not permit him to focus only on one discipline. One writer described him as a dilettante: "an artist, athlete, scholar, scientist, art patron, sports patron, philanthropist, and amateur in architecture, medicine, and music."[13] Architecture appeared to be a palliative, a ready cure for any setback, an observation made by Alva Johnston: "Any disappointment in a romantic matter caused him to console himself with architecture."[14] This observation is borne out by his ready impulse to build in Palm Beach following his unfulfilling, tempestuous quest of Isadora Duncan.

Blond and elegant, Paris cut a dashing figure and shared his father's interest in pretty girls. Although married, he fell in love in 1909 with Isadora Duncan, a bohemian, uninhibited dancer whose organic style foreshadowed modern dance. In her autobiography, she refers to him as "Lohengrin," the knight of the Holy Grail who is dispatched to save a maiden.[15] To his frustration and disappointment, Singer could only rescue Isadora from chronic financial difficulty. Always in need of money, Isadora was guided by an artistic spirit that did not want to be constrained by anyone in any way. She was initially consumed by the relationship, acknowledging to be "in the hands of an expert voluptuary."[16] In the end, she valued freedom and her life in Europe more than any attachment.In his biography of Duncan, Peter Kurth summarizes Paris Singer as "a gracious but inveterate tyrant," a trait that could only have repulsed one whose lodestar was independence.[17] Unable to fathom Isadora's refusal of his gift in 1917 of Madison Square Garden as a site for her dance school, an exasperated Singer finally decided to make his home in America. For a man accustomed to having his own way, he could only extract himself from an impulsive, unconventional temperament that he could never comprehend.

After five years of the emotionally enervating pursuit of Duncan, Paris Singer began to turn his attention to Joan Bates, a senior nurse who had helped him establish military hospitals after the outbreak of World War I. The last of the hospitals was created at Oldway, his English country mansion in Devonshire, and was named the American Women's War Relief Hospital. Oldway, originally known as the "Wigwam," had been built by Paris Singer's father in 1873 and was later transformed significantly by Paris after the death of his mother in 1904.[18] The extensive renovation reflected his French tastes and included fresco paintings and Gobelins tapestries. This was the third of his residences that he had transformed into a military hospital, all of which had originally been supervised by Joan Bates. After deciding to move to America, Singer brought her to Palm Beach ostensibly to oversee the recuperation of Addison Mizner. Later in 1918, Paris Singer finally divorced his wife and, a year later, married Bates, well liked and described by one of Mizner's friends as "a charming, dignified and handsome woman of suitable years."[19] Palm Beach would become their home.

Joan Bates correctly diagnosed Addison Mizner's wound and prescribed exposure to the sun as a cure. The original destination suggested by Singer for his new friend was not Palm Beach. Entranced by Mizner's stories of his time in Central America, Singer originally proposed a trip to Guatemala to avail themselves of its warm weather and to learn more about its interesting history and architecture. This trip was made impossible when a series of earthquakes, beginning in November 1917 and lasting until late January 1918, destroyed large parts of Guatemala City and Antigua. With this tragedy, Singer suggested they go to Palm Beach instead. That this pair of men arrived at this particular moment was a gift of Fortune. What they found in this resort community was a relatively undeveloped town that had experienced significant change in the last decades of the nineteenth century.

The white settlement of the area known as Palm Beach did not occur until the last half of the nineteenth century. Lake Worth's remote location and the difficulty of transportation did not move General Worth, who camped on the island at the end of the Second Seminole War in 1841, to give a name to this remote outpost.[20] Federal settlement movements offered 160 acres to pioneers who would defend the area against Native Americans who, unsurprisingly, saw the new settlers as a threat to their long-established life in the area.

In 1876, the Dimick and Brown families moved to the island and purchased land at one dollar per acre in through-island sections running from the ocean to the lake.[21] In the middle of the island, there was a fresh water slew, and families built the first houses on the lakefront, suffering through a hurricane that destroyed their houses and goods. The families persevered and developed a sustainable agriculture that was supplemented by fishing and hunting the abundant waters and jungle of the island.

A fortuitous accident in 1878 changed the nature and appearance of the island when the 175-ton brig *Providencia*, traveling from Trinidad to Spain, wrecked on a reef carrying cargo of twenty thousand palm coconuts. Will Lanehart and H. F. Hammon salvaged the freight and the coconuts were sold to settlers for $2.50 per hundred. The *Providencia* also carried a cargo of "aqua dente," a Cuban rum, and settlers celebrated their new coconut fortune with a party.[22]

By May of 1880, conditions on the island had not sufficiently improved for Frank Dimick who, discouraged, sold his land to Edmund and John Hale "Doc" Brelsford before moving to North Carolina. E. N. "Cap" Dimick, Frank's brother, and his wife Ella, added eight rooms to their house to create the "Coconut Grove House," the island's first lodging.

Edmund and "Doc" Brelsford came to the lake from Ohio on a hunting and fishing trip and by the fall of 1880 had moved their families to Palm Beach. The Brelsfords brought the first music to the lake. Edmund played violin and Doc played cello, with their sister, Minna, on piano. Edmund was a founder of the Palm Beach Yacht Club (PBYC) and was its first commodore. When PBYC erected its clubhouse near the Coconut Grove House, the Brelsfords assembled a seven-piece orchestra to play on opening night. PBYC was the prominent social venue in the 1890s and member Henry Phipps notably hosted Mr. and Mrs. Andrew Carnegie. Henry Flagler was a frequent visitor as well.[23]

As leading citizens of Palm Beach, the Brelsford brothers continued to develop business enterprises that would heighten the reputation of their beautiful island and built a thirty-ton schooner called the *Bessie B* that sailed between Jacksonville and Palm Beach. When the inlet closed, preventing passage, the Brelsfords dug, largely by hand, a cut of four hundred feet, eight feet wide, and nearly twenty feet deep in one part. In 1884, the Brelsfords opened a store that included the first US Post Office. Given the thousands of palm trees that resulted from the wreck of the aptly named *Providencia*, the brothers had chosen Palm City as the name of their town, but it was taken, so they settled on Palm Beach instead.[24]

The burgeoning land boom of the 1880s was energized by a growing stream of winter visitors to Palm Beach. C. I. Cragin, a wealthy soap manufacturer from Philadelphia, was the first to build a second home in Palm Beach and selected a lakefront site. Cragin was followed shortly by Denver railroad and land developer Robert R. McCormick, who bought a lake-to-ocean tract from Albert Geer for $10,000 and built a Shingle-Style house on the lake originally named Croton Cottage and known today as the Sea Gull Cottage.[25]

The oldest standing house in Palm Beach, the Sea Gull Cottage is an excellent example of the early architecture of the town. Although moved twice since its construction, it was originally located about three hundred yards north of the future site of Flagler's Whitehall.

With improved conditions and the beginnings of a seasonal lodging market, "Cap" Dimick expanded the Coconut Grove House, eventually offering fifty rooms in the lakefront hotel. The accommodations were unsophisticated with a cistern and outdoor sanitary facilities, and because maid service was not provided, guests brought their own servants. Rooms, including meals, were two dollars per day or ten dollars per week and guests were warned that the woods were full of snakes, alligators, wildcats, and bears. Notwithstanding the primitive facilities and the probability of deadly wildlife, the hotel accommodated 238 guests from January to March of 1892, erecting tents for the overflow when required.[26]

In 1892, Charles J. Clarke saw Palm Beach from his yacht, *Alma*, and bought two and a half acres for $800. In March 1893 Clarke purchased the Dimick Hotel and twenty acres from lake to ocean for $49,000. The *Tropical Sun* reported:

Jungle Road, circa 1905. This early view of what would become County Road, one of the principal streets in Palm Beach, illustrates the thick vegetation that existed before the arrival of Addison Mizner and Paris Singer in 1918. The area that would become Worth Avenue, though only a half mile farther south, was still dense jungle at this time. The cottage on the left belonged to the photographer, Walter Histed, who later rented space to Mizner for his studio and residence.
Courtesy of Historical Society of Palm Beach County.

During the past ten days there have been the liveliest times in real estate that were ever experienced in the Palm Beach and Lake Worth Region. C.J. Clarke's purchase of the Cocoanut Grove House property from Captain E.N. Dimick gave rise to much speculation among the old guests, who are much attached to the beauties of the place. In growth and possibilities the spot has no equal, and Mr. Clarke is to be congratulated on his rare possession.[27]

C. J. Clarke was also a founder of the Palm Beach Yacht Club, and in 1892 bought the PBYC and fifty acres of land from the Lake Trail to the ocean to consolidate his properties. In 1892, Clarke became commodore of the PBYC and was subsequently known as "Commodore" Clarke.

In 1892, another man bought a few acres in Palm Beach, the consequences of which would be immeasurable. Henry Morrison Flagler, one of the founding partners of Standard Oil, had successfully entered the railroad industry and was driving his Florida East Coast Railway to Florida's tip.

Flagler, sailing around Palm Beach in 1892, decided to buy two acres on Palm Beach and, after seeing pictures of McCormick's home, bought the lake-to-ocean tract and the house from McCormick for $75,000, and also purchased four hundred feet of lake frontage from the Brelsford brothers for $50,000.[28]

Flagler and his railroad associates attended a reception hosted by Palm Beach business leaders. During the reception, Flagler's colleagues requested that the community raise $30,000 to bring the railroad to Palm Beach, a task they accomplished in short order.[29]

The promise of Flagler's Florida East Coast Railway dramatically changed the value of Palm Beach real estate, causing property to increase from one dollar per acre in 1876 to over $7,500 per acre in 1892. Those with property in 1893 and 1894 became very wealthy, indeed. On May 1, 1893, the Dade County Bank was opened with "Cap" Dimick as president. On the same day, Henry Morrison Flagler started construction of the Royal Poinciana Hotel.[30]

As Palm Beach grew, its economy and political interests required a greater degree of autonomy and Palm Beach County was carved from Dade County in July of 1909, with West Palm Beach established as the county seat. To accommodate orderly growth, the County encouraged the creation of subdivisions from jungles and agricultural property. J. R. and E. R. Bradley's Floral Park was the first subdivision with a development announcement in 1910. Floral Park was composed of 230 fifty-foot lots platted along Sunset Avenue from the lake to the ocean. The freshwater marsh in the center of the island was filled and the remainder of the marsh, known as "The Styx," was cleared of the black hotel workers and their families. A California realtor, Lewis Henry Green, was brought in to promote and auction the lots. Green attracted buyers to the auctions with prizes such as rugs, pianos, and china and successfully sold all of the lots within a few hours on February 9, 1912.[31]

In 1911, the Town of Palm Beach was incorporated by an overwhelming majority of thirty-four of the thirty-five eligible voters with "Cap" Dimick elected mayor. Following the establishment of his bank, Dimick created Palm Beach Improvement Company. Among his land holdings, Dimick controlled a large block from just north of today's Royal Palm Boulevard south to today's Worth Avenue, from lake to ocean. In those days, however, the land was considered too remote and very dense. His Royal Park development was well south of Flagler's railroad bridge, so the transportation of goods and materials was complicated by distance and poor roads across thick and swampy jungle. The portion of the land closest to the lake required that a dredge dig a half million yards of fill from Lake Worth.

In 1910, Dimick secured a permit from the County, created the Lake Worth Bridge Company, and completed the Royal Park Bridge on October 1, 1911. Having enabled out-of-town buyers to drive to the site, and using Floral Park auctioneer, Lewis Green, Dimick set up the auction at the foot of the new bridge in 1913. Lots were offered at $375 each and sold out quickly.[32]

By 1918, the Palm Beach that most seasonal visitors experienced was largely the creation of Henry Morrison Flagler. Having already enjoyed Florida's warm weather and simple charm, Flagler recognized the possibility for development and knew that the lack of transportation and hotels were impediments to attracting northern vacationers. Having spent a gratifying winter of 1883–1884 with his second wife in St. Augustine, he returned in 1885 to build a grand vacation hotel. The Hotel Ponce de Leon, constructed in the Spanish Renaissance style, was the first major commission given to the young firm of Carrère & Hastings in New York. To provide transportation to his resort destination, he purchased three small railroads to service the route from Jacksonville to St. Augustine, eventually consolidating them into the Florida East Coast Railway Company.

With the intention of developing a resort hotel in Palm Beach, he further extended the railway to reach West Palm Beach by April 1894. In February of the same year, Flagler opened the Royal Poinciana Hotel, also designed by Carrère & Hastings. Two years later, the smaller Palm Beach Inn was constructed on the beachfront property of the Royal Poinciana. Flagler subsequently added cottages to the inn, one of which was Croton Cottage, his original home that had been moved from the lake to the oceanfront. When guests began requesting rooms "over by the breakers," Flagler changed the

Henry Morrison Flagler, a founder of Standard Oil, married Mary Lily Kenan in 1901 and gave her a Beaux-Arts mansion in Palm Beach as a wedding present. Known as Whitehall, it was the most elaborate mansion in town. His two hotels, the Royal Poinciana and the Breakers, attracted wealthy Americans and made Palm Beach the winter resort for the Gilded Age elite.

Courtesy of Historical Society of Palm Beach County.

name to The Breakers in 1901. Despite some negative comments from Henry James and a few others, the hotels quickly became very popular.

At the time of their opening, these hotels were quickly praised by the social elite as luxury destinations, an assessment that helped to establish Palm Beach as America's premier winter resort. To ensure the satisfying experience expected by his clientele, Flagler had a railroad spur built to deliver guests by private train right to the door of the Royal Poinciana. The first train arrived on March 14, 1896, ferrying four Vanderbilts among a total of seventeen passengers.[33] During the 1901 season, the *Palm Beach Daily News* noted that "there will be more wealth represented on Palm Beach than anywhere else on the continent. The Rockefellers, Vanderbilts, Goulds, and Astors are scheduled to arrive. They are not alone, as a large number of millionaires are coming each day."[34] Clearly, Flagler had succeeded.

The fashionable and powerful seeking winter refuge in Palm Beach at this time had a short season that extended from the end of December to George Washington's birthday on February 22, the date of the annual Washington Birthday Ball, which was recognized as the highlight of the social season.[35] With only a few cottages and a handful of estates in Palm Beach at this time, virtually all of the resort population stayed in Flagler's hotels. The brief season and the confining social

The Vanderbilt party in front of the Royal Poinciana Hotel, 1896. Cornelius Vanderbilt II and his wife Alice arrived in Palm Beach with family and guests on their private train car. Henry Flagler's East Coast Railway made it easy for wealthy Americans to travel from the North and Midwest to Palm Beach in a style appropriate for their privileged position in society. Upon arrival, guests would find a band playing to welcome them.
Courtesy of Historical Society of Palm Beach County.

life would change when Addison Mizner and Paris Singer began to reinvent the architectural landscape and sense of community.

When Paris Singer and Addison Mizner arrived in Palm Beach, they found a broad range of houses, from the small and simple to the classically splendid. Before architectural grandeur crept into the Palm Beach landscape, most homes were bungalows and cottages mostly designed by the builders. Among the first to build on a large scale were Standard Oil beneficiaries Mr. and Mrs. Charles W. Bingham, who had their Cleveland architect, Forrest A. Coburn of Coburn & Barnum, design a home in 1893. Figulus, a Shingle-Style house sited on a 160-acre lake-to-ocean parcel purchased from Dr. R. B. Potter, was the first privately owned residence built on the ocean in Palm Beach as well as the first through-island estate.[36] The house was constructed by Lainhart & Potter, founded in 1893 and one of the region's first contracting, realty, and development firms.

The first grand mansion, not surprisingly, belonged to Henry Flagler. After marrying for a third time, he commissioned Carrère & Hastings to design Whitehall as a wedding present for his wife, Mary Lily Kenan from North Carolina. Sited on the lakefront near Croton Cottage and completed in 1902, the Beaux-Arts marble mansion was recognized immediately for its magnificence. The *New York Herald* deemed it "More wonderful than any palace in Europe, grander and more magnificent than any other private dwelling in the world. . . ."[37] Later, other important residences began to appear.

Around 1906, Henry and Anne Phipps began spending winters in Palm Beach at Rosewood Cottage on Lake Worth's

Figulus, Palm Beach. Known also as the Bingham-Blossom House, the residence for Mr. and Mrs. Charles William Bingham of Cleveland was the first privately owned residence on the ocean in Palm Beach. Designed and constructed by local builder George Lainhart, Figulus was completed in 1893 in the Shingle Style. Although most homes in Palm Beach before World War I were relatively modest, this situation began to change during the war.
Courtesy of the Library of Congress.

west bank near the present site of Horace Trumbauer's First Church of Christ Scientist. Mrs. Phipps, greatly admiring the Philadelphia Museum of Art that had just been completed by Trumbauer, conveyed the land upon which the church was built, and was instrumental in retaining the architect to design it.[38] About ten years later, Henry Phipps bought and subdivided an oceanfront parcel in Palm Beach's north end where family members built splendid winter cottages. Mr.

Whitehall, the home of Henry Morrison Flagler and his wife, a seventy-five-room marble mansion designed and built by the New York firm of Carrère and Hastings, was completed in 1902. As Palm Beach at that time was a relatively small town with very few important houses, Whitehall represented a grand architectural statement. After the arrival of Addison Mizner in 1918, formal architectural styles would be replaced by Mizner's Mediterranean Revival style with its asymmetry, stucco, ironwork, and uneven red barrel roof tiles.
Courtesy of Historical Society of Palm Beach County.

and Mrs. Henry Carnegie Phipps and Mr. and Mrs. Frederick (Amy Phipps) Guest commissioned F. Burrall Hoffman Jr. to design Palm Beach homes in 1916, Heamaw and Villa Artemis, respectively. Michael P. Grace, the father-in-law of John Phipps, also had an unknown architect design and build on the parcel a classically inspired home eventually known as Los Incas. Among these, the only surviving estate is the Guests' Villa Artemis, a two-story home famously defined by a classical temple on a balustraded terrace that looks out to the Atlantic Ocean. At the same time, Miami architect Harold Hastings Mundy completed Blythedunes, a Tuscan oceanfront house for Robert Dun Douglas just north of the Phipps' estates.

Though impressive, these early houses in Palm Beach displayed little evidence of a sophisticated Mediterranean Revival influence.[39] There was, however, a Spanish-style commercial complex known as the Beaux Arts Fashion Building & Promenade on North Lake Trail designed by August Geiger, a Miami architect who opened a Palm Beach office in 1915. By the end of World War I, Geiger and Mizner were the only practicing architects in Palm Beach and, by 1920, Geiger had closed his Palm Beach office to practice solely from Miami. Although Geiger was then credited with introducing the Spanish style to South Florida, it would be Addison Mizner who realized its fullest dimensions in terms of plan, section, orientation, and materials.

Another important early house was conceived at the same time that Addison Mizner arrived in Palm Beach in 1918. Frances Bingham, the daughter of Charles Bingham, married Chester C. Bolton who later served in the US House of Representatives from 1929 to 1939. Following his death,

Frances Bingham Bolton served that seat until 1969. In 1918, the newly married couple was given an oceanfront parcel just south of Figulus and retained Cleveland architect Abram Garfield, the youngest son of President James A. Garfield, to design Casa Apava. Garfield's design approach blended the scale of English country manor house with the massing and detailing of Spanish Mediterranean Revival. The builders of Casa Apava were the Brown & Wilcox Company of Palm Beach, which began the project in 1919 and completed the estate in 1920.

Fortunately for Addison Mizner, there were some competent builders in Palm Beach at the time of his arrival such as Brown & Wilcox and Lainhart & Potter. George Lainhart and George Potter were both pioneers in the early development of Palm Beach. Lainhart, a New York native, came to the region as a carpenter and surveyor and, according to the Palm Beach County Historical Society, was hired in 1889 to forge a road from Palm Beach to Miami. Potter, who left Cincinnati for Florida in 1873 hoping to ease his asthma, was a surveyor who mapped out much of West Palm Beach before starting the first Palm Beach real estate firm, Porter & Potter. Important to the career of Addison Mizner was Cooper C. Lightbown, who moved to Palm Beach from Washington, DC, in 1912. Lightbown, a seasoned contractor who built the Phipps and Grace residences, became an important contributor to the growth and success of Palm Beach. One of the community's prominent civic leaders, he was twice elected mayor of Palm Beach with the support of Mizner and was honored when the first airport in Palm Beach was named for him.

The construction of larger houses predicted a general movement toward personal residences. As a result of the prosperity created by World War I and the arrival of Addison Mizner, this trend accelerated significantly; however, there were other factors. For many lodgers and an increasing number of seasonal residents, the polite amusements provided by the hotels were insufficient so, for the adventurous and speculative, a more exciting kind of entertainment was available. Colonel Edward R. Bradley and his brother John provided such an attraction by opening Bradley's Beach Club in 1898. To circumvent state gambling laws, Bradley operated a private club that admitted as a member anyone who was not a resident of Florida. Other rules stipulated that no one could be admitted who did not look twenty-five years of age, did not wear evening clothes, or appeared to be under the influence of alcohol. An original rule dictated that ladies had to be escorted to gain admittance; however, that regulation was amended in 1899 to enhance the club's popularity.[40]

Bradley's dining room could seat over two hundred guests and the gaming room initially offered roulette and hazard. In

Afternoon tea at the Cocoanut Grove, Royal Poinciana Hotel, circa 1910. Prior to the arrival of Addison Mizner and Paris Singer, social life in Palm Beach was centered on Henry Flagler's two hotels, the Royal Poinciana and the Palm Beach Inn, renamed The Breakers in 1901. The daily schedule of events included sports, teas, and dinner dances. After the opening of the Everglades Club in 1919, winter residents began to build their own houses and to adopt the more relaxed lifestyle introduced by Mizner and Singer.
Courtesy of Historical Society of Palm Beach County.

1923, *chemin de fer* was added and produced over $3 million in wagers during the first year.[41] One resident witnessed a gentleman lose $100,000 at the club one night, a misfortune that "worried him not the least."[42] Although huge sums of money were being bet every night, the club never suffered a robbery.[43] Bradley appealed to women by allowing them to gamble and by fitting out the establishment with soft lighting that flattered the complexion. When guests crossed the Flagler railroad bridge to enter Palm Beach, they passed right by this alluring spectacle. The *New World*, a New York newspaper owned by Joseph Pulitzer and his family, proclaimed: "The real reason for the popularity of Palm Beach is not its climate or its hotels; it is Bradley's."[44]

While members of the carriage trade continued to enjoy Palm Beach's various amenities, they were unaware of the dramatic changes that would soon occur as a result of the arrival of Paris Singer and Addison Mizner. Singer originally bought his small bungalow during a visit to Palm Beach in 1917 because he had a bad experience at The Breakers where he was staying. Mizner's initial impressions in 1918 were no different from those he formed during his earlier visit in 1906. Later recalling his arrival with Singer, Mizner wrote: "we rattled over a rickety old wooden toll bridge and into a jungle and on to Peruvian 'Avenue'. . . . next door to our 'villa' were two more atrocities just like the one I was in."[45]

His initial impression notwithstanding, Mizner quickly imagined the architectural possibilities for Palm Beach. As he surveyed the town with Singer, he could only have compared the incongruity of the clapboard hotels and the polished mansions with the Mediterranean charm of the Villa Vizcaya he had visited in Miami. As he sarcastically noted, "The blue skies and pastelle [sic] ocean didn't look like a New England farmhouse to me."[46] He also would have seen Villa Zila, the Prairie-style house completed in 1914 and designed for William and Zila Koehne by Marion Mahony Griffin of Chicago. Griffin was among the first women licensed to practice in the United States and was Frank Lloyd Wright's first employee following his departure from Adler & Sullivan. Mizner knew that the climate and natural features of South Florida called for stucco, barrel tiles, and ironwork. While seeing academic regularity in the existing buildings, he imagined random massing and uneven roof lines. As his late New York houses suggest, he had deftly developed the art of adaptation, of taking the Spanish and Mediterranean styles he had studied and making them appropriate for a lifestyle oriented to entertaining on a large scale.

However uninspired Mizner initially was with Palm Beach and Singer's cottage, they were tolerable because he had begun to make progress with his health. Upon arrival, he was "weak as a bridegroom" but, as Joan Bates predicted, he benefitted from the salutary effect of the sun, which allowed the wound to heal.[47] In her, Addison found not just a nurse but a new friend. Comments from his unpublished manuscript indicate that he had encountered a kindred spirit: "She gave me a quick glance of her clear Irish blue eyes and there was a wonderful twinkle in them that instantly made us pals for life."[48] Within three weeks, he was well enough physically to move around the porch by using crutches and sufficiently fit mentally to begin thinking creatively once again. This tropical strip of land that now inspired and energized him would very soon bestow considerable benefits on the architect.

Mizner's artistic invigoration began with a modest project. Happy to see his friend and collaborator renewed, Paris Singer gave Addison a sketchpad, pencils, and watercolors to begin working on the renovation of his bungalow. This simple house had originally been conceived as a small development villa of no architectural distinction. Mizner's imagination set about to transform this unassuming clapboard structure into a fantasy that would become known as the "Chinese Villa." When Singer first reviewed Mizner's sketch, he was quite pleased and remarked that he liked a bit of color. To his great amusement, Addison "didn't find out for years that he [Singer] was color-blind and couldn't tell the difference between green and red."[49] The day after seeing the sketch, Singer arranged for carpenters to begin work the next day. The final result was a synthesis of Chinese and Japanese elements accentuated with bold color. Addison recalled in his memoirs: "I was having great fun. With the color box I striped each three rows of shingles a different color, and lacquered posts and panels all over it."[50] Further gratifying his sense of humor, he crowned this folly with a five-foot-long stuffed alligator "to defy good taste."[51]

If Mizner's playful effort at embellishing Paris Singer's modest cottage strayed from the boundaries of accepted taste, his next effort would establish a norm of refinement and sophistication that would create an enormous demand for his ideas and services. Addison Mizner's prominence and reputation would soon soar. The architect was on the threshold of celebrity.

CHAPTER TEN

A MOORISH TOWER

Having successfully collaborated on a lark, Paris Singer and Addison Mizner would next embark on a signature project that quickly became an architectural landmark and just as quickly contributed greatly to the stylistic transformation of Palm Beach. What is known today as the Everglades Club began as another of Singer's hospitals for wounded soldiers. Having sons fighting in the war and having already established such hospitals in France and England, Singer was inclined to build another hospital in America. Having witnessed the salubrious effects of the climate on his new friend, Singer was confident that Palm Beach would be an appropriate location to treat the injured. Undeveloped land was in abundance and, by the end of April 1918, Singer had acquired Palm Beach real estate valued at $250,000.[1]

With Singer's commitment to build a Palm Beach convalescent home and hospital for these soldiers, Mary Fanton Roberts, the publisher of *Touchstone* magazine, formerly *The*

The cover of Touchstone *magazine, August 1918. By the time of his arrival in Palm Beach with Addison Mizner in 1918, Paris Singer had already transformed properties in England and France into convalescent hospitals for wounded soldiers of World War I. To honor his American heritage, he wanted to do the same in Palm Beach. Singer and Mizner collaborated to build the Touchstone Convalescent Club for this purpose but, when the war ended in November 1918, the hospital became the Everglades Club, one of America's most exclusive private clubs.*

Courtesy of Historical Society of Palm Beach County.

Craftsman, the public voice of Singer's efforts, began to organize lectures for New York society matrons to qualify them as companions and nurses. In appreciation of Fanton's success, Singer, Touchstone's largest patron, decided to name the hospital The Touchstone Convalescent's Club.

Sometimes, great achievement begins with a dream, and the early vision of what would become the Everglades Club appears to have been conceived in reverie. One spring day Paris took Addison on a ride in his motorcar and stopped at a point on the ocean side of the island. When asked what kind of building he envisioned there, Addison reflected and responded: "A Moorish tower, like on the south coast of Spain, with an open loggia at one side facing the sea, and on this side a cool court with a dripping fountain in the shade of these beautiful palms."[2]

Two days later, they ventured out again, but this time to the lake side, and once more Singer asked Addison for his thoughts. Addison imagined "something religious" with a chapel, cool cloisters, and a courtyard of oranges. Moreover, he saw something organic as if it had existed for centuries and been enlarged from time to time: "It could be a mixture, built by a nun from Venice, added onto by one from Gerona, with a bit of new Spain of the tropics."[3] It had not required much time at all in Palm Beach for Addison Mizner to realize that its bright sun, deep shadow, balmy climate, and dense foliage lent themselves to a Mediterranean style of architecture that he had been formulating in his mind for so many years.

Mizner's time in Guatemala and Spain had ignited a passion for the variety of architectural expression represented by centuries of cultural and religious upheaval, melding, and reinterpretation that was both accepted and propagated by rulers and clergy. The architectural experience that so affected Mizner in his youth and early manhood was profound and indelible.

Mizner sketch of Salamanca Detail
Mizner's sketches from his early years, as preserved in his scrapbooks, are valuable to understanding his approach to picturesqueness and the role of architectural change over centuries.
Drawing courtesy of the Society of the Four Arts, Palm Beach, Florida.
Photograph by Craig Kuhner.

Mizner's ostensible educational reasons for attending the University of Salamanca notwithstanding, his young life in a pre-Roman city enabled him to experience the centuries-old process of conquest and loss that Addison would distill into his accretive approach to architecture. Courtesy of Wikimedia Commons. Photograph by Tamorlan.

What he had begun to understand, first from Polk and then from White, was that the highest power in architecture is not to replicate the past but to interpret it and to bend it toward one's view, a specific need, climate, and site. In Palm Beach, Mizner awakened to what was truly possible across all of these architectural dimensions; and in Paris Singer, his patron and friend, he had shared vision and ample capital.

With Singer's purchase of a half-mile-wide parcel of land running from the Atlantic Ocean to Lake Worth, the project took shape. With this financial commitment, Paris persuaded Addison to remain in Palm Beach and formed the Ocean and Lake Realty Company with Mizner as president. Following Singer's investment, Mizner returned to New York to collect his possessions and to hire two draftsmen to support his design of The Touchstone Club. Mizner returned to Palm Beach in June and began work on the plan.

There is no evidence that Mizner worked from any sort of formal program for the club. The only mandate appears to have been speed to completion. Generally speaking, the original scheme was to build the club on the south side of Worth Avenue, against the jungle on the south and fronting Lake Worth on the west. Across Worth Avenue from the club, and looking south over the basin of Lake Worth, ten two-story, square planned villas, forty feet by forty feet, would be located, each composed of seven bedrooms and baths, a small kitchen, and servant's rooms. The identical structures were arranged in two rows parallel to Worth Avenue: the front row, arrayed as diamond shapes to maximize the views from two sides, and on the second and rear row, square shapes that looked through the diamonds. Each building had stucco walls, red-tiled roofs, and porches and balconies. Differentiating the buildings were their soft Mediterranean colors of mauve, blue, pink, green, and white. The design was a rather simple conception and related in no formal architectural way to what eventually was designed and built across Worth Avenue on the lakefront.

This 1919 photograph shows the ten villas across Worth Avenue west of the Everglades Club. Initially planned for use as hospital rooms for recovering World War I veterans, the end of the war enabled the conversion to apartments for Everglades Club members.
Courtesy of the Library of Congress.

Mizner and Singer agreed that they would clear as little jungle as required to locate the villas on the parcel, which was generally bounded by Worth Avenue on the south, Cocoanut Row on the west, and Peruvian Avenue on the north. In a newspaper interview, Mizner stated that "We want to make everything we do look like a part of the natural Florida scenery, not like a battle between man and nature, and we want to work in soft colors instead of glaring ones. The second thought that struck me in studying the situation here is that this is a country where people live out of doors." Mizner continued, "In all of the pictures of Florida landscapes you see either graceful palms or a tall pine slanted over by the winds. That's what this country means. It must not be cut down with an ax, run over with a road scraper, and packed with a steam roller. Most of it wants to be unimproved, nice and soft and Oriental. And as much of the time as you can, you want to live in a room that is open on three sides, arranged by development of the grounds so there is a little privacy there, with perhaps a little fleeting vista out into the blue of the lake or the ocean, but not with the Atlantic City boardwalk effect leading elaborately up to a showcase porch. This is a country of romance and every little accessory to romance must be preserved or else we won't have Palm Beach atmosphere at all."[4]

The club was Mizner's first opportunity to design a large building, and over the many months of their nascent friendship, Mizner and Singer constantly discussed architecture and the development possibilities of Palm Beach. Singer was buying land at an increasing pace, and he and Mizner had grown to appreciate each other's views of architecture and decoration, sharing a commitment to what might be considered an Old World appearance. The site of the club, fronting on the gently curving portion of Worth Avenue lining a picturesque basin of Lake Worth, presented Mizner a design challenge that would be met with his clever planning approach.

To meet Mizner's aesthetic and cinematic sensibilities, he allowed the tallest portions of the building to remain parallel to the yacht basin. But he would build several layers of lower buildings north and west of the main mass of the club to maintain a fixed sidewalk width between the building façade and the northwest-curving curb of Worth Avenue. The main rooms of the club's first floor were formally planned below the mass of the building. The service areas were planned west and north along Worth Avenue and were devised so as to break forward, toward the street, and away from the main plane of the building. Mizner featured the service areas to create the effect of years of building additions with complex roof shapes and varying wall heights. The effect was also to provide a human scale at the sidewalk while encouraging the eye to rise to the mirador that housed Singer and Mizner's apartments. The architectural notion that the mass of the building would have smaller structures at its edge to suggest age and accretion was a device that Mizner would raise to motif.

For the club, Singer and Mizner both imagined a building that looked as if it had been there for centuries, but Mizner aspired to build with sufficient quality to assure that the building would eventually be as old as it looked. In imagining what would become the Everglades Club, Mizner first drew upon his recent experience in New York and his practical education in the building arts, learned since his San Francisco days with Polk & Polk. Singer did not imagine a permanent structure for the club and Mizner reported that:

In an early photograph of the Everglades Club from Worth Avenue, the sense of the pressing jungle is profound and would have made Mizner reminisce about his childhood in Guatemala.
Courtesy of Historical Society of Palm Beach County.

It took me some time to convince Paris it would be better to build something well; that is, out of fireproof construction instead of a makeshift. It was the first of July before we had decided to do something that could be used as a club when the war was over. Finally, he okehed [sic] a very rough sketch of the Everglades Club. . . . The afternoon of his departure we roughly staked out the main building. It was the tenth or twelfth of July [1918].[5]

In the summer of 1918, Singer and Mizner retained Cooper C. Lightbown, the builder of the 1916 Phipps and Grace mansions, known as Los Incas, Heamaw, and Villa Artemis, to become the building contractor for the Everglades Club. Lightbown's demonstrated understanding of the principles of Mediterranean architecture and construction were welcome in a place with few qualified builders.

Lightbown was born in Washington, DC, on November 30, 1886 and began work as a carpenter with Charles Lightbown, his father. In 1910, Lightbown married Dyoll Prathers and worked in DC as a carpenter and building contractor. The Sunday, February 11, 1911, edition of the *Washington Post* features an article about a Mission-style home that the Lightbowns were building in Chevy Chase, Maryland, evidence of Lightbown's clear Mediterranean architectural interests. In 1912, the Lightbowns moved to Palm Beach to build a home for an unknown Washington, DC, client. Enjoying the weather and sensing growing opportunity, the Lightbowns decided to stay in Palm Beach where Cooper became one of Mizner's most important collaborators following the success of the Everglades Club. Clearly, Lightbown's construction of the Phipps and Grace houses, and Singer and Mizner's Everglades Club, led directly to his construction leadership of El Mirasol, the Warden House, Casa Bendita, Amado, Audita, and,

fortunately in the downturn years of 1926 and 1927, the Bath and Tennis Club and Mar-a-Lago.[6]

Lightbown was unfailingly courteous and complimentary of Mizner's creativity and construction acumen, and appreciative of his construction materials businesses. In 1922, Lightbown traveled to Italy, France, Spain, Switzerland, and England to vacation and study architecture. Upon his return, he gave a talk at the Congregational Church, and stated:

> The style of architecture which is being developed in Palm Beach is unique. It certainly is not Spanish—it comes nearer being Italian. But the combination of ideas worked out by the school of architects of which Addison Mizner is the pre-eminent exponent, is typically Palm Beach. I believe the day is coming when it will be referred to as the Mizner school of architecture and students will come here from all parts of the world to study it, just as they now go to Europe.[7]

Nevertheless, with credit to Lightbown for the construction of the Everglades Club, as well as many of Mizner's most important future residences and commercial structures, prior assumptions regarding Mizner's exclusive role in the actual construction must be fairly reevaluated. Prior biographies of Mizner have suggested that he was, in fact, the builder, but that is not borne out by the record of Lightbown's leadership in the construction of so many important houses and clubs for Mizner, but also for Wyeth, Urban and others. It is also fair to say that since neither Lightbown nor Mizner had constructed a large building, that they mutually benefitted from the close collaboration required for the Everglades Club and for the largest estates of El Mirasol, Casa Bendita, and Playa Riente.

That Mizner and Lightbown respectfully collaborated over many years, and on many of Mizner's most important estates, is a wonderful story in and of itself. Lightbown had designed and constructed houses with Spanish influence in Washington, DC, and in Palm Beach prior to Mizner's Palm Beach arrival, and he would visit Europe to study Mediterranean historical styles and methods of building. One can imagine that Mizner and Lightbown genuinely enjoyed the collaborative experience and that Mizner found a kindred soul in Lightbown's dedication to and understanding of Mediterranean styles. As Palm Beach's fourth mayor, Lightbown's commitment to modern planning and development principles were certainly sources from which Mizner would find value in his planning of Boca Raton.

In Mizner and Lightbown's hands, the club would become a formidable structure in the jungle of 1918 Worth Avenue. Mizner's plan, beginning with the procession at the Worth Avenue main entry, was an act of centering and recentering, changing axes to allow the member or guest to penetrate the building's first floor in an organized and dramatically unfolding fashion. As one entered the building, one glimpsed a cloister and beyond, the Court of Oranges. Arriving at the cloister, one turned right to enter the lounge, which was the first large space in the club. At this juncture, one could sense the organization of the remainder of the club. Prior to the 1925 additions, the lounge had large west-facing windows fronting onto the lakefront terrace, which was shared by the south-facing dining room (typically Mizner's "Nun's Chapel"). The dining room was paneled with wood salvaged from a Spanish monastery and had a pecky cypress ceiling supported by huge pecky cypress beams and rafters. Some beams were constructed to appear bowed by the weight of the roof, again attempting to create the impression of age. The terrace stepped down in a series of smaller terraces to the lake. The lounge and dining room on the stepped terraces would have been light-filled and would have encouraged both member and guest to see the muted and faded colors of painting on the wooden beams and coffers of the rooms. A few monumental formed concrete staircases predicted the eventual use of exposed staircases to engage the eye, reinforced the building's story, revealed the path, and allowed guests to gracefully climb the shortened risers.

The stair connected to the mezzanine, which contained the offices, a boardroom, and balconies overlooking living and

At eighty-five feet by forty-four feet, the Everglades Club living room was meant to suggest baronial scale. The open, pecky cypress trusses were designed to suggest the weight of centuries. The first party was hosted by Addison Mizner on the afternoon of February 4, with music provided by Irving Berlin.

Photograph by Frank E. Geisler reproduced by Craig Kuhner.

The Armada Dining Room, seventy by forty feet, is detailed with linenfold paneling and frescoes by Achille Angeli.

Photograph by Frank E. Geisler reproduced by Craig Kuhner.

dining rooms. A floor above, the second floor included nine bedrooms and a sitting room. The tower, or mirador, rose above all and had a three-story apartment for Singer overlooking the western terrace and the lake. The first floor of Singer's apartment had the living room, dining room, and service areas connected to the club's back-of-house. The second floor had two bedroom suites served by a common sitting room, from which a balconied stair connected to Singer's master suite with the other bedrooms, dressing rooms,

an efficiency kitchen, and a large ornately tiled "Moorish" bathroom.

Singer's bathroom and many of the other tiled rooms of the club were important to Mizner's "Moresque story" of the club. Over time, an apocryphal story referenced some "2000 year old" tiles which guests, upon seeing, fell down in prayer. The tiles that Mizner used at the Everglades Club and for many successive projects were, in fact, of African origin and had been produced by the Chemla Pottery of Tunis. Chemla tiles

The cast concrete grand stair led to offices and the Singer and Mizner apartments. Mizner's many cast concrete stairs in Palm Beach and other places were novel and popular, however they were misinterpreted by critics as having been left out of the original plans by the architect. Photograph by Craig Kuhner.

were produced from the 1870s through 1977 by the Chemla family companies such as the Tunisian Tile Company and The African Tile Company and distributed in the New York area by The Robert Rossman Company. Mizner would have been introduced to these tiles during his New York practice.

Jacob Chemla, a Tunisian scholar and artist, and the founder of the pottery works, had researched and developed the means to replicate the "Arab" tiles used on the Bardo Palace and the Mosque of Kairouan in Tunisia, the first mosque to be built in the Maghreb in the Islamic calendar year 50 (670 AD). Chemla, and successively his son, developed the chemistry to replicate the color and glazes that had been developed more than one thousand years earlier. A popular 1915 article in Gustav Stickley's *The Craftsman* proposed the renewal of Tunisian tile in buildings and residences and specifically those of the Chemla family.

Mizner's use of Chemla tile found much broader expression in his Palm Beach work. In Singer's personal bathroom in his Everglades Club apartment, Mizner used historic Tunisian and North African patterns and motifs to exotic effect. Photograph by Craig Kuhner.

In an undated ad, likely from the early 1920s for a Chemla family offshoot, Tunisian Products, Inc., in New York City, a list of recent installations includes the "Deering Estate, Miami, Florida, Paul Chalfin, Architect," "Everglades Club, Palm Beach, Florida, Addison Mizner, Architect," and the "Edward I. Stotesbury Residence, Palm Beach, Addison Mizner, Architect".[8]

Geisler's 1928 photograph of the Everglades Club captures Mizner's romantic vision of a waterside settlement where boatmen ferrying produce for sale would land to negotiate with the Mother Superior.
Photograph by Frank E. Geisler reproduced by Craig Kuhner.

Mizner would learn quickly that his vision, and his mandate, would not be realized by the skilled craftsmen to which he had become accustomed in New York. The few competent ironworkers, furniture makers, stonemasons, and carvers in Palm Beach were preciously guarded by the small companies for whom they worked. With the few exceptions of large mansions such as Vizcaya, Figulus, Casa Apava, Heamaw, Artemis, and Los Incas, many buildings were wood-framed and -sided. Workers did not possess the training in the building arts required to fulfill Mizner's and Singer's vision of an "Old World" building based upon modern use of the newer technologies that had become integral to both commercial and estate residential architecture.

This significant problem of the absence of craftsmen would wither under Mizner's indefatigable nature. In a herculean effort that would eventually become one of Mizner's most important legacies, he set about creating the shops and kilns necessary to produce building materials and decorative fixtures required for his design, while simultaneously managing his architects' production of design and construction documents, as well as overseeing the various projects in construction. In short order, Mizner bought a sawmill, built kilns for the roof tiles, and imported clay from Georgia for the production of roof tiles. For lighting fixtures and ornamental iron grilles, he controlled a blacksmith shop. And, to produce furniture, he bought the black-owned Novelty Works.[9]

The Court of Oranges served as the Everglades Club's setting for breakfast before Mizner's seawall enabled the creation of more land west of the club and the extension of the Venetian Terrace to the lake and a boat landing on Singer Basin.
Photograph by Craig Kuhner.

The "Patio de las Escuelas Menores" in Salamanca, a place that Mizner would have crossed during his student days, could easily have been the inspiration for Mizner's cloister bounding the original Court of Oranges. The Plateresque, "in the manner of a silversmith," arches developed in late Gothic and early Renaissance buildings in late fifteenth century Spain, reached the peak of their artistic expression in Salamanca.
Courtesy of Wikimedia Commons. Photograph by Diego Delso.

Shortly after building began, on the first day of August, the carpenter's union walked off the job demanding fifty cents more per hour than the $5.50 per day they received, which was fifty cents more than prevailing wage. Wasting no time, Mizner announced on August 2 that Singer had threatened to move his hospital to California.[10] Not since the community's response to Flagler's request that the community raise $30,000 to substantiate Palm Beach's commitment to growth had the community faced the loss of a development so closely tied to a successful future. Judge E. B. Donnell and *Palm Beach Post* publisher Joe Earman stressed the patriotic nature of the hospital, thereby convincing the carpenters to return to work. Having lost little time, the work proceeded with unusual speed, a characteristic that would become very important over the coming years.

While work was again proceeding apace, changes began to occur. As fall approached, Paris Singer had begun to consider that, with the war drawing to a close, he might need to reconsider the purpose and, thus, the name of his project. How long he had been thinking about this is unknown but, in September, he altered the name of his clubhouse from The Touchstone Convalescent's Club to the Everglades Rod and Gun Club.[11] Local legend states that, while attending a dinner party one evening, Singer was seated next to Mrs. George W. Jonas, the wife of the mayor of Palm Beach. In the course of the dinner, he said to her: "I am going to give you the privilege of naming my club. I don't want any Spanish name, just something pertaining to Florida, something wild and wooley."[12] His dinner partner replied that she liked "the Everglades Club." Singer, announcing the new name to all of the guests, then proposed a champagne toast to formalize it.

As fall progressed, Paris Singer's thoughts regarding the purpose of his club became more clear. Anticipating the end to the war, Paris Singer and Addison Mizner acknowledged that the project could be used as a club when peace came. In late December 1918, an article in the *Palm Beach Post* stated that "It is probable that the accommodations of the hospital, cottages and club may not be limited to the class for whom the enterprise was originally designed."[13] Nonetheless, Singer proceeded with his original purpose in mind. While leaving the design and construction in the capable hands of Mizner and Lightbown, he continued to travel to New York for the purpose of identifying and attracting an appropriate staff for his convalescent hospital. By the end of 1918, Singer had hired an eminent physician from New York to be in charge of the hospital as well as a doctor trained at Stanford University to be responsible for the research laboratory.[14]

The residential buildings were the first of the facility to be completed in November of 1918, and were composed of seven villas and a medical center across Worth Avenue from the Club. The medical center was composed of residential units for resident assistants and nurses. An operating room offered a full array of surgical equipment and fittings. The white villa, the first completed, became Mizner's office and drafting room and contained his precious architectural library, which he brought back from his June trip to New York.

As work continued, Mizner was, no doubt, designing as he built. His close supervision was required to assure Singer that the ultimate product would meet their very high standards. Mizner actively engaged in the design and construction of the landscape, devising new ways of moving large trees and creating croton nurseries from which he would eventually draw much of the planting materials that would finish the grounds of the club. For the interior furnishings, Singer had much of his private collection of antiques, mostly Spanish in origin, shipped to Palm Beach so that the club would open in a highly finished state. Arriving, to Mizner's great delight, were monastery paneling, Alpujara rugs, large pieces of furniture, fine paintings, and tapestries.[15]

On the lakefront, Mizner dug the yacht basin and built the seawall, and as the club opening was not far away, the dredge digging the yacht basin broke down before providing the fill for the terrace. Mizner "arranged" for a tugboat towing another dredge to have "problems" in front of the club and, before the tugboat could be fixed, the club terrace was completed.[16]

On November 11, shortly after the completion of the villas, the Armistice was signed, ceasing hostilities in the Great War and prefiguring a rededication of resources to American life and, importantly for Palm Beach, the promise of life lived to its fullest. The wartime destruction of Europe dictated that the French and Italian Rivieras would not be viable leisure destinations in the near future, ensuring that Palm Beach, by dint of the booming US national economy, the convenience of transportation, and the presence of broad family wealth, became a closer, more sustainable, and far more attractive alternative.

Some of Mizner's New York houses may have been Spanish or Mediterranean in concept, plan, and massing, but their weakness, and the general weakness of all so-inspired housing built in the Northeast, was the houses' inability to blend with their surroundings. The foliage is largely deciduous, meaning that their setting was seasonal with cold, snowy winters. In South Florida, there is but one season and it produces a diversity of tropical vegetation in a variety of year-round green hues. The ease of cultivating flowering plants and year-round lawns provided Mizner the perfect means by which he would completely suspend disbelief, thereby transporting his guests to a place of fantasy, wholly conceived, constructed, decorated, and landscaped to satisfy the romantic yearnings of the wealthy.

Mizner's success is in having leveraged a demonstrated national interest in Mediterranean design to its fullest expression in the jungles of South Florida. More easily imagined and plausible, Mizner's design for the Everglades Club, at the edge of the jungle, could have as easily been in Guatemala or another equatorial waterside setting. The complex's massing, varieties of outdoor settings, and single-room sections enabling one never to be more than a half-room's distance from sunlight or the outdoors, created a sensual setting for leisure that did not broadly exist in America at that time outside of New Orleans, Mobile, or San Diego, all occupied by Spain. Mizner's interior planning abetted his quest for cinematic "borrowing." The interest of seeing beyond the room that one occupied was accommodated with views to people in the next interior room, on the loggias, terraces, and patios, or at a railing on a level above. One could see as well as be seen by most of the people gathered most of the time. Mizner's design for the Everglades Club was his first large building meant to be occupied by large numbers of people, and in its original and successive forms, it succeeds quite well by meeting Mizner's design intentions and by fostering changes in architectural and decorative taste.

From its opening the Everglades Club was always in construction, adding amenities, and essentially changing the first floor plan in dramatic ways, placing Mizner in charge of the planning, design, and execution during his absence in France for the summer of 1919. The Everglades Club afforded expanded notions of a cottage community, and as additions were made to the primary building and as new buildings were added east and west, the club was able to absorb a growing membership, fueling the creation of dozens of large estates. In addition, the demolition of older houses in the core of the city allowed for larger homes to be built closer to the club.

Mizner cleared sixty acres of jungle for the construction of the Seth Raynor–designed nine-hole golf course, and personally managed the creation of nurseries for trees and shrubs that he temporarily relocated for future use. Mizner developed pruning and root-ball techniques that enabled the removal and reuse of large and older specimens, techniques that, at this time, were thought to be deadly. In 1920, the golf course opened along with the clay tennis courts to provide unmatched facilities on the southeast coast of Florida.

Donald Curl best describes the frenetic pace of renovation and redevelopment and new construction through 1925: "Following the creation of the golf and tennis complexes, Singer extended Golfview Road to County Road and created a small subdivision within the grounds of the club. The course-fronting lots sold quickly to members wishing to have their own homes at the club, many of which would be designed by Marion Sims Wyeth, a Princeton and Ecole des Beaux Arts graduate who arrived in Palm Beach in 1919. In particular, Wyeth designed villas in this subdivision for E. F. Hutton, Clarence Geist, and Jay F. Carlisle."[17]

During the summer of 1919, Mizner remodeled the Everglades Villas and converted the medical house into thirteen bedrooms and baths for bachelor members, while also supervising the construction of a building east of the clubhouse along Worth Avenue with shops on the ground floor and maisonettes above. Across Worth Avenue, Mizner added a two-story building to house maids and valets.[18]

The emerging architectural context of Southeast Florida must be closely examined to accurately locate the Everglades Club within an architectural trend. By 1918, those already attracted to Palm Beach had no more purpose than to create

Mizner's interest in enabling multiple views of outdoor spaces, looking up and down, created a variety of views that approximated his memory of the visual complexity found in ancient cities.
Photograph by Frank E. Geisler reproduced by Craig Kuhner.

a seasonal family retreat in an exotically lush and temperate place that would be made more reliably accessible by Flagler's railroad. That most members and their spouses knew, or knew of, each other effectively created a wealthy and well-connected

CHAPTER ELEVEN

SOCIETY ARCHITECT

In collaborating to create the Everglades Club, Paris Singer and Addison Mizner not only established a Palm Beach landmark but brought significant social change to the resort. Paris Singer's tightly regulated club offered elegance, entertainment, and exclusivity to socially avid newcomers and introduced them to a charming architectural style characterized by an open, flowing parade of rooms and outdoor spaces. The desire to replicate such a style in personal residences propelled the demand for Mizner's architectural services and simultaneously diminished the appeal of the more structured culture that then existed in Palm Beach. Mizner's Mediterranean Revival villas stood in distinct contrast to the

In establishing the Everglades Club as the standard by which a Palm Beach style might be measured, Mizner embarked upon a staggering accomplishment of designing, building, and providing the building materials and decorative arts for about thirty-five houses through the 1924 season.

Development of the precinct around the Everglades Club enabled Mizner to build several houses and buildings within view of each other. Addison must have been pleased by the view of the Everglades Club from Casa de Leoni across the Singer Basin.

Photograph by Frank E. Geisler reproduced by Craig Kuhner.

extremes of the simple Shingle style homes and the grand classical structures that were built prior to his arrival and even to the few Palm Beach houses that betrayed a Mediterranean Revival influence.

Change was also occurring in American society. The horrors of World War I exposed the world to vast social and material destruction and fostered a modern attitude among many that broke with the patterns and mores of the past. The 1920s revered speed, technology, and innovation and was, not surprisingly, a period of excitement and exhilaration for those who could afford to indulge themselves. It was an age of mass communication in which movie stars, professional athletes, gangsters, and socialites were esteemed. Addison Mizner was well suited to this decade: he was a kinetic individual in a frenetic time. The five-year period between the opening of the Everglades Club in 1919 and his foray into real estate development in 1924 proved to be an immensely successful and professionally gratifying time for the architect. This period was defined by prolific output and by the creation of enduring friendships among the wealthy that prompted his identification as a society architect.

Since Addison Mizner had always felt comfortable among the wealthy and distinguished, integrating himself into a new web of social relationships in Palm Beach was no different from what he had done his entire life. His gregarious nature, humor, and erudition had always opened doors in society. Paris Singer and many others who had spent considerable time with Addison consistently confirmed one biographer's description of him as "an epidemic of good humor, radiating bonhomie as far as he was visible or audible."[1] What made him especially attractive was his thrilling past and the inclination to use colorful language in a manner that was entertaining and not offensive. He said things that, uttered by others, would have invited rebuke or even condemnation. His irreverence and linguistic facility had always appealed to those in the highest social stations in Palm Beach, just as they had earlier in New York and San Francisco.

In choosing to vacation in Palm Beach in the 1920s, visitors were witnessing a transformation of its culture and lifestyle. The social changes brought on by the war and the popularity and influence of the Everglades Club had created among some a more informal attitude and a broad desire in Palm Beach to live and entertain in a private residence. Additionally, Paris Singer brought to his new home the more relaxed manners and dress that he had assimilated during his many visits to the French Riviera. Since Paris Singer and Addison Mizner were catalysts for many changes occurring in Palm Beach and since the Everglades Club resonated so completely with all visitors and guests, it was natural to select Mizner as the architect for a seasonal home there.

Mizner and Singer's collaboration also brought about a shift in architectural styles owing in part to their visit in 1918 to James Deering's Villa Vizcaya. Both men returned to Palm Beach having directly experienced the villa that had been the primary focus of the July 1917 issue of *Architectural Review,* an issue that Mizner would likely have seen and studied. Some have speculated that Vizcaya had greater influence on Mizner's approach to the Everglades Club than can be found. Mizner's long-held embrace of Spanish, Moorish, and other Mediterranean architectural styles had been evident for several years at this stage and there was, in the American mind, a growing desire for Mediterranean architecture and decoration, the beginning of which had been evident in South Florida for many years among many prominent Americans.

At the Everglades Club, Mizner's scenographic approach extended the modest planning and massing approaches that he had explored in New York and for the first time, climate and fertility conspired to make his indoor/outdoor approach to residential life very attractive to the socially credentialed flocking to Palm Beach at the close of the Great War. They were experiencing, many for the first time, Mediterranean Revival architecture completely sympathetic to its surroundings. A pink stucco castle with arcades, loggias, wrought-iron balconies, and rejas must have been quite a sight from Lake Worth. Carved from the jungle, the landscaping was dramatic and the plant choices were clever and represented a new approach to landscape development. The interiors were delightfully surprising with important furniture and textiles, fine paintings, and unique tiles. Mizner had created a magical realism that evoked comfort, unpretentious elegance, and exotic romance—just what a war-weary world welcomed.

Shortly after the club's opening in January 24, 1919, Mizner addressed a group at the Women's Club in West Palm Beach. A report of the February 20, 1919, meeting described Mizner as having "sauntered on to the stage in an offhand manner with his hat in his hand and a quizzical smile on his face." He then began to speak about design and architecture: "The most important thing in a home is simplicity. Decoration can come along later and disfigure it, but original simplicity will always stand: any cook can make a cake with a bridegroom on top of it and sugar plum kisses all around it but that isn't architecture.

"Ladies, architecture is a development. It rose from the tombs, rolling up through the ages . . . An architect must know everything. He must be a plumber and an electrician, a brick mason and a tile-layer—the latter I know because I had to teach my men over on the island to make tiles." He also ventured that an architect "might be an artist."[2]

Between 1919 and 1924, Mizner would become one of the most important social architects of his time, designing and building

more than thirty-five large homes and other clubs, residential developments, and retail stores. This was an extraordinary accomplishment for any architect, but even more astounding for an architect who also built factories to make the materials, decorative elements, furniture, and furnishings; ran his own small construction company; and had the stamina to maintain a vigorous social life in seasonal Palm Beach.

To examine the range and importance of Addison's accomplishments, it is useful first to consider what he had learned about architecture and construction from his presence in Polk's office in the mid-1890s, from his personal involvement in the exuberant residential development on the North Shore of Long Island, and from his achievement at the Everglades Club. Having seen many important Long Island and Newport estates as well as the Villa Vizcaya in Miami, Mizner had witnessed the extraordinary effort and time required to produce such magnificent homes.

In choosing to work in Palm Beach at this moment, Mizner realized that he would have to improve upon construction methods and architectural detailing if he was to meet the demands of both climate and weather, not to mention the demands of clients that their homes be delivered between social seasons. He would also have to build not only well, but quickly, while simultaneously juggling all of the potentially profitable enterprises that were required to meet the expectations of a new resort community.

Mizner had learned to work with hollow-tile construction in New York and decided to achieve the mass required for his Mediterranean models by using hollow-tile and stucco. He would also create cast stone architectural details as a substitute for cut stone, thereby eliminating the requirement for the skilled European stonecutters and artisans who were unavailable in South Florida. But even with his changes in technology, the speed gained from ownership and operation of most of the required supply chain, and his valuable and successful relationship with Cooper Lightbown's construction company, he could not have been prepared for the number and size of the estates and residences that would come his way.

Seven estates and properties stand out as examples of Mizner's approach and best work in the period 1919 to 1924: El Mirasol (1919), La Bellucia (1920) Casa de Leoni (1921), Casa Bendita (1921), William Gray Warden (1922), Playa Riente (1923), and the Vias Parigi and Mizner, which included Addison Mizner's Villa Mizner (1924). In each, Mizner broadly explored a range

Southeast Elevation of the Villa Vizcaya, 1912–1916.

Villa Vizcaya was the brilliant Biscayne Bay product of James Deering, a worldly industrialist, and his creative team. Of the early South Florida estates derived from Mediterranean, or in Vizcaya's case, Renaissance Revival, Mizner was deeply impressed by the marriage of taste, architecture, antiques, and money. However, Mizner did not embrace the classical rigor of Vizcaya's symmetrical massing, fenestration, and solidity, instead preferring irregular and accretive massing, narrow sections, and transparency.

Courtesy of Wikipedia. Photograph by Leonard J. DeFrancisci.

The aerial photo of Lake Worth to Ocean shows, left to right, Mizner's Louwana (1919) for Gurnee Munn and Amado (1919) for Charles Munn, Mizner's Casa Bendita (1921) for John S. Phipps, Heamaw, Los Incas, and Mizner's first Palm Beach estate, El Mirasol (1919) for Ned and Eva Stotesbury. These early lake-to-ocean estates established Mizner as the preeminent society architect of his time. El Mirasol and Casa Bendita were demolished in the early 1950s and 1961, respectively.

Courtesy of the Robert Yarnall Richie Collection, DeGolyer Library at Southern Methodist University.

of planning and architectural approaches, honing his environmental approach in coming to clearly understand the south Florida, ocean- and lakefront character in all of its sunbathed beauty. In the Vias Parigi and Mizner, he would create a real estate development model that is still popular today: the mixed-use development with commercial and retail on lower floors and residential above.

Addison Mizner's clients for many of these and other commissions were leaders of an American city that is generally unassociated with extravagance and conspicuous display. Among the most prominent Americans had always been the leading families of Philadelphia. Formerly the capital of America, Philadelphia proudly bears a rich Colonial history that has produced a hereditary leadership that reaches back to the early eighteenth century. Philadelphia's pre-Revolutionary past is distinguished by the families of Morris, Wharton, Willing, Shippen, Cadwalader, and Bingham, among others. Even with significant social change and the rise of new fortunes resulting from the Civil War, the status and influence of the oldest families prevailed. The stability of Philadelphia's social structure created an air of assurance among its members that made it difficult for new money to penetrate. Social historian Dixon Wector described it as "a cruel sun in which sapless gentility may wilt, and a stony soil where the parvenu seldom strikes successful root."[3]

This self-awareness is illustrated by a story that, whether entirely true or not, captures the confidence of Old Philadelphians. While in exile in 1796, the Duke of Orleans, the future King of France, Louis Philippe I, was visiting Philadelphia and became enamored of the daughter of Senator William Bingham. When the exiled royal asked Bingham for permission to marry his daughter, Bingham replied: "Should you ever be restored to your hereditary position, you will be too great a match for her; If not, she is too great a match for you."[4] It was the wealthy from this traditional city that importantly patronized Addison Mizner in Palm Beach in the 1920s. Though most of these patrons could not claim descent from Philadelphia families of the 18th century, they were, in fact, successfully operating within the city's old social network.

The general tendency among the Philadelphia patriciate was to avoid ostentation, and this conservative outlook naturally extended to their homes and furnishings. Historian Nathaniel Burt describes this tendency: "Most old Philadelphians prefer to live with the furniture that God, abetted by will and testament, gave them and houses approximating as closely as possible the Old Family Place."[5] He further describes them as "house snobs" who could identify a "solecism in curtains or chairs as surely as an Oxford grammarian can smell out the misusages of 'which' and 'shall.'"[6] One literary wit visited the city around 1920 and, unable to escape the heavy evidence of the past, remarked, "Moss, moss on everything!"[7] This was the sensibility and sense of place inherited by many of Mizner's Philadelphia clients when they arrived in Palm Beach.

As president of the Drexel Company investments firm and J. P. Morgan's Philadelphia partner, Edward T. "Ned" Stotesbury had spent his life in Philadelphia, becoming one of the wealthiest men in America. Roughly thirty years after the death of his first wife, Ned Stotesbury married the widow Eva Roberts Cromwell in 1912. Before Eva Stotesbury had become the recognized grande dame of Palm Beach, a position to which she aspired in New York, she had been married to Oliver Cromwell, a prominent New Yorker and son of the founder of Sullivan and Cromwell, the white shoe New York law firm.

Following the wedding, the newlyweds boarded Ned's private car for Palm Beach where they stayed for a month at the Breakers, prolonging the curiosity of Philadelphia society about Eva Stotesbury. Eva had married the richest and most eligible Philadelphia widower, upsetting many widows that would have gladly taken her place, and she had lived in Chicago, New York, and Washington, all cities at odds with Philadelphia's sense of itself. While waiting, Philadelphia wondered how it would treat Mrs. Stotesbury when she finally decided to arrive in Philadelphia.

As Florida wrapped up in February, the social columns speculated about Mrs. Stotesbury's arrival and learned that

Mrs. Edward T. Stotesbury, circa 1930. Philadelphians Ned and Eva Stotesbury gave Addison Mizner one of his first residential commissions in Palm Beach after the opening of the Everglades Club in February 1919. "Queen Eva" was recognized as the social leader of Palm Beach, a position that was emphasized with the building of El Mirasol, one of the largest projects ever undertaken by Addison Mizner.
Courtesy of Historical Society of Palm Beach County.

she had actually been in Philadelphia quietly for a few days and would be attending the opera on the evening of February 12. The hall was packed but the performance was not the most important aspect of that evening. The Stoteburys arrived precisely on time, and hundreds of opera glasses turned to meet her arrival. Dressed in white satin with a net of crystal and silver spangles, she was swathed in a great purple cloak lined with white fox at the collar and sleeves. The Stotesbury pearls, coiled in four, lay on her bosom and at the base of her neck rested the Morgan diamonds, both wedding presents. On her head rested a diamond tiara, said to be the most magnificent that had ever graced the Metropolitan Opera House. A few days later, the announcement of the invitation list to Philadelphia's 1912–13 Assembly season was posted and the Edward Stotesburys were conspicuously absent. Within the season, however, the Stotesburys were included, and there are many different stories of the pressure applied to cauterize the slight.[8]

Eva was most certainly not a Philadelphian, but then, neither was Ned. Although he had been born there and came from a respectable family, he had not enjoyed any special advantage in his career owing to family influence. Ned Stotesbury had started as a clerk at Drexel and, through hard work and diligence, he had eventually elevated himself to senior partnership. To demonstrate Stotesbury's value to Drexel, historian Stephen Birmingham relates a story of Stotesbury having offended Edward Biddle, a son-in-law of Anthony J. Drexel, head of the bank:

> One day . . . Biddle came to Drexel saying, "Your clerk has insulted me. Either he or I must go." "What clerk?" croaked Drexel. "Stotesbury." "Then you'd better go." And go Edward Biddle did.[9]

In his first marriage, all was work, so now Ned promised his new wife that nothing would ever be denied. He had the wherewithal to provide Eva with anything that she wanted in Philadelphia except acceptance. Eva realized that she was a parvenu and set herself to competition for acceptance in Philadelphia, swiftly learning two important things: that Philadelphians took great pride in their beautiful parties and that she needed a social sherpa to guide her through the wild. In Katherine MacMullan, Eva found a woman of intellect, passion, resourcefulness and deep local knowledge of Philadelphia, but not a *Philadelphian*. Twenty-plus years her junior, "Mrs. Mac," as she was known, had studied Philadelphia rite and ritual for years and was encyclopedic about rivalries, skeletons, and maneuvering through the varieties of carrots and sticks that Eva would employ.

Eventually, the Stotesburys were entertaining three times and two hundred people a week, suggesting that thousands would cross their threshold annually, and remarkably she knew all of their names and frequently the names of their children. "Quite often Eva had no idea who might be coming to her dinners until Mrs. Mac had given a quick pre-party briefing."[10] In the end, none of this mattered. Eva would never become a *Philadelphian*, and she understood that simple fact very well.

Before they married, Ned had been lassoed by Lord Joseph Duveen, the legendary art dealer who had sold him Gainsboroughs, Romneys, and other important paintings and antiquities, a trend continued by Eva. In time, as was Duveen's goal, space was becoming dear at Ned's old Walnut Street home, so the Stotesburys needed an estate to meet Eva's intended scale of living and entertaining. By late 1915, Ned Stotesbury purchased 365 acres in Chestnut Hill and entertained sketches by architects eager to satisfy the insatiable hunger of both Eva and Duveen. In 1916, Duveen recommended Horace Trumbauer as architect, Jacques Greber of Paris as landscape designer, and Sir Charles Allom of London as interior decorator. Eva agreed with Duveen's recommendations and five years later, in October 1921, Whitemarsh Hall opened to a huge party that included all of Philadelphia's social and banking set. Undeterred by Prohibition, four bars were arranged and matched by four orchestras.[11]

It has been suggested that Eva built Whitemarsh Hall as a diversion from the viciousness of the Philadelphians, and that is probably somewhat true. At one hundred thousand square feet, with six stories and three basements, Whitemarsh Hall was the grandest of estates. The house boasted a commercial switchboard for all of the telephones as well as a full-time staff of forty-five plus seventy gardeners. And, of course, the estate was as full as Lord Duveen could make it, but as Fiske Kimball, the Director of the Philadelphia Museum of Art noted, "The furnishings made a great impression of great magnificence. One scarcely realized how few of them were actually antique."[12] What Mrs. Mac failed to disclose was that as life became grander and more frenetic, the further Eva was distancing herself from Philadelphia and Philadelphians.

Almost simultaneously with the beginnings of Whitemarsh Hall, Eva was also planning El Mirasol, a new home in Palm Beach. Eva approached Addison Mizner allegedly while she was measuring a terrace at the Everglades Club: "Oh, Mr. Mizner, you have made me so discontented with the plans that I have done for 'El Mirasol'; I don't think I will ever be content with them after seeing this."[13] A few weeks later, the Stotesburys released their architect, F. Burnham Chapman, and asked Mizner to design the house. This may be the first instance in Palm Beach when a family sought to assert its social prominence by the design and construction of a large residence. After Chapman had been dismissed, Mizner began

El Mirasol, 1919. Aerial photograph of El Mirasol looking east. Mizner's 1919 approach to the design of Palm Beach residences was clearly established by his approach to El Mirasol. The spine of the house was organized along the north-south axis with the oceanfront or eastern façade providing terraces for the capture of ocean breezes, and the western loggia serving as a large patio for afternoon and evening enjoyment. Note the chimney in the northwest portion of the residence. This area was typically the service wing with kitchens and accommodations for staff. Prevailing breezes drove food and cooking odors away from the residence.

Courtesy of the Robert Yarnall Richie Collection, DeGolyer Library at Southern Methodist University.

the design of his first residential commission in Palm Beach. Little did he know how resonant the Everglades Club would be and that, as a result of his being retained by the Stotesburys for their magnificent Palm Beach home, he would become the social architect of choice.

The Stotesbury parcel at 348 North County Road on the north end, just south of the Grace estate, ran from ocean to lake. Mizner, no doubt, realized the importance of the context of this commission to his future as a Palm Beach architect, particularly as his first client was contemporaneously shared with Horace Trumbauer. It was a statement of the times that a family enjoyed the resources to plan, design, construct, and decorate two very large estates at the same time.

By 1919, Eva Stotesbury was the acknowledged bellwether of Palm Beach society, a position that eluded her in Philadelphia and was surprising because Palm Beach in the early twenties was dominated by Philadelphia families, many of whom would also become Mizner clients. Eva Stotesbury's home was the first of four commissions received by Addison Mizner within a month of the Everglades Club opening, and the architect, keenly understanding the stakes, threw himself into the design but was probably not prepared for the sophistication of a client who was spending the 2017 equivalent of $125 million on a new estate near Philadelphia. Mizner complained that Eva was constantly changing her mind, and it was in this context that Mizner mentioned his envy for the doctor who could chloroform his patient.

Mizner preferred, and the pattern became, signing a contract and approving the concept at the end of the season before returning north, thus providing him complete control over design and construction, landscaping, and furnishing. El Mirasol proceeded in this fashion, and the Stotesburys returned to Florida on Tuesday, January 29, 1920, to their new Wells Road mansion completed on the Sunday and Monday before. It is unfortunate that no architectural plans for El Mirasol have been found. From aerial photographs, however, it is evident that the mansion was generally organized the same as others in the vicinity with the largest massing on the north-south axis, with gardens and lower buildings developed east and west of the tallest massing and oriented to eastern views of the ocean, and western views of the gardens and the sunset.

In siting houses in Palm Beach, Mizner generally kept with local precedent, which was to site the house on top or near the coral ridge of the property and generally near the shore. As with most of Mizner's houses, the orientation was for views east and west. In many houses, particularly the larger houses, the entry was on the north or west façade and onto a floor below the main floor. On the lower level were the kitchen, service areas, and servants' area, usually a narrow building

El Mirasol, 1919. The Ocean Boulevard façade of El Mirasol from the former Ocean Boulevard, destroyed by the 1926 hurricane and never replaced.

Photograph by Frank E. Geisler reproduced by Craig Kuhner.

El Mirasol, 1919. The west patio off the Moorish cloister. The patio was the scene of frequent parties hosted by Ned and Eva Stotesbury.

Photograph by Frank E. Geisler reproduced by Craig Kuhner.

El Mirasol, 1919. The moorish cloister illustrates the means by which Mizner encouraged guests to move through the houses easily.

Photograph by Frank E. Geisler reproduced by Craig Kuhner.

El Mirasol, 1919. In the living room, the chandeliers were hung without regard to the geometry of the room, a Mizner device that suggested the passage of time.

Photograph by Frank E. Geisler reproduced by Craig Kuhner.

El Mirasol, 1919. When entertaining at El Mirasol, Eva Stotesbury would stand at the top of the main stair as guests arrived.

Photograph by Frank E. Geisler reproduced by Craig Kuhner.

running north-south. The entrance hall was large and had a fireplace that faced a cloistered patio with fountain. At the entry, it was typical of Mizner to locate dressing rooms with showers, as this was closest to the path to the ocean.

At El Mirasol, a wide staircase, reflecting Mizner's scenographic interests, connected the entry vestibule with the main floor landing at a place that allowed a bejeweled Eva to stand to greet her guests from the top of the stair. The position overlooked the ocean from the top of the ridge. On this floor were a substantial living room with six large French doors, three opening onto the ocean terrace and three opening onto the western patio loggia. This is an architectural device to which Mizner would return again and again.

The living room could accommodate 175 people and had a coffered, pecky cypress ceiling from which old Spanish chandeliers hung, and was headed by a dais with a large fireplace. To the south, the dining room had two large French doors facing the ocean and stepped down to the terrace. The sanctum sanctorum, the library, opened off the living room and faced north. Above the living areas, the Stotesburys' private quarters occupied the top floor and were ventilated by grilled openings in the ceiling and connected to protected intakes ensuring generous and discreet ventilation.

The Stotesbury's had embraced Mizner's vision of resort architecture and, unlike any aspect of Whitemarsh Hall, Mizner had given them a sun-drenched Mediterranean mansion replete with Spanish and Moorish tile, rugs and furniture, religious ornaments and tapestries, and pews and glazed urns full of all manner of exotic vegetation, including a manicured green lawn that crept into Mizner's larger landscape design. Beside the lavish gardens near the mansion, Mizner designed an aviary, small zoo, and an orange grove and, for Mr. Stotesbury, a vegetable garden and chicken house. As the estate ran from ocean to lake just north of Wells Road, the estate was bifurcated by County Road. Mizner cleverly planned the landscaping to completely obscure County Road.[14]

El Mirasol was the center of a very active Palm Beach social life that included lectures and performances and, of course, lavish parties and the annual February 26 birthday party for Mr. Stotesbury. On Valentine's Day in 1922, Mrs. Stotesbury's daughter, Louise Cromwell, married General Douglas MacArthur there. All El Mirasol events were deeply covered by the press, and a former U.S. ambassador to Spain exclaimed the El Mirasol "far surpassed anything in Spain with the exception of the Royal Castle of the King and Queen."[15]

Mizner continued to add to El Mirasol every year until around 1925, when the Stotesbury's turned to Bar Harbor and the creation of their summer cottage, a highly controversial project not unlike Whitemarsh Hall in Philadelphia. El Mirasol stood as Mizner's first mansion, and its inspiration was explosive: Palm Beach was completely captivated by this exotic approach to resort life. In short order, El Mirasol and the Everglades Club served as a proof point of Mizner's ability as an architect, builder, interior designer, and visionary and confirmed the architect's position of primacy in this small community of privilege. With Eva Stotesbury's decision to have Addison Mizner design her Palm Beach house, she created a style of gracious living that her guests would well remember. Others would follow her lead.

Louwana, 1919. When Philadelphian brothers Gurnee and Charles Munn purchased ocean-front land from and north of the Henry C. Phipps estate, both brothers retained Mizner for the design and construction of their homes and both were built along the ocean ridge with the service and entry on the ground level with the principal rooms on the second floor overlooking the ocean. Louwana, built by Gurnee Munn, was a relatively small house compared to its neighbors.
Photograph by Craig Kuhner.

In the same year that Mizner designed El Mirasol for the Stotesburys, he received commissions from other influential Philadelphians. Charles A. Munn Jr. and his younger brother Gurnee had purchased an oceanfront parcel of land that had been part of the Henry C. Phipps estate on the north end. The brothers had long been coming to Palm Beach with their family, which was one of the first to arrive by private rail car. Although the Munn brothers had grown up in Washington,

Amado, 1919. Amado, built by Charles Munn, was also a relatively modest house built for family enjoyment.
Photograph by Frank E. Geisler reproduced by Craig Kuhner.

DC, each married a girl from a prominent Philadelphia family. Charles married socialite Mary Astor Paul, an heiress to the Drexel banking fortune, and Gurnee wed Marie Louise Wanamaker, whose father Rodman was a department store magnate with stores in Philadelphia, New York, and Paris. The brothers divided the land and had Mizner build *Louwana* for Gurnee on the north side and *Amado* for Charles to the south. Owing to the popularity of both couples, these houses were very familiar to the elite of Palm Beach. One Christmas, Flo Ziegfeld gave Louise Munn a Christmas present of a full orchestra for a week, a gift that produced an unforgettable series of parties for seven consecutive evenings.[16] These houses also served as constant reminders of Mizner's architectural flair.

In the three-year period from 1921 to 1924, Addison Mizner received a further six commissions from Philadelphia couples. In 1922, the year after Mizner designed Casa de Leoni for Leonard Thomas, the architect was commissioned by William Gray Warden II and Barclay Harding Warburton. The next year, commissions came from Daniel H. Carstairs, Rodman Wanamaker, and Anthony Joseph Drexel Biddle Jr. Since these people were friends, it was not unusual for the families to be interconnected. Barclay Warburton, the publisher of the *Philadelphia Evening Telegraph*, married Mary Brown Wanamaker, who was the sister of Rodman Wanamaker and the aunt of Mary

Villa Mizner, 1924. Within a few years Mizner realized the creation of a Mediterranean village, anchored first by the Everglades Club, and by 1924 the creations of the Via Mizner and Via Parigi sharing Worth Avenue across from the club with Casa de Leoni.

Photograph by Frank E. Geisler reproduced by Craig Kuhner.

Louise Munn, each of whom was Addison's client. Although he never designed a house for T. Coleman du Pont, this Philadelphian provided support to Addison and became the chairman of the board of the Mizner Development Corporation.

Beginning in the remarkably productive year of 1923, Addison received three commissions from Anthony Joseph Drexel

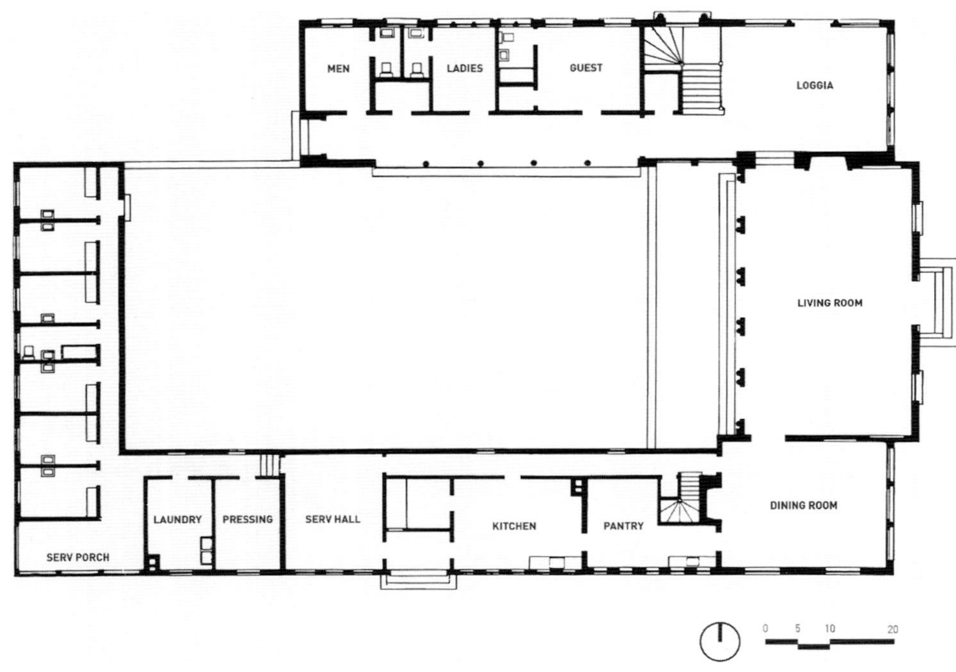

El Sarimento, 1923. With the purchase of a recently completed house and an adjacent lot, A. J. Drexel Biddle retained Mizner to design a large house. In Mizner's original plan, and approaching from an arrival west of the residence, entry to the courtyard north colonnade led to the grand stair, the northeast loggia, the oceanfront living room, and the southeast dining room. The kitchen, laundry, and service quarters were on the south wing. Joseph Urban's 1927 replanning of El Sarimento relocated the front door to the dining room, which became an entrance hall and enlarged the courtyard by demolishing the service wing. Along the expanded courtyard, Urban added a south-facing, ballroom-sized dining room to the ground floor of the south wing.
Plan reproduced by Chase R. Cothran.

Biddle Jr. and his extended family. The Biddles traced their lineage to 1681 in America and to the 1720s in Philadelphia. Family prosperity was enhanced in the nineteenth century when Edward Biddle III married Emilie Taylor Drexel, one of the heirs to a considerable banking fortune. In the twentieth century, Anthony Joseph Drexel Biddle was an eccentric publisher who kept alligators as pets, loved theatricals and boxing, and was the inspiration for a play and movie entitled *The Happiest Millionaire*. Remarkably, he taught hand-to-hand combat in the Marine Corps not only in World War I but also, at the age of sixty-six, in World War II. A contemporary at the time said that he "knows more ways to kill you with his bare hands than any man alive."[17] He also produced a son who became a leader in Palm Beach and a client of Addison Mizner.

Anthony Joseph Drexel Biddle Jr. was known as "the leader of Palm Beach's smart set" and was involved in all manner of social and sporting activities.[18] He became an early vice president of the Everglades Club and was one of the founding members and the first president of the Bath and Tennis Club. He would be appointed ambassador to Norway by President Roosevelt in 1935 and subsequently ambassador to Spain by President Kennedy in 1961. In April 1915, Anthony's sister Cordelia married North Carolinian Angier Buchanan Duke. A social sensation, the wedding was followed by a reception

El Sarimento, 1923. Unfortunately, there are no original photographs of Mizner's El Sarimento. In 1928, Geisler captured Urban's redesign of the residence in this photograph of the new entrance doorway.

Photograph by Frank E. Geisler reproduced by Craig Kuhner.

at which Eva and Ned Stotesbury presented the bride a gift of a large sapphire. On this occasion, Anthony Biddle Jr. met Angier's sister Mary and married her only three months later.

El Sarimento, 1923. The original north façade of El Sarimento illustrated a feature that Mizner frequently employed in the creation of internal monumental stairs, the large and highly decorative window that dominates the façade and identifies the grand stairwell.

Photograph by Frank E. Geisler reproduced by Craig Kuhner.

Although the family was well acquainted with Palm Beach and had vacationed there for many years, it was only in 1923 that a Biddle actually built a significant home in Palm Beach. Anthony Biddle Jr. commissioned Addison Mizner to build a villa on South Ocean Boulevard that, consistent with the Philadelphia value of restraint, was substantial but not pretentious.

Known as *El Sarimento*, a variant of the Spanish surname of Biddle's great-grandmother, the villa was entered from the west and was unusually symmetrical by Mizner standards. Typically, the entrance façade featured a dramatic composition that extended almost the full height of the structure. Recessed wings flanking the main block boasted the Biddle family coat of arms in carved stone, centered just below the roof line. The same year, Mizner also designed a house for Cordelia and Angier Duke.

In the course of the design and construction of El Sarimento, details were being studied not only by Mizner's client, Anthony Biddle Jr., but also by his father-in-law, Benjamin N. Duke, and Benjamin's brother, James Buchanan Duke. Having made a fortune in tobacco as well as in textiles and energy, the Duke family had many philanthropic interests. In 1924, James B. Duke established the Duke endowment with $40 million and specified that a portion of the annual income be directed to Trinity College in Durham, North Carolina, whereupon the institution was re-chartered Duke University in honor of the family. The benefactor desired to expand the existing college and, believing that the architect's design aesthetic would reflect the high educational aspirations of the family, Duke awarded an important commission to Addison Mizner. On February 27, 1924, the *New York Times* reported that Mizner would design fifteen to twenty buildings for the university and stated that "no architect is known to have ever received a similar commission whereby an entire group of university buildings was planned in harmony by one brain."[19]

Addison had to be greatly pleased with the trust that James B. Duke had placed in him. In the article in the *Times*, Mizner stated that he considered this "the crowning commission of his career."[20] Ultimately, Addison Mizner never designed anything for Duke University. Although there is no report of exactly what transpired after the agreement, the project was subsequently awarded to Horace Trumbauer, who had done important and costly work for James B. Duke in New York City and in Somerville, New Jersey. The various Gothic buildings that make up much of the West Campus today were originally recognized as the collective work of the firm, Horace Trumbauer. It was later revealed that a significant portion of the work, including the revered Duke Chapel, was specifically the work of one of Trumbauer's associates, Julian F. Abele, the first black graduate of the University of Pennsylvania.

What actually happened regarding the Duke commission is a matter of conjecture. With an office of considerable size in 1924 and a backlog markedly reduced from the previous year, Mizner could have handled the magnitude of the project. The enormous sums of money being made in Florida real estate development had been occupying Mizner's mind for some time. His brother Wilson, whose antennae were always

Wilson Mizner, circa 1925. Addison's brother left New York in 1922 to join his brother in Palm Beach. The stick pin in his tie belonged to the wealthy Charles Yerkes, the deceased husband of Myra Adelaide Yerkes to whom Wilson was briefly married in 1906 before divorcing. With his mercenary outlook, Wilson most likely would have discouraged Addison's taking a large commission from the Duke family in favor of embarking on the potentially lucrative real estate development project in Boca Raton.
Courtesy of Historical Society of Palm Beach County.

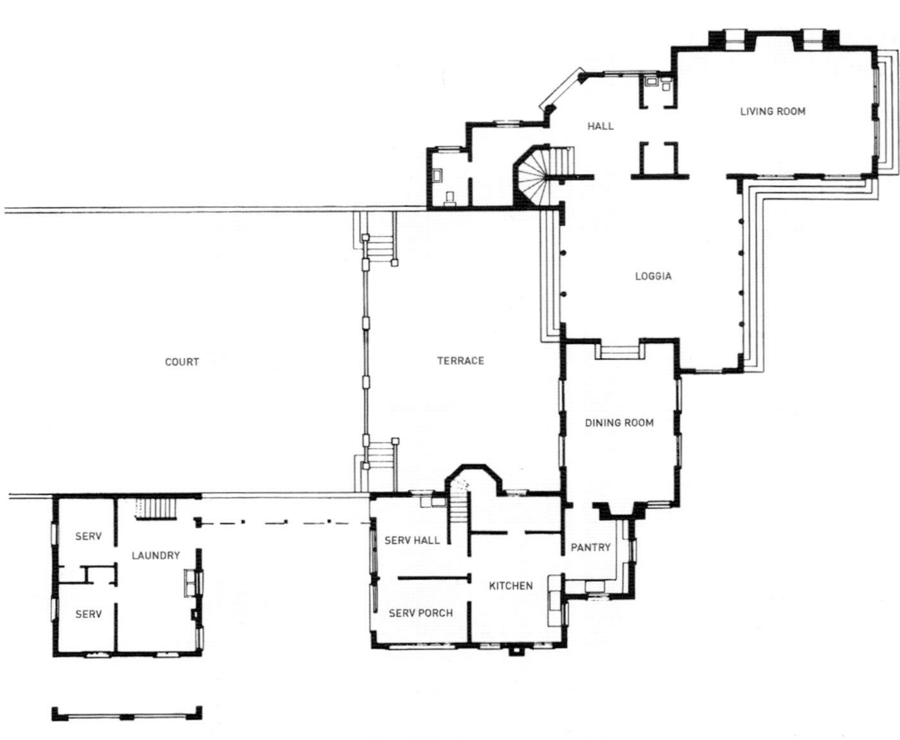

La Bellucia, 1920. Kingsley purchased an oceanfront parcel in a remote area south of Palm Beach. A contagion of stepped façades, northeast to southwest, were devised by Mizner to capture every available breeze, but had the dramatic effect of creating several inside corners where Mizner never mirrored adjacent façades.
Plan reproduced by Chase R. Cothran.

La Bellucia, 1920. Mizner would not duplicate the chamfered entry until 1928 with the design of the Gedney residence in Manalapan, Florida.
Photograph by Craig Kuhner.

La Bellucia, 1920. The western approach up to the coral ridgetop. The emptiness beyond the ridge promises an ocean view.
Photograph by Craig Kuhner.

La Bellucia, 1920. In effectively creating a series of folded planes, Mizner maximized the opportunities for ocean breezes and unique views. He also created a deep, second-floor, covered balcony in the inside corner of the main structure allowing a cover for the main doors serving the ocean terrace.

Photograph by Craig Kuhner.

La Bellucia, 1920. The eastern elevations illustrate Mizner's approach to creating the means to catch the prevailing breezes.

Photograph by Craig Kuhner.

sensitive to moneymaking schemes, had also taken note of this phenomenon. Recognizing the vast amount of time required to plan and execute the Duke project and considering the febrile nature of the Florida real estate market, perhaps Addison decided that he could do the same amount of work for his own development project and reap significantly greater reward. The degree of Wilson's involvement in this decision is not known, but it was a decision he would have encouraged, especially in light of the potential payoff. It would not

be long before Addison Mizner would redirect his energy and resources to real estate development on a massive scale.

Although Philadelphians figured prominently in his Palm Beach commissions, Addison Mizner had been very successful in adding other prominent names to his growing roster of clients. In 1920, the architect was commissioned by Willey Lyon Kingsley, a physician and capitalist from Rome, New York, to build far south from Palm Beach on a deserted stretch of beach. Kingsley, a member of private clubs in New York, Paris, and

La Bellucia, 1920. The view of La Bellucia from the beach.
Photograph by Craig Kuhner.

steps down to a walled court. It was unusual for Mizner to locate the kitchen and servants' wing on the southern end of the home, but because so much of the plan is east of the servants' wing, the practical effect is the same in terms of dispersing kitchen odors and smoke across the western court by the prevailing southeasterly breezes.

Casa de Leoni was Mizner's first Venetian Gothic residence and could not have been better connected to its site, the first lot west of the Everglades Club and directly on Lake Worth. Leonard Thomas, a former husband of Tessie Oelrichs's niece, had served as secretary in the US Embassy in

Casa de Leoni, 1921. Mizner's 1904 tour of Venice with Tessie Oelrichs left indelible Venetian Gothic impressions, which Mizner employed early and often in his Palm Beach residences and estates.
Photograph by Frank E. Geisler reproduced by Craig Kuhner.

London, chose to name his home [La] *Bellucia*, translated as beautiful Lucy, in honor of his wife. Again, the house is sited atop the coral ridge to capture both ocean breezes and views. The two-story house is entered on a northwest-facing chamfered corner, an entry approach that Mizner did not use again until the Gedney house in 1928. The vestibule serves the exposed stair entered through a deep opening to the living room and a wall-thickness opening onto a large loggia that steps up to the ocean-facing dining room and to a west-facing terrace that then

Casa de Leoni, 1921. Mizner's Venetian main door borrowed the Lion of St. Mark, the winged lion sculpture that adorns the Piazza San Marco among many other buildings and places in Venice.

Photograph by Frank E. Geisler reproduced by Craig Kuhner.

Casa de Leoni, 1921. This 1977 photograph of Casa de Leoni shows the waterfront, eastern addition along Worth Avenue.

Photograph by Craig Kuhner.

Rome and the American legation in Madrid.[21] Thomas was the son and heir of one of Edward Stotesbury's partners in Drexel and Company and was familiar with Mizner's motifs and approach and felt confident that his Palm Beach residence would resonate with his desires and expectations. In fact, Thomas planned to complete his home with the import of Italian furniture and a gondola, and to hire an Italian cook and servants.

Mizner planned the home around a patio facing and stepping down to the lake, with its footings and foundations resting on lake bottom so that the home appeared to rise directly from the water. It must have been at the forefront of Mizner's design approach to consider Casa de Leoni the western bookend of his mise en scène with the Everglades Club. After later occupying the Villa Mizner on Worth Avenue, Mizner must have been delighted with his view from the mirador of Villa Mizner

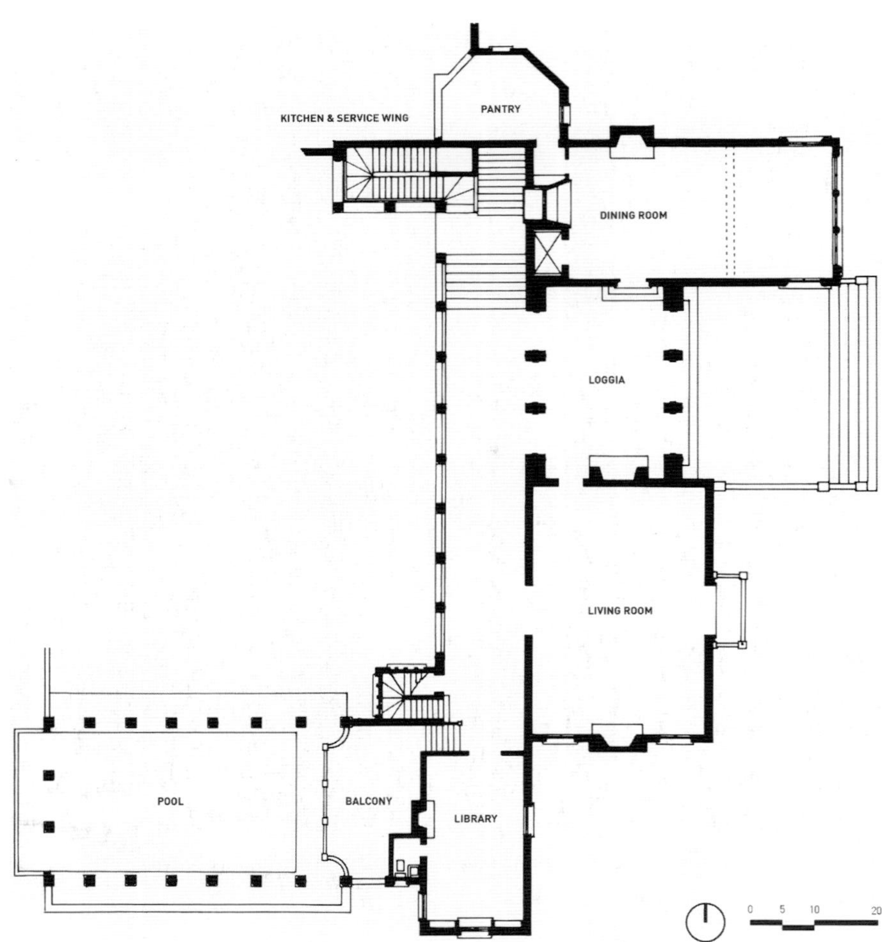

Casa Bendita, 1921. The single-room width of Phipps' grand residence illustrates Mizner's environmental sensitivity in the design of his Florida houses. The openness on two sides assured that each house maximized the natural cooling of ocean and western breezes. More importantly, in early morning or late afternoon, the bright sunlight must have rendered Casa Bendita almost transparent.
Plan reproduced by Chase R. Cothran.

Casa Bendita, 1921. The first of Mizner's large-scale houses, its C-shaped plan was improved upon by the 1928 addition of the western, pool pavilion (far right), one of Mizner's most striking embellishments.
Photograph by Frank E. Geisler reproduced by Craig Kuhner.

of his group of waterfront buildings and the Venetian architectural vocabulary of lancet-arched windows with elaborate trefoil tracery, stone balconies, and a gondola slip. At the entry off of Worth Avenue, the front door is crowned with a carved St. Mark's lion over the door. Casa de Leoni, because of its exposed condition on the lake, remains one of Palm Beach's most attractive reminders of Mizner's accomplishments, more so at almost one hundred years of age.

The Phipps family had enjoyed Palm Beach since the Flagler era. Henry Phipps, the father of John S. Phipps, was

Casa Bendita, 1921. Mizner's picturesque massing, accomplished by the use of solid and "hollow" forms such as the double-height stair and the upper and lower loggias, was masterful.

Photograph by Frank E. Geisler reproduced by Craig Kuhner.

Casa Bendita, 1921. The 1928 addition of the colonnaded pool improved the massing of the house and added a signature outdoor space.

Photograph by Frank E. Geisler reproduced by Craig Kuhner.

an original partner of Andrew Carnegie who had visited Henry at the Palm Beach Yacht Club in the late nineteenth century. Henry's gift of property to his children allowed John Phipps to commission Casa Bendita, sited on a coral ridge adjacent to Henry's home, Heamaw. From County Road, a long winding drive arrived at the base of a four-story octagonal tower that anchored the north end of the home and was used as a way of directing circulation up and on to the first

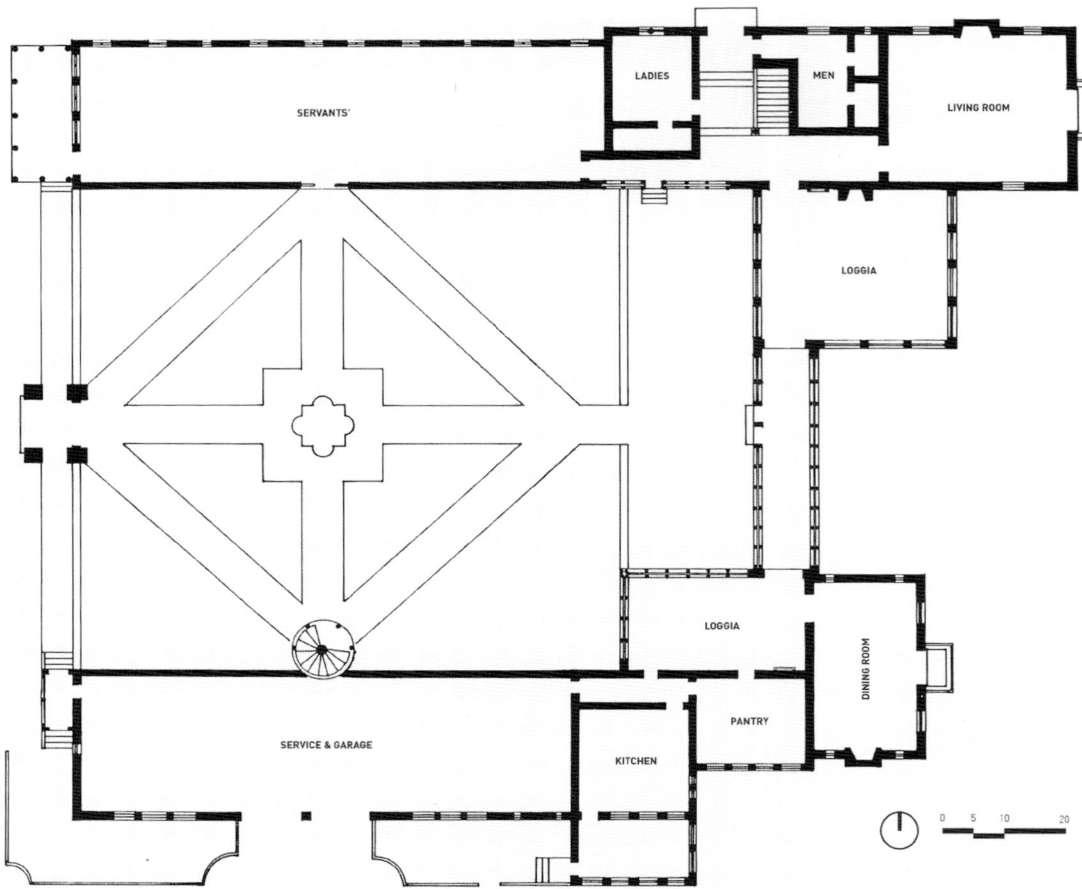

Warden Residence, 1922. The open square site plan of Mizner's Warden residence was the first of his Palm Beach houses to replicate his successful, Long Island design approach to the Stephen Brown residence. The Wardman house was saved from destruction by the conversion to six condominiums in 1983.
Plan reproduced by Chase R. Cothran.

Warden Residence, 1922. The long façade on Seminole Avenue concerned Warden, who believed that the residence would appear ostentatious. To answer Warden's concern, Mizner reported that he drew the Seminole Avenue in context with its neighboring houses, but reduced the scale of Warden's residence so it would appear smaller than its neighbors.
Photograph by Craig Kuhner.

and second floors. From the northern entrance a stair led up to a patio and open cloister from which branched the principal rooms, the dining and living rooms, and terminating in the library. The stairs at either end of the cloister rose to the Phipps private quarters and guest rooms.

In the mid-1920s, Mizner added a colonnaded pool to the southwest corner of Casa Bendita, one of his most successful spaces. With high columns on three sides, the pool was protected from the high sun but still provided ample direct sun and reflected light. The western edge of the pool extended beyond the colonnade allowing two columns to be supported on pedestals resting in the pool, which allowed bathers to sit in the water in direct sunlight. Mizner surrounded the colonnaded pool plinth with a baluster that allowed the western façade to be understood as large volumes tautly controlled,

Warden Residence, 1922. The main stair hall of the second floor. Entering the monumental doorway on Seminole Avenue, guests rose to the second floor in the north light of the monumental stair windows.

Photograph by Craig Kuhner.

allowing the first and second floor cloisters to appear as carved from a solid surface. This was a direct environmental response to the harsh western light, and must have rendered late afternoon views within and without the building as a geometric play of shadows. Mizner, for the first time, controlled volumes and their reticulation in masterful ways that are more Renaissance than Revivalist and predicted the disciplined approach that he would take in the design of Playa Riente.

The son of a founder of the Atlantic Refining Company and a member of the Standard Oil Trust, William Gray Warden

Warden Residence, 1922. Watercolor for ceiling decoration in the Warden house by Addison Mizner and the actual ceiling, circa 1922. Although this decoration sketch presents vivid colors, the values would have been significantly softened and muted in the actual finishing process. Made of pecky cypress, the coffered ceiling was first whitewashed, then painted with watercolor, and finally rubbed to produce the appearance of a seventeenth-century ceiling. Mizner taught his artisans how to create the antique patination he favored.

Watercolor courtesy of the Society of the Four Arts. Both photographs by Craig Kuhner.

Warden Residence, 1922. Six years after construction, the lush vegetation of the U-shaped, one-hundred-foot-by-eighty-foot courtyard suggests that Mizner had realized his Guatemalan aspirations in the creation of a large, enclosed courtyard. The dense foliage presented Warden and his guests a tropical oasis from their courtyard windows and ensured privacy.
Photograph by Frank E. Geisler reproduced by Craig Kuhner.

remained affiliated with Standard Oil and served as the chairman of Pittsburgh Coal Company.[22] Warden was a wealthy

man, but his modesty encouraged him to ask that Mizner design a small unostentatious house. On the other hand, Mrs. Warden asked Mizner to design a large villa. What follows is an excellent example of Mizner's propensity to create a story at his client's expense, when the truth does not actually square with the story.

Mizner claims to have made a drawing of the site in context. Probably an elevation, the full front of the proposed building was drawn at half scale, whereas the houses on either side were drawn at full scale. Letting Mrs. Warden in on the trick, he showed the drawing to the Wardens and Mr. Warden expressed his approval that the new home looked "truly insignificant." In October, according to Mizner, Warden arrived in Palm Beach on an inspection trip. Warden reportedly liked what he saw and requested a set of elevations with which to return to Philadelphia. Mizner claimed that he replied, "Elevations! Bill, you look intelligent at times; how could I send you elevations when the house isn't finished yet?" The truth is that both Wardens inspected the house in June and were quoted in the *Palm Beach Post* as "very much pleased with the results." This Mizner story, one of many, contributed to Mizner's mythic architectural nonchalance.

The site of the Warden villa is an entire oceanfront block between Root Trail and Seminole Avenue and along Ocean Boulevard on the east. Mizner approached the design on this

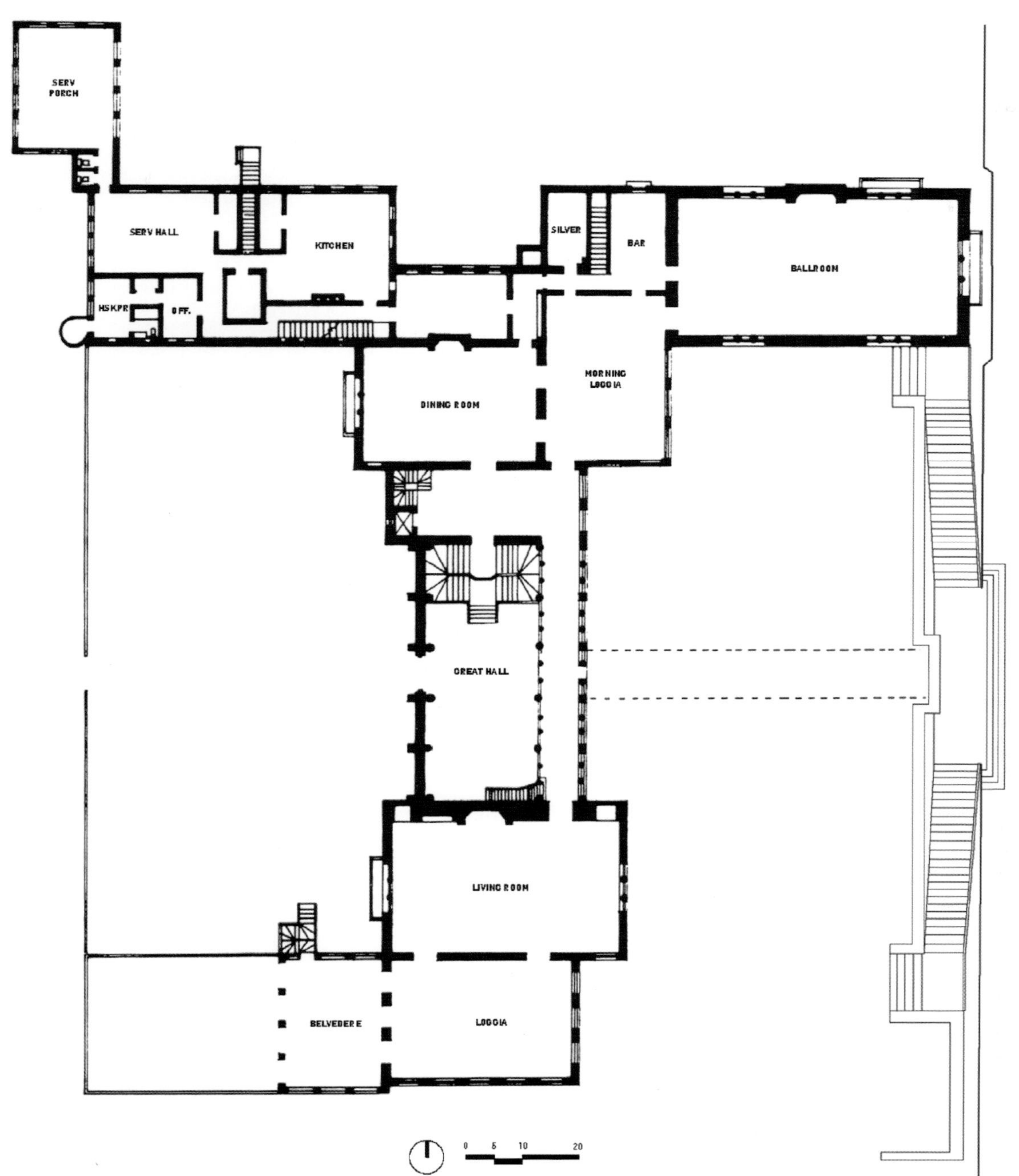

Playa Riente, 1923. The grandest of Mizner's Palm Beach estates, Playa Riente was an excellent example of social competition. Nell Cosden, primarily responsible, with Mizner, for the design of Playa Riente, and Eva Stotesbury shared Mizner's services in competing for the largest houses in Palm Beach. Plan reproduced by Chase R. Cothran.

suburban site by establishing two long east-west blocks along Seminole and Root Trail. The primary view on Seminole is composed of the major eastern portion of the façade and the minor northern portion of the façade, which is the servants' wing. Connecting the two wings are a large loggia against the oceanfront living room and a cloister between the loggia and the south wing loggia and the oceanfront dining room.

Playa Riente, 1923. Mizner's only residence to incorporate a highly formal seawall, Playa Riente, from the ocean, projects a civic scale that could easily be mistaken as having been built centuries ago in Italy or Spain.

Photograph by Frank E. Geisler reproduced by Craig Kuhner.

On the western end of the complex, a cloister connected the service and garages with the servant's wing. The result is a 185-foot by 175-foot patio bounded by the servants' wing and the garage building.

Entering from Seminole Avenue, there are changing rooms on either side for the convenience of beach users and a large stepped vestibule that also shares a large stone staircase that lead to the second floor. The floors are black tiles throughout. To accommodate the weight of the tile and its substantial setting bed, Mizner used steel to support the second floor, which accommodated the owner's suite and a sleeping porch over the living room. Five guest suites were distributed over the servants' wing. A bachelor's wing was placed over the garage and accessed by a spiral stair from the courtyard.

In the Warden villa, Mizner approached his first suburban residence by creating a large single room-width enclosure to make a large courtyard for the private enjoyment of many guests in many different areas. The success of Mizner's plan may have contributed importantly to the salvage of the building when it was threatened by demolition in the late 1970s. After much debate and legal action, the Warden villa was converted to condominiums.

The architectural aspect that supported this conversion was Mizner's approach to creating a large courtyard surrounded by a narrow section two-story building that lends itself to

Playa Riente, 1923. This view from the garden illustrates Mizner's intent to create a formal central entry that upon approach is revealed to connect directly to longer views of the ocean, on axis, through a subgrade tunnel and through the seawall.

Photograph by Frank E. Geisler reproduced by Craig Kuhner.

subdivision. Mizner could never have anticipated the idea of subdivision, but in this case, his approach may have saved an important villa.

When Mizner moved to Port Washington in Nassau County, New York, there were many wealthy families in residence, among them some of Mizner's future Palm Beach clients, including Angier Duke and Joshua Cosden who had second homes there. By 1919, Joshua Cosden was a charter member of the Everglades Club and would come to know Mizner well,

but the relationship between Addison and Joshua's wife Nell Cosden was special and would become very close over time.

Playa Riente, 1923. The main entrance portal and view to the ocean. Any first-time visitor would look out at the ocean lawn from the second level and wonder how they had glimpsed the ocean upon entry.

Photograph by Frank E. Geisler reproduced by Craig Kuhner.

Cosden began as a Baltimore streetcar conductor but had the brains and the boldness to develop a $50 million fortune from oil exploration. Socially ambitious, popular, and interesting, the Cosdens decided that building the biggest villa in Palm Beach would firmly establish their social leadership.

The Cosdens bought a site on the coral ridge, the only piece of property on North Ocean Boulevard that had no road separating the site from the ocean. Mizner's initial impressions about the site did not change from his first. He imagined "an old Gothic palace built out into the sea." After the Cosdens agreed to retain him, Mizner worked feverishly on the sketches that would captivate the couple, a key feature of which would be the great sea wall with a tunnel and steps to the beach.

Playa Riente was palatial in every sense of the word. It was much larger than the Everglades Club and was designed at a civic scale with the appearance of a castle that might lie at the center of any substantial European city and might house a community beyond its owners, including a militia for its own

Playa Riente, 1923. The main entrance hall and the north stairway illustrate Mizner's mastery of scale and authentic detail. From his Salamanca student days, Mizner retained an image of the French Gothic Grand Hall and Golden Stairs in the Cathedral of St. Mary of Burgos in northern Spain, a variation to which he would return in the design of La Ronda in Bryn Mawr, Pennsylvania, in his later years.
Photograph by Frank E. Geisler reproduced by Craig Kuhner.

Playa Riente, 1925. The minor south stairway in the main entrance hall was hidden in shadow, primarily receiving morning and afternoon light from small eastern and western windows.

Photograph by Frank E. Geisler reproduced by Craig Kuhner.

defense. While the skills required to design and build Playa Riente were an extension of the collaboration between Mizner

and Cooper Lightbown, it was Mizner's inspiration and belief, and the Cosden's belief in his vision and ability, that drove him to perform at the highest level of his career.

Mizner's architectural references included the grand stair at Burgos that he replicated in the main entrance hall as the north stairway as well as many other Gothic references handled with exceptional subtlety and deftness. Nell Cosden and Mizner spent a great deal of time together and went to Europe, spending several weeks in Spain during which Nell bought furniture, tapestries, rugs, and art. For the grand salon, Nell and Addison bought a canary yellow carpet with floral motifs and reputed to have been woven in 1595 by nuns for a cathedral in Granada. In the dining room, the Cosdens, on Mizner's recommendation, brought in Federico and Achille Angeli from Florence after Nell had admired their work at the Davanzati Palace in Florence. The Angelis' frescoes also decorated Nell's bedroom and private loggia.[23]

The ballroom, also known as the music room, had panels painted by Jose Maria Sert, a prominent Spanish artist. The panels depicted Sinbad the Sailor and were painted over silver leaf with trompe l'oeil crimson draperies depicted as divided to reveal a riot of people, oceans, trees, and animals.[24] Cosden prided herself on her work during her collaboration with Mizner on Playa Riente and came to know a great deal about both the design and engineering required for the creation of her massive villa.

Mizner's greatest house was in the hands of its owners for only a few short years. By 1926, the Cosdens' fortunes had shifted and they sold Playa Riente to Mrs. Horace Dodge, the widow of the automaker. They also sold their Sands Point and Newport houses at the same time and used the money raised to begin again. They made another fortune only to lose everything in 1929.

Playa Riente sealed Palm Beach's reputation as a global resort.

Addison Mizner was now involved in the busiest season of his career. The year 1923 not only brought him the commission from the Cosdens for Playa Riente but several others from Philadelphia friends. He also designed and built an additional six residences and one club in the same year. The Gulfstream Golf Club came about when William Warden and others complained of the constant difficulty of getting tee times at local golf courses. Mizner was quickly charged with conceiving plans for a new club and, since the office was already consumed with large commissions, the architect himself was able

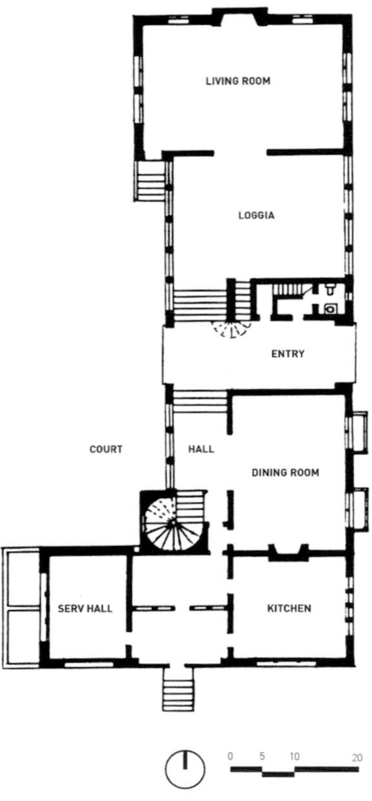

Carstairs Residence, 1923. Described by Mizner as a farmhouse of the King Ferdinand period, the wide central hall could have allowed carts and carriages to pass through. The entry bifurcated the house with the living room and loggia on the southern half and the dining room, kitchen, and service wing on the north.
Plan reproduced by Chase R. Cothran.

Carstairs Residence, 1923. The Ocean Boulevard elevation and entry.

Photograph by Craig Kuhner.

Carstairs Residence, 1923. The Central Hall of the residence connecting arrival with the courtyard.

Photograph by Craig Kuhner.

Carstairs Residence, 1923. The 1928 view from the garden to the garden portal.

Photograph by Frank E. Geisler reproduced by Craig Kuhner.

to provide a concept for Warden in just six hours. The western entrance façade was defined by an arcaded loggia fronted by a balustraded terrace that is impressively approached by a double flight of curving stairs. A reviewer in an article in *Architectural Forum* called it "the most attractive 'Spanish-Italian adaptation' in the United States."[25]

Addison Mizner had emerged among his new friends not simply as an architect but, more importantly, as a tastemaker. He was not merely providing a utilitarian service but was the purveyor of a new and elegant style of living, an architectural style that provided a relaxed and gracious setting for a modern style of entertaining. Nowhere was this attractive lifestyle more in evidence than in his own personal residences. His large, open reception rooms not only showcased a curated collection of historical objects but facilitated convivial behavior. Every year on New Year's Day, Addison held an eggnog party attended by the most socially prominent names in Palm Beach.

An accomplished host, Addison was adept at bringing together Society and Bohemia where clients and potential clients mingled with artists, musicians, and occasionally the unconventional personality. An aficionado of music, he frequently entertained guests with performances and concerts. Among those who performed for Addison were the New York String Quartet, Frances Alda of the Metropolitan Opera, Irving Berlin, and Jerome Kern. In spite of the Volstead Act

Gulfstream Golf Club, Gulfstream, Florida, 1923. Created by Warden, Vanderbilt and others, Gulfstream solved the problem of competitive tee times at the Everglades Club. The beautiful landscape of today's setting showcases the palatial, oceanfront nature of the club in ways that Mizner could only have imagined. Mizner reportedly created the concept for Gulfstream in just over six hours.

Photograph by Craig Kuhner.

recognized for Jamaican rum cocktails served by his butler in antique silver mugs.[26] These components, when combined with the dramatic environment of his homes, proved a potent concoction for cultivating relationships.

Described as "the most delightful and entertaining of men," Addison Mizner was fascinating company for women and, not surprisingly, a highly sought-after guest and escort at private dinner parties and grand social functions.[27] He was equipped with a ready mind that could expound on the subtleties of

Addison Mizner, Peggy Thayer, and Nell Cosden, 1923. Addison was in the process of building Playa Riente, the spectacular home of Mr. and Mrs. Joshua Cosden, when Nell Cosden accompanied Addison to Spain during the summer to shop for art and furniture. Since her husband was unable to go at the last moment, she took Peggy Thayer as a traveling companion. Addison and Peggy became infatuated with one another during this trip.

Courtesy of Historical Society of Palm Beach County.

that established Prohibition in 1919, Mizner, like most Palm Beach hosts, served cocktails during his parties and was art, history, and culture and possessed a rapier wit that could puncture the pretensions of the most inflated peacock. Women considered Addison not only entertaining but also trustworthy. He was frequently entrusted with confidences and received letters that were effusive in their affection.

Eleanor "Nell" Cosden was Addison's kind of person. She was a woman of beauty, spirit, and intelligence, all traits that he valued. As a matter of fact, she was so attractive that, upon first meeting her, he thought that her intelligence could not possibly measure up to her allure. This notion was summarily dispelled when he found that "she could read a plan better than I could, even to the plumbing chases and the electrical conduits."[28] While quite stylish and sufficiently wealthy to maintain a stable of thoroughbred racehorses and wear pearls that cost $600,000, Nell was authentic, exceedingly generous, and well liked by everyone. After her husband Joshua was unable to travel on the buying trip to Spain with Addison, Nell invited a friend to go in his place. This young lady was Peggy Thayer, an attractive former debutante from Philadelphia who was not only beautiful but venturesome.

Margaret "Peggy" Thayer, born in 1899, was not only well bred and fashionable but also an accomplished sportswoman. Some thought that she could compete for the US tennis championship if she dedicated herself. She won medals in swimming, went lion hunting in Africa, and even rode a wild, bucking bronco in Wyoming. At the same time, her refinement and charm were such that, after meeting Edward, Prince of Wales, the future Edward VIII, he invited her to attend an intimate party he hosted before sailing back to England after a visit to America.[29] During the trip to Spain with Nell Cosden, Peggy and Addison became attracted to one another. In his memoirs, Addison described her as "a wicked little devil" who loved to tease him.[30] At this point, Addison was forty-nine years old and Peggy only twenty-two, a disparity that, judging from his memoirs, appeared to discomfit him. At the end of this trip, he left Nell and Peggy in Nice, a separation he described in his memoirs as "a terrible parting." This large, strong man, known for his reservoir of humor, said goodbye as "tears were standing in my eyes."[31] It is not surprising that Addison described this time as "the happiest two months of my life."[32]

On his return to America, Addison stopped first in New York where he saw Peggy. There she informed him of her intention to move to Palm Beach to open a retail shop. She had a business in Rittenhouse Square in Philadelphia where she sold continental soaps, cheeses, and fashion items and planned to do the same on Worth Avenue. It became the "Peggy Thayer Shop." She was a kindred spirit, polished, and receptive to nonconformist behavior. No one can know exactly why Addison did not pursue this relationship further. Perhaps Peggy was not interested in anything more than friendship. Certainly

Addison was quite aware of the difficulty posed by a twenty-six-year difference in age but, most probably, he was tepid due to the realization of his own homosexuality. Although ultimately left with another deep friendship, Addison had experienced perhaps the most affecting female relationship of his adult life. Subsequently, Peggy's name was associated with prominent bachelors and, although she married in 1925, they remained good friends.

Addison benefitted from other female relationships in Palm Beach. One went back to his early years in New York City. Through his social network, the architect had met the James E. Martins, a couple that represented the merging of two

Casa Florencia, 1923. This view from the mirador shows the master quarters of Casa Florencia. Accessed from the main stair of the entry, the Satterwhites' private quarters were above the living areas and accessed a private loggia and roof garden above the cloister that connected the living room to the ecclesiastical dining room in the parallel wing and one side of the large courtyard.

Photograph by Frank E. Geisler reproduced by Craig Kuhner.

Casa Florencia, 1923. Built shortly after and inspired by Villa Flora, both among Mizner's best residences during his extraordinary 1923 season, Casa Florencia, commissioned by Preston and Florence Brokaw Satterwhite, possessed a large collection of fifteenth-, sixteenth-, and seventeenth-century paintings and furniture. As reported in the Palm Beach News *on January 5, 1924, the Satterwhites were so taken by Mizner's design success that they commissioned sculptor Percival Dietsch to create a bas-relief portrait of Mizner for the façade of the residence. In 1952, Casa Florencia was razed and buried onsite, creating a large mound.*

Photograph by Frank E. Geisler reproduced by Craig Kuhner.

distinguished New York families. Florence Brokaw Martin, the daughter of a prosperous merchant, was already independently wealthy when her husband, a retired Standard Oil executive, died in an automobile accident on Christmas Eve in 1905. Known as "the Widow Martin," she had benefitted from the considerable estate of her deceased husband. When Addison attended Mardi Gras in 1906, she was a member of the party and, before returning to New York, they traveled together with other members of their group to Palm Beach. When Florence Martin subsequently married Dr. Preston Pope Satterwhite, they began collecting fifteenth-, sixteenth-, and seventeenth-century Spanish and Italian art and antiquities. Living in New York and on Long Island where Florence had inherited the magnificent Martin Hall from her husband, the couple commissioned old friend Addison Mizner to design a Palm Beach oceanfront home appropriate for their collections.

Mizner began working on the home that would be named *Casa Florencia* in 1923. The entrance and stair hall were positioned on the north side of the villa and the library and living room were on the east side providing views of the ocean.

Casa Florencia, 1923. With stone walls, a vaulted ceiling with ribbed groins, and a raised apse with stained glass windows that was separated from the dining area by a high, iron altar screen, the setting was beautiful if suppressive of the frivolity of large festive occasions. Photograph by Frank E. Geisler reproduced by Craig Kuhner.

The living room was expansive with large arched windows to provide light and the south end of the room had a dais and stone balustraded railing that led to the library. The elaborate dining room was also on the east side in a separate wing reached from an arcaded cloister. With stone walls and ribbed groins, the end of the spectacular room was defined by a raised apse framed by a lancet arch and an iron-grilled altar screen. Mizner used stained-glass windows in dramatic fashion to fill the elliptical opening. Although magnificent, the dining room for many guests was rather forbidding and not exactly conducive to merriment.[33] The Satterwhites were so pleased with the results that they commissioned sculptor Percival Dietsch to create a bas-relief portrait of Mizner that tastefully surmounted the exterior architrave of a stained-glass window.

That Addison Mizner had special relationships with women is not to suggest that he lacked the same kind of friendships with men. Addison's unconventional past always provided a fruitful source of material for anecdotes and stories appropriately recounted to men in salty language, or what Paris Singer called "Tavern English."[34] One friend described his remarks as "pungent, uninhibited, scurrilous and often plain vulgar. Yet, somehow, they were never offensive and always funny."[35] After Alex Waugh sent material to Alva Johnston, an author who was writing a biography of the Mizner brothers, he received a reply thanking him for his effort but also informing him that the stories were unfortunately unusable. Johnston loved the "amusing incidents" and concluded, "but the tragedy is that many of them are quite unprintable and this is the more sad for they are so funny."[36] Addison had always been a remarkably adept raconteur and within his anthology were, not surprisingly, many tales fit only for the ears of men.

Sometimes he would forsake his female friends for their husbands. Eva Stotesbury had arranged for the eminent composer and pianist Sergei Rachmaninoff to give a solo recital at El Mirasol. This evening was the kind of remarkable occasion that famously solidified Eva's position of social primacy in Palm Beach. Two hundred guests gathered to listen to the expressive pianist play his works. Ned Stotesbury took little interest in the social world of his wife and managed to sneak away from the performance. At intermission, Eva noticed his absence and immediately set off to search for her truant spouse. Finally she found him in his study playing pinochle with Addison. Exasperated, she demanded to know why they were not downstairs enjoying the virtuosity of the great pianist. Addison, unruffled, looked up and said, "Oh, I thought it was the piano tuner."[37]

Although Addison made his living by catering to people of privilege, he did not do so at the expense of those less fortunate. He always shared his friendship indiscriminately and enjoyed associations with dedicated employees, skilled workmen, and colorful characters. One such individual was Wendell Weed, an eccentric old gentleman who faithfully did odd jobs for Addison. When Wendell fell on hard times, Addison cared for him and created a position as greeter for guests arriving to shop at Via Mizner. Dressed in white conspicuously accented with a red cummerbund and fez and armed with a red golf umbrella, Wendell became a minor celebrity in Palm Beach and sometimes received work from Addison's friends. Addison also bought him clothes and made sure that he received medical care.

Cooper Lightbown was another example of someone Addison went out of his way to support. In the mayoral election of 1922, Addison wanted to thwart the reelection of George Jonas, so the architect encouraged the competent Lightbown to run in opposition. Addison gave speeches on his behalf and created handbills that he personally signed and distributed to the public. As a result, Lightbown became the fourth mayor of Palm Beach and successfully served in that position through 1927. Just after the election results were posted, Mizner was confronted by the loser who was "in a rage."[38] Addison tamed him by grabbing and twisting his nose, an action that produced a feeble response: "You nearly broke my glasses."[39] At that point, the loser disappeared. Noting the efficacy of his action, Addison later observed, "Mizners have always thought that the enemy's nasal appendage was like the handle of a frying pan."[40]

Wherever Addison Mizner went, he had the gift of being able to establish enduring relationships. Alex Waugh, who traveled with Addison to Europe to buy antiques, remarked that "all doors seemed to open to him."[41] Addison frequently received invitations from important friends and, on one memorable occasion, he took Waugh to the home of the Duke of Alba, one of the most sophisticated connoisseurs of Spanish art and antiquities. There they browsed one of the most important collections of art, books, and manuscripts in the world, an opportunity that Waugh would not have otherwise had.

Addison's hotel suite in Spain was frequented by noblemen, collectors, historians, and archaeologists. One day, there was a phone call that a tired Addison did not answer. The phone rang again and, when Waugh answered, he was informed by the front desk that someone important insisted on coming up to Señor Mizner's room. There was a knock at the door and in walked King Alfonso XIII of Spain. Addison's greeting to his old friend was "Well, you old son-of-a-bitch. Why didn't you say it was you?"[42] On another trip, a former American ambassador's wife approached Addison and curiously, perhaps enviously, enquired: "I saw you at the king's races yesterday; you were with the very smartest people in Spain—all the court set. How did you get to know them?"[43] When entertaining

Nell Cosden, Peggy Thayer, and Louise Munn in Spain in the summer of 1922, they dined with the Duke of Alba and lunched with the Marquis de Villa Vieco, among others.

In Mizner's entire career, there were very few with whom he had an antagonistic relationship and one was E. Clarence Jones. Born in New York, Jones was one of the first New Yorkers to make Palm Beach his winter refuge. He had established a banking firm in his own name in 1889 and became a member of the New York Stock Exchange. A bachelor for many years, he married the beautiful widow of playwright Henry Blossom in 1921. As a purveyor of stock tips, a sportsman, and the first president of the Everglades Club, he was an influential figure in the Palm Beach community.[44]

Perhaps under normal circumstances, Jones and Mizner would have enjoyed a harmonious relationship; however, the conditions under which their relationship developed were hardly normal. With the death of Charles T. Yerkes in New York at the end of 1905, Clarence Jones set his eyes on Yerkes's very rich widow. In spite of his position and influence, Myra Yerkes was not impressed with the serious banker; instead, she was smitten with the charming, carefree roué, Addison's brother Wilson. The ignominy of the slight, probably augmented by Wilson's cavalier attitude, no doubt left a bruise that Jones still bore. Now, thirteen years later, he had the opportunity to exact revenge.

Clarence Jones had commissioned Addison to build him a furnished house for $10,000. According to Addison's memoirs, the architect absorbed another $3,000 to complete a house that fulfilled his standards. Apparently satisfied with the results, Jones asked him to purchase some more furniture. In order to be able to pass along the trade discount to his client, Addison ordered on his own account $2,400 of furniture from Giles, a retailer in West Palm Beach.[45] Jones refused to pay the bill and arranged to have Giles sue Addison for non-payment. Jones then connived with a deputy sheriff to have Mizner served with a subpoena in the presence of Eva Stotesbury. Addison learned that the deputy had been paid twenty-five dollars if he would confront the architect in front of the influential Mrs. Stotesbury, thereby shaming him and causing irretrievable damage to his reputation.[46]

Addison was predictably furious. Finally confronting Giles, he concluded his tirade with the salvo "I hope you drop dead right where you stand."[47] Eva Stotesbury and others, forever faithful to their friend, saw right through Jones's charade and were entertained as Addison shared the story over tea shortly after the episode. When the telephone rang a few days later, Louise Munn informed Addison that Giles had dropped dead yesterday, exactly where the architect had specified. A year later, one of the women who had heard the story at the tea asked Addison if he could possibly produce the same result with her detested stepmother.

Concha Marina, 1921. Over time, Concha Marina would be modified by other Palm Beach architects including Wyeth, Fatio, Volk and others into the present day.

Photograph by Frank E. Geisler reproduced by Craig Kuhner.

Clarence Jones was also able to punish Addison in another way. An officer of the Everglades Club, he was involved in devising a new set of rules that forbid the presence of dogs in the club and also did not allow ladies to be admitted above the first floor. Since Addison kept chows and had an amazing throng of female friends, the effect of this new rule was to remove the club as a place of residence for Addison who, since its opening, had kept an apartment on the fifth floor. This forced expulsion induced Addison to build his own house, but each new house that he conceived for himself was immediately desired by someone else. After three tries, he had to give up this idea because his office had become extremely busy with private commissions.

Since Addison believed that Clarence Jones had engineered the elimination of the Everglades Club as a residence for himself, the architect was forced to arrange other accommodations. Following this expulsion from the club, Addison built a house for himself at 720 South Ocean Road, a location that was removed from the center of Palm Beach at that time and offered the architect privacy. Known as *El Solano*, the house was purchased within a year of completion by Harold S. Vanderbilt, who immediately had Addison enlarge the house. For his office, Addison had been renting a building known as "the mule shed" from the English portrait photographer, Ernest W. Histed, and since he was now homeless again, he remodeled the structure to include living quarters for himself.

Concha Marina, entrance to patio, 1921. Mizner's elegant approach to section is ironic in that the heavy, segmented arch of the exterior entry on one side is opposed by a very light, cloistered courtyard façade. Flanking the path to the courtyard are the windowless masses of the kitchen and service quarters."

Photograph by Frank E. Geisler reproduced by Craig Kuhner.

In spite of a short recession in America in 1920 and 1921, Addison continued to receive several commissions and decided to build another residence for himself. *Concha Marina*, sited just

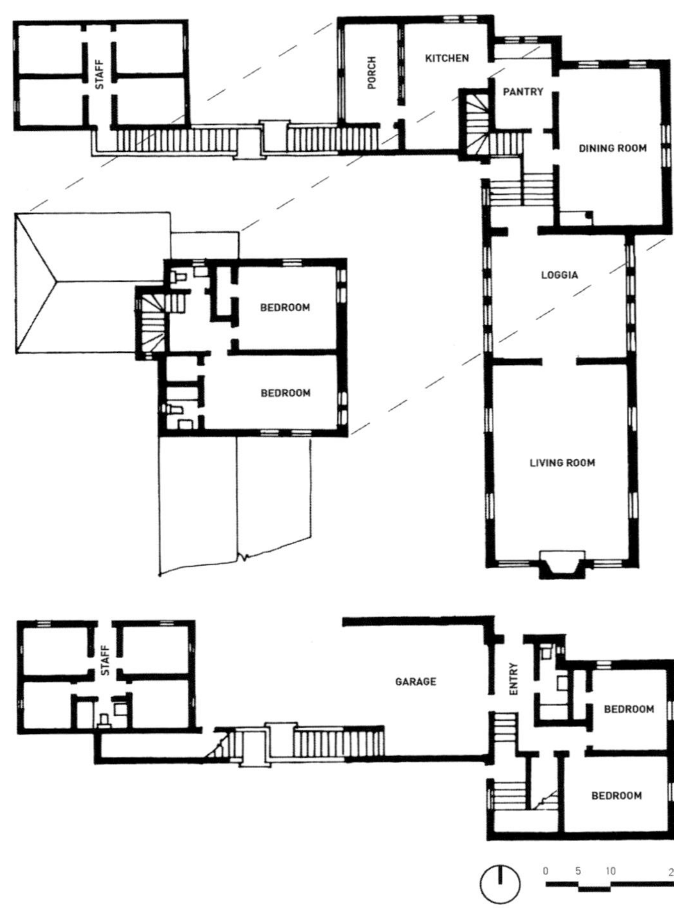

Concha Marina, 1921.

Plan reproduced by Chase R. Cothran.

Sin Cuidado, 1922. Following the sale of Concha Marina, Mizner bought a lot much farther south at 1800 Ocean Boulevard, hoping to avoid the attraction of a buyer. His new home, Sin Cuidado, was designed to meet the topography of the site. Entering on a lower level situated on the downhill slope of the coral ridge, and shared with the garage, two bedrooms, and the service quarters, guests rose to the main level loggia and living room, which faced the ocean. Continuing on the same main stair and up six steps was the dining room. Continuing farther still the stair landed at a foyer serving two oceanfront bedrooms.

Again, the home was sold. The buyer was Edward S. Moore, in 1922.

This view from Ocean Boulevard provides no hint of the dramatic topography of the terraced court-yard. Mizner created an L-shaped plan that appeared quite modest on the ocean elevation. The tall corner portion of the residence was three stories, the lowest of which was concealed beneath the coral ridge.

Photograph by Frank E. Geisler reproduced by Craig Kuhner.

Sin Cuidado, 1922. The unusual topography of the Sin Cuidado parcel enabled Mizner to develop a dramatically terraced courtyard, an opportunity that he had not enjoyed since his Port Washington, Long Island days.

Photograph by Frank E. Geisler reproduced by Craig Kuhner.

Via Mizner, 1924. With the sale of his third house to Moore, and the continuing success of his practice and Mizner Industries, Mizner, while traveling in Europe in the summer of 1923, planned a new building across Worth Avenue from the Everglades Club to house his practice and offices for all of his commercial ventures, and importantly, a showroom at ground level for his products. This was the beginning of Via Mizner, a shopping complex that would influence mixed-use retail development for generations. Via Mizner, on Worth Avenue, connecting to Peruvian Avenue, was imagined by Mizner as a warren of small meandering alleys that could have arisen from the abandonment of a castle's lowest floors by the regent's standing army. The arcaded street level and the alleyways accommodated small shops, restaurants and offices, while the upper areas were occupied by offices and apartments. Villa Mizner, his last home, rose four stories above retail at the street level.

Photograph by Frank E. Geisler reproduced by Craig Kuhner.

north of his former house but still remote from Worth Avenue, was an L-shaped house with a single-story section facing the ocean and a two-story section facing the jungle. The architect

was able to occupy the house only for a few months before selling it to George and Isabel Dodge Sloane. Once again, he moved back to the "mule shed" and immediately began

Via Mizner, 1924. In addition to the work begun in 1923, in 1924 recognizing the real estate success of his first phase of development, Mizner added to the experience with the westward adjacent creation of Via Parigi, a tribute to Paris Singer's financial involvement in both projects. Both projects served as catalysts for the retail development of Worth Avenue by encouraging the conversion of street-front houses to retail and commercial use.

In Via Parigi, Mizner developed his first retail operation for the sale of Mizner Industries' products.

Photograph by Frank E. Geisler reproduced by Craig Kuhner.

planning his next house. This time he bought a lot much farther south at 1800 South Ocean Boulevard, thinking that its distant location would dissuade anyone from purchasing it. *Sin Cuidado*, completed in 1922, was a small house with an ocean façade that included a dining room and living room joined by a loggia. Within two years of designing this house, he agreed to sell it to Edward S. Moore, who immediately asked the architect to expand the house considerably. The result of Addison's frustrating efforts to create a home for himself was to extend farther south the boundaries where people lived in Palm Beach.

Mizner had grown weary of designing and building homes for himself only for someone to buy them, forcing his return to the "mule shed" next to his office. With the growth of the Everglades Club there was a nascent neighborhood along Worth Avenue, and Mizner considered the opportunity to create a place for his office and offices for his manufacturing companies, and perhaps a place for himself. As he developed the idea, he remembered the medieval built fabric that surrounded the castle or the cathedral in Spain. He imagined that he would build towers at the base of which were places where people might live, go to market, and enjoy the life within a crowded and meandering market. Mizner dreamed of the street within a street, with winding paths doubling back on themselves with the occasional short dead end or pocket fountain and a stair leading to a second, third, or fourth level.

Via Mizner, 1924. The entry to Mizner's tower was conveniently, yet anonymously, located off of Worth Avenue and was served by a monumental stair and an elevator, both of which rose to the mirador at the tower's top. The entry was protected by a decorative iron gate.
Photograph by Frank E. Geisler reproduced by Craig Kuhner.

Villa Mizner, 1924. The living room and its entrance foyer, the dining room, and kitchen occupied the second floor, which also enjoyed terraces from every room. On the day of Mizner's memorial service, the Stotesburys arrived to a full living room and listened to the service from the entry foyer, interrupted occasionally by the chattering of Mizner's Capuchin monkeys that moved about the terraces.
Photograph by Frank E. Geisler reproduced by Craig Kuhner.

Villa Mizner, 1924. Mizner's large living room was the center of his afternoons at home. Fifteen-foot ceilings accommo-dated large tapestries and windows that allowed the many antiques and products from Mizner Industries to exhibit so well that photographs were used in Mizner Industries advertising programs. The pecky cypress–beamed and –paneled ceilings were glazed and painted to resemble the painted remnants of an old Spanish hacienda or convent.
Photograph by Frank E. Geisler reproduced by Craig Kuhner.

Villa Mizner, 1924. Mizner's dining room, like the rest of the rooms in the Villa Mizner, was distinguished by antique objects that he had collected throughout his life. Most notably in this room is the linen fold wall paneling that he brought home from the University of Salamanca. In dramatic fashion, the architect designed a monumental fireplace to the same height as the molding that crowns the paneling. Walnut, leather, wrought iron, glazed tile, and silver objects combine to great effect in this room where he regularly entertained friends.
Photograph by Frank E. Geisler reproduced by Craig Kuhner.

As the inspiration for Via Mizner, Addison determined that he would develop two parcels opposite to greater effect. The other would be called Via Parigi in honor of his friend and investor, Paris Singer. This urban approach was completely new at that time in the United States. Now, of course, it is considered urban thinking. Mizner saw the small, ground-level shops as opportunities for ladies and men to create businesses that traded in small specialty products of the highest quality and that would give the resort a unique mix of fashionable products such as clothing, scents, and candles. Mizner's arcades became further evidence of his genius and entrepreneurship, and the accolades that he received further encouraged him to think more grandly about the possibilities in new towns and cities.

In Via Mizner, Addison determined to build a high villa for himself, reachable by elevator and with views of his Palm Beach. The Villa Mizner was to be five stories high with shops on the ground floor and his private apartments upstairs. At the lowest level were his living room, dining room, and kitchen and above it, two floors each of two bedrooms and bathrooms. At the top, in the mirador, was Mizner's studio with the best views in Palm Beach.

The rooms are generous and well detailed as one would expect. The living room is thirty-five by forty feet with carved windows, a pecky cypress ceiling, and a dark terra cotta floor surrounding a central oak floor panel. The finishes, furniture, and furnishings are from Mizner's long-held collection of artifacts and cohere to produce an encyclopedia of Mediterranean design as well as a scrapbook of Mizner's life. The dining room paneling was a gift from King Alfonso and was from the private apartments of King Ferdinand and Queen Isabella of Spain in Salamanca, the dark wood lighted with whitewash, as done by Stanford White at Rosecliff.

The mirador is the Villa's most wonderful space. Twenty-five by thirty-three feet, with fifteen plain glass windows on three sides, through which the scene appears exactly as Mizner might have imagined: irregular tiled roofs to the ocean and the lake.

Villa Mizner, 1924. From the mirador, Mizner could see many of his houses and buildings, most prominently, the nearby Everglades Club, Casa de Leoni, and Casa Maria Marrone, built in 1926 for Barclay H. Warburton at the end of Worth Avenue on Lake Worth.

Photograph by Frank E. Geisler reproduced by Craig Kuhner.

The floor finishes are varied and the pecky cypress ceilings are a riot of color. The walls are washed in pale greens, yellows, and pinks, depending on the sun angle, and there is a terrace, accessible from the dining room. This was a favorite place for Mizner's menagerie, particularly the monkeys that would throw their peanut shells down on unsuspecting shoppers.

In Via Mizner and Via Parigi, Mizner demonstrated a maturity and mastery of proportion and human scale. Mizner felt that he now knew Palm Beach in all of its dimensions as a place. He was confident and felt that he had accomplished a great deal of which he could feel justifiably proud.

As a result of his success, Addison Mizner was working very hard managing a multifaceted business. As an escape from the ever-present exigencies of the workday, Addison found gratification at the dinner table. He loved to eat and consumed large quantities of food. A favorite dessert was ice cream, reportedly made specially to make it richer, topped with ginger.[48] Later in Palm Beach, he became especially fond of his cook's hot chocolate cake.[49] When dining at Addison's house, guests were served on silver plates that his father had acquired in Guatemala. A close friend observed that his plate was actually larger than those presented to others.[50] When Addison grew to weigh approximately three hundred pounds, he managed to lose about forty pounds with the help of his doctors; however, he said the loss made him feel worse, not better. Despite his weight, he was indefatigable and immensely strong. On a construction site, he watched two workmen struggle to lift a huge bathtub. Frustrated with the lack of progress, Addison brushed them aside and lifted the massive object from the truck and carried it into the house by himself.[51]

Although passionate about eating, Addison was much more circumspect about drinking. Perhaps his broad experience in life had made him well aware of the detrimental effects of alcohol. He had already witnessed the harm done to his brother by excessive use of alcohol and drugs. In a practical sense, he was dedicated to running his businesses and realized that late nights and dissipation could only impede his ability to function professionally. Deprecating sloppy behavior, he also ensured that guests were served in moderation at his own parties. Although he drank little, he did like to smoke in the early Palm Beach days; however, this desire appears to have diminished as he got older. One of the first observations made by Joe Earman, the editor of the *Palm Beach Post*, was that the architect had a preference for smoking.[52] As he approached his last years, Ozie Belle Brown, Addison's housekeeper beginning in 1929, stated that she rarely saw him smoke in the four years she spent with him.[53]

As a result of his sound relationships developed in New York and expanded in Palm Beach, Addison Mizner became recognized as a society architect. Though naturally gregarious, he worked hard to create and sustain these friendships. He loved to entertain and did it well. Also, he regularly received invitations to important parties and was frequently honored to be seated to the right of his hostess. As his business progressed and prospered, he gradually felt disinclined to go out as much;

however, once at a party, he invariably enjoyed himself. Alice DeLamar, a close friend for virtually his entire life in Palm Beach, flatly said that he did not like to go out, but this observation was made over thirty years after the architect's death. Although Mizner was recognized as a storyteller of the first order, he was not a constant talker. DeLamar described his voice as mellow and deep and his speech as "brief and to the point" with "a touch of wit."[54]

Owing to size and strength of personality, Addison Mizner was always recognizable in the community. By nature an informal person, Addison wore a tuxedo when necessary but his willingness to dress formally also waned as he got older. During the day, his dress was casual because he would spend the morning in the office and the afternoons at construction sites. In Palm Beach, he drove an unusual car that Alex Waugh described in his memoirs as a "super-dreadnought," a customized vehicle whose salient virtue was that it accommodated his girth.[55] He had a Mack truck chassis stripped of anything unnecessary and fitted with two bucket seats. In his memoirs, Alex Waugh recalls seeing Addison roaring around the community with his shirt blowing in the wind.

This description of Addison's comportment, when combined with stories of his earthy language, creates the image of an entirely carefree individual, an unconventional character unbothered by pressing events and impervious to discipline.

This perception has been further enhanced by the willingness of some biographers to make Addison complicit in some of the comic antics of his brother, Wilson. The brothers indeed spent much of their lives in the same cities and collaborated on many adventures; however, Wilson's capacity for mischief far exceeded that of his brother. When Addison left New York to go to Palm Beach with Paris Singer in 1918, Wilson remained in New York. Unsurprisingly, his venal activities placed him in precarious circumstances. He was badly beaten by thugs and became debilitated from cocaine addiction. By 1922, Wilson lay ill in a New York hospital as a result of heart trouble. At this point, still faithful to his mother's entreaty to look after his little brother, the solicitous Addison invited Wilson to Palm Beach to recuperate.

To his credit, Wilson was able to overcome the cocaine addiction; however, that resolve was not applied to any other aspect of his life. In 1923, having visited California, he returned to Palm Beach with a girlfriend named Florence Atkinson whom he introduced as his "wife." This would later be revealed to be a falsehood, much to the embarrassment of Addison. Being the good brother, Addison also arranged a position in Mizner Industries for his brother; however, this appointment hardly enhanced the efficiency of the operation. Generally, Wilson remained self-centered and only looked out for himself.

Wilson Mizner Residence, 1924. Palm Beach home of Wilson Mizner at 237 Worth Avenue, circa 1925. Addison Mizner built this house for Wilson, who temporarily lived there with a woman who Palm Beach inhabitants wrongly thought to be his wife. Addison had the dining room decorated with mural paintings, a decorative touch that Wilson had painted over in white. When asked why he did this, Wilson replied, "so I can see the mosquitoes."

Courtesy of Historical Society of Palm Beach County.

Jealous of Addison's affection for their nephew Horace Chase, who was now managing one of Addison's businesses, Wilson concocted a tale to diminish Horace's stature. There was a critical ironwork project that had to be completed for an important party to be held at El Mirasol for Eva Stotesbury. Mysteriously, the blacksmith who was assigned to complete the project disappeared on a drinking binge that lasted three days. The failure to fulfill this obligation for one of his most important clients greatly enraged Addison. Wilson assured his brother that the negligence belonged to the irresponsible Horace. When Horace was fired, Wilson cheerfully assumed his nephew's former responsibilities.

Wilson's ingenuity and attraction to financial gain were in conspicuous evidence just after his arrival in Palm Beach. It was announced in local newspapers on October 29, 1922, that a corporation with an authorized capital stock of $1 million was being formed to establish the motion picture business in the Palm Beach area. "The Palm Beach Motion Pictures, Inc." would be centered in a studio building in which Wilson Mizner planned to produce his own pictures and which could also be made available to other producers. The article acknowledged Wilson as a playwright and producer of movies and concluded that he "is competent to judge the merits of California and Florida as points of location for making moving pictures."[56] Although this project did not move forward, it was a prelude of other rash and fruitless schemes that Wilson would enthusiastically endorse to his brother.

Though unconventional and roguish, Wilson Mizner was popular in Palm Beach and was found attractive by many. In the course of his five-year stay in Palm Beach, he attracted sophisticated women like Anita Loos, the author of *Gentlemen Prefer Blondes,* and Eleanor Chase, the future wife of architect Maurice Fatio. At heart, he was still an irredeemable miscreant whose behavior was aberrant in a community that generally adhered to conventional comportment. In 1924 Addison built a house for Wilson at 237 Worth Avenue that was a duplex. The ground floor was rented and the upper floor belonged to Wilson and his "wife," Florence. Alice DeLamar walked by one day and saw an unkempt Wilson, dressed in a nightshirt and smoking a cigar, supported by the balcony railing with several days' growth of beard on his face.[57] Such was the nature of Wilson's life. The tendency among some biographers to view Addison through the prism of his younger brother only diminished the architect and supported the many myths that have come to be regarded as fact.

Unlike Wilson whose life gained pace only with the approach of nighttime, Addison was dedicated to his profession and began his days early. Arising before six every morning, he was able to work in his studio without interruption before being besieged with a multitude of questions and decisions as the office began its day. In the afternoons, he would visit the sites of various projects where he oversaw construction and made any alterations in design that might be required. After work, the architect dedicated himself to the Palm Beach social life that allowed him to develop the relationships that fed his business.

Addison was adept at developing talent both in the office and at the various workshops within Mizner Industries. The design and review process within the office saw the participation not just of senior designers but of draftsmen and apprentices as well. The senior designer and draftsman often shared the same office to ensure communication and both were present during conferences between Addison and the client. The atmosphere in the office was collegial and inclusive. One associate commented that there was "a feeling you are with him. . . . It was a pleasure working for Mizner."[58]

Historian Donald Curl interviewed many associates from Addison's office who spoke of the genuine interest he took in their work and of the professional guidance offered by the architect. Addison had asked one associate to detail the balusters and hand rail for a stair and, after reviewing the results, patiently sat with him to explain why the proportions were incorrect.[59] In his antiques business, Alex Waugh recounted how Addison would quiz him about the provenance of an object and, after hearing the answer, would further explain the time, place, and social conditions attached to its creation. He said, "I learned more from Addison than years spent at a university would have taught me, and his recapitulations were more permanently telling in their effect."[60]

It was the high level of confidence and trust that Addison had created among the different components of his staff and construction teams that allowed him to begin traveling to Europe during the summers. These excursions were important because they gave the architect the opportunity to escape the minutiae of everyday activities to renew his creative spirit. His curious eye was always consuming new concepts and details that would be recorded with photographs or postcards and subsequently added to his scrapbooks. Also, these trips allowed him to shop for antique furniture, furnishings, and accessories, those inimitable objects that gave his interiors their own special quality. Importantly, this quest for ideas and objects fed the creativity that drove his business.

Addison Mizner's architectural education and practice have been called into question by some biographers, specifically by those willing to sacrifice fact in the interest of recounting an entertaining tale. In reality, he ran an office whose organization and operation were consistent with that of other professional architects. Each project was begun with consultations to ascertain the taste and preferences of his client. Addison himself then prepared sketches and sometimes watercolors of the elevations to convey the appearance and general arrangement of the house. A senior designer would then develop plans with the frequent input of Mizner and finally a draftsman would complete construction plans for the builder. Some have propagated the notion that his plans were incomplete or impracticable. The stories of omitting stairways and forgetting bathrooms, while amusing to imagine, are simply not true.

Addison Mizner's objective was to create something that appeared to have existed for two or three centuries. This look conveyed the imperfections that time and constant use inevitably impart: faded woods, uneven boards, and broken bits of stone in carved ornament. Once built, his houses underwent a process of conferring the appearance of antiquity. He was known to use burning tarpaper to smoke up a ceiling and to apply condensed milk to painted plaster walls before rubbing them with steel wool to produce an aged effect. Not only were roof tiles applied unevenly but, before application, the roof line would sometimes be built up in places to create the illusion that it sagged. For external doors, cypress boards would be sandblasted to simulate a weathered look. Mizner found that the separate applications of a lime whitewash and creosote would, after interacting with the natural oils of cypress, create a mottled effect. After one of his artisans had installed an important carved stone fireplace, Addison walked up to it and began to knock off bits and pieces with a hammer. He then asked the incredulous craftsman to repair the damage he had just witnessed. All of these practices were carefully conceived to produce the blemishes of age.

Addison Mizner's contracts stipulated that his office would handle the interior decoration of the rooms on at least the principal floor. With a strong sense of history, Addison always had a specific vision for the interiors of each house. As was the case with many other facets of his business, it was more efficient to have someone else execute the plan after it had been specified by the architect. He used a local designer by the name of Lilias Piper on many of his houses but, as the number of projects increased, he began to contract with others.

Addison Mizner had come to know the Duchess of Richelieu through her charity work and began to use her to handle interior decoration. Born Elinor Douglas Wise in Baltimore, she married the eighth Duke of Richelieu in 1913 and lived with her new husband part of the year in New York. Having studied voice in Paris, she was famous for traveling around the country to raise money for wounded veterans of World War I.[61] Mizner also used Ruby Ross Wood, one of America's pioneer interior decorators, who lived in New York and had developed a clientele that included members of the Vanderbilt and Astor families. She began her career working for the John Wanamaker store and, as a result, started to do work for Addison's friend Rodman Wanamaker. She supplied Addison with fabrics for upholstery and drapery application and with hand-woven rugs from Portugal and Majorca.[62] Regardless of the level of involvement of these decorators, photographs of the original interiors in Mizner's houses bear the unmistakable stamp of the architect and suggest that, for the most part, the decorators were working to his aesthetic goals.

Addison Mizner was not just a talented architect; he had proved to be an innovator, a successful entrepreneur, and skillful business manager as well. Considerable demand for his services was indicated by the large number of private residences he had just completed for the 1923–1924 season. The spectacular results of his work impressed visitors and caused his reputation to spread. As a society architect, he enjoyed the patronage of the rich and powerful and spent his evenings socializing with them. Under these circumstances, it was natural for the architect to be emboldened by such success. To this point, Mizner had confined his efforts to fulfilling individual commissions but, with the unrestrained growth that South Florida was experiencing, he decided to embark on a development project of immense scale that would consume the next two years of his life. Like much of Addison Mizner's existence, this would be an adventure.

One of the reasons that Addison Mizner could consider undertaking a project of such huge scope was that he had enabled himself to control virtually all of his critical supply chain. In considering Mizner's distinguished architectural legacy, one could easily overlook the extraordinary enterprise he exhibited in establishing many businesses that supplied extremely sophisticated products to satisfy the needs of a refined and discerning clientele.

CHAPTER TWELVE

AN ENTREPRENEUR

Before building the Everglades Club, Addison Mizner had to confront a significant obstacle to construction and finishing: the critical absence of materials, skilled labor, and furnishings. According to Mizner, there were fewer than thirty houses on the island at this time and virtually all were constructed of wood. In contrast to the vernacular woods of South Florida, he preferred a more permanent building material, something more appropriate for his preferred architectural style. Additionally, all healthy men in the area were performing military service and those that remained were either old, frail, or lacking in construction experience. Finally, the war had made it impossible to import the furniture, tapestries, and architectural parts that were used to complete his Mediterranean Revival–style interiors. While these deficiencies

Carved capital, circa 1923. There was hardly anything that Mizner Industries could not produce. As this style of composite order was not part of Mizner's regular stylistic vocabulary, the capital would probably have been commissioned by another Palm Beach architect. Mizner Industries was integral not only to Miner's projects but, because of the high level of artisanship, also to those of the other architects working in South Florida.
Courtesy of Historical Society of Palm Beach County.

might have posed insuperable problems for most people, they were merely momentary obstacles from the ingenious architect.

In considering the impressive architectural legacy of Addison Mizner today, one should not underappreciate his entrepreneurship in establishing a colony of skilled artisans capable of producing the most sophisticated array of products required to finish houses: from roof tile, ironwork, and pottery to millwork, furniture, and leaded glass. Not only did this feat require expert knowledge of all trades and materials, but it demanded an inordinate amount of energy and patience to establish a variety of business and to educate workers in each craft. In this time of want, Mizner proved to be a man of broad dimension in his skilled ability to conceive remarkable villas one after the other and, at the same time, to create lines of products that satisfied his complex requirements as well as those of other architects and designers. Both clients and architects demanded a finished product of the highest quality, both in terms of design and execution.

In the Palm Beach years from 1919 to 1925, Mizner designed, built, and furnished well over thirty-five villas and all of them had to be completed in the offseason between April and December. To have accomplished this, especially considering the enormous scale of his projects, is nothing short of miraculous. The capacity to overcome challenge developed during his adventurous years of travel now began to pay dividends.

Florida in 1919 was a lightly populated state without significant industry and, worse for Mizner, South Florida was an even more remote and less developed part of the state. After the opening of the Flagler hotels, there was not much construction activity in the area around Palm Beach. In such an environment, all materials were purchased at a premium and any labor had to be developed from local resources. Alex Waugh began to work for Addison in 1922 and remarked: "Nothing was available, no tile, a shortage of the right timber, no hardware, cement like unto gold dust, paint hard to come by, rolled steel joists a dream. . . ."[1] What materials could be found were very expensive due to America's entry in World War I. The average price of twenty-nine leading building materials in the United States had increased 136 percent from 1914 to the end of 1919. Also, these materials were produced on an "as needed" basis and, since housing construction had come to a halt during the war, so too had the production of residential construction materials. As an example, domestic brick production in 1913 was eight billion units while, in 1919, it was only four and a half billion.[2]

Complicating the situation further were the more exotic requirements peculiar to Mizner's style of architecture. Among the materials that characterize Mediterranean Revival architecture are red barrel roof tiles, glazed floor tiles, and ironwork for gates, balconies, and windows. None of this was available from Europe due to the war and anything available in America was inappropriate both from the standpoint of design and quality. The solution to these immense problems would issue from the architect's determination and extensive knowledge of the building trades. His cast of mind motivated him to want to know how things worked, and this flame of curiosity routinely illumined the complexities of design and construction. Mizner's ingenuity and curiosity were innate but were certainly brought to the fore by necessity during his pioneer experiences.

Among Addison Mizner's many talents was an understanding of craft. During his two and a half years in the office of Willis Polk in San Francisco, he not only learned architecture but became intimately familiar with the building trades and developed an appreciation for the inherent beauty of materials. Alva Johnston remarked that Addison "picked up crafts as a born linguist picks up languages, and soon had more than a smattering of carpentry, house painting, bricklaying, masonry, plastering, plumbing and kindred lines."[3] Throughout his excursions to Central America and Europe, he had genuinely appreciated the work of the many artisans required to create a harmonious architectural composition. For him, the signature of the hand communicated an expressive language understood only by the initiated. To transform unskilled laborers into skilled artisans with a sympathy for the subtleties

Entrance façade of St. Edward's Church, Palm Beach, 1926. This elaborately carved Spanish baroque façade was made by Mizner Industries to the specifications of architect Mortimer Dickerson Metcalfe. By pouring a mixture of lime gravel and cement into molds, Mizner was able to create rough architectural parts that were then carved and finished by skilled artisans. Being able to produce such massive and distinctive stone parts allowed the architect to control costs and construction schedules.
Courtesy of Historical Society of Palm Beach County.

of various crafts, he established his own guild system. If he had nothing else to do, this would have been a formidable task in itself; however, he was busily engaged in every aspect of a project, from design to installation.

Addison Mizner's approach to architecture was akin to the medieval tradition where the entire construction project was overseen by the master mason, a process that included making his own materials. The master mason, like Mizner, was an individual who had risen to his position through the possession of a thorough knowledge of every facet of building. Mizner was aptly described as a practical technician who "could lay brick as well as any bricklayer, could cut stone, glaze and color tile, polish marble, fit wood, band iron, all the while instructing those of lesser talent and experience exactly how it should be done."[4] In fact, Mizner, a member of the local Florida union of painters, decorators, and paperhangers, was one of the rare architects to hold a union card.[5]

Beyond the mere possession of knowledge, Mizner importantly had an aptitude and willingness to mentor others. Alex Waugh recalled his own learning experience: "Addison was encyclopedic in the subject and had an uncanny ability of imparting knowledge so that it stuck."[6] Since many of his workers were Hispanic, it helped greatly that he spoke a fluent Spanish liberally sprinkled with colorful vernacular that his audience appreciated. Only later was he able to bring to

Palm Beach European craftsmen that would supervise the various specialty workshops, a collection of companies later to be known as Mizner Industries.

Addison Mizner's first challenge as he began construction on the Everglades Club was finding roof and floor tiles that would be appropriate in color and finish for the period Renaissance buildings whose spirit he was trying to capture. The shipping embargo put in place during the war left him only with domestic tiles he described as "stamped out and looked like painted tin when they were laid and were a horrible, lurid

La Ronda, 1928. To simulate the appearance of old buildings, Mizner produced red barrel roof tiles that varied in color and were applied unevenly. Tiles in Spain were inefficiently formed by artisans using their thighs as molds. To produce the large quantities required, Mizner made wooden molds in the shape of the human thigh that enabled him to create the appearance of a hand-formed tile.
Photograph by Craig Kuhner.

color. . . ."[7] His only alternative was to make them himself, a decision that necessitated the establishment of his own factory. Paris Singer supported Addison and agreed to finance a venture that began with the purchase of an existing business, The Novelty Works. Because the quality of product required by Mizner could only be made with skilled hands, he decided to name the business *Las Manos*, Spanish for "hands," suggesting that his tiles would be handcrafted.

Addison established the operation near the train tracks on Bunker Road in West Palm Beach to facilitate the receipt of materials. He experimented and found that clay from Georgia would yield the most satisfying results. He constructed drying sheds and three primitive kilns that were fired with pine logs from local forests. Once again, he had to investigate through trial and error the firing process whose temperatures would create the uneven, irregular surfaces that replicated the appearance of handmade tiles. Mary Fanton Roberts, the publisher of *Arts and Decoration* magazine, arrived in Palm Beach at the same time that Addison was beginning to experiment. In recalling her first visit, she said that "we all went at day dawn to see the first opening of the kiln—from which the tiles were taken by the Italian workman, overburnt and ruined."[8] Mizner eventually determined that, after partial drying, roof tiles of high quality and appropriate appearance were produced by baking at 2,600 degrees for four days.[9]

In Spain, the barrel shape of the tiles would have been formed over the thigh of the craftsman, an Old World method that was inefficient for his needs. Addison's solution was to create a wooden mold in the shape of a thigh, a form that could be efficiently reproduced to allow for large production runs. To achieve the appropriate shape, the molds were narrow on one end with solid wood in the center to create the subtle shaping of the thigh. Mizner then determined that the molds had to be sanded to prevent the clay from sticking to the wood. With this approach, his kilns initially produced approximately sixty-five thousand roof tiles per month.[10] More important to the architect, these tiles were irregular, undulating, and variegated in color, giving them the critical appearance of being handcrafted. He eventually increased the number of kilns when the quality of his product attracted the attention of other architects who were beginning their practices in the Palm Beach area. Mizner loved the irregular look of his tiles and preferred to emphasize the unevenness of a roof by having inexperienced men lay the tiles to ensure that it had the appearance of having been ravaged by time and weather.

Just as essential to Mizner's style of architecture was the Mediterranean floor tile. The process for making floor tiles was similar to that of roof tiles and involved having the workers shape each tile with their bare hands. In the beginning, he produced an unglazed square tile that was treated and waxed to produce a warm brown that satisfied the architect's discriminating eye. Later, he would expand the assortment to glazed tiles offered in various sizes and six shapes and thirteen colors.[11] Once again, Addison had to test various combinations to produce the desired colors. Alex Waugh wrote about the complex process of creating a color called *Mizner Blue*: "the average layman does not realize that a cerulean blue starts life, before firing, as maybe a muddy buff color. So, who, then, knew how to mix the pigments and just how long to leave the tile in the kiln. All these problems had to be worked out by very untrained labor."[12] The experimental nature of the manufacturing process and requirement of training labor were constant.

One feature of Mizner's Mediterranean architecture was the creation of openness by eliminating the barrier between interior and exterior space. One decorative object that was effectively employed in both areas was pottery in traditional sixteenth- and seventeenth-century Spanish shapes. Considering the variety of projects and the regular use of cloisters, loggias, and patios, his needs were substantial, so the sizes offered ranged from a small flower pot to a basin that could hold an orange tree. For the pottery collection, Mizner imported the glazing materials from Italy in various shades. Once again, he instructed his workmen on the subtleties of application and he fashioned kilns that produced an uneven heat to provide the

Warden Residence, 1922. Stairs at William Gray Warden house, 1922. The widespread use of tiles in Mediterranean buildings required Mizner to have access to a ready source of high-quality tiles, a demand he could only satisfy by making them himself. Using clay from Georgia and a firing process that created uneven surfaces and irregular colors, Mizner made tiles that appeared handmade. The Mizner blue tiles above were improbably produced from a clay that was originally buff colored.
Photograph by Craig Kuhner.

desired modulation of tone and color. These products became so successful that he eventually opened an alfresco showroom in the courtyard of the Via Mizner and another on South County Road.

Addison Mizner had developed a manufactory that would quickly become the largest employer in West Palm Beach, and he needed management assistance. In 1919 he was contacted by his sister, Min Chase, who informed Addison that her son Horace had just been discharged from military service and needed employment. She requested her brother to look up the son in New York. Typical of the loyal Addison, he dropped what he was doing, traveled to New York to locate Horace, and brought him back to Palm Beach. Addison's idea was that his nephew could manage the Las Manos pottery operation. As Addison noted, Horace "was the best natured slob I ever saw," but was "the most untidy war hero in the world."[13] Horace was charming, good natured, and convivial but was less disposed to bring order and efficiency to a growing business. The hiring of Horace Chase was less a sound business decision than a generous act of avuncular charity.

With the completion of the Everglades Club, Addison Mizner had immediately ascended to a level of celebrity he had never known. He was now sought by Palm Beach's grandest *habitués* to build homes, the realization of which brought him the title of society architect. This spate of attention caused a rift with Paris Singer who realized that, henceforth, he would have to share the professional services of Mizner. To the displeasure of Addison, Singer wanted to sell Las Manos potteries. At this point, Addison borrowed money to purchase the business, correctly reasoning that his own architectural projects would cover operational costs. Las Manos was the foundation for what would become in 1925 Mizner Industries, a series of workshops that crafted virtually all products required to construct and furnish his villas. Addison remarked that the level of design and execution was extremely sophisticated: "we were making something that could not be bought in the U. S. A."[14] Most South Florida architects recognized the same and became patrons.

In conjunction with the production of roof and floor tiles for the Everglades Club, Mizner also had organized workshops to produce furniture and wrought iron products. As he began to build houses for his growing clientele, the need became much greater for more diverse forms of furniture in larger quantities. In 1923, he established a larger furniture factory to address increased demand. The guiding principle of Addison Mizner for decorative furnishings was "If you can't get it, make it. But make it good and make it authentic."[15]

Since the furniture requirements for his projects were enormous, it was impossible to travel to Europe to satisfy such a large demand for period antiques. At the most sophisticated level, supply is limited and what exists is not always in pristine condition. The advantage that Addison's furniture workshops offered was the capability to repair pieces damaged in transit, to create missing parts for imperfect originals, and to reinforce properly pieces that would be subjected to heavy use. A good example is the chair. It was extremely difficult to find antique chairs in large sets and equally challenging to provide a three-hundred-year-old chair that did not need structural restoration. Mizner's shop could produce any quantity of chairs to satisfy the design requirements, and it could finish them in such a way as to be compatible with antique furniture in the same room. In a similar manner, chests were historically moved frequently, so it was not unusual to find that legs on antiques were wobbly or badly replaced. The Spanish word for furniture is "*meubles*," meaning "mobile," a term that suggests the portable nature of furniture. Such functional pieces, when retrieved for modern usage, frequently required replacement or repair.

The sources of inspiration for Mizner's reproduction furniture business came from two sources: original antique furniture that he regularly imported and from photographs of antique furniture that he meticulously maintained in his scrapbooks. When on a buying trip in Europe, Addison bought not only furniture but furniture parts, such as the leg of a chair or table that he found particularly interesting. Scholarly in his knowledge of decorative arts, he knew exactly what the rest of the piece should look like and instructed his workshops accordingly. Also,

his scrapbooks were organized by category, "Trestle Tables" as an example, and each category contained sometimes a hundred iterations to provide numerous variations of form and decoration. This not only satisfied his curiosity but allowed him to avoid duplication when furnishing the homes of demanding clients who insisted on exclusivity and differentiation.

The artisans that he taught became familiar with the materials and methods used in the finest examples of period Spanish furniture. Walnut, the principal wood used for fine furniture by the *ebanistas*, or cabinetmakers, in the sixteenth and

Drawer panel, Mizner Industries, circa 1925. This carved panel illustrates the high quality of craftsmanship that was a hallmark of all products of Mizner Industries. The depth and clarity of the carving speaks to the sophisticated artisans that Mizner employed. Although Mizner eventually brought European craftsmen to work in various aspects of his workshops, he also trained many unskilled laborers who were originally unfamiliar with the decorative arts. Photograph by Craig Kuhner.

seventeenth centuries, was imported to the Mizner workshops and was properly cured before cutting. Mizner, the master, instructed his apprentices until they were intimate with the Old World methods of joinery, decoration, and finish. Joints were cut by hand and reinforced with the use of dowels. Like the antiques that inspired them, edges of the reproductions were softened, showing the wear and usage of centuries; surfaces were irregular, betraying the natural movement of wood over time; and the color of wood varied, owing to the effects of exposure to sunlight. Finally, artisans polished and waxed each piece by hand, imparting a soft patination that revealed all the scars of time intentionally created in the shop.

Many writers have criticized Mizner's furniture operation for creating "fakes." His intention was not to deceive but rather to replicate the pleasing proportions, details, and personality of the original pieces. Beyond the aesthetic reason is a practical one. It would have been impossible to furnish one of his large rooms with exclusively antique furniture. Since, by necessity, he was forced to mix old with new, the reproduction furniture used in a room would have to live harmoniously side by side with other pieces that might be three hundred years old. To do otherwise would have created a visual incongruity to the refined eye. The furniture made in his shop, still to be found in Palm Beach interiors today, withstood the destructive effects of the South Florida climate as well as the ravages of time.

Mizner's furniture operation gave him the flexibility to make two levels of product. If one of his clients had a very sophisticated antique piece and wanted to replicate it to create a pair, Addison could accommodate such a request. On the other hand, if he or another architect were working with a hotel that required large, repetitive quantities of furniture, Mizner Industries could take advantage of economy of scale to supply high quality at a reasonable price. He also designed a selection of rattan chairs, settees, and tables and a small assortment of iron furniture to be used on patios or courtyards. Since Spanish chairs were upright and rather severe by modern standards, he made fully upholstered seating to provide comfort and convenience. A capacious overstuffed chair designed for large men was called the "Papa Mizner chair" and a smaller version was the "Mama Mizner chair." Advertising from the 1920s compares the experience of sitting in Mizner upholstery to "resting in a fleecy cloud."[16] Whatever he made, the primary focus was always quality, an attribute determined by good design, appropriate materials, and a high level of craftsmanship.

As Addison Mizner traveled to Europe during the Palm Beach offseason to buy antiques for his many projects for the coming season, he decided to start an antiques business. In Paris in the summer of 1922, Mizner happened to run into Alex Waugh, a young acquaintance from England who was

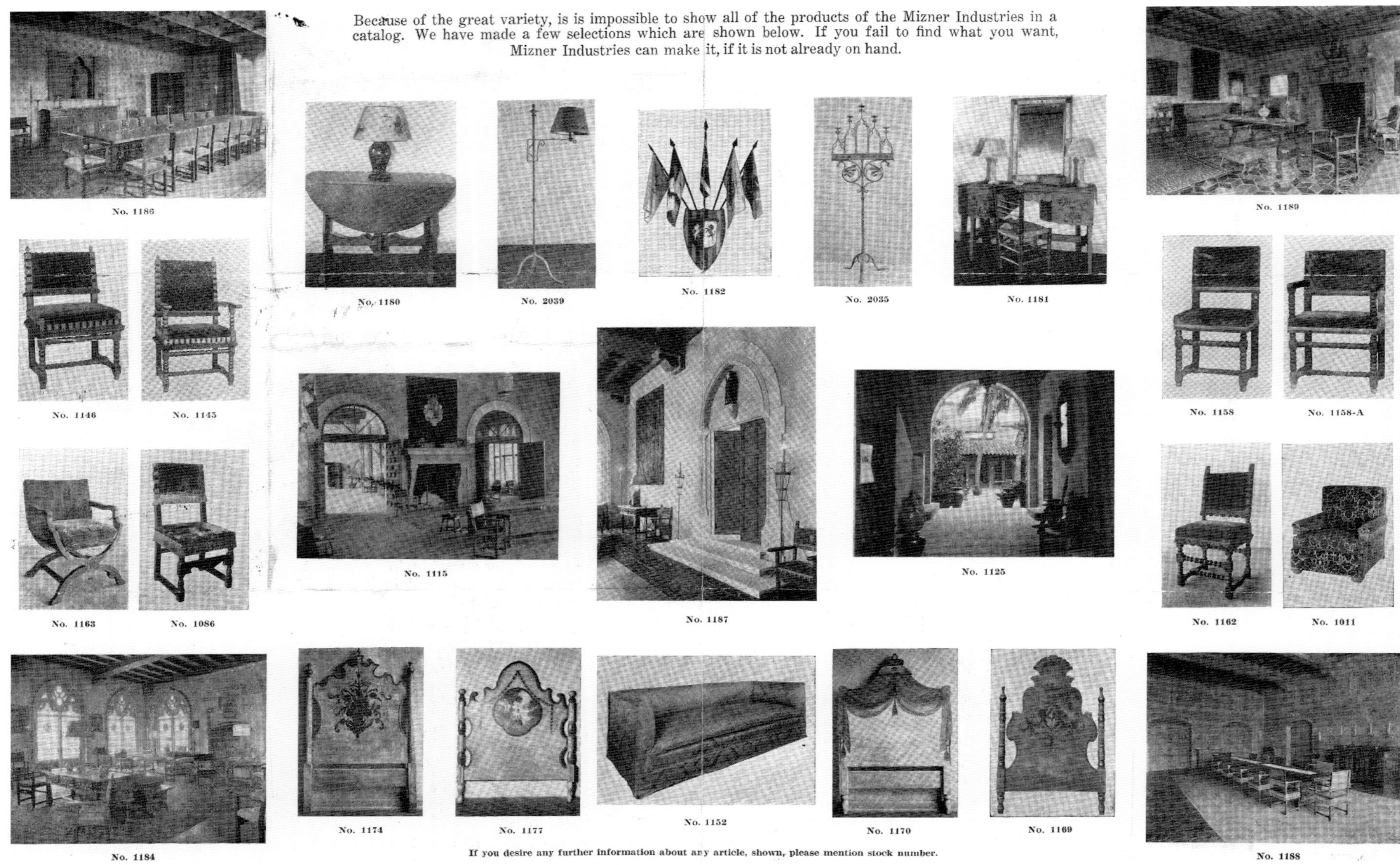

A page from the furniture catalogue of Mizner Industries. Due to a lack of skilled artisans in South Florida in 1918, Mizner established his own workshops to fill the decorative needs of his sophisticated projects. Mizner produced floor and roof tiles, ironwork, stained glass, carved stone, and even tapestries. This page illustrates a broad assortment of furniture, including fully upholstered chairs and sofas.

Courtesy of Boca Raton Historical Society.

very knowledgeable about English eighteenth-century fine and decorative art. When he learned that the Englishman was looking for a job, he hired him on the spot to travel with him to Spain on a buying trip and, upon returning to Palm Beach, to run his antiques business. This was a good business decision because there was more demand than supply, and there was the cachet that accrued to Addison from offering such a high level of quality that was previously found only in New York City. Displaying his erudition and his willingness to teach, he instructed his new employee about the richness of Spanish history and decorative arts.

As ironwork was essential to the architectural expression of Mizner's Mediterranean Revival style, he was constantly searching for iron grilles, grates, gates, lanterns, and even parts of old pieces. With his encyclopedic mind, he could imagine a new composition just from looking at a fragment. His forge also gave him the flexibility to create compatible iron pieces that did not exist centuries ago such as the backplate for a light switch. Alex Waugh described Mizner's creative approach as a

Spanish bed, circa 1600. Addison Mizner had long been attracted to Spanish furniture when he began importing Hispanic antiquities for resale in 1904. With its spirally fluted posts and elaborately carved cresting of angels flanking a coat of arms on the headboard, this was a particularly fine example of Renaissance Spanish furniture. Mizner found that selling antiques was very profitable and, beginning in the early 1920s, took long trips to Spain every summer to replenish his inventory.

Courtesy of the Preservation Foundation of Palm Beach, Palm Beach, Florida.

La Ronda, Great Hall, 1928. Extensive use of ironwork was a distinctive characteristic of Mediterranean Revival architecture. Mizner Industries produced all manner of iron products including the rejas, doors, stair railing, and chandelier seen in the magnificent and dramatic stairway of one of Mizner's grandest houses.
Photograph by Craig Kuhner.

mystery that could create something from nothing: "Addison would spend hours going over all these oddments and out of them would emerge some most lovely things—stair balusters which started life hundreds of years ago as a garden railing."[17] Beyond the array of structural iron products, Mizner also produced more delicate objects such as tole.

Once again, he taught everyone associated with the metal shop the process of forging and educated them to perceive the nuances of craftsmanship and finish appropriate to the period. He later enticed Italian craftsmen skilled in Old World methods to join him in Palm Beach. The shop used machine tools but much of the process was executed by hand. To make rejas, the protective window grilles typical of Spanish Renaissance architecture, Mizner's artisans banded the joints even though soldering them would have been both quicker and less expensive to produce. He preferred the traditional method because it resulted in a product that was more aesthetically pleasing and more structurally sound. Similarly, he preferred a finish that had the same aged patina of the antique ironwork he brought back from Spain. To achieve this look, he allowed the wrought iron to rust by leaving it overnight in an acid solution. The next day craftsmen would wax the pieces and then rub them with rottenstone.[18] As with everything he did, nuance and detail were important components in creating products that were faithful to the original. As was the case with all of the product categories made in his shops, it was through trial and error that he discovered the important subtleties that were always imparted to his craftsmen.

Addison not only spent a significant amount of time teaching others but also continued to educate himself. In looking through his scrapbooks, especially those relating to ironwork, it is evident that he constantly made simple, loose sketches of objects to refine his eye to proportion and balance. He also constantly worked to improve his understanding of craft by collecting data and articles on techniques and processes relating to iron construction. His scrapbooks suggest a serious dedication that belies the deprecating commentary of some critics who considered him an amateur. The habit of continuously educating himself brought him into contact with artisans that he was able to entice to work at Mizner Industries. Among those were Percival Dietsch, a German artist and draftsman who created designs for the workshops and Joseph Messinna, a Roman who became the foreman of the tile and pottery operation.[19] He also hired another Italian from Florence who assumed responsibility for the ironworks and a woman from England who was a trained specialist in working leaded glass.[20]

With the great success of his various manufacturing businesses, Addison consolidated all production facilities under the name of Mizner Industries in 1925. The companies that were combined were Addison Mizner Inc., the parent company that included the architecture practice; Las Manos, the factory that made tile, pottery, and stone; and Antigua Shops, which sold antiques, reproduced furniture, and manufactured iron. To this assortment he had just added a manufacturing component to supply the leaded and stained glass frequently used in his houses, hotels, and clubs.

Stained and leaded glass were hallmarks of the Mizner style and could be found in virtually all of his large projects. Tinted glass was not only architecturally distinctive in that it was set into important stone surrounds, but it also served to soften the bright Florida sunshine. The sensation of light passing through tinted glass resulted in an inviting, soft atmosphere in a room, an effect Addison liked to create in his interiors. After a late afternoon concert in his own home, he was moved to describe the impression: "daylight died through the soft tints of the colored glass."[21] Addison's objective was to design architecture that was picturesque and interiors that were evocative of a romantic past. Refracting natural light in such a manner was one way to achieve this.

Mizner's creativity and curiosity constantly led him to experimentation. Always in need of complex and dynamic expressions that served as points of contrast in his compositions, he was in need of furniture, carved doors, or room paneling to create this visual interest. Such rare objects were expensive whether he acquired originals on buying trips to Europe or had them reproduced in his workshops. After much trial and error, in 1928 he created Woodite, a composite material that he was able to patent. Woodite was a mixture of wood shavings and a cohesive compound that could be poured and cast into the shape of any decorative or architectural element. This innovation provided the latitude to customize anything that would appropriately complement and enhance his projects at a reasonable cost. He could take molds of architectural elements such as doors, moldings, or elaborate decorative details to fashion Renaissance-style paneling for an entire room. Complex carvings on furniture could now be reproduced economically and the finished product had the visual authenticity of the original. It reproduced all of the characteristics of the original wood: graining, knots, holes, and worn spots. Woodite was hard enough to be

Villa Flora, Moorish Window, 1923. An important part of Mizner Industries was the cast stone works. It was difficult to find and ship old stone and it was expensive to carve new stone, so Mizner ingeniously developed a method of casting stone in molds. After casting, his artisans would then refine the carvings to produce the crisp detail that he demanded. Photograph by Craig Kuhner.

La Ronda, Coffered Ceiling, 1928. Elaborate and complicated millwork was a regular feature in most of Mizner's large houses and a coffered ceiling of such complexity would have been extremely expensive to make in his workshops. In 1928, Mizner created an economical alternative that he patented as Woodite, a composite material that simulated the look and performance of wood and that could be cast into any shape.
Photograph by Craig Kuhner.

sawed, nailed, or carved and it could be stained, painted, or gilded.[22]

From the beginning of his architectural practice in Palm Beach, Addison Mizner faced a similar issue of supply and cost with ornamental stonework. Even if cost were not an impediment to his clients, period medieval and Renaissance architectural elements of stone were difficult to find, complex to reassemble, and inefficient to ship due to bulk and heavy weight. The time required for consolidation, packing, and shipping was slow and made meeting tight deadlines difficult. A solution could not be found locally as Florida stone was rare. He had first tried to create critical architectural parts by pouring cement into molds, a process that produced unsatisfying results in both quality and color. Experimentation eventually produced a better product that was used not only by Mizner but, like all of the products of Mizner Industries, extensively specified by other regional architects.

By using a new mixture composed of lime gravel and cement, Mizner now could manufacture surrounds, balustrades, columns, and capitals that more faithfully represented the antique that he preferred. The process created rough parts that could subsequently be sculpted and finished and it reproduced cracks, open seams, and chips, all of the imperfections found in the originals that were highly valued by the architect. As in other divisions of Mizner Industries, Addison gradually

E. F. Hutton Brokerage Office, 1930. Addison Mizner thought the characteristics of keystone both distinctive and appropriate for his Palm Beach architecture. A material that does not retain heat, keystone's holes and rough texture create an interesting, variegated color. Unfortunately, Mizner started this business in 1929 just before the Wall Street Crash. Like other products of Mizner Industries, keystone was specified by other Florida architects.
Photograph by Craig Kuhner.

brought to his stone works European artisans whose skills were oriented to Old World techniques and whose sensibilities knew how three-hundred-year-old stone fragments should look and feel. German craftsmen have a long heritage in stone carving and Mizner had several working for him. In 1924, Joe Mueller arrived from Germany to supervise a team of 106 men that included two of his countrymen that filled the important positions of drafting and mold-making.[23] Together with Mizner, they introduced products that reproduced the look of travertine and marble. Always searching for ways to diminish costs, Mizner also developed a process to produce precast plastering for walls and ceilings.

In 1929 Addison Mizner made a considerable investment to begin producing quarry keystone that could be used for outdoor terraces, stairs, and walls. To start the business, Mizner spent approximately $75,000 in plant, equipment, and installation with the most significant expenditure for a huge saw powered by a fifty-horsepower engine.[24] The limestone was extracted in eight-ton blocks and brought by railroad to West Palm Beach from the quarry on Windley's Island in the Florida Keys that was leased from the Florida East Coast Railway. The blocks were cut into two-inch slabs that were then planed and, if necessary, carved. It was estimated that the forty employees could handle a carload of stone a day. That this was another Mizner product that would be used by local architects and builders was immediately confirmed when Maurice Fatio, an important Palm Beach architect, immediately specified keystone for three projects, one of which was his own house.[25] It was unfortunate that Mizner made this investment just before the Wall Street crash in late October. Nonetheless, Mizner acquired another quarry in 1931 near Bradenton on the west coast to fulfill stone supply contracts for two Florida post offices. This is another example that illustrates the reach that Mizner Industries had as a purveyor of building products well beyond the architect's own needs.

Another innovation devised by Mizner out of necessity was bronze sliding doors and windows. In his desire to blend outdoor and indoor space, he used heavily fenestrated rooms. In desiring to give his clients the functional freedom to control the elements, he developed a new framing system that could survive the weather and could be operated without complication and effort. Beyond functionality, he wanted a product, unlike those then available in the market, that was not visually heavy and that would not rust. He found that doors and windows made of bronze would satisfy all of his requirements, both in terms of unchallenging performance and tasteful appearance. His products had the added advantage of being made to disappear by sliding into a concealed frame in the wall or floor when open. The Mizner workshops also produced textiles such as flags and tapestries.

Mizner Industries was a unique operation that supplied an extremely refined array of architectural components and decorative art to a highly sophisticated market of affluent, influential clients and demanding, cultivated architects. A passage from historian Donald Curl attests to the respect accorded Mizner Industries and its importance to the South Florida building community:

> Every architect and builder in the Palm Beaches, and many throughout South Florida, looked to Mizner industries for the items needed to decorate their houses. Thus, Mizner tiles on the roof and on the floor, Mizner ironwork for grills, gates, screens, and lighting fixtures, Mizner cast stone for window- and door surrounds, columns, and capitals, and even Mizner lead and stained-glass windows, enclosed in Mizner bronze frames, can be found in practically every Palm Beach house built in the 1920s.[26]

This praise was borne out financially as Mizner Industries turned a profit of approximately $39,000 a year from 1923 until the end of the decade.[27] This is noteworthy considering that the efficiency of Mizner Industries was always compromised by regularly having feckless family members or retainers running various aspects of the business. It should be noted that business was curtailed significantly in the period 1926–1929 due to the real estate bubble and two hurricanes. As home building increased in South Florida in the 1920s, Mizner Industries also faced competition from manufacturers of decorative products from Palm Beach to Coral Gables. Perhaps the impact of the business is best illustrated in 1925, a year in which net profit was $152,000, an even more impressive figure when considering the company absorbed a bad debt of $150,000 that year.[28] With this venture, Addison Mizner not only made money but developed a business that was vertically integrated, making it possible to fulfill his very specific needs and to satisfy exigencies of both budgeting and scheduling.

If all that Addison Mizner did was to create this manufacturing business, he would merit regional recognition; but he also simultaneously started an architectural practice and developed artisanal workshops from scratch within a compressed period of time, a truly remarkable accomplishment. Only a man with Mizner's encompassing erudition could have conceived of such a grand project, and only a pioneer with his boundless energy could have succeeded in such an ambitious endeavor. Mizner Industries could only have been created by a master builder. The architect would now direct knowledge and energy to the largest project he had ever conceived.

CHAPTER THIRTEEN

THE GREATEST RESORT IN THE WORLD

Addison Mizner was endowed with an expansive, fertile imagination aspiring to the grand gesture. In 1925 he conceived his most ambitious idea, a utopian vision of such broad dimension that it could only be realized in an environment where the necessary variables were in harmonious alignment. Since arriving in Palm Beach in 1918, he had benefitted from a concord of timing, location, ethos, and concentration of wealth that nurtured his prodigious talent and bestowed fame and wealth. Now in his most productive years, the architect decided to develop his own resort in Boca Raton, an unremarkable farming village twenty-five miles south of Palm Beach. This sweeping project offered the potential for achieving a level of affluence beyond anything he had ever known and for being perceived among the social elite not simply as a friend but as an equal. In his mind, he was quite simply in the right place at the right time.

While the opportunity to create his own unconstrained vision of urban design was irresistible, so too was the potential to enhance his financial situation. While his Palm Beach

Among the first buildings constructed in Boca Raton were the administration buildings where the Mizner Development Corporation was installed. At this point, the building was under construction as can be seen by the palm tree that has not yet been planted. This photograph reveals the undeveloped nature of Boca Raton in 1925.
Courtesy of Boca Raton Historical Society.

architectural practice provided the means to sustain a very nice lifestyle, he now had an expanding list of family retainers that required his support. Brother Wilson and nephew Horace

Chase were already on his payroll. Hoping to improve the ill health of his brother Henry, an Episcopal cleric, he had arranged for him, his wife, and daughter to move to Florida. He assisted his sister, Min Chase, and her husband who had lost Stag's Leap, their Napa Valley home, and he doted on their daughter Ysabel, his favorite member of the family. Noted for his generosity, friend Alice DeLamar wondered if his family was not taking advantage of Addison's kindness. Conditions in America gave him no reason to doubt his ability to provide for his family.

While many things in life were subject to flux, prosperity in America by 1925 had come to be seen as a constant. A short recession in 1921 notwithstanding, economic growth and escalating stock values since 1914 supported the notion of an ever-rising arc of prosperity. Americans, viewing their country as a land of bounty, had become convinced of a better future, a general belief affirmed in 1909 by Herbert Croly, the founder of the *New Republic*: "From the beginning Americans have been anticipating and projecting a better future. From the beginning the Land of Democracy has been figured as the Land of Promise."[1] With an optimistic temperament and daring pioneer spirit, Addison Mizner was the embodiment of this belief.

By 1925, business growth had created a level of prosperity that had introduced many Americans to a world of comfort and leisure. In January of that year, President Calvin Coolidge addressed the Society of American Newspaper Editors: "After all, the chief business of the American people is business. They are profoundly concerned with producing, buying, selling, investing and prospering in the world."[2] Led by automobile manufacturing, many industries prospered during the 1920s. Residential home building in the suburbs, road construction, oil, rubber, and steel all benefitted immensely from the enormous success of car sales. American ingenuity not only created a higher standard of living for most but also dramatically increased the number of million-dollar incomes from seventy-five in 1924 to 207 in 1925.[3] The decade of the 1920s was becoming a period of affluence and dissipation, a time of spending and speculation. The availability of easy credit and seductive advertising proved intoxicating, inducing families to live beyond their means. The propensity among the more adventurous for new styles of dress, dancing, and speakeasies gave rise to the rebellion and indulgence of the "Roaring Twenties."

Florida, benefitting substantially in this climate of optimism and confidence, was developing the reputation as an Eden. By 1925, the state's population had grown to 1,264,000, an increase of 31 percent since 1920.[4] Transportation was markedly improved as construction of both railroads and public roads increased dramatically. The development of the Dixie Highway, begun in 1914 by Carl Fisher, connected the Midwest with the South and brought vacationers streaming into Florida. There was a desire among many to escape the crowded industrial cities of the North and Midwest that had begun to develop during World War I. Finally, there was the attractive incentive that the state of Florida had no state income or inheritance taxes.

Supported by the chambers of commerce of various cities, the state also mounted an advertising campaign that promoted the easy lifestyle and sunny climate. The allure of Florida was especially potent when northerners in the middle of winter read advertising copy describing Florida as a land "bathed in passionate caresses of the southern sun."[5] Formerly a place strictly for the wealthy, Florida had now become a destination for the middle class as well. Kenneth Roberts of the *Saturday Evening Post* estimated that more than two and a half million people came to Florida during 1925.[6] Growth was so visibly perceptible in Miami that it moved William Jennings Bryan, former presidential candidate, to remark: "Miami is the only city in the world where you can tell a lie at breakfast that will come true by evening."[7] Optimism, mobility, and temptation induced many pioneers to venture south, and effective advertising and publicity offered proof that Florida real estate was a good investment.

The significant increase in tourism was naturally accompanied by augmented sales of real estate, and the velocity of

William Jennings Bryan was a great orator and the Democratic nominee for the office of the presidency three times. After retiring from politics, he and his wife built a house in an area of Miami that would become Coral Gables. Considering the city alluring, he promoted tourism and the development of Miami by making speeches. Here he sits poolside in Coral Gables speaking before a group of people about the virtues of the region. He said that "Miami is the only city in the world where you can tell a lie at breakfast that will come true by evening." Courtesy of Library of Congress.

activity was such that land values increased to an unprecedented level. In the four years from 1921 to 1925, the assessed property values in the city of Miami increased 560 percent from almost $64 million to over $421 million.[8] In 1925 it was estimated that there were two thousand real estate offices and twenty-five thousand agents in Miami selling land at a time when "inside" lots within a forty-mile radius of the city were selling for between $8,000 and $20,000 and actual seashore lots sold for between $20,000 and $75,000.[9] Palm Beach property was even more expensive. A New York lawyer had been offered $240,000 for a parcel of land ten years before the boom and sold it in 1923 for $800,000. A year later, it was converted into building lots that sold for an aggregate price of $1.5 million.[10] During the 1924–1925 season, Florida investors bought approximately $300 million in real estate.[11]

Speculation was rampant and many investors were never present in the state for the purchase or sale of their property. Land could be purchased with a "binder," a non-refundable down payment that required that the balance be paid in thirty days. The speculators intended to sell the land at a profit before the balance came due, and they made money as long as prices continued to rise. As part of its promotional campaign, the state of Florida was actively involved in placing stories in northern newspapers that validated the security of Florida real estate and trumpeted the profits that were being realized. A man walking down the street in New York City in 1925 saw a sign in a shop window relating the story of a man who made $500,000 in a month in Florida real estate.[12]

This was the feverish situation in 1924 when Addison Mizner first decided to go into the development business. He was further emboldened by his own architectural and social success that engendered a desire to build at a far greater scale and to create a new mode of living in South Florida. Mizner's vision for a new town derived from many different urban planning and architectural trends that had started in the 1880s and were very important topics of discussion in the San Francisco office of Willis Polk during Mizner's apprenticeship. Polk firmly believed that cities could be intelligently planned by embracing the principles of the Academic movement and the City Beautiful movement. Polk and his contemporaries believed that the successful future of San Francisco depended on the creation of a city whose beauty matched that of its environment.

The Cloister Inn, Boca Raton, 1925. Addison Mizner had been greatly influenced by the Chicago World's Fair during his visit in 1893 and embraced the City Beautiful movement that it represented. Desiring to create Boca Raton as the "first tailor-made city in the world," the architect believed that the beauty of the buildings should be the equal of the captivating environment. The Cloister Inn was a good example of the harmony and beauty that was intended to define Boca Raton.
Courtesy of Boca Raton Historical Society.

The City Beautiful movement's most successful and compelling display was the 1893 World's Columbian Exposition in Chicago. The leaders of the exposition's design team were Daniel Burnham and John W. Root who, with many other famous architects, determined that the architecture of the exposition should be unified. They agreed that the neoclassical style would be employed and that the height of the cornice line would be regulated. Richard Morris Hunt, McKim, Mead & White, George B. Post, William L. Jenney, and the firm of Adler and Sullivan would turn the fair into a laboratory for the City Beautiful movement, thereby strengthening the agenda of the era's Progressive reformers who believed that cities must be both beautiful and efficient.

In January 1891, the architects gathered in Chicago for a planning and design meeting at which they decided to paint all of the buildings around the Court of Honor white, a decision that resulted in the description, the "White City." Mizner learned a great deal about planning, design, and the City Beautiful movement while in the office of Willis Polk and in the company of so many architects for whom the movement was a guiding light. Over the next three decades, many cities around the country were beautified by heeding the ideals of the City Beautiful movement.

While Mizner's decision to develop a great resort city must have been informed by what he had learned in San Francisco, a more successful experiment in City Beautiful planning and design was less than eighty miles south of Palm Beach in Coral Gables, a suburb of Miami. This development was the vision of George E. Merrick, the son of a Congregationalist minister from the environs of Pittsburgh. Merrick moved to South Florida in 1898 at the age of twelve, departed to study law in the East, and returned in 1911 upon the death of his father. As a county commissioner, he became an administrator of the highway system in Dade County and was fascinated by the ways that transportation controlled growth patterns.

In 1922 he began to plan and build Coral Gables on three thousand acres of land. In the next three years, Merrick spent $20 million on infrastructure and buildings, including one thousand Mediterranean Revival houses to complement the city's core, which included the Biltmore Hotel and a number of country clubs.[13] He used a uniform style of architecture called "modified Mediterranean" and developed what was described in advertising as "America's Most Beautiful Suburb."[14] Mizner could not have been unaware of this development, just as Merrick must have certainly been aware of Mizner's accomplishments in Palm Beach.

In addition to Merrick's Coral Gables, there were other examples of financially rewarding Florida real estate development right before his eyes. After completing the Dixie

Highway, Carl Fisher devoted himself to developing Miami Beach, turning a mangrove swamp into a resort destination that was incorporated in 1915. At the same time that Addison Mizner was considering his grand project, his friend Paris Singer was contemplating a proposed resort on the barrier island just north of Palm Beach that he had just purchased. Singer's many exploits in Florida real estate were well known, especially to Mizner. All of these men were examples of entrepreneurs who had already realized handsome profits from local development activities.

Before turning to Boca Raton, Addison Mizner first conceived in 1924 a plan for Mizner Mile, a strip of land in Boynton Beach intended as an elegant beachfront resort. This was Mizner's first attempt to substantiate his vision for a comprehensive ocean city, the first to be entirely conceived and built by an architect. Mizner Mile, situated on Old Ocean Boulevard, was to include a club, polo fields, houses designed by Mizner, and a two-thousand-room hotel modeled on "the lines of a Spanish monastery."[15] Though it was not ultimately realized, he learned valuable lessons that would apply to his design of Boca Raton. In retrospect, Mizner probably conceived the master plan too quickly and was too optimistic that the local citizenry, small as it was, would welcome the fundamental change in Boynton's relationship with the ocean, even if conceived by the legendary Mizner.

Local history suggests that Mizner planned to exchange the design of a new Boynton City Hall for city commissioners' permission to build his hotel and club. The commissioners were attempting to raise money for this project, and Mizner assumed that a simple *quid pro quo* would satisfy the community. Early in 1925, Mizner finally persuaded the three-member commission to give him a sixty-two-hundred-foot stretch of Old Ocean Boulevard, the central artery running through the town. For Mizner's purposes, the road was inconveniently situated too close to the ocean to provide oceanfront lots with sufficient size and privacy for the luxury market.

After Mizner's group built a parallel road west of Ocean Boulevard, the Boynton community began to sense its loss of beach access and organized protests. Before legal action could be taken by the community, the Mizners took matters into their own hands and attempted to destroy the old road. In true Mizner fashion, Wilson showed up late one evening attired in white tie and tails to direct the bulldozers to their surreptitious task. When angry residents put a stop to the demolition, the Mizners abandoned Mizner Mile. The poor performance by the development group generated unfavorable publicity and, at this stage in his career, Mizner could scarcely afford to embarrass himself, or his backers, with the humiliation of having been run from a town ten miles south of Palm Beach. As a result, Addison designed plans for the Boynton Woman's Club without fee in an effort to make amends to the city.

Now focused on development, an enthusiastic Mizner failed to recognize his loosening hold on Palm Beach architectural leadership as well as the loss of former clients to new and worthy competitors. Another disturbing fact was that he had squandered significant capital in the Boynton fiasco; however, this was mitigated by the fact that Mizner Industries, the favored source for building materials and decorative products, was providing the architect with sufficient capital to continue his experiments in development. Most critically, Mizner had wasted almost a year and that simple fact would ultimately prove to be a significant factor when considering his eventual plight in Boca Raton.

With his quest for a new city unsated, Mizner and his investors turned in March 1925 to Boca Raton, eighteen miles south of Boynton, to create "the world's most architecturally beautiful playground."[16] Articles immediately began to appear in the *Palm Beach Post* announcing the acquisition of oceanfront property in Boca Raton by Rodman Wanamaker for a syndicate led by Addison Mizner. Mizner had formed the Mizner Development Corporation and counted among his directors such names as William K. and Harold Vanderbilt, Paris Singer, Rodman Wanamaker, Elizabeth Arden, Clarence H. Geist, Irving Berlin, and the Duchess

T. Coleman du Pont was president of E. I. du Pont de Nemours and Company and a two-term senator from the state of Delaware. Du Pont was one of the investors in the Mizner Development Corporation and served as the chairman of a board that included William K. and Harold Vanderbilt, Rodman Wanamaker, Irving Berlin, and Elizabeth Arden. With the resignation of du Pont from the board, Mizner's Boca Raton project was doomed.
Courtesy of Library of Congress.

of Sutherland. The chairman of the board was T. Coleman du Pont, former president of E. I. du Pont de Nemours and a newly elected US senator. Mizner began his company by selling a total of $5 million in stock mostly to his directors; however, he did allocate $500,000 of stock to the "average Floridian," a subscription that was consumed in less than a week.[17]

The corporation continued to purchase land, eventually amassing approximately fifteen thousand acres that included two miles of oceanfront property and, on May 31, it placed large advertisements in local newspapers announcing the sale of residential lots in Boca Raton. The ads announced "The First Tailor-Made City in All the World" created for "men of large affairs" and assured that all residential buildings would be "architecturally supervised by Addison Mizner."[18] Such colossal scale demanded an architect with a large reservoir of imagination and originality. The name of the architect promised luxury; the names of his directors conferred cachet. The only thing more remarkable were the plans.

Addison Mizner's plan for Boca Raton was vast and all-encompassing. This was an urban planning project that was to be the culminating statement of an already distinguished career in architecture. His audacious conception embraced not simply grand houses that had become his trademark in Palm

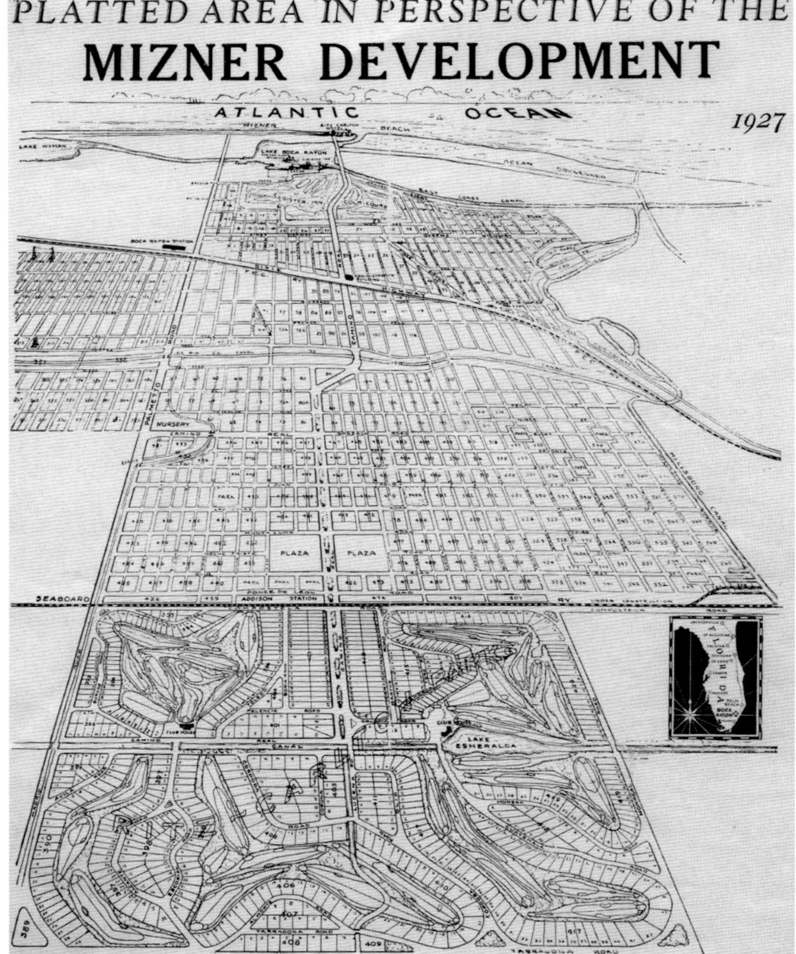

Plat of Boca Raton, 1925. Mizner's ambitious, and only, urban plan was thoughtful and imaginative and was influenced by his 1893 extended stay in Chicago at the height of the World's Columbian Exposition. The first large example of the planning principles underlying the City Beautiful movement had been planned by Daniel Burnham and others known by Mizner, including Willis Polk, his employer and Burnham's representative in San Francisco for the city's urban planning initiative.
Courtesy of Boca Raton Historical Society.

Beach but also an industrial area, residential areas for workers, as well as a subdivision dedicated to blacks. An advertisement stressed that Boca Raton was a development where "the most modest home builder in Boca Raton is assured an enjoyment of life in every way equal to that of its largest and most elaborate estate owner."[19] Infrastructure projects included an air terminal to accommodate passenger planes and hydroplanes, a deep water inlet, and yacht basin. He intended to weave sixty-one miles of canals throughout the development to create "the Venice of America."[20] The Mediterranean Revival style he so loved would be articulated in its most expressive form to create a dramatic and scenographic masterpiece.

As was his practice in Palm Beach, Mizner assumed responsibility for overall design, planning, and construction to ensure unity and integrity. He was consumed with everything, from approving small details of streets to designing grand villas for the elite. As an example, desiring to eliminate anything that might blemish the visual harmony, he placed conduits underground to hide all electrical wires. His purview even extended to cultivating forty acres of plants, bushes, and flowers to provide sufficient plantings for landscaping the large project. All details funneled into his grand vision, expressed in an interview in the summer of 1925: "It is my plan to create a city that is direct and simple; to make homes that are direct and livable, to make streets that are suitable for traffic, to make shops that

are inviting and parks that are beautiful . . . to give Florida and the nation a resort city perfect as study and ideals can make it."[21]

Mizner's first objective was to buy building materials and organize a construction site. Said at the time to be the largest requisition ever made in the state of Florida, he ordered a massive quantity of materials that included six million feet of lumber, fifty-seven hundred tons of structural steel, two thousand tons of reinforcing steel, nineteen thousand tons of crushed rock, thirty-five thousand tons of concrete, fourteen thousand pounds of nails, and seven thousand palmetto trees.[22] He then took the tropical wilderness of Boca Raton and transformed it into a work site that accommodated hundreds of workers and various manufacturing plants. In order to receive the pleasure yachts, Mizner also oversaw the widening and deepening of the inlet that connected the ocean with Lake Boca Raton.

The focal point of the theatrical paradise was the Camino Real, a 160-foot-wide boulevard that extended two and a half miles from the eastern beach to a golf course community in the west. The Camino traversed the Intracoastal Waterway with a "Venetian" bridge that contained a three-story tower with an apartment for the bridge keeper. As this axis ran westward, it led to an expansive plaza that housed Addison Station, an impressive terminal for the newly proposed route of the Seaboard Airline Railroad. From there, it reached the western

Promotional material, The Mizner Development Corporation, 1925. The central feature of Boca Raton was to be the Camino Real, the main entrance road to the city. Dramatically bisecting this road was a grand canal flanked by palm trees and graced with gondolas. This picturesque watercolor of the canal was used in corporate promotional material. Courtesy of Boca Raton Historical Society.

terminus represented by the Ritz-Carlton golfing community. To maximize profits, Mizner created premium lots on both geographical extremes. Expensive oceanfront property was balanced with highly desirable lots in the westernmost section of Boca Raton sited around the golf course in Ritz-Carlton Park.

Adding to the allure of Boca Raton was a picturesque canal that bisected the Camino Real for well over half its length. It extended from the El Rio canal, an existing waterway running north and south, through a group of shopping arcades to the center of the Ritz-Carlton community in the west. With the beginning of Mizner's canal, the width of the Camino Real expanded to 220 feet. The literature of the Mizner Development Corporation stated that the canal was modeled on the Botofago district, a stylish beachfront community in Rio de Janeiro. In reality, the actual details of Mizner's conception related very closely to a canal located in a less sophisticated neighborhood farther west of the Botofago. As was the habit of the corporation's public relations department, truth was bent sufficiently to create imagery appropriate for the splendid development.

Florida developers knew from the example of Carl Fisher in Miami what was required to market, promote, and sell a large resort development in South Florida. In addition to a plat map codifying lots and a description of infrastructure and entertainment facilities, Addison Mizner immediately needed a hotel to house prospective buyers. A compelling hotel served as a social and commercial nexus where the most effective sales pitch could be made in a gracious, charming environment. Anticipating the need to accommodate a large number of visitors, Mizner designed the Castillo del Rey, a thousand-room luxury hotel sited on the beach that was to be "the world's most complete and artistic hostelry."[23] With a budget of $6 million, the Castillo could unquestionably fulfill that claim.[24]

It was announced in May that the Ritz-Carlton Investment Corporation would operate the hotel. This was a prestigious collaboration for Mizner, one that certainly enhanced his commercial aspirations; however, it did problematically alter the building schedule. Desiring to reduce the number of rooms and to change interior configuration, the Ritz-Carlton commissioned the New York firm of Warren & Wetmore to customize the interior space while leaving Mizner in charge of the building design. Recognizing the delay resulting from the involvement of another architectural firm and desperately needing a hotel for promotional purposes, he announced on May 29, 1925, that a smaller one-hundred-room hotel would be built on the west side of Lake Boca Raton. Designed with a cloister surrounding a courtyard, the hotel would be named The Cloister Inn and would be operational by January 1926.

In addition to the immediate need of a hotel, Addison Mizner tried to anticipate all of the luxuries demanded by his audience to ensure the idyllic resort they envisaged. Well understanding the habits and desires of the elite, he planned to exploit the popularity of the "sport of kings" with a race course, hunt club, bridle paths, and polo fields. Advertising pointed out that "Polo time is all the time—it's always *June* in Boca Raton."[25] He even planned to board Tennessee saddle horses. When his friend Birdie Vanderbilt considered boarding her horses in Boca Raton for the winter, he thought that his stables could hold the same exalted distinction in winter that Saratoga occupied in summer. The planned inlet would be of sufficient size to permit large yachts to enter and dock. In addition, three golf courses were being planned, two for the Ritz-Carlton by William J. Flynn and one for Mizner by renowned designer Donald J. Ross.

Thoroughly aware of the importance of evening entertainments to the leisure class, Addison astutely gave responsibility for developing them to his brother. Wilson was habitually a nocturnal creature and understood better than anyone the possibilities for amusement after the sun disappeared. Forever a buccaneer in search of booty, Wilson had the idea for a nightclub appropriately called the Pirate Ship Cabaret to be anchored in Lake Boca Raton near The Cloister Inn. He even went so far as to purchase ships and barges in Baltimore for the purpose. His intimacy with the world of theater ensured a steady stream of accomplished performers for the cabaret intended to seat four hundred. Boca Raton would not want for amusing diversion.

With the coming of fall, Mizner announced plans for his own house, a castle on a compact island in Lake Boca Raton. The entire composition derived from the organic nature of ancient castles where owners, from century to century, imparted their own distinctive tastes to create a cohesive whole, yet one bearing the stylistic vocabulary of different periods. Mizner imagined the process himself: "A Spanish fortress of the Twelfth Century captured from its owner by a stronger enemy, who, after taking it, adds on one wing and another—and then loses it in turn to another who builds to suit his taste . . . Perhaps later, the whole thing is restored to the Gothic period."[26]

The picturesque Castle Mizner was to have a drawbridge operated by motor, a "boat grotto" to accommodate a forty-five-foot yacht, and various rooms for staff and guests. He also borrowed from the Villa Mizner in Palm Beach by including a four-story tower topped with a mirador to provide sweeping vistas of the town and ocean. The castle was estimated to cost well over $1 million, a sum that had little significance for the architect. As a colleague noted: "Mr. M. didn't worry much about cost."[27] A dramatic design, Castle Mizner was to be gifted to the city of Boca Raton to be used as a museum after the architect's death. One contemporary reporter commented that it represented "a cornerstone to American architectural prestige" and "a monument to American money."[28]

When the lots from the first plat went on sale on May 14, the Mizner Development Corporation announced the next day that over $2 million in sales had been realized. The second offering brought in an additional $2 million in sales with $1 million booked in the first twenty minutes.[29] Acknowledging that part of the ready demand for Boca Raton property stemmed from the involvement of the great architect, there was no doubt that the hysteria for buying Florida real estate was being fueled by easy credit. The lax system permitted binder holders to resell the property and the febrile climate allowed them to do so at ever higher prices. This continuous escalation created a real estate bubble. As the tide continued to rise, the corporation announced that sales had increased to $6 million by summer. During the rest of 1925, the corporation was able to sell prestigious lots as well as over three hundred lots to developers of smaller homes.[30]

Capitalizing on the excitement, Mizner opened sales offices in various cities in Florida and in several northern cities including New York, Philadelphia, Boston, Baltimore, Washington, DC, and Savannah, Georgia.[31] He also made it easy for prospective buyers to visit by arranging bus service from Worth Avenue in Palm Beach to Boca Raton. Wilson Mizner used

Castle Mizner, 1925. In Mizner's sketch for his own villa in Boca Raton, his romantic scenography is fully developed. Replete with battered seawalls, crenellated battlements, a drawbridge, and portcullis, Mizner imagined his sanctum sanctorum as a highly secure place to which he would retreat from the world with family and friends. The building's organization was typical of Mizner's work in that the building was centered by a tall tower from which the massing pinwheels out and down to the base.
Courtesy of Boca Raton Historical Society.

his experience and expertise in hustling to coach the Boca Raton salesmen how to speak persuasively about the resort.

Alice DeLamar was walking down the street one day when she was stopped by a cacophony of "strident oratory." The

Worth Avenue, Palm Beach, 1925. The Mizner Development Corporation offered regular transportation service from Worth Avenue in Palm Beach to Boca Raton to make it convenient for prospective buyers to visit and experience the resort. Standing in front of the group ready to board the De Luxe Pullman Bus is Wilson Mizner. Among his various duties at the Mizner Development Corporation was to instruct the corporate salesmen how to sell luxury property. Courtesy of Boca Raton Historical Society.

clamor was coming from the Mizner real estate sales school in which approximately forty young men were receiving "loud-mouth instruction from one of these gasbag experts."[32] One of Wilson's ploys was to have his students emphasize frequently the involvement of T. Coleman du Pont and other notables to inspire confidence. This would eventually come to the attention of du Pont with repercussions for Addison Mizner.

Another factor that contributed to the frenzied situation was seductive advertising and publicity. Not to be outdone, Mizner's corporation enlisted the aid of Harry Reichenbach, one of the most effective and outrageous promoters in the entertainment business. The new promoter was exalted in *Photoplay* magazine as one who "specializes in imagination" and creates value for his clients by producing "sensational manifestations."[33] Reichenbach learned his craft by traveling around the world twice as the press agent of a magician known as The Great Reynard. So well known had his reputation become that, when any report with an outrageous claim appeared in a newspaper, editors referred to it as a "Reichenbach."[34]

Harry Reichenbach, Wilson's friend from mining days, was being paid $3,000 a week, three times what he was earning only three years earlier.[35] A master of deception and hyperbole, he once attempted to stage the "kidnapping" of one of his clients to Mexico to enhance her value with movie studios. With this hoax, Reichenbach succeeded in gaining recognition for the actress; however, he also earned a reprimand from the office of the president for stretching the truth and complicating relations with a neighboring country.[36] Under his direction, advertising for Mizner's Boca Raton made many bold claims that would have harmful repercussions. With rich associations in New York theater and Hollywood cinema, Reichenbach and Wilson Mizner brought many celebrities from the world of entertainment to Palm Beach and Boca Raton.

Harry Reichenbach's marketing philosophy was "get the big snobs, and the little ones will follow."[37] He knew that snobs wanted to associate with social superiors and therefore desired to attract to Boca Raton titled foreigners and well-known personalities from the world of entertainment. Board members Irving Berlin and the Duchess of Sutherland already served this purpose. When a competing developer announced that he had successfully enlisted the support of the exiled king of Greece, Reichenbach contemplated having the king kidnapped.[38] The Mizners were successful in gaining the support of Marie Dressler, a stage and screen actress and future Academy Award recipient, who helped to promote the resort and became known as "the Duchess of Boca Raton."[39] Apparently stimulated by Addison Mizner's inventive artistry, she considered selling Boca Raton real estate a creative endeavor. She admired the theatricality of what she was witnessing: "Groves are created overnight by uprooting large palms and planting them around houses . . . to lend a touch of tropic romance to a scene."[40]

Issues that began to appear in 1925 as worrisome signals escalated to a point that heralded the presence of severe problems by the arrival of fall. During the summer, tourists decided to come to Florida to investigate Florida real estate during the offseason to avoid the crowds. With restaurants and hotels closed, the multitude of visitors encountered a dearth

Marie Dressler, Addison Mizner, and Richard Barthelmess in Boca Raton, circa 1925. Among Addison's friends were Hollywood actors such as Dressler, who was enthusiastically involved in promoting Boca Raton real estate and became known as the "Duchess of Boca Raton." The Mizners used celebrities and socialites in their advertising and publicity to enhance the exclusivity of their development.
Courtesy of Historical Society of Palm Beach County.

of housing, a shortage that led to a rise in rents. Many were reduced to sleeping in their cars or in tents set up by developers. Beset by heat, humidity, and mosquitoes, visitors were also inconvenienced by a shortage of food. Writing letters home, they recounted the terrible conditions and admonished friends to avoid coming to Florida.

Negative information also began to surface in the press. There was a spate of articles that began to appear in northern newspapers, reporting rampant fraud related to Florida real estate. As a countermeasure, Florida governor John W. Martin led an entourage to New York in October to address the bad press. Accompanying the governor was T. Coleman du Pont, the chairman of Addison Mizner's board, who stated that the negative publicity relating to the real estate situation in Florida was exaggerated. In an effort to dispel the notion that Florida was experiencing problems, the mayors of Miami, Miami Beach, Coral Gables, and Hialeah jointly proclaimed the last day of 1925 and the first two days of 1926 "The Fiesta of the American Tropics," a grand celebration promoting fun, fellowship, and dance. Exaggerated language and capital letters were used to emphasize an idyllic existence by promising "that through our Streets and Avenues shall wind Glorious Pageantry of Sublime Beauty Depicting in Floral Loveliness the Blessing Bestowed upon us by Friendly Sun, Gracious Rain, and Soothing Tropic Wind."[41] Although an exciting three days, the Fiesta had no effect whatsoever on prevailing conditions.

Unfortunately, it was not only bad press that dampened demand for South Florida property. An enormous increase in building was the natural consequence of the land boom in South Florida and, as a result, the spike in construction created an inordinate demand for building materials that overwhelmed the railway systems. In August, there were significant disruptions in transportation services that created interruptions in the delivery of supplies. In that month, the railroads announced a statewide embargo on all materials except petroleum, livestock, and perishable goods and, although the restrictions were lifted in February, the damage to the building business was irreparable. Of the hundred railroad cars that came in every day, only eighty were unloaded due to congestion.[42]

The transportation disruptions caused many hardships, including shortages of water and food. This, combined with electricity outages resulting from high demand, created unbearable conditions for tourists and workers alike. Another casualty was the mail service. As the Mizner Development Corporation had seaplanes to ferry potential investors to Boca Raton, it decided to offer its services to the postal service, proposing to carry special delivery mail to and from Palm Beach, Miami, and Boca Raton. To run this operation, the Mizners made an offer to Colonel Billy Mitchell, a World War I hero and the former commander of all US air combat units. As the corporation was also in discussions to procure eight additional aircraft to augment its fleet, the newspaper deemed the operation "one of the most ambitious enterprises in the country."[43] Since Mizner was denied critical construction materials as a result of the complications, the offer to deliver the mail might have represented a gambit on the part of the architect to get preferential treatment from the state government in securing building supplies. Regardless, nothing came of the proposal as larger events began to consume the Mizners.

With the disruptions that occurred in transportation in South Florida in 1925, there were shortages of many staples, which complicated living conditions. Another result was the inability of the government to deliver the mail. Mizner offered to carry the mail between Palm Beach, Miami, and Boca Raton in his seaplanes, perhaps to induce the state to give the architect preference in gaining access to critical building supplies for his Boca Raton project.

Courtesy of Historical Society of Palm Beach County.

In 1925 many investors who had made significant gains trading in Florida property began to liquidate their holdings to realize profits. It has been estimated that approximately 90 percent of those who made "binder" purchases in Florida property during this time had no intention whatsoever of ever occupying it.[44] Then, the Internal Revenue Service declared that taxes had to be paid on the paper profits of real estate transactions. This caused many speculators to liquidate property to be able to satisfy tax obligations. As a result of so much selling, prices began to fall and a panic ensued. This suddenly created a vast market for overpriced land that lacked buyers. Burdened with debt, many investors went bankrupt. As more and more investors had come to Florida earlier in the decade, an enormous amount of capital was injected into the real estate market for the development of houses, resorts, retirement communities, and golf clubs. Bank deposits, having risen precipitously from $180 million in 1922 to $875 million in 1925, began to shrink in 1926.[45] This, combined with irresponsible management practices, eventually resulted in bank failures, especially among smaller banks. By the end of 1926, over 150 banks closed in Florida and Georgia owing to the banking panic.[46]

The Florida real estate bubble proved devastating for many people; however, there were reassuring indicators to suggest that Mizner's Boca Raton might be spared the calamity befalling other regional developers. Sales of his real estate in the first six months totaled a healthy $25 million.[47] Another reason for optimism in October was the announcement by the corporation that sales for the month had totaled $6,700,000.[48] Moreover, it was reassuring to know that Mizner was appealing mostly to the wealthy, a minuscule segment of the market that is ordinarily the last to be negatively affected by a downturn. Finally, the directors of his corporation, representing the highest echelons of business, entertainment, and society, buttressed the notion of stability and confidence. On August 6, at a meeting of the board, du Pont expressed the directors' approbation of Mizner's management decision "with our unqualified approval."[49] Addison Mizner was aware of the fragility of the Florida real estate situation; however, he had to be modestly sanguine when considering his unique position in the market.

In an effort to sustain momentum for Mizner's Boca Raton, Harry Reichenbach ginned up the publicity. Dubbing Mizner "the Aladdin of Architects," he stated in one advertisement that "Yachts discharge directly at the lake entrance to this hotel" when, in reality, there was no hotel.[50] At a point when little had been built in Boca Raton, one of his ads proclaimed "No Existing World Resort of Wealth and Fashion Compares with Boca Raton."[51] To reassure investors, another ad averred "Where Promises Are as Good as the God-Given Soil."[52] If anyone doubted the inescapable appeal of the resort, he removed them with "The Riviera, Biarritz, Mentone [sic], Nice, Sorrento, the Lido, Egypt, all that charms in each of these finds consummation in Boca Raton."[53] For Reichenbach, nothing was too outrageous.

Reichenbach oversaw a national advertising campaign that had frequently listed the names of the board of directors and

Gold and Sand

Mizner Development Corporation

Developers of Boca Raton

Mizner Development Corporation advertisement, June 26, 1925. This ad in the Palm Beach Post *is representative of the inflated language used to promote the development by Harry Reichenbach, the director of advertising and public relations. Here, he stated that "Florida sands are the greatest gold mine ever discovered. You do not have to dig it, nor mine it, nor smelt it. When you buy Florida land you were getting not gold in a creek bed—but minted gold of the realm."*

Courtesy of Boca Raton Historical Society.

unabashedly included the following in one ad: "The owners and controllers of the Mizner Development Corporation are a group of very rich men—men of unlimited means, who propose to build from the creative genius of Addison Mizner, what will probably be the most wonderful resort city in the world . . . the combined wealth of the stockholders . . . probably represents considerably over one-third of the entire wealth of the United States . . . It is reasonable to suppose that every lot buyer . . . should make quick and large profits."[54] While such brazen essays of reassurance had been tolerated, some directors were becoming uneasy.

As revenue from the purchase of land began to slow, a strategic move was taken by Reichenbach to stimulate sales by reassuring prospective buyers. The corporation's publicity now included the following: "Attach this advertisement to your contract for deed. It becomes a part thereof."[55] This constituted a pledge on the part of the company to fulfill its construction obligations. The furious activity in the Florida real estate market had generally obscured the distinction between the "developer," a well-intentioned individual or entity of integrity, and the more pejorative "promoter," a self-serving profiteer interested only in recurring transactions. This pledge clearly placed the Mizner Development Corporation in the more respectable category.

Reichenbach's excess had finally crossed a boundary that was to have dire implications for Addison Mizner. T. Coleman du Pont especially objected to his name being used in any advertisement for the Boca Raton project because the inclusion of directors' names suggested that they were personally guaranteeing claims made in the advertising. An ad in September 1925 directed readers to "note the names who make this guaranty" and then listed future projects such as the seven-hundred-room Ritz-Carlton Hotel, three golf courses, polo fields, tennis courts, and more.[56] Du Pont, fearing that he and all listed directors could be held liable in the event that such projects were not completed, complained about the manner in which publicity of the corporation was being handled. When du Pont's call for the resignation of Wilson Mizner and Harry Reichenbach went unheeded, he and Jesse Livermore resigned on October 24, 1925, when the board of the Mizner Development Corporation convened for a meeting.

It appeared only a short time earlier that the thoughtful approach taken by the Mizner Development Corporation would render it impervious to the ubiquitous fiascoes littering the world of Florida real estate. These and subsequent board resignations revealed otherwise. Du Pont made a statement to the *New York Times* on November 24, 1925, outlining the reasons for his resignation and, four days later, sent a letter to the newspaper in which he objected to the use of his name in the corporation's advertisements. The only inference to draw from his statements was that there was mismanagement that signaled future financial problems. The foundation of legitimacy established for the Mizner Development Corporation by the association with du Pont and others had been eroded. Following these defections, sales for Boca Raton real estate dwindled considerably and the value of lots plummeted. Wilson Mizner had offered $50,000 for a desirable lot owned by socialite Lytle Hull. Insulted by the paltry amount and choosing to keep the property, Hull found that the property was worth only about $200 after the bubble.[57]

Addison Mizner was not easily daunted. Operating with an accelerated construction schedule and severe financial problems, Mizner and his staff worked heroically to finish the Cloister Inn. This building, representing potential salvation, would serve as a graphic reminder to all of the promised elegance and splendor of Boca Raton. Although construction of the hotel was not finished as Christmas approached, its state of near completion was such that Mizner could still use the amazing hotel for a large party that he hoped would astonish his audience and restore confidence in his project. On Christmas Eve, he hosted a dinner for friends and former clients at the new hotel. Service was provided by the staff of the Ritz-Carlton, which recently had agreed to manage the operations of the hotel.

The initial impression conveyed by the Cloister Inn's western entrance facade was one of gracious, languorous charm,

Main Entrance, the Cloister Inn, Boca Raton, 1926. The main entrance to the hotel featured an imposing Romanesque stone arch fronting two important doors. In company literature, the front doors were purported to have been three-hundred-year-old doors from the University of Salamanca. In reality, the doors were made in Mizner's workshops in West Palm Beach of pine from Dade County, local cypress, and imported walnut.
Courtesy of Boca Raton Historical Society.

a perception that was reinforced by the design and configuration of the public spaces inside. The easy flow of the hotel was not unlike the chain of spaces created by Mizner at the Everglades Club seven years earlier. Upon approach, guests encountered an impressive structure with a low profile, a building inspired by a Spanish convent of the eleventh century. Typical of Mizner's designs, the building had roof lines that rose to different heights and a tower that dramatically soared two stories above the highest roof. Entrance was gained through a porch composed of a large Syrian Romanesque arch supported by a pair of short, masculine columns with elaborately carved capitals. The huge doors were purported to be three-hundred-year-old originals from the University of Salamanca. In reality, these doors were made of Dade County pine in the workshops of Mizner Industries. The lobby, forty feet square and two stories high, was generous and decorated with tile floors, plaster walls, and a beamed ceiling. On the east side was a staircase with low risers that suggested an elegant ascent.

Harmonious as a composition, the hotel had public rooms that were large, dramatic, and informed by historical precedent. The loggia was thirty feet by fifty feet and provided access to a dining room, smoking room, and lounge. The dining hall, inspired by a fifteenth-century Catalonian hospital, was eighty-four feet by forty feet and partitioned by five Gothic arches that rose to a beamed ceiling. Its large windows were glazed with green, yellow, and rose stained glass to soften the Florida sun. The ballroom, a generous room distinguished by a fireplace that a man could stand in, had the appearance of a baronial hall. Its massive beamed ceiling was anchored throughout with wrought iron chandeliers from Mizner Industries. Perhaps reflecting his intended aesthetic or maybe resulting from financial constraints, each room was sparsely furnished in a manner that "harks back to earlier monastic

Main dining room, the Cloister Inn, Boca Raton, 1926. The large dining room was partitioned by five Gothic lancet arches under a beamed ceiling. The strong Florida sunlight was filtered through a series of stained-glass windows. All of the furniture, ironwork, ceramics, and tiles in the room were supplied by Mizner Industries.
Photograph by Frank E. Geisler reproduced by Craig Kuhner.

days . . . and reeks of the atmosphere of early religious orders in its simplicity."[58] It is known that he used much of his own

antique furniture in the public spaces to control costs. A January 1926 article in the *Palm Beach Post* stated that the cost of the hotel was $1 million, "making it one of the best appointed and most costly hotels in the state."[59] The architect had created a destination of privilege and leisure.

This beautifully conceived theater was ready for an audience on February 6, 1926, when Mizner hosted five hundred members of Palm Beach society to celebrate the formal opening of his hotel. All guests, treated to a lavish dinner and served by waiters liveried in red coats with gold braids, were greatly impressed with the evening. The success of the dinner was in jeopardy until the last moment as the electric cooking ranges needed to prepare the food did not arrive until two hours before the designated time to begin serving dinner.[60]

This proved to be an extravagant dinner estimated by many to be one of the superlative social events of the Palm Beach season. Among the guests that evening was the wife of Stanford White who gratified Mizner by commenting that "Addison is the foremost genius of the age. Since Stanford White, there has been no one with such exquisite sense of artistry. This building is superb."[61] Another guest was Alexander P. Moore, the former American ambassador to Spain, who said that the hotel was "as radiant as anything there is in Spain."[62] Ida Tarbell's description came close to mirroring the intention of the architect when she wrote that "The Cloister was simple

Dinner at the Cloister Inn at Boca Raton, December 1925. Before the formal opening, Addison Mizner invited fashionable Palm Beach to dine on Christmas Eve to showcase the splendors of his new resort, despite the fact that not everything had been completed. Notice that the walls have not yet been plastered. Addison is seated against the wall on the left and Wilson is leaning back in his chair laughing (center). The brothers' niece, Ysabel Chase, is seated to the left of Wilson.

Courtesy of Boca Raton Historical Society.

to severity in its whole yet rich in delights."[63] In an article in *Arts & Decoration*, Giles Edgerton succinctly described the hotel as a "Spanish gem."[64] Clearly, Addison Mizner enjoyed the critical accolades; what he needed more than anything was commercial success.

The administration buildings at Camino Real and Dixie Highway were another symbol intended to exhibit the exquisite taste of Mizner's Boca Raton resort. The North and South Buildings represented the architect's Boca Raton headquarters and contained rooms for his architectural staff, his apartment, a sales office, and an alfresco restaurant that served tea and lunch. The North Administration Building was inspired by the house of El Greco in Toledo, Spain, and reflected many features of its antecedent. The southern façade had an enclosed patio with hanging galleries. The northern façade faced the Camino Real and featured a dramatic baroque composition, albeit a more delicate design than typically found in baroque conception of the seventeenth century. A pair of slender Ionic columns rose to support a segmented pediment interrupted by a projecting balcony containing French doors. A distinctive feature of the original Toledo house duplicated on the porch of the administrative building was the unusual "cannonball" capitals that surmount the columns supporting the entablature.

Just before the opening of the hotel, the Mizner Development Corporation unveiled its most exclusive parcel of real estate called *El Distrito de Boca Raton*, composed of fifty-eight oceanfront lots intended exclusively for the socially prominent. Careful to ensure beauty in this sophisticated enclave, Addison Mizner reserved the right to approve all architectural designs.

The first sale in the Distrito was for $150,000 to Countess Millicent Salm.[65] Born Millicent Rogers and married for the moment to an Austrian count, she was a fashion icon, patron of the arts, and the granddaughter of one of the founders of Standard Oil. With this felicitous beginning, others followed. Although he designed several luxury residences for friends Irving Berlin, Marie Dressler, and others, he never saw one of them built. Artistic virtuosity and tony denizens were to have made the distrito the "rendezvous of the elite of the world."[66]

Mizner publicity continued to paint an attractive image of sales and construction activity in 1926. It was important to reinforce the impression of landowners' building houses as opposed to simply re-selling lots. It was reported that a house was under construction for the family of the Reverend Henry Mizner, one of Addison's older brothers. This house was among the more modest houses that were constructed in the neighborhood known at the time as Mizner Plat 11. Within a couple of years, this group of houses was recognized by the names that the neighborhoods have today, Spanish Village and Old Floresta. Although historian Donald Curl thought that none of the houses in Spanish Village was actually designed by Addison Mizner, they featured characteristics of the architect's work. Despite the fact that one hundred were originally planned, only twenty-two were actually constructed by builder Harry Vought, who priced them modestly at $7,000.[67] To the west of

this was Old Floresta, the more elaborate neighborhood where twenty-nine homes were designed by Mizner and constructed by Dwight Robinson. Intended for employees of the corporation, these houses had generous living rooms with beamed ceilings and fireplaces with stone mantels.

In January 1926, Addison Mizner sent a letter to each owner of Boca Raton property acknowledging problems in the Florida real estate market. He differentiated his exclusive real estate from the mass of ordinary property by citing the success

Old Floresta, Boca Raton, 1925. Mizner developed ten small house prototypes, labeled "A" through "J," of various sizes for use in the creation of neighborhoods such as Old Floresta. By mirroring the plan, he effectively created twenty types enabling the use of no more than one type per street. The house shown is House "E" and was intended for executives and directors of his development company.
Courtesy of Boca Raton Historical Society.

the corporation had enjoyed in the seven months its property had been on the market and by affirming that $2,300,000 of his lots had been resold "with profits to the original purchaser in every case."[68] With the market flat, the corporation then decided to auction a parcel of oceanfront lots in northern Boca Raton. Although every lot was sold in two days, the auction brought in only $250,000, hardly sufficient to sustain business operations.[69]

With no revenue from the sales of lots, the corporation lacked the operating capital to continue construction and acquisition of additional land. Unable to collect for services, contractors initiated litigation against the corporation in May 1926. Devoid of options, the board of directors voted in July to cede control to Central Equities Corporation of Chicago, owned by Rufus Dawes and his brothers. One of the brothers, Charles Dawes, was serving at this time as vice president of the United States in the Coolidge Administration. Recognizing the value of the Boca Raton project, Rufus Dawes promised to retain Addison Mizner to manage the company and oversee all architectural development. This created the illusion among some people that the Boca Raton project would be realized. The *Palm Beach Post* reported on October 19, 1926, that "The dream which Addison originally had for Boca Raton seems assured of materialization" and went on to suggest that the value of South Florida real estate was secure.[70]

In the end, Central Equities contributed only a fraction of the promised money and probably only postponed the bankruptcy of the Mizner Development Corporation. In "Addison Mizner: Promoter in Paradise," a comprehensive article in the *Florida Historical Quarterly* outlining Mizner's Boca Raton development project, attorney and author Raymond B. Vickers summarizes the ultimate effect of Central Equities' involvement: "The Dawes brothers had secured for themselves the unencumbered assets of the Mizner Development Corporation, leaving its debts and other liabilities for the bankruptcy court."[71] On July 26, 1927, the Mizner Development Corporation was judged by the court to be a bankrupt company, leaving 173 creditors with over $4 million in unsecured claims.[72] The debt was finally settled three years later at a tenth of a cent to the dollar. As an example of this resolution, the Palm Beach Bank and Trust Company, which had made loans to the Mizner Development Corporation totaling $58,000, was paid $58 in 1930.[73]

Vickers describes the architect's complicity in the complex events that contributed to the failure of Florida banks and outlines in detail the intricate relationships between the Mizner Development Corporation and local bankers, a connivance that resulted in losses incurred by their depositors. Conflict of interest was rampant, evidenced by the fact that the Mizner Development Corporation sold stock to local bankers who in

Addison Mizner, February 1926. This photograph was taken just before the grand opening of the Cloister Inn on February 6, 1926. This formal occasion featured an extravagant dinner for almost five hundred members of Palm Beach society including the Stotesburys, Warburtons, and Wanamakers. Another in attendance was the widow of Stanford White who, to the great satisfaction of Mizner, thought the hotel superb.
Courtesy of Historical Society of Palm Beach County.

turn made loans to the corporation as well as to themselves. The banks also accepted fake collateral for credit extended. Failing to maintain appropriate liquidity, banks recklessly made loans far in excess of their capital.

The Mizner Development Corporation essentially made the Palm Beach National Bank a subsidiary by acquiring over 50 percent of the bank's equity, a privileged position that allowed it to guarantee loans to customers purchasing Boca Raton lots.[74] Donald Herbert Conkling, a director and stockholder of several local banks and also publisher of the *Palm Beach Post*, owned fifteen hundred shares in the Mizner Development Corporation.[75] He was in a position to ensure good publicity in his newspaper for Mizner's project, which would enhance the value of his stock. Such practices between bankers and developers were not at all uncommon during this time. Also, in an effort to protect their market, it was the general habit of local newspapers to provide favorable publicity to developers and to downplay the reality of the real estate bubble.

While the facts and the outcome are indisputable, the level of direct involvement by Addison Mizner in these events can never be known. While most certainly aware of the remedial steps being taken to sustain the operating capacity of his corporation, Addison Mizner likely had neither the aptitude nor the inclination to devise a complex plan of bank fraud. Alice DeLamar, who knew Addison very well and considered him family, said that he "was never meant to be a businessman."[76] Mizner's inability to manage his own finances throughout his life was also evidence of his lack of interest in business affairs.

Addison's indifference to finances is reinforced by a story related by Alva Johnston in which an agitated Harry Reichenbach ran into Addison's office one day to tell him that a corrupt colleague was decamping to Europe with a quarter million dollars belonging to the Development Corporation. Upon hearing this, Addison merely turned away and said, "Don't bother me with these things."[77] Also, it should be remembered that Addison had the bad judgment to make his brother Wilson the treasurer of the corporation. A superlative conniver, Wilson neither needed the assistance of anyone else to conceive clever financial schemes nor had the inclination to seek approval for such actions. Most probably, Addison did not actively manipulate the financial affairs of his corporation; however, as he did acquiesce, either tacitly or explicitly, he was ultimately responsible for the results. DeLamar flatly stated that Mizner lacked "financial sense and business shrewdness."[78]

By the fall of 1926, Addison Mizner did not need a portent to signal that his grand dream for Boca Raton was doomed. What arrived was a much more forceful and straightforward affirmation. One of the most destructive hurricanes in the history of Florida overcame the region in the middle of September and damaged South Florida, including Boca Raton and Palm Beach. The storm—estimated to be the costliest tropical storm in history when adjusted for inflation—resulted in the loss of hundreds of lives and caused severe damage.[79] In Boca Raton, the wife of the mayor later commented that "railroad cars were being knocked off the tracks and telegraph poles were snapped like toothpicks."[80] The destruction left the architect overwhelmed and made the intervention of the Dawes brothers necessary. In July 1926, Stella Crosley announced in an article in *The Nation* that "the Florida boom has collapsed. The world's greatest poker game, played with building lots instead of chips, is over."[81]

Because the concept for Boca Raton was so grand and the area to be developed so vast, it is a simple conclusion in the aftermath to note simply that Mizner failed to realize his objective. But Addison always had focus and tenacity, both of which he utilized during the frenetic activity in Boca Raton in 1925 and 1926. The amount of work that was completed in the span of a year was remarkable. It is this accomplishment that underscores his dedication and indicates the sincerity of his desire to complete the project and fulfill his obligations.

A letter dated December 4, 1926, from the Mizner Development Corporation signed by the chairman of the executive committee, James R. Nicholson, outlined to the Central Equities Corporation, soon to take control of the Mizner

The ballroom, the Cloister Inn, 1926. This generous room featured a fireplace centered between two large entrance doors surmounted with half-round arches of decorative ironwork. The scale is illustrated by the fireplace that is sufficiently tall to allow a man to stand inside. Mizner used many antiques from his personal collection that mixed seamlessly with the many objects made in Mizner's workshops.

Courtesy of Boca Raton Historical Society.

Development Corporation, all that had been accomplished. In the category of general development, three thousand acres were cleared; land was cleared for forty-two miles of streets and thirty-two miles were graded; one hundred and eighty thousand square feet of concrete sidewalks built; seven bridges constructed; thirteen miles of water mains installed; and fifteen wells for water supply drilled and connected. It reported that forty-six houses had been built and thirty-five more were under construction. Two golf courses, the Cloister course and the Ritz-Carlton course, were fully completed with functioning water systems and an equipped radio broadcasting station had been finished. In addition to administrative buildings, there was the Cloister Inn that cost approximately $2 million. The letter states that total expenditures for development, improvements, and buildings amounted to over $4 million.[82]

In less than two years, the circumstances of Addison Mizner's life had unexpectedly changed with far-reaching consequences. Emboldened by six years of recurring good fortune and animated by an encompassing vision, Mizner undertook a project described by Donald Curl as "monumental in scale and magnificent in concept."[83] The combination of its colossal nature, incorporating thousands of acres, and inopportune timing, beginning almost at the height of the real estate bubble, foreordained disaster. Perhaps Mizner was a casualty of his own overreaching ambition; however, in fairness, he had become conditioned to the fixed certainties that ordered the world of his wealthy friends. For six years in Palm Beach, he had witnessed the privileged few gratifying themselves with colossal statements of pride that he himself had created. The elite appeared to exist beyond penalty of any kind. In the end, his foresight was no worse than that of anyone else in being unable to prophesy the collapse of the real estate market and the end of shameless indulgence. The siren call of Boca Raton proved irresistible.

In early 1925, Addison Mizner savored the euphoria that an artist experiences when a successful design assumes definitive form. He sincerely believed in his idealistic conception of the perfect resort city. As 1926 came to a close, this sublime idea had been displaced by the distressing realization that his dream would never become reality. The profound dismay and frustration he endured at this point was in proportion to the intense exultation he had enjoyed only eighteen months earlier. In the end, Addison Mizner was psychologically ravaged and financially devastated. For a man who habitually identified the dawning of a new day with possibility and potential, he was now uncomfortably shrouded in darkness. This reversal of circumstance would regrettably shape the rest of his life.

CHAPTER FOURTEEN

REBIRTH AND RECOGNITION

The magnitude of planning "the greatest resort in the world" and the labyrinth of resolving an interminable array of convoluted problems left Addison Mizner little time for anything else. In spite of being consumed with the complexities of Boca Raton, Mizner did accept a couple of commissions during the period of his involvement with Boca Raton. One was a project to design a new church for the congregation of the Riverside Baptist Church in Jacksonville, Florida. This was the only commission for a religious building that he ever accepted. With a focus on Boca Raton, he originally refused the invitation due to a busy schedule. Realizing that this was an opportunity to honor his beloved mother with a fitting memorial, he finally relented to the request and refused compensation for his efforts.

Mizner had never designed a religious building but had, from his earliest days in California, Guatemala, Spain, and all of his European travels, seen, remembered, and collected images of churches and ecclesiastical buildings. Consistent

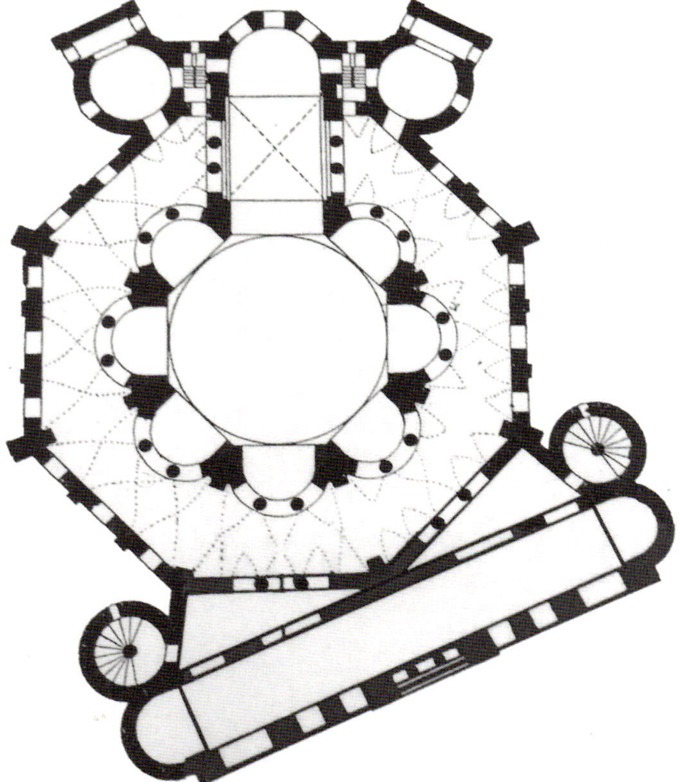

San Vitale, Ravenna, Italy, circa 548. San Vitale is an octagonally planned church and one of the most important examples of Byzantine art and architecture. Mizner would have been quite aware of San Vitale's plan and may have considered its appropriateness as a model for a Baptist church.
Courtesy of Wikimedia Commons.

An evening photograph of San Vitale illustrates the core of the church and the flying buttress vaulting that occurred over time, a feature that would have particularly interested Mizner.
Courtesy of Wikimedia Commons. Photograph by Tango7174.

with his established architectural interests and patterns of design, Mizner approached the Jacksonville church in 1926 with a plan solution that drew from familiar but novel sources, in this case from a later Byzantine architecture and particularly from early octagonal churches such as San Vitale (AD 547) in Ravenna or Saint Sergius (AD 527) in Constantinople. Architectural historians have suggested that a source of inspiration is the thirteenth-century Iglesia de la Vera Cruz in Segovia, Spain, but this church has a twelve-sided exterior and the circular interior is centered by a two-story gallery.[1]

In selecting an octagonal plan, Mizner rejected the typical longitudinal axes of the Romanesque and Gothic cathedrals. He determined that the Jacksonville Baptists would have a church that derived from churches from the earliest periods of Christianity that eventually became mosques during the Moorish and Ottoman periods before returning to their original Christian use in later centuries. In this way, Mizner concocted a story for this project that enabled him to mix styles and architectural periods.

The Riverside Baptist Church resides at the corner of Park and King Streets in the historic Riverside neighborhood of Jacksonville, and is one and one-half stories tall. While octagonal in plan, the uninterrupted, central octagonal space has two long and two short orthogonal wings projecting from the octagon walls that suggest a cruciform base. These one-story projections provide the main street entry (NW), the secondary entry (NW), the cloister and garden entry (SE), and the blind elevation that conceals the high altar (NE) on axis with the main entry. From the interior, none of these projections are evident beyond Mizner's organization of major and minor interior façades of the octagonal plan. In the center of each major interior façade, those of the main entry and the high altar, Mizner created arches that surmount the half-story stringcourse that surrounds the interior walls. Above the entry, there is a porch with three windows, and at the altar, a high three-arched composition with metal screens within the arches and a gate for access to the high altar. Flanking the high altar are baptisteries and other liturgical spaces that reside behind the same kinds of screens that protect the altar. The ceiling appears to be a massive structure of pecky cypress beams, which had been conventionally constructed and sheathed with pecky cypress woodwork.

The Riverside Baptist Church, 1926. Mizner's design for the Riverside congregation was an exceptionally well-executed example of a post-medieval ecclesiastical building, and interesting because of its embrace by most of the Baptist congregation. Those who did not care for the design were free to depart the congregation.

Photograph by Craig Kuhner.

The Riverside Baptist Church, 1926. Having reluctantly agreed to design the Riverside Baptist Church in Jacksonville, Florida, Mizner must have had his beloved mother in mind in committing to his only ecclesiastical structure.

Photograph by Craig Kuhner.

The Romanesque massing of the church is tightly constrained, and a construction type that suggests great mass behind flat, stuccoed walls. Mizner accomplished the visual mass by building double walls with a cavity between. The effect is satisfactory and the interior, with its apparently thick walls that were washed with buttermilk and burnt umber, has a patina that suggests centuries of existence.

The façade is highly formal, and more formal than any Mizner façade up to that date. Exhibiting a firm grasp of Romanesque architecture, the openings for windows, doors, and entry-façade porches are small and deep. Mizner used Lombard arched corbels to extend the clay tile roof, and the way that Mizner uses different scales of arched corbels to substantiate the major and minor façades is a nuanced approach that suggests architectural growth since his design of the Everglades Club eight years earlier.

For Mizner to have conceived and built a church better suited to high church ritual than to Baptist oratory caused some of the congregation to withdraw from Riverside.[2] However, the building has been in continuous use since its construction and Addison Mizner would be justifiably proud of this accomplishment and the fact that its apparent age might date its construction to the late eighteenth century.

Addison Mizner was also able to find time for his friend and patron, Paris Singer. Well versed in the art of making money in the Florida land boom, Singer had planned to develop a luxury resort on the small island just north of Palm Beach. In 1925 he was able to have the county construct a bridge connecting the mainland at Riviera Beach with his newly acquired Singer Island. Singer originally wanted to build two magnificent hotels to house prospective buyers, one large and the other more intimate, to reflect the sophisticated quality of lifestyle envisioned by the developer. He turned to his friend Addison Mizner who began to design the larger hotel named The Blue Heron. With sales activity weak and prospects dim, Singer made the decision to halt construction in 1926 after having spent $2 million on the project.[3] The Blue Heron not only turned out to be a financial disaster, but it resulted in Singer's being arrested for fraud arising from allegations of false advertising. Although cleared, Singer was forced to endure the ignominy of the negative publicity attached to the entire fiasco. A last consequence of this calamitous venture was a strained friendship resulting from his inability to compensate Mizner for his architectural services.

When Addison Mizner was finally able to look beyond the rabble that was Boca Raton, he found a landscape for architectural services much more crowded than what he had formerly known. Having been consumed with his grand vision for two years, he had essentially removed himself from the market for a sufficient span of time to allow other architects to gain traction among the elite. Marion Sims Wyeth, a graduate of Princeton and the Ecole des Beaux Arts in Paris, was someone Mizner knew well as he had arrived in Palm Beach in

1919, only a short time after Mizner himself. They alone had commanded virtually all important commissions for villas in the early 1920s.

In 1925, a sophisticated young European arrived in Palm Beach from New York where he had begun to practice architecture in the United States in 1920. Maurice Fatio, born in Switzerland and educated at the University of Zurich, was handsome, socially polished, and well versed in architectural styles and was already familiar with South Florida as a result of earlier work at Jupiter Island. His first commission in Palm Beach actually came at the expense of Addison Mizner. Having first asked Mizner to design a house for him, Joseph Widener changed his mind and gave the commission to Fatio. Other architects soon followed: Howard Major, Joseph Urban, and John Volk. Urban, an Austrian designer familiar with European modernism, and Wyeth collaborated on the monumental Mar-a-Lago for E. F. Hutton and his wife, the former Marjorie Merriweather Post.

Despite the fact that Mizner was now losing business to these young architects, he never let competition stand in the way of friendship. He socialized with them and enjoyed their company. Among those regularly invited to his fashionable parties were the Fatios, Wyeths, and Volks. As Marion Sims Wyeth said, "We talked about architecture. We were never rivals."[4] Additionally, Mizner's esteem of Fatio's ability was so high

Johnnie Brown was a monkey raised by Mizner in Palm Beach and one of a few reasons that Mizner blamed E. Clarence Jones for changing the rules that originally allowed pets to be kept in Mizner's mirador apartment in the Everglades Club. The Club's decision to disallow pets and also women above the first floor, effectively urged Mizner to design his first personal residence, El Solano, at 720 South Ocean Boulevard. Mizner's love for Johnnie Brown, "The Human Monkey," led him to erect a tombstone in a courtyard of Via Mizner. Photograph by Craig Kuhner.

that he offered to enter into a partnership with him. Fatio had set up his own practice in Palm Beach after having established a partnership in New York with William Treanor. Wishing to remain on his own, the younger architect declined Mizner's offer yet the two remained very good friends.

The year 1927 would prove to be difficult for Addison Mizner. He was perhaps frustrated and further demoralized to find that he was no longer first among equals in the Palm Beach architectural hierarchy. Early in the year, he was stricken with pneumonia and recuperated at a slow pace. Already weakened by the stress and tension of trying to save Boca Raton, he had to endure the additional burden of losing several close relationships. Always inordinately fond of exotic animals, he experienced especially close attachments to his monkeys. Johnnie Brown, his favorite, died suddenly. He wanted to keep Johnnie close and had him buried and memorialized with a tombstone just outside the entrance to the Villa Mizner. With business suffering, his nephew Horace Chase left Mizner Industries to go to Europe where it was less expensive to live. Accompanying Horace was Addison's trusted friend Alex Waugh who had very capably run the antiques business. Paradoxically, the defection of his troublesome brother might have been the most dismaying.

At once a contrast and likeness to his brother, Wilson Mizner occupied an unusual position in Addison's life. While Addison Mizner had a wealth of friendships, no one was as close and intimate as his younger brother. A supreme nuisance and a boundless source of exasperation, Wilson was the kindred spirit who alone could provide solace and comfort through an idiosyncratic perspective peculiar to the Mizner family. Given the choice of confronting or avoiding adversity, Wilson consistently chose the latter. When it became apparent that Boca Raton was in jeopardy, Wilson began searching for anything to extricate himself from South Florida.

As formal employment was always a rare and transitory experience for Wilson, he used his capacity for repartee to find a job that would remove him from Florida creditors. In August 1925, he went to New York to begin working on a script for a musical comedy called *Naughty Cinderella*. He began to go out with one of the actresses, Pauline Armitage, well known in New York theater circles, and, according to some, eventually proposed marriage. When she had a nervous breakdown and subsequently committed suicide by jumping to her death from the fourteenth floor of the Shelton Hotel, many placed the blame for the tragedy at the feet of Wilson. The negative publicity attached to the actress's death reached Palm Beach in February at the height of the social season and served as another source of scandal that bedeviled Addison. Back in Palm Beach, the situation was so bad by the end of 1926 that Wilson encountered an endless stream of court orders: "I never open my door but a writ blows in."[5] By June 1927, Addison's brother had permanently moved to Hollywood.

Addison was also forced to witness the sale of the assets of the Mizner Development Corporation in a public auction, a humiliating reminder to friends of his colossal failure. In March 1927, creditors filed involuntary bankruptcy proceedings against Addison's company in Jacksonville. In October, Clarence Geist, a developer of gas and electric utility companies, tried to buy the assets of the corporation, including the Cloister Inn, for $5,000 with the agreement to assume responsibility for all outstanding obligations and to guarantee clear title to all contract holders. When that was deemed insufficient, he then bid $71,500 with the same guarantees, an offer that was accepted.[6] Geist brought in the architectural firm of Schultze & Weaver that greatly expanded the Cloister Inn and the new owner reopened it in 1930 as The Boca Raton Club, a private men's club.

Mizner was able to focus on architecture once again when John R. Bradley, distinguished horse breeder and brother of Beach Club owner Colonel Edward Bradley, commissioned him for a new house in 1927. This project took him away from Florida to Colorado where the landscape and environment were different from the subtropical Palm Beach he had known for the past eight years. Located on a flat plain at the base of the Rocky Mountains, Colorado Springs has a mild and dry

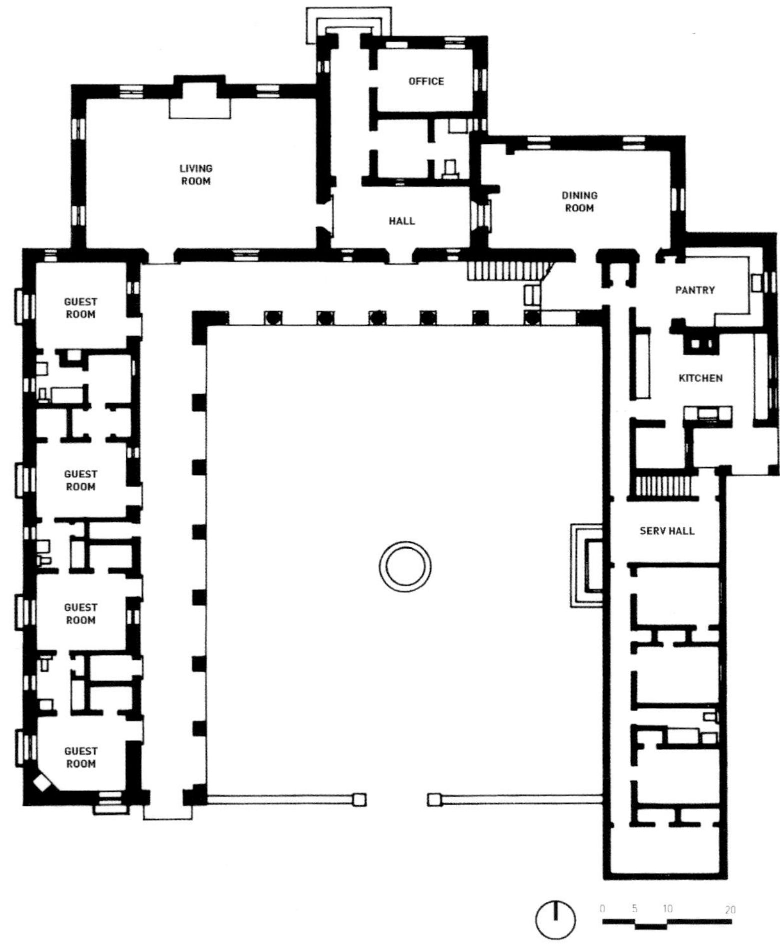

Casa Serena, 1927. Mizner, for the first time, remembered the architecture that had had such a profound effect in his youth, the Spanish and Mission styles. The planning approach for Colonel Bradley's ranch in Colorado Springs was based upon the adobe massing of a C-shaped plan. The massing was intended to appear accretive over time, and Mizner's use of a mirador to conceal the elevated water tower was inventive. Plan reproduced by Chase R. Cothran.

climate. Mizner responded appropriately to these features with a design that combined the Adobe design of the southwestern plains with Spanish mission sources. This was his only project that reached back to Spanish Colonial architecture. Using a south-facing U-shaped plan that enveloped a patio, the main block of Casa Serena rises three stories with a flat tiled roof, typical of the Pueblo Revival style. Two elements of the main structure give dimension to the composition: the projecting roofed balcony of the master bedroom on the second floor and a water storage tower that rises four floors. Compared to his Florida work, this ranch house was defined by its simplicity and lack of ornamentation. Casa Serena finds service today as one of the main buildings of the Fountain Valley School in Colorado Springs.

One of the most rewarding tokens of friendship is the unanticipated gift. Poignantly aware of the tribulation and hardship that misfortune can impose, Addison had been reflecting on the difficult plight that had befallen his estranged friend, Paris Singer. Mindful of his own painful experience, Mizner magnanimously wrote him a letter of reconciliation in 1927. Having re-established his most important friendship in Palm Beach, Addison was allowed to renew his name to the membership list of the Everglades Club for 1928. Singer acknowledged the value of their relationship and the pain of estrangement: "It is the one name that has any real right to be there [on the Everglades list of members], and when you took it off you gave me one 'right in the jaw'!"[7]

During this period of difficulty, he took the time to repay the kindness of another old friend. Addison had not forgotten that Elsa Maxwell had been in league with Lady Colebrooke during his rehabilitation before leaving New York in 1918. With a promoter's eye for what creates interest and allure, Maxwell helped bring about the transformation of the Lido in Venice into a highly desirable summertime resort destination in the early 1920s. Seeking to alleviate the financial problems of his principality, Prince Pierre of Monaco later sought assistance from Maxwell in bringing about a similar metamorphosis in Monte Carlo. Among the new amenities suggested by Maxwell were a huge pool next to the sea, a casino and outdoor pavilion, and tennis courts that could be used to stage an international tournament every year at the conclusion of Wimbledon. The centerpiece was a new hotel adjacent to the pool, the plans for which were produced by Addison Mizner as a gift for his entertaining friend.[8] Although beset with complications in his life, Addison was still able to retain a sense of gratitude and a readiness to demonstrate appreciation. These unbidden deeds would now be reciprocated.

Mizner's friends, led by Alice DeLamar, conspired to honor him with the publication of a book entitled *The Florida Architecture of Addison Mizner*. This thoughtful act touched the architect

Alice DeLamar (center), Lucia Davidova, and friends at Sloppy Joe's in Havana, circa 1930. DeLamar became one of Mizner's dear friends in Palm Beach and referred to him as "my favorite uncle." After Mizner's calamity in Boca Raton, DeLamar underwrote and over- saw the production of a book on the work of the architect that was published in 1928. This publication, an unexpected gift to Mizner, led to several commissions and a renewed apprecia- tion of his architecture.

Courtesy of Historical Society of Palm Beach County.

and, more importantly, gave impetus to his business after the book was published the following year by bringing renewed attention to his genius. DeLamar, introduced to Addison in 1920 by his nephew Horace Chase, was immediately drawn to the warmth, humor, and erudition of Addison. She later defined the affinity she felt by describing them as "Horace my favorite brother; Addison my favorite uncle."[9] As a guest at the first house that Mizner had designed for himself, she noticed

that it gave the appearance of having been lived in for several generations. Finding the mansions of her youth dreary and funereal, she loved the openness and charm of his new home on South Ocean Boulevard. Mizner then began providing ideas for her own home, a project she eventually completed on her own with the assistance of draftsmen from Mizner's office.

Alice DeLamar's father had created a mining empire and later became a Wall Street investor. When he died, she became heiress to a fortune of $10 million.[10] Having grown up in mansions on Madison Avenue and at Glen Cove, Long Island, she was intimately familiar with Gilded Age splendor; however, she derived little satisfaction merely from opulence and began to cultivate a more refined sensibility. As a young lady, she began studying art and spending summers in Paris with her mother. She later met Bernard Berenson, the distin- guished connoisseur of Renaissance art, and was guided by him in assembling her own art collection. In Addison, she had found another refined spirit with whom she could discuss art and architecture. Although reserved and reticent, she imme- diately treated Addison "like my own family" and, in his time of distress, essentially became his patron in 1927.[11]

Friendship and admiration impelled her to supervise and fund a book about "the artistry" that Mizner had brought to Florida. She wanted to acknowledge her friend with "flowers to the living instead of the dead."[12] Commissioning journalist Ida

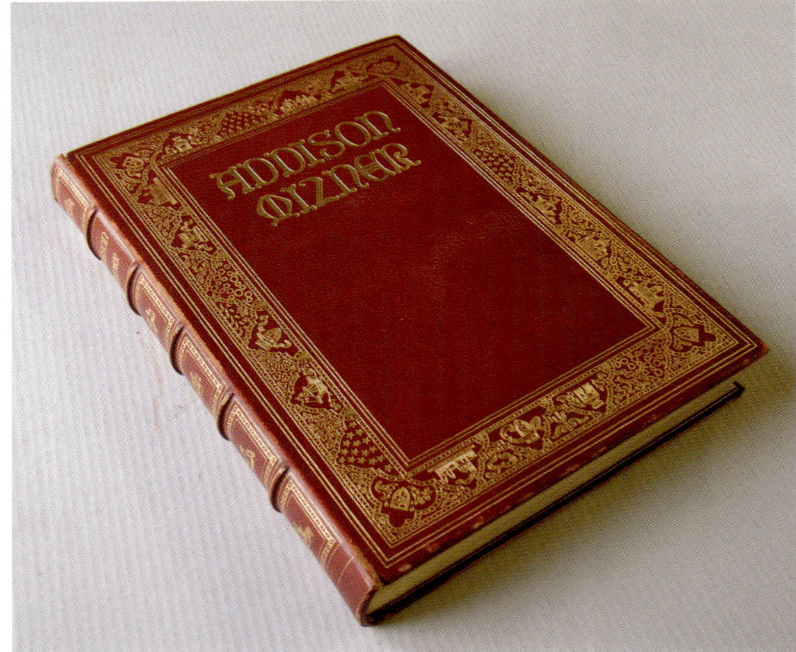

The Florida Architecture of Addison Mizner, Edicion Imperial, 1928, *underwritten by Alice DeLamar and written by Ida Tarbell, featured 185 plates of Mizner's architecture photographed by Frank E. Geisler. To give Geisler the best perspective for his photography, DeLamar drove him around Palm Beach in a pickup with his camera elevated in the bed of the truck. Mizner greatly appreciated DeLamar's effort and referred to her as "my Lorenzo the Magnificent."* Courtesy of Society of the Four Arts. Photograph by Craig Kuhner.

Tarbell to write the text and Frank Geisler to photograph the houses, DeLamar was able to have the book published in 1928. In addition, she created one hundred copies of an *Edicion Imperial*, a leather-bound, gold-tooled version with slipcase cover, that Mizner autographed and gave to special friends and clients. Mizner's gratitude to Alice was expressed in a letter: "I have been so ill since The Book took shape that I have never made

it quite clear how much I appreciated the greatest compliment ever paid a living architect."[13] His appreciation only increased after witnessing the salutary effect it had on commissions.

In 1928, no doubt aided by the publication of the handsome book that showcased his innovation and creativity, Addison Mizner received many commissions. The book graphically reminded its owners of the estimable legacy that the architect had already created in a relatively short period of time. With some reviews describing his work as "monumental" and comparing it to that of Italian Renaissance masters, Addison once again drew the interest and attention of those requiring architectural services.[14]

During his tenure in Palm Beach, Addison had always sustained a frenetic pace to satisfy his many clients, a pace that would have exhausted most. It was the sudden absence of this familiar velocity that had to unsettle a man who only flourished in motion. The sudden spate of activity that came his way was welcomed not only for the needed revenue it produced but also for the psychic gratification that had been absent for the past two years. After the contentious debacle that was Boca Raton, Mizner was happily able to focus once again on architecture and to enjoy the rewards of creating beauty.

After completing an addition to the home of John F. Harris, Mizner received a commission for a new house in Manalapan, just south of Palm Beach, from Jerome Gedney, the attorney who handled the acquisition of the assets of the Mizner Development Corporation for Clarence Geist. This commission must have been somewhat emotional for Mizner as Gedney had played a prominent role in Mizner's loss of the corporation and the subsequent expansion of the Cloister Inn by Schultz and Weaver, and the change of name from the Cloister Inn to The Boca Raton Club. Mizner's creation had been publicly subsumed in almost every way to his detriment and profound embarrassment.

The Manalapan site, extending from ocean to lake and dropping significantly toward the lake from a coral ridge, provided the architect a dramatic feature that he was to use to his advantage. In many respects, this was Mizner's best use of a relatively high coral ridge that he had executed to this time. Mizner created terraces on the west side of the house that led down to the lake, from which one could look up and back to a house that projected a dominant sense of height. Mizner, for the first time since La Bellucia in 1920, employed a chamfered northeast-facing entrance that layered dressing rooms on either side to create the compression that Mizner felt allowed the home to "open" as one penetrated deeper into the plan and turned left to see the loggia. By progressing through and beyond the entrance, one understands the logic of the plan. With a high, vaulted ceiling and an oculus to provide

Gedney Residence, Manalapan, Florida, 1928. The Gedney residence was built for Jerome D. Gedney, the New York attorney representing former Mizner backer Clarence Geist. This may have been particularly awkward as Geist assumed control of the Mizner Development Corporation, effectively ruining Mizner financially.
Photograph by Craig Kuhner.

light, the spacious entrance led to a long hall flanked on the ocean side by a thirty-five-foot-long living room and a cloistered courtyard on the opposite side. Defined by varying roof lines, the house was more of a modest hacienda than a great house and had a low profile that created a strong horizontal line. The rooms were generally arranged as Mizner had for some time: the dining room with its great fireplace was on the western patio with the kitchens and serving rooms, and on the east, the very large living room, small library, and guest room. The south side of the house had two bedrooms, also on the patio. The small second floor was by a spiral stair at the southern end of the loggia, with the master bedroom and bath situated over the first floor guest room, and two more guest bedrooms over the lower-level patio guest rooms.

The massing effect was Mizner at his best. As one approached the house, the massing built from the one-story entry to the two-story masses at the ends of the wings. The effect was that the house had two distinct appearances from the ocean side and the patio, with two different approaches to sunlight, breezes, and the outdoor enjoyment of the home.

In 1999, the eight-thousand-square-foot house, scheduled for demolition and now named L'Encantada, was bought for $3.2 million by Maryland horse breeding brothers Jim and Ranney Morgan and Palm Beach real estate investor Gary Ross. The intent was to divide the house into three

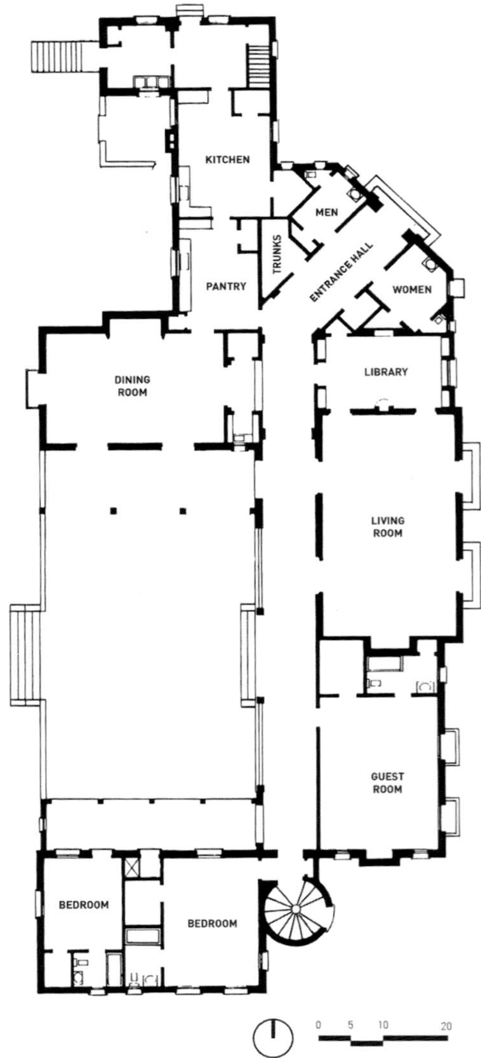

Gedney Residence, 1928. The Gedney house plan reprises Mizner's northwest, chamfered entry of La Bellucia.

Plan reproduced by Chase R. Cothran.

Gedney Residence, 1928. The Gedney residence was one of Mizner's most successful projects. Long and low, the massing of the house rose and fell against the nearby shoreline. Upon entry, guests discovered a cloistered interior courtyard facing west, with a fountain at its center. Photograph by Craig Kuhner.

several-hundred-ton parts and move them, by barge, from Manalapan, first to St. Lucie County, and then to Palm Beach County.[15] After dividing the house, the problems of loading the barges and then getting under way over ocean could have ended badly in many different parts of the voyage. At one point a barge ran aground and incurred $86,000 in fines and cease and desist orders and later encountered six-foot waves that could have rolled the parts into the ocean. This fiasco resulted in continuing owner disputes. At the end of the $15 million investment, the house ended up at 101 Seaspray Avenue in Palm Beach.[16] Mizner's last great South Florida villa survived what would have destroyed most houses, but as Mizner built his villas to last, this test proves that he understood constructability very well. Unfortunately, the house could not survive the lingering dispute between Ross and the Morgans and in 2001, one of Mizner's most important and well-designed houses was razed.

In spite of the marketing boost from the publication of *The Florida Architecture of Addison Mizner*, the architect still faced formidable competition from the array of talented architects now practicing in Palm Beach. As a result, he began to accept more commissions outside of the state of Florida. His last hotel project came from Howard Coffin, a resident of Detroit and cofounder with Roy D. Chapin and others of the Hudson Motor Car Company in 1909. Having become entranced with the beauty of the coastal regions of Georgia while attending the Vanderbilt Cup auto races in Savannah in 1911, Coffin purchased Georgia's Long Island in 1926 and renamed it Sea

Island. Desiring a small hotel to test the appeal of Sea Island as a resort destination, he sent his young cousin, A. W. "Bill" Jones, on a trip to Florida to investigate hotels. After visiting the Cloister Inn in Boca Raton, renamed the Ritz-Carlton Cloister, Jones recommended that they commission Mizner for their project. Jones, well aware of the lofty reputation of the great architect, was intimidated before his initial meeting with Mizner; however, unaware of the architect's financial problems, he was surprised to be showered with profuse charm and attention on his initial visit to Mizner's Palm Beach office.

Mizner built a three-story hotel with public rooms on the first floor and guest rooms on the second and third floors. The L-shaped building was framed on the third side by a loggia, creating a U-shape that enclosed a cloistered patio. In approaching the entrance, visitors could appreciate the theatricality of projecting planes and varying roof lines and the enchantment of an entry façade shouldered by a round stair tower. Bill Jones and Howard Coffin were unsure of the prospects of the proposed resort so, rather than build a large hotel, they chose to have Mizner construct a forty-room temporary wood building without concrete foundations. Completed in October, the hotel was christened with a gala opening attended by many dignitaries, shortly followed by a visit from President Calvin Coolidge during the holidays. Success was immediate but interrupted by the Depression, an event that prevented the construction of the proposed larger hotel.

During construction of The Cloister, Mizner was asked by Bill Jones to build a small house for him and his wife. In September 1926, Jones had married Katherine "Kit" Talbott, the daughter of a wealthy and prominent couple from Dayton, Ohio. Only a year earlier, Kit's brother Harold had married Peggy Thayer,

The Cloister, Cottage Number 10, Sea Island, Georgia. When Addison Mizner designed and built The Cloister at Sea Island in 1928, he was asked by A. W. "Bill" Jones to build a house for him and his new wife. The result was this charming cottage, modest by Mizner's standards and reminiscent of the smaller homes he designed in Boca Raton. Instead of building with the same materials he used in South Florida, the architect chose tabby construction, indigenous to the southeastern coast and composed of lime, sand, oyster shells, ash, and water.
Photograph by the author.

who had become infatuated with Addison Mizner during the summer of 1922 on their trip to Spain with Nell Cosden. As was the architect's wont, he worked closely with each client's wife to ascertain her role within the house and to refine appropriate ideas for design. In the course of discussing plans for the interior, Kit asked Addison if he was going to design a mantel for the fireplace. Favoring simplicity, Addison stated that there would be no mantel as "some son-of-a-bitch will just put a clock on it."[17] Although his empire had been shaken and his image impaired, Mizner's propensity for salty language remained intact. Playful and spirited, Kit was unfazed, if not amused, by Addison's comment.[18] The house, the only one designed by the architect on the island, was modest but very charming. Occupied by the Joneses until 1940, the house was constructed of tabby, a type of building material used in the coastal Southeast made with oyster shell. Though tabby was not used in Florida, the architect wanted to use a material appropriate to the region.

Perhaps Addison Mizner's most satisfying commission in 1928 was a grand mansion for Percival Foerderer in Bryn Mawr, Pennsylvania. Foerderer, a Philadelphia businessman and philanthropist, dropped out of medical school to run the family leather tanning business when his father became ill.[19] Friends with Edward Stotesbury and Rodman Wanamaker, Foerderer appreciated the results Mizner produced for his fellow Philadelphians. Having wintered in Palm Beach during the 1920s, he also knew that the architect possessed the imagination to handle the scale required for an estate of 249 acres.

Mizner obliged with a magnificent mansion, *La Ronda*, a tour de force that harkened back to his earliest and grandest Palm Beach houses. A walled forecourt introduced the entrance façade defined by a castellated third floor tower that served as a mirador. The great stone hall actually recalled the same room at Playa Riente with its monumental height, ribbed groins, and Gothic fenestration. The series of windows on the south side of the great room overlooked a fountain and provided a full view of the garden. The windows were distinguished by their great height, leaded glass, and the crestings of cinquefoil Gothic tracery that were set into lancet-arched openings. The elaborate ceiling, inspired by a Gothic castle in Spain, was made by Mizner Industries. The experience of planning the expressive articulation of this house, recalling the early days of glory in Palm Beach, surely had to provide the architect a sense of exhilaration.

Mizner was clearly planning for a different climate, more like Long Island or San Francisco than Palm Beach. His planning was tightly controlled with only one loggia and small terraces, but still with rooms, large and small, separated by only a wall and door between. He flanked the entry with restrooms to achieve the compression between entry and the surprise of the Great Hall, which stepped down into the twenty-eight by

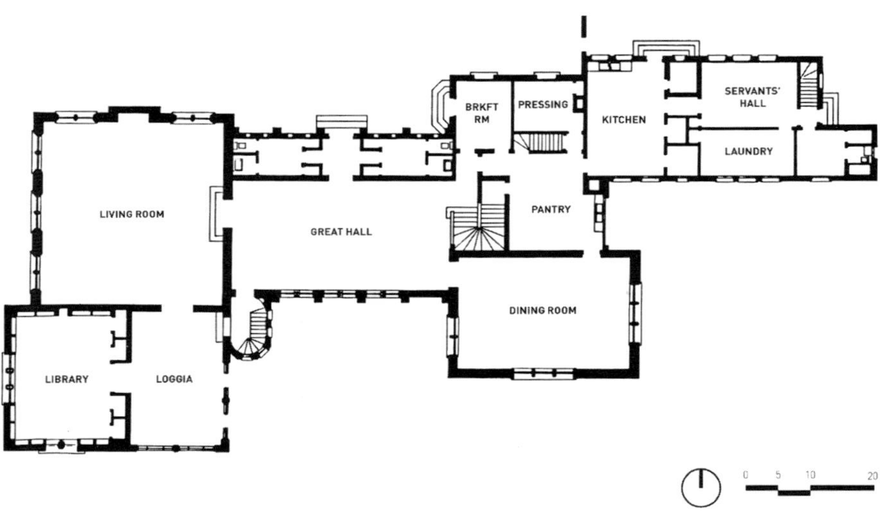

La Ronda, 1928. Due to stronger competition in Palm Beach, Mizner looked further afield for commissions. Percival E. Foerderer, a wealthy leather merchant, retained Mizner for a new estate in Bryn Mawr, Pennsylvania. Foerderer was a winter resident of Palm Beach and familiar with Mizner's work. Mizner's 1928 plan derived from his earlier Palm Beach houses, most importantly Playa Riente, Casa Bendita, and El Mirasol. The plan was tightly controlled with the massing recognizing its environmental conditions in the Mid-Atlantic.
Plan reproduced by Chase R. Cothran.

La Ronda, 1928. The south patio and gardens of La Ronda were bounded by the dining room, the great hall, and the loggia, which is shared by the library and living room.
Photograph by Craig Kuhner.

La Ronda, 1928. The view of the mansion from the great lawn belies the fact of the estate's 249 acres. The residence was located at the end of a long drive through a gatehouse, and past garages and staff quarters to a walled entrance court on the north side of the house.
Photograph by Craig Kuhner.

thirty-six foot living room. East of the living room was the heavily coffered dining room and the kitchen and service wing. The west wing of the second floor held two bedrooms and a master suite of bedroom, sleeping porch, baths, and a small secretary's office. The exterior stair tower also accessed the master suite and a mirador in the battlement. A second mirador contained the children's playroom and a sleeping porch.

Mizner employed many of the devices learned from ancient sources in Italy and Spain that he had used at Casa Bendita and Playa Riente, particularly the Davanzati Palace in Florence and Gothic castles in Spain. The interiors were almost wholly stone—walls, vaulted ceiling, and floor—the carving

La Ronda, 1928. The large north entrance plaza at La Ronda.
Photograph by Craig Kuhner.

La Ronda, 1928. The great hall was reminiscent of the scale and detail of Playa Riente.
Photograph by Craig Kuhner.

and casting for which was equal to the quality at Playa Riente if not at that scale. Suspended bronze stairs, complex leaded glass, and large wall-hung tapestries cohered to become, with the random massing of square and round towers, a place that might have been six hundred years old. Mizner Industries supplied practically all of the decorative detail, furniture, keystone, and tile. With La Ronda, Mizner proved that he had not suffered any loss of capacity, creativity, or stamina in the creation of one of his best estates.

Mizner also traveled to California to plan and build a house in Montecito for Alfred Dieterich, for whom he had built a house in 1912 in Millbrook, New York. Dieterich sold his family estate in New York after the death of his father in 1927 and subsequently invited Mizner to collaborate with him once more. Dieterich had originally commissioned George Washington Smith, a very prominent Santa Barbara architect working in the Spanish Colonial and Mediterranean styles, to design the house; however, he released the popular Smith to hire Mizner, someone with whom he had enjoyed an excellent relationship.

The house, christened *La Bienvenida* by its owner and built in Park Lane, an enclave of two hundred estates, had forty rooms and occupied approximately seventeen thousand square feet. Designed around a central patio, the mansion boasted forty rooms, including a fourteen-hundred-square-foot living room, a south cloister with a vaulted ceiling twenty feet in height, and a capacious library that scorned Prohibition with its secret passageway leading to a wine cellar. The thirteen-acre grounds required seventeen full-time gardeners and featured a glorious garden with cascading water provided by seventy small stylized shells.

The living room was thirty-four feet by forty-two feet with arched Venetian windows, a large stone fireplace, and an elaborate chambered ceiling inspired by a cloister ceiling at the library at the University of Salamanca. Both the cast stone fireplace and ceiling were made by Mizner Industries and shipped to California from Florida. The ceiling was made from Woodite and was painted and decorated on site. In an interview conducted by historian Christina Orr in 1975, an employee of the architect described how Mizner climbed the scaffolding to show his painters the technique and desired result: "(He) painted the sample for the painters to follow. He went up there at eight o'clock in the morning and wouldn't come down for lunch until he had one section completed. . . . He did a beautiful job. He worked out all the colors and showed the painters what to do."[20] Despite advancing age and bad health, Addison focused on delivering an appropriate design and finish, even if he had to do it himself. He remained the master builder.

The flurry of activity in 1928 gave the impression that Mizner's architectural practice had been revived; however, the

Casa Bienvenida, 1928. Between 1927 and 1931, Mizner's practice was truly national for the first time in his career. The A. E. Dieterichs, for whom Mizner had designed a New York house during his Port Washington years, asked Mizner to design a house in Montecito, California. The Dieterichs had commissioned George Washington Smith, the most prominent architect of Santa Barbara, but released Smith and retained Mizner.

The thirteen-acre estate on Park Lane enabled Mizner to design a forty-room, seventeen-thousand-square-foot hacienda-type house with an austere façade and three-sided cloister surrounding the courtyard. Mizner collaborated with a California landscape designer in the creation of gardens inspired by Generalife gardens in Granada, Spain. Courtesy of the Santa Barbara Historical Museum.

crescendo of momentum was stifled by another natural disaster in September. A devastating hurricane destroyed hundreds of homes in West Palm Beach and claimed approximately two thousand lives in Palm Beach County.[21] In Palm Beach, the storm flooded Ocean Boulevard and damaged many buildings, although none of Addison Mizner's houses were reported to have been structurally damaged. Addison remarked that, according to his agent in Palm Beach, "the houses of many of my friends there are practically intact" and that "My own property, including an entire subdivision in Palm Beach, has suffered a loss of about $5,000."[22] The destruction required much repair and re-building but it dampened demand for luxury homes with the predictable result that Addison Mizner's business suffered in 1929.

The most significant work for Addison Mizner in 1929 was to design the Florida Embassy Club for Colonel Edward R. Bradley. Patronized by the bellwethers of industry and society, the exclusive club was modeled on the clubs of New York and London and offered dancing and dining. As Mizner's health was failing, associates Byron Simonson and Lester Geisler had begun to assume responsibility for more work in the office. Instead of adhering to the sixteenth- and seventeenth-century design that had characterized most of his work in the last ten years, Mizner conceived an eighteenth-century neoclassical Spanish Colonial building. A loggia for dining surrounded a dance patio that was illuminated with colored lights, producing dramatic effects during the evening. The Embassy Club eventually suffered financially and was subsequently redesigned by Marion Sims Wyeth in 1947 to serve as the Society of the Four Arts.

Prominent leaders of Palm Beach established the Memorial Fountain Commission to raise a subscription to build a memorial park on South County Road in honor of the town's founders. When the chairman, Harold Vanderbilt, requested local architects to submit plans for the design, Maurice Fatio graciously wrote a letter to the *Palm Beach Daily News* imploring the commission to award the design to Addison Mizner, stating that his plan "could not be improved upon."[23] This was a magnanimous gesture on the part of the younger Fatio, a suggestion that was approved. Mizner's composition has a central reflecting pool flanked by stone walkways, manicured hedges, and symmetrically arranged palms. Above this on the terrace to the south is a central fountain and bowl supported by four rearing chargers. This feature, inspired by the Fountain of the Sea Horses at the Villa Borghese in Rome, serves as the focal point in the Town Hall Square Historic District. Mizner's last commission of the year was a group of retail stores and apartments only three blocks north of the fountain at South County Road and Seaview Avenue.

As if hurricanes were insufficient to ravage the professional prospects of Addison Mizner, another catastrophe befell him that proved to be the *coup de grace*. The stock market crash in October of 1929 was a tragedy that not only signaled the

Memorial Fountain and Plaza, 1929. In 1929, members of the Palm Beach Garden Club endeavored to beautify Palm Beach by creating a memorial fountain dedicated to honor Henry Flagler and Elisha Dimick. The Fountain Fund raised $25,000 and engaged Mizner to design the fountain. When Harold Vanderbilt, the commission's chairman, decided to invite other architects' involvement, Maurice Fatio sent a letter to the Palm Beach Daily News *saying that "In view of the fact that Mr. Addison Mizner is the originator of this beautification proposal and has himself submitted a fountain design to adequately meet the requirements. . . ." With that statement, Fatio withdrew from the competition, and the commission then accepted Mizner's plan. Mizner's design was elegant, dramatic, and was clearly derived from the Alhambra in Granada, Spain.*
Photograph by Craig Kuhner.

end of the architect's career but also caused the ruination of the lives of so many others. The unbridled exuberance and seemingly unbounded prosperity of the 1920s, fueled by a stock market that quadrupled in value in a decade, came to end. The implications for Addison Mizner were unavoidably grim. Had the architect been younger and stronger, his pioneer spirit would have propelled him forward to a better day; however, at this point in his life, beset with financial problems, bad health, and emotional turmoil, he no longer possessed the vitality that had always sustained him in times of crisis.

Addison's health was deteriorating as a result of ulcers, heart and leg problems, and being overweight. Less physically active now, his weight increased to approximately three hundred pounds. In 1929, Ozie Belle Brown came to work for Addison as his cook. Having worked for prominent families in Palm Beach, she must have been an excellent cook because Addison gave her a 25 percent raise and accommodations to accept his employment. She enjoyed working for Addison and described him as a man who "loved to eat and who liked everything."[24] Addison's nephew, Horace Chase, humorously observed that "Addison's idea of a square meal is to sit a foot away from the table and eat till he touches."[25] Beyond indulging at the dinner table, Ozie observed that Mizner was not much of a drinker or smoker at this time. Though casual

Addison Mizner dressed as Wendell Weed, circa 1928. Weed, an eccentric man looking for odd jobs when he met Mizner in 1918, was eventually employed by Mizner as a greeter for shoppers visiting the Via Mizner on Worth Avenue. Mizner, copying the attire of Weed, is dressed in white with distinctive red accents: a fez, cummerbund, and umbrella. This photograph attests to the expanding waistline of the architect in his later years.
Courtesy of Preservation Foundation of Palm Beach, Palm Beach, Florida.

about many things, he was punctilious about the table setting, preferring to dine privately with plates, cups, and objects of silver and gold.

When Mizner became highly successful in Palm Beach, the architect began to be less discreet in his personal life. While he had romances with Bertha Dolber and Peggy Thayer that were documented in his memoirs, he had also enjoyed relationships with men throughout his adult life. Certainly one of his best friends outside of the immediate family was Alice DeLamar, who knew much about Addison's personal life. She spoke about an emotional relationship with a young man, Jack Baird, during Addison's last years in San Francisco before leaving for New York in 1904. This was the same time period in which he was informally engaged to Bertha Dolber. This is not to suggest that Mizner was romantically linked with Bertha and Jack simultaneously or that his feelings for Bertha were not genuine. It does speak to the mores of the time that did not sanction homosexuality. A convenient solution for a gay person then would have been to marry a tolerant female.

Later in Palm Beach, an opportune solution to create the appearance of propriety was for Mizner to hire desirable young men for his business, a personal convenience yet a professional burden. DeLamar describes a profile that Mizner preferred: thin, attractive, well-dressed young men who possessed enough decorum and taste to attend Palm Beach parties, frequently as escorts for older ladies. As these men were generally searching for an advantageous marriage or relationship for themselves, they were not really interested in business and therefore made poor managers for Mizner Industries. It is unknown to what degree Addison was emotionally attached to these partners, but DeLamar recorded that the relationships were always fleeting and psychologically painful. During Mizner's difficult years after the debacle of Boca Raton, it would only have been natural to seek companionship and solace in a relationship. Humiliated and disgraced in public, he would have welcomed a connection beyond mere gratification or friendship.

It is worth noting that Alice DeLamar's comments about Addison were submitted in a letter to Alva Johnston, a Pulitzer Prize–winning author that she knew was publishing a series of articles about Mizner in the *New Yorker* in 1952. In essence, these were private thoughts intended not to be divulged at the time for fear of causing harm to the reputations of friends and acquaintances. She wanted Johnston to understand Mizner as completely as possible before writing his four magazine pieces that would subsequently be published in a book, *The Legendary Mizners*. As a true friend who considered the architect part of her family, she was sympathetic to Addison's difficult condition as she herself was gay. As she said to Johnston, "you cannot have a basic understanding of Addison's character without some insight into these more indiscrete [sic] sidelights . . . for in the long run an idea of his emotional weaknesses will only add up to a better appreciation of the lovable side of his character."[26] His frailties were present but not easily perceived as they were always concealed behind a veil of humor and bonhomie; however, Addison Mizner, like all human beings, needed companionship and affection.

Because of Mizner's popularity, many pretended to be unaware of his indiscretions, although they were played out in a public forum for anyone who was interested. Jack Roy was a memorable young man whom Addison made manager of his furniture factory despite his having no experience whatsoever in management or any familiarity with artisanship. He later repaid Addison by running off with Wilson's discarded girlfriend, Florence Atkinson. Until that time, Atkinson had been recognized in Palm Beach society as Wilson's wife. The scandalous fiction perpetrated by his brother and the quick, furtive departure of Roy and Atkinson brought unwanted shame to the architect. Addison met Jerry Girandolle in New York and, after giving him a new Cadillac, also made him manager of the furniture factory. Later, Addison was attracted to the young painter he used on the Cosden house, Achille Angeli, described by DeLamar as "a strikingly handsome young fellow."[27] These men were in their twenties when Addison met them and none provided him with meaningful companionship or intimacy. For Addison Mizner at this time, only frustration and disappointment were to be found in pursuing youth.

The vagaries of the investment world punished many but left others unscathed. Although some Palm Beach winter residents had been diminished by the Crash, they still had significant assets and were able to sustain a splendid lifestyle. On one hand, Paris Singer, devastated by speculative real estate investments and a reduced stock portfolio, moved to Saint-Jean-Cap-Ferrat on the French Riviera to escape embarrassment. At the same time, Joseph Widener's financial situation remained sufficiently robust to begin building Il Palmetto, his grand Italian Renaissance estate in Palm Beach designed by Maurice Fatio.

In spite of the Crash, it was announced by the Chamber of Commerce in 1930 that "Palm Beach was enjoying one of its largest seasons" and it was variously reported that the many Palm Beach clubs were bustling.[28] This proved to be of little benefit to Mizner. Illustrating the extent of his fall and the dramatic ascent of his competition was the fact that, in 1930, Mizner received one modest commission in Palm Beach while Maurice Fatio received eight, most of them for substantial residences.[29]

In general, the propensity for extravagance yielded to an attitude of restraint that reduced the demand for large projects in Palm Beach. With neither prospects nor money,

Barclay Warburton and Addison Mizner at Mizner Industries, circa 1929. Warburton, a Mizner client, became the mayor of Palm Beach in 1928 and visited his friend a year later at the opening of the stone works, the newest addition to Mizner Industries. Even after the fiasco of Boca Raton in 1926, Mizner Industries remained one of the largest employers in the area until the Stock Market Crash in 1929 and provided Addison with a source of income during trying times.

Courtesy of Historical Society of Palm Beach County.

Addison Mizner was sadly forced to rely on financial support from friends. Some, like Irving Berlin, provided loans while others paid his bills. Edward Moore, who had purchased Sin Cuidado, the home on South County Road that Addison had originally built for himself, continually provided assistance. The munificence of friends could not prevent Mizner's problems from compounding. The architect was again plagued by the residue of Boca Raton when a group of investors sued the officers of the Mizner Development Corporation for $1,450,000 for conspiring to inflate the value of Boca Raton land.[30] There appeared to be no end to his problems.

Throughout this difficult time, there was no offer of support from either his brother Wilson or his niece Ysabel Chase Hollins, both of whom were living in California. To Addison's great sadness, his carefree nephew, Horace Chase, had died in a plane crash in 1928. A year later, his niece Ysabel appeared to place herself in favorable circumstances as she married McKim Hollins whose sister Marion had won the US Women's Amateur Championship in golf. Their father was Harry Bowly Hollins, socially prominent in New York and friends with Vanderbilts and Morgans. Occupied with a busy social life, Ysabel devoted less and less time to her uncle. Beset with problems that intensified alcoholism, McKim Hollins would later squander his money and be forced to sell his family's house.

Wilson was always aware of Addison's fondness for his nephew and niece and, according to Alex Waugh, selfishly viewed them as impediments to benefitting from Addison's estate. Whether true or not, Wilson's self-centeredness and disregard for his brother were evident at this time. Though removed from Palm Beach, Wilson continued to accumulate bills that ultimately fell at the feet of his brother. Reminding Wilson that he too was financially strapped, Addison remonstrated as best he could through correspondence, encouraging Wilson to consider making monthly payments to begin satisfying his Florida obligations. Ensconced in the safe harbor of Hollywood, Wilson merrily brushed off any hint of advice to the great frustration and disappointment of the architect.

Yet, in spite of the apparent indifference of his relatives, Addison remained loyal and was unavoidably drawn to the remaining two members of his family. He seriously considered leaving Palm Beach for Carmel, California, where he had earlier purchased a large tract of land with a farmhouse and garden that he had begun renovating during trips to the West Coast. To be able to build an architectural practice in the state, he went to the trouble of taking Florida examinations to obtain a special license that would also have been recognized in the state of California; however, when he ultimately took stock of his health, he realized that his physical and emotional limitations would forbid starting over. For a man who always remained sanguine, it must have been terribly distressing to confront at every turn the futility that now enveloped his life.

Although Mizner spent considerable time in 1930 on projects for Alexander Camp in Dallas and Hugh Dillman in Grosse Pointe, Michigan, he lost the commissions to Maurice Fatio and Horace Trumbauer, respectively. He did design Palm Beach offices for E. F. Hutton & Co. on South County Road, just north of Royal Palm Way. Hutton, married at the time to Marjorie Merriweather Post, was one of the first to open a brokerage office in a resort town such as Palm Beach. Built of keystone and sited on a corner, the horizontal structure had a canted entrance. Double doors were flanked by masculine, quoined piers with finials and surmounted by a blind pointed arch in which a clock was encased. This handsome building had a more restrained presence than the typical Mizner residence. Perhaps his psychological mood moved him at this moment to embrace a more sober historical style that was in itself a reaction to dramatic exuberance.

Addison Mizner's Christmas card showing the magnificent front door of the Villa Mizner. The legend reads "The door from which eggnog and Christmas Greetings flow." His Christmas card would have been followed by an invitation to his annual eggnog party on New Year's Day. With his considerable skill at entertaining the elite, Addison became deservedly known as a society architect.
Courtesy of Historical Society of Palm Beach County.

In spite of pressing issues, Addison Mizner still presented a public image of the gregarious, cheerful bon vivant that his Florida friends had always known. In 1931 he hosted his annual New Year's Day party at the Villa Mizner and greeted all the illustrious names that constituted the beau monde of Palm Beach. Early that year, he gave a series of parties for visiting friends, including the Archbishop of Santo Domingo and Syrie Maugham, his old friend from New York. In April, Addison traveled to Washington in hopes of landing a commission for a new federal post office for Palm Beach, an award that would have given impetus to his business. Despite having spent a lot of time on the project throughout the year, Addison was frustrated by a government that continued to deliberate the merits of building the post office.

In the late 1927, Mizner began a commission for a winter home from William J. Williams, the founder of the Western Southern Life Insurance Company of Cincinnati. Casa Coe da Sol, completed in 1931, was the first and only house commission that Mizner had ever taken on the west coast of Florida. The site was composed of two lots with two existing houses on Boca Ciega Bay in St. Petersburg that enjoyed dramatic sunset views of the bay. The lot and house at 500 Park Street had been owned by Albert Lang in 1930. Previously, the Williams had bought an old bungalow at 510 Park Street that faced the yacht basin and redecorated it just before they asked

Mizner to design a new home on their consolidated lot. Edith Petronis, the second owner of Casa Coe da Sol, spoke extensively with Oscar J. Steinert, the original contractor for the

Casa Coe da Sol, 1931. The Williams family, having grown fond of the hand-painted murals of the master bedroom, asked Mizner to incorporate the master bedroom from the existing house on their property into the new house. The photo shows the bedroom having been raised to the level of the second floor. Visitors to the home can see the roof of the old house in the attic of the Casa Coe da Sol.

Courtesy of Amy Petronis Rand.

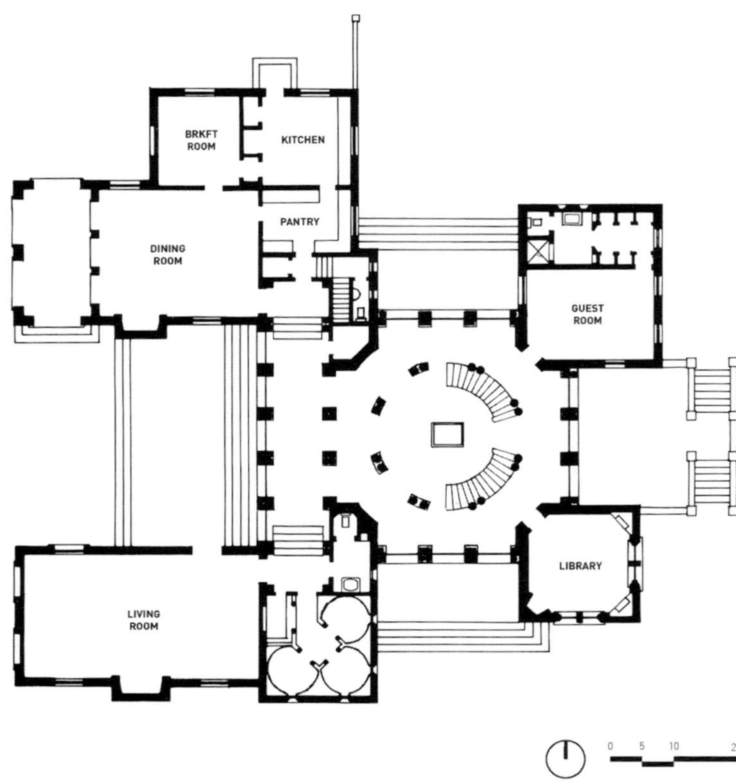

Casa Coe da Sol, 1931. Mizner, with the considerable assistance and perhaps influence of Byron Simonson, a longtime Mizner draftsman, created a plan that was unlike any he had ever created. The highly formal four-square plan is organized around two symmetrical, curved stairs that land on the center axis of the second-floor colonnade. This strong core allowed Mizner to vary the squares in plan and massing to create his signature accretive effect.
Plan reproduced by Chase R. Cothran.

house, and with Mrs. Byron Simonson, the widow of Mizner's on-site clerk of the works during the construction of the project and learned a great deal about both Mizner's direction of the project and the Williams' direction and work with Mizner over the five-year design and construction period.

In the Williams' original bungalow, Mrs. Williams liked her bedroom and bath with the sea bottom ceiling mural so much that the couple insisted that it be incorporated in the design of the new home by raising it into the structure to become the northwest bedroom. The old shingled hip roof can still be seen in the attic.

This seventeen-room mansion was Mizner's last large estate. At about eleven thousand square feet, Casa Coe da Sol is smaller than most of the houses Mizner had typically designed in Palm Beach and is a fitting "last" house, unique in all of Mizner's career in that it has a solid, not an open or outdoor, core. Conceived as a four-square plan around a large circular double-columned, peristyle stair hall, the entry is through the east façade flanked by the two eastern square volumes. The paired columns on the lower level are Doric on flat bases, and the upper columns are Ionic on pedestals, and connected by bronze railings.

Upon entry, the view to the bay is clear across a large round, low fountain, the middle of which is occupied by a full-size marble bathing nude. Directly above the fountain is a twelve-foot,

Casa Coe da Sol, 1931. The entry was typical in that a guest would take either of two sets of steps to gain access to a small porch that fronted the front door and flanking windows.
Photograph by Craig Kuhner.

multi-tiered crystal chandelier that was replaced in the 1970s, suspended through a geometric, stained-glass ceiling. At the entry are two suspended concrete stairs, curving upward and about the fountain space, that meet at the landing on the second floor, which serves the bedrooms.

The massing of the main structure is roughly ninety-seven by ninety-nine square feet overall, and composed of differently scaled masses of generally consistent height. Mizner's approach to the design is consistent with his historical approach, and in keeping with that, the large volumes west of the four-square,

Casa Coe da Sol, 1931. The grand stair and its colonnade were powerful organizing elements for the core of the house, and the geometric pattern of the very large laylight above allowed Mizner to use a darker blue tile to hold the floor against a very bright room above.
Photograph by Craig Kuhner.

the living room on the south and the dining room and loggia on the north, are separated by a large terrace that steps

Casa Coe da Sol, 1931. As is frequently the case in the treatment of Mizner's houses over time, the loggia has been filled with glass doors and windows in expanding the living areas of the house.

Photograph by Craig Kuhner.

down to the lawn and to views of the bay. From the rotunda and through equal openings between the four-square masses, one moves to exterior terraces and down to the landscape.

Mizner's effect is that the four-square portion of the home appears to have been built first, with the western additions having been built later.

That Mizner relied upon a two-story rotunda is unique and that the rotunda is central to the plan was new to his approach. Mizner clearly was thinking differently about design, generally, but it is important to note that Byron Simonson had rejoined the firm in 1931 and was given design authority in Mizner's later years.

Evidence of recent trends in architecture are dramatically present in the Williams home. The coffee room in the southeast wing adjacent to the living room is highly stylized with a trefoil plan with tiled banquettes and segmented arches reminiscent of Moorish arches. The master bath is more dramatic and is a very good example of art deco, unique in Mizner's work. Notably, Mrs. Williams forbade Mizner from "antiquing" any part of her home, the result being that the home looks more contemporary than Mizner's earlier work. There is no pecky cypress or stained woods, and Mizner's earlier religious motifs are absent.

The Williams were devotees of early modern architecture and the home was furnished with many of Mizner's traditional pieces. There were also many pieces of Paul Frankl's art deco cabinet work, contemporaneously important in New York and with a reputation among young architects and designers that

Casa Coe da Sol, 1931. The bath of the master suite was an expression of the owners' interest in art deco and modernism in general. Many of the original furnishings in the Williams house were by Paul Frankl, a noted art deco furniture designer from New York.
Photograph by Craig Kuhner.

looked to modernism as an honest style. In 1928, Frankl published a book, the foreword of which was written by Frank Lloyd Wright.

It is not known why Mizner departed from his historicist treatment at Casa Coe da Sol, but it is an important house not least because it is the most intact house in terms of architecture, finishes, and furnishings that exists. That it is Mizner's last large villa is important because of the ample evidence that he was evolving as an architect and interior designer.

In 1971, Casa Coe da Sol was bought by Mr. and Mrs. Henry Petronis, who moved into the property in July. Edith Petronis protected the house and, with her husband, restored the house to its former glory. In many cases, Petronis was able to find the original manufacturers such as Kokomo Glass Works in Indiana for the atrium skylight. The exterior was restored and all of the lighting fixtures were repaired and cleaned, original rugs from W & J Sloane were cleaned and repaired, and all of the original paint colors were restored. Edith Petronis performed a great public service as Casa Coe da Sol was added to the National Trust of Historic Places in July 1980 and is available for tours on a regular basis.[31]

Despite woeful conditions of health and finance, Addison once again hosted his well-attended party on New Year's Day 1932 and, notwithstanding the fact that younger architects were regularly receiving the important commissions in Palm Beach, he graciously continued to invite his competition. With an invitation list of four hundred people, Addison's New Year's Day parties were regularly covered by local newspapers

Casa Coe da Sol, 1931. The cafe was a highly stylized version of a small European coffee bar. The trifoil plan lent a commercial air to the house. There is nothing recorded as to the intent of the owners, Mizner, or Simonson in creating this whimsical feature.
Photograph by Craig Kuhner.

and also reported in the *New York Times*.[32] In the aftermath of his Boca Raton failure, an observer could not be faulted for assuming that the society architect would inevitably lose some of his social luster; however, Mizner continued to entertain fashionable society regularly. Not only did his guest lists continue to include the leaders of Palm Beach and celebrities from the world of entertainment but also members of the aristocracy and royalty. In the 1929 season, Addison gave a musicale described as "the largest affair to date" and then hosted a party for Viscountess Fielding from England and Princess Aspasia, the widow of the former king of Greece, Alexander I.[33]

In 1931 he had begun to write an autobiography, beginning with the story of his parents and ending with the death of his mother in 1915. Believing that no one would be interested in the challenges and achievements of his architectural career, he focused on personal relationships, adventure, and storytelling. As his riotous life was a series of amazing and fascinating stories, the book, published in September 1932 as *The Many Mizners*, made for good entertainment. Although a gifted raconteur, some friends thought that his tales were much more entertaining in conversation than in print; however, one reviewer acknowledged the book to be "one of the most rollicking, rowdiest pieces of humor that any reader will encounter."[34]

Mizner's intention was to write a second volume that covered the rest of his life; however, he was able only to complete 123 pages of a typescript that covered the years 1918 to 1924. Once again thinking that his readers wanted to be amused, he subordinated his professional career to entertainment. His writing provides a window into a clever mind that always saw the humor in life and reacted accordingly. Larded with fewer improbable escapades than found in *The Many Mizners*, the second volume was replete with stories of the impressive personalities that were his everyday companions. The first page begins with Alva Belmont, one of the dominant figures of Gilded Age New York and the mother of Consuelo Vanderbilt, the former Duchess of Marlborough. "Miss Alva," was "chattering away so fast that I couldn't get in a word edgewise, and she knew that I couldn't reach anything to throw at her."[35] The last page ends with two of the most important figures in American music: "Irving Berlin wrote two or three hits at my piano, and Jerry (Jerome) Kern . . . and others would play by the hours in the afternoons."[36] The tone always conveyed the easy familiarity he enjoyed with an endless parade of social paladins. Such was the life of a society architect.

Addison Mizner received a commission in 1932 for his last Palm Beach house from Kenneth D. Alexander, an automobile dealer in West Palm Beach. The smallest of his Palm Beach homes, it was a narrow structure that presented a simple

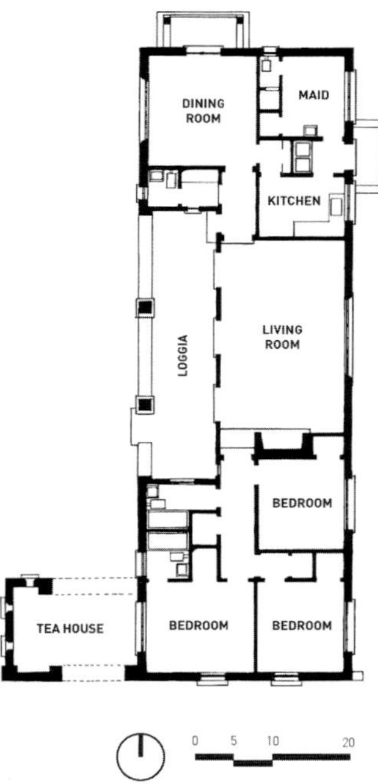

Alexander Residence, 1932. The plan for the Alexander house was modest, but rigorous. The long plan offered an interesting approach to working within a tight Palm Beach lot. Plan reproduced by Chase R. Cothran.

Alexander Residence, 1932. Mizner's taut façade is carved away for the major openings and windows.
Photograph by Craig Kuhner.

Medieval Revival entrance to Brazilian Avenue. While only a one-story house with three bedrooms, modest by Palm Beach standards, the architect was still able to imbue it with architectural interest. The living room, spacious with a high, beamed ceiling, was distinguished by a large stained-glass window on the east side and three French doors on the west side that looked onto a loggia and garden beyond. This arrangement took advantage of the sun to magnify a relatively small space with soft, diffused light.

Though the fees generated from the Alexander house and a subsequent project for a movie theater in Belle Glade were well received, they could not begin to cover his expenses. It was at this point that he learned that Mizner Industries was forced to declare bankruptcy, a painful realization since it owed him over $36,000.[37] Without any source of meaningful income, he could no longer afford to keep his ranch in Carmel; as a result, he transferred ownership to his niece, Ysabel Chase Hollins. Then in June, he learned of the death of his good friend Paris Singer who had passed away in London. This was a difficult loss that no doubt prompted reflection. The appearance of Paris Singer in 1918 represented a happy renewal of his life and his sudden absence was a reminder of the downward trajectory that now defined his existence. Perhaps looking to escape a life that was fragmenting in front of him, Mizner decided to travel to California.

After so much distressing news, Addison happily learned in June 1932 that his niece Ysabel had just given birth to a baby girl named Kim Mizner Hollins. Once again, the magnetic lure of family beckoned. Addison, even in frail health, did not shrink from driving himself over three thousand miles. He visited his niece in Pebble Beach and periodically went to Los Angeles to check on brother Wilson who had been stricken with pneumonia in August. Wilson, as usual, had managed successfully to re-invent himself as a visible figure in Hollywood. During this time, the brothers were photographed together at the racetrack at Del Monte. The caption identified the pair: "Mr. Mizner is a brother of Wilson Mizner, the wit." In typical Mizner fashion, the delighted Wilson gave Addison a copy on which he had written "This should put you in your place."[38]

Avoiding work was a practice that Wilson Mizner had refined his entire life. As he said, "I hate work like the Lord hates St. Louis."[39] Just as he had done on Broadway, Wilson was now getting paid to write: in this case, screenplays for Warner Brothers Pictures. Despite being in a financial depression, Jack Warner gave Wilson a job because he "knew Mizner could write the sharpest dialogue in the business."[40] In reality, this meant that he was providing inimitable nuggets of dialogue to the actual writers, a natural practice that did not require much effort. At the studio, he was called "the Archbishop" because he liked to nod off in a big red lounge chair that resembled a church throne.[41] When awake, Wilson's contributions added authenticity to the newly popular genre of films about gangsters and underworld figures that made stars of James Cagney and Edward G. Robinson and that made Warner a lot of money. When working on the movie *20,000 Years in Sing Sing*, a story about warden Lewis E. Lawes, Wilson was very surprised to meet the penitentiary's warden on the set one day: "Warden, I never expected to meet you without an iron grille between us."[42] Wilson was also the inspiration for various shady characters in movies, roles portrayed by such notable actors as Clark Gable and William Powell.[43]

Another endeavor that suited his indolence was becoming a restauranteur. He partnered with Jack Warner, his employer who put up the money, and Herbert Somborn, a former husband of Gloria Swanson, who owned land on Wilshire Boulevard. Together the three men opened the Brown Derby, a celebrated restaurant across the street from the Ambassador Hotel where Wilson lived. Wilson was always present but felt the need to be careful. Ever alert to those who might be seeking him out for past misdeeds, Wilson held court there every night at a table shielded behind a one-way mirrored wall that conveniently allowed him to spot anyone approaching while, at the same time, prevented others from seeing him.

Warner and Somborn looked to Wilson to provide ambience and entertainment, a task at which he succeeded. The Derby was intended as a comfortable haunt where Hollywood celebrities could relax and avoid curious, overbearing fans. It stayed open late, provided superb service, and employed very attractive waitstaff. It was reported in gossip columns that such luminaries as Douglas Fairbanks, Sr., Charlie Chaplin, Darryl Zanuck, Tallulah Bankhead, and others could regularly

Addison and Wilson Mizner were photographed together at the Del Monte race track in 1932. Abandoning Addison and the troubles of Boca Raton in 1927, Wilson moved to Los Angeles where he became well known as an owner of the popular restaurant, the Brown Derby, and as a writer of screenplays. The caption of this newspaper photograph was "Mr. Mizner is a brother of Wilson Mizner, the wit." This explanation greatly pleased Wilson. Addison's visit to the West Coast was the last time the brothers saw one another.
Courtesy of Kim Mizner Hollis.

be found in Wilson's booth number fifty.[44] Frequently seen there was Anita Loos, the author of *Gentlemen Prefer Blondes* and Wilson's former girlfriend from Palm Beach days who remained a close friend. It was said that while discussing marital woes there one night with Wilson, John Barrymore exclaimed, "The only way to fight with a woman is with your hat. Grab it and run."[45] Wilson, the master of such humor, had the habit of "insulting" his exalted friends with humorous observations that they relished.

While visiting Wilson at the Ambassador Hotel in December, Addison had a heart attack. With this, he decided to return to Florida by way of Mineral Springs, Texas, where he intended to avail himself of the spa there. By Christmas, he was so sick in Texas that the local doctor would not allow him to take the cure. Unable to renew his health, he pressed on with his journey in sometimes difficult conditions and managed to return to Palm Beach in early January 1933. Before he left Mineral Springs, the doctor had provided a grim diagnosis of his condition and, as Addison humorously related, gave him "an identification card as to where to ship the corpse."[46] His black humor proved prophetic.

The new year dawned with more bad news. On January 12, Addison Mizner experienced a series of heart attacks that further complicated his weakened condition. He was then informed that there would be no new post office and federal building in Palm Beach. Having decided to cancel the contract for the project that Mizner had spent a considerable amount of time conceiving, the government would not be compensating him for any of his work. On January 26, he learned of the death of Alva Belmont, the dear friend that he met just after arriving in New York in 1904.

Four days later, he endured another heart seizure. Ysabel Hollins and Wilson Mizner had been apprised of his situation and Ysabel quickly paid a short visit to Addison in Palm Beach. Wilson, in bad health himself at this time, was working on a screenplay and sent his brother a telegram that could only be appreciated by a Mizner: "STOP DYING AM TRYING TO WRITE A COMEDY."[47] More sympathetically, Wilson also contacted a cardiologist in Miami to have the doctor examine his brother. The ominous diagnosis came as no surprise to Addison, who continued to receive communication from his solicitous relatives. On February 4, Addison received a telegram from Florence Atkinson, now reunited with Wilson, informing him of the stunning news that Wilson had been made an honorary captain of the Los Angeles Police Department. Even *in extremis*, Addison appreciated the absurdity and wired back: "THANK GOD MAMA IS DEAD."[48]

Fully cognizant of his fate, he had recently told visitors: "I've seen everything, been everywhere, and done everything. Now I can wait for the door to open."[49] On February 5, just as the sun was setting in Palm Beach, Addison Mizner died.

CHAPTER FIFTEEN

MASTER BUILDER

Addison Mizner was an active participant in the pageant of life. He enjoyed the company of men, women, and animals and relished the adventure that was living.

He was a man of large appetites: for food, friendship, ambition, work, adventure, humor, and learning. Loyal to family and friends, he was comfortable with both the grand and the lowly and he radiated a warmth and humanity that created bonds immediately. It was the combination of this social ease with his knowledge and experience that enabled him to become a society architect, attracting some of the wealthiest, most accomplished, and powerful women and men of his time as clients. In the course of a couple of months, he formed a fast friendship with an aesthetically sophisticated and somewhat

Addison Mizner holding a macaw and supporting his favorite monkey, Johnnie Brown, circa 1925. When Mizner arrived in Guatemala with his parents at the age of fifteen, he was presented with a pet monkey, a gift that began a lifelong infatuation with exotic animals. When Johnnie died, Mizner had him buried near the doorstep of his own Villa Mizner. Courtesy of Historical Society of Palm Beach County.

reticent Paris Singer, resulting in an invitation that changed his life and defined his career in architecture.

Addison Mizner was an anomaly within his own family. Among the children born to Lansing and Ella Mizner, only Addison realized the level of achievement originally envisioned by his parents. The Mizner offspring constituted a confounding paradox: born to industrious and reputable parents who provided intellectual stimulation and access to superior education, the children inexplicably lacked the wherewithal to succeed and basically lived unremarkable lives. Apart from Addison, the touchstones of ambition, tenacity, and respectability that defined the parents appear to have had scant influence on the next generation of Mizners.

The most stable and principled of the brothers was Henry, who served the Episcopal Church by running a missionary outpost in a slum area of St. Louis. When Minnie Mizner married Horace Chase, her prospects were very bright; however, financial irresponsibility and an unhealthy focus on society brought about a life of significantly reduced circumstances. William became a doctor in Oakland but only managed to develop a modest practice. The most educated of the children was Lansing Jr., known as Lan. Although a lawyer, he never considered the law to be an honorable profession and was content to be a club man like his brother Edgar, an ineffectual entrepreneur. Neither Lan nor Edgar ever married or owned a house, and each was living in a hotel when death called. Realizing Lan's lack of ambition, Mama Mizner told him: "you have the ability to make of yourself a distinguished man if you were only more self-reliant and would persevere."[1] If Ella Mizner had issued this earnest encouragement to all of her children, only Addison, for unexplainable reasons, would have heeded such a call.

Although Wilson Mizner achieved celebrity, he was no better than the other siblings. Imbued with the same values and provided identical advantages, Wilson and Addison constituted different sides of the same coin. Wilson was recognized for clever thoughts recorded by other people who frequently appropriated them as their own; Addison left substantial monuments that confirmed him as one of the most inventive architects in the early twentieth century. Each was a commanding figure in his own right but, together, they constituted an unforgettable force that, in the words of Alex Waugh, "produced not an addition but a multiplication of their parts."[2] The tendency by some writers to produce an entertaining joint biography of the brothers has created an impression that Addison was party to much of Wilson's knavery. As a result, the portrait of Addison that has been passed down is distorted and foreshortened. Wilson's many capers, considered highly entertaining today, were frequently committed to the detriment of Addison. Despite the negative impact that Wilson repeatedly brought to his life, Addison was forever loyal to his reprobate brother. Addison's closest relationship throughout most of his life was with Wilson.

Addison always benefitted from a positive temperament and captivating sense of humor. He once remarked that his greatest gift was to be able to forget the bad and remember the good. When Wilson sent the telegram commanding him to "Stop dying. Am trying to write a comedy," Addison, very much aware of life's finality, responded with his own telegram: "Am going to get well. The comedy goes on."[3] Such a lighthearted response at this moment appears unnatural; however, employing humor was his way of mocking the inevitable and of dealing with adversity. To this outsized man, the human condition was indeed a comedy. Well acquainted with human imperfection, Addison himself was proof of man's capacity to be both virtuous and selfish and to commit deeds both noble and reckless. In his mind, the anguish resulting from life's jolts could be diminished with humor.

One important trait that enabled Addison Mizner to thrive in an unconventional life was the pioneer spirit inherited from his family. Like his forebears, he relished challenge and adventure. At Addison's memorial service, the bishop read "Weighing Anchor," an anonymous poem that touched on the mysterious voyage that the architect was now taking. The poem described a lonely voyager who slips his mooring and sails away to an unknown sea. Forsaking the protection of a safe harbor, Addison always relished the open seas and the adventure that it promised. He was happiest when on the journey itself and, in many ways, his life was a quest for adventure and beauty.

To the pioneer, instinct was just as important as intelligence and skill. A venturesome and peripatetic life demanded an ability to adapt to ever-changing conditions and to identify and seize opportunity. In Palm Beach, he was presented with circumstances far more favorable than any he had previously known in his life; yet, the mere presence of advantageous conditions did not ensure success. After collaborating on the Everglades Club with the benevolent and visionary Paris Singer, Addison used his instinct and talent to forge ahead on his own to create unexpected recognition and wealth.

That Addison Mizner even found himself in Palm Beach in 1918 was unexpected. Like many individuals who reach great heights, they benefit to some extent from accident and chance. Addison Mizner suffered significant injury to his leg at the age of fifteen and once again at the age of forty-five. Both times, enduring great pain, he recuperated by temporarily leading a sedentary existence, a way of life contrary to his energetic nature. Yet, each period of immobility produced unanticipated discoveries that were critical to his crowning achievement in Palm Beach.

Claflin Residence, 1923. The Arthur B. Claflin house on Lake Worth in Palm Beach was another of the grand houses Mizner produced in 1923. Stretched out north and south along the lake, Mizner created a series of public and private courtyards between the east-west oriented wings producing a variety of indoor and outdoor settings, all with views of the Lake and sunset. The pictured courtyard is the Water Gate from which guests would arrive and depart from yachts moored just offshore.

Photograph by Frank E. Geisler reproduced by Craig Kuhner.

In 1888, after injuring his leg, the bedridden patient began to draw, cultivating a talent that had lain dormant until that moment. Additionally, when his father was making preparations to move to Guatemala to assume his ambassadorial post, he decided to take the fifteen-year-old Addison with him to supervise his recuperation. Just about to turn sixteen, Addison could have been left in San Francisco to attend boarding school if not for his health. The awakening of a creative temperament and exposure to an alluring Spanish Colonial culture were important to his artistic formation and essential to his professional achievement. With an aversion to traditional education, Addison would never have made these crucial discoveries through formal study.

Thirty years later, after suffering another wound to the same leg, he was forced into a period of convalescence that allowed him to meet Paris Singer, a kindred spirit who became his collaborator and patron. Enthralled with Mizner's descriptions of Guatemala, Singer suggested they vacation there to enjoy the country's beauty and to allow Addison to benefit from the sun. But for the 1917 earthquake that ravaged the country, there they would have spent their time. Events may never have taken Mizner back to Palm Beach; however, the resultant destruction forced Singer to identify another place to visit. By choosing Palm Beach, Singer allowed himself and his reflective patient to see old scenery in an entirely different light. It was at this time that the architect recognized the consonance between his architectural ideas and the climate and history of Palm Beach. While energy, ambition, and imagination contributed to Mizner's ultimate success, so too did serendipity. These events, the unforeseen consequences of recuperation, represented inflection points in Mizner's life.

While Mizner demonstrated the capacity for great achievement, he was also capable of imprudence. By 1927, after having ascended to great heights socially and financially, he experienced a dizzying and humiliating fall. The failure of his development in Boca Raton cast his reputation on the rocks, strained some friendships, left him bankrupt, and caused critics to claim that Addison had misled and bilked investors. Although sufficiently competent in finance to start and operate various businesses simultaneously, Mizner simply had little interest in financial matters according to the comments of those who knew him well. Possessed of an artist's temperament, Addison was focused on creating the most beautiful resort community in the world, not on concocting a devious plan to defraud investors. While ultimately responsible for all corporate activities, Addison was negligent in allowing others to operate the finances of the company in a reckless manner.

Once Addison made the decision to undertake the Boca Raton project, he directed his focus and energy to planning, design, and construction. If there were signals in the real estate business in 1925 that would have alerted him to an overheated market, he failed to see them, as did most others. In addition to financial mismanagement, timing and scale proved to be complicating factors that contributed to the downfall of his venture. Signs of a bust began to appear just after Mizner began to build and, just over a year later, a devastating hurricane signaled the end of the land boom. At this point, bankruptcy was a common phenomenon in the Florida real estate business. Had he begun this project two years earlier, the outcome might have been different; however, the mammoth scale of the planned city also represented another difficult challenge. When the assets of the Mizner Development Corporation were auctioned in 1927, there were fifteen thousand acres of land that constituted the development.[4] A project of such size would have required much more time to complete than the architect had planned or was granted.

The accusation that Mizner was unscrupulous can best be assessed by comparing his behavior and accomplishments with those of the unprincipled hustlers to which critics compared him. Many developers, interested only in churning sales transactions, had no intention of building infrastructure, amenities, or recreational facilities. Mizner, endeavoring to fulfill his obligations, completed an astounding amount of work in fifteen months: thousands of acres cleared; streets and sidewalks built; water mains and wells installed; and

This pencil sketch of Addison Mizner was done in 1926, the trying year that saw the bankruptcy of the Mizner Development Corporation and the end of his spectacular plans for the "perfect city" of Boca Raton. Although his health was beginning to deteriorate, he still retained his boyish features. The architect would live only six more years. Courtesy of the Oakland Museum of California.

administrative buildings, houses, hotels, and golf courses constructed. This activity, representing expenditures of over $4 million, was not the accomplishment of a man intending to deceive. Had it been his plan to swindle investors, he most likely would not have invested much of his own money in such a scheme. To the contrary, the failure of Boca Raton left him financially ruined. Twenty years earlier, Mizner's entry in the 1904 *Cynic's Calendar* read: "Tomorrow would be sweet if we could kill yesterday."[5] While certainly ruing the decision to risk everything in Boca Raton, Addison neither complained nor sought relief in self-pity but, instead, did his best to mend a shattered life.

Many architectural journalists and biographers have criticized Addison Mizner for his lack of professional education despite the fact that he was formally licensed to practice architecture. Although formal university programs in architecture existed in America before the twentieth century, it was not unusual for someone interested in the profession, just as in law or medicine, to learn it as an apprentice in an established firm. This was the path followed by many, including icons Stanford White and Frank Lloyd Wright.

Unlike White and Wright, each of whom opened his own architectural firm at the age of twenty-six, Addison Mizner was almost thirty-eight years of age when he formally began practicing architecture on Long Island. Although a man of professional variety until establishing his practice, he had spent a significant amount of time in those years developing knowledge of drafting, construction, and design with Willis J. Polk. In his apprenticeship with Polk, he mostly handled drafting as the design work was done by Polk and his father. When not in the office, he spent considerable time on construction sites where he received a thorough education in the building trades. This would have been the general exposure that any serious architectural apprentice would have had, although few would have experienced Addison's breadth of exposure to the trades or attained his level of expertise in them.

The depth of Mizner's design education can be better understood by considering the quantity of material he collected in his personal library. The photographs, postcards, sketches, and watercolors that constituted his architectural vocabulary filled twenty-five large scrapbooks, each logically arranged according to subject matter. With each volume containing up to two hundred pages, there are between three and four thousand pages with multiple images per page, many with written annotations. In addition, his library of art, architecture, and furniture was enormous, consisting of books written in English, French, Spanish, and Italian. Through travel and patient study, Mizner was largely self-taught.

What differentiated Addison Mizner professionally from many architects was a complete command of his chosen design idiom of Spanish and Mediterranean architecture. He said that the affinity for Hispanic culture went back three generations in his family. As the son of a California pioneer, Mizner grew up in an environment influenced by the colonial manners and

Since his first introduction to Spanish culture in Guatemala in 1889, Addison had always been smitten with the people, art, and architecture of Spain and its colonies. Here he is visiting friends in 1926 at the Monastery of Santa Maria de Guadeloupe, a monastery southwest of Toledo that dates from the thirteenth century and one of the most important cloisters in Spain. In the course of his many travels to Spain, he not only absorbed architectural ideas and concepts but formed many friendships with a broad range of people. Courtesy of Historical Society of Palm Beach County.

cultural expressions of a European nation. At the age of fifteen, his fascination with Spanish and Mediterranean culture was awakened when he lived in Guatemala and it continued throughout his life with recurring visits to Central America, Spain, and Italy. This education was supplemented by trips to England, France, and Asia as well as by frequent visits to the grand houses of Newport and Long Island. His habit was to sketch ornamentation, buildings, squares, gardens, and furniture, making notes and including measurements to understand proportion, detail, and spatial relationships. Mizner's deep experience in the world, at a time when most Americans and many architects had neither traveled nor lived in as many countries as he, provided a bountiful source of reference and possibility.

If Addison Mizner had truly lacked an adequate education, as many have suggested, he would certainly not have been able to design and build the remarkable variety of very large houses in Palm Beach that he so skillfully did. Several critics stated that Mizner could not do construction drawings. Responsible for managing the efficiency of his office, Addison logically devoted his own time to design and construction. The intermediate step of preparing construction drawings was a discipline that was executed by a full complement of well-trained technicians that he managed. For Addison to have spent his time on drafting would only have subtracted from his creative time. By any measure, Addison Mizner's architectural education was sufficient; considering his chosen idiom, it was exceptional.

Some critics saw Mizner's work as derivative, inextricably linked to the Hispanic Revival style of California. In reality, the Hispanic architecture developing in Florida during the 1920s, including the work of Mizner, was not part of the broad enthusiasm for Spanish Colonial revival styles in California. This was treated thoroughly by Christina Orr-Cahall, the former executive director of the Norton Gallery in Palm Beach, in her PhD dissertation for Yale University. As Hispanic Revivalism was seen by academics to suppress creativity and innovation in American architecture, the misplaced association of Mizner to the movement automatically damned the architect in the eyes of many.

After his death, Addison Mizner was included in the *Dictionary of American Biography* with an entry that was written by Turpin C. Bannister, one of America's foremost architectural historians. Bannister received his PhD from the Harvard Graduate School of Design and was a founding member and the first president of the organization that became The Society of Architectural Historians. His assessment of Mizner's architecture stated that a "more critical appraisal of his work reveals dubious structural durability, gross detail, and excessive theatricality. . . . His real significance lies in expressing concretely in $50,000,000 worth of buildings, the escapism of the rootless plutocracy and in symbolizing the irresponsible promoters who exploited it to the hilt."[6] This is a harsh denunciation that is, by objective standards, unfair. Other critics have made similar assessments.

Bannister cited the "dubious structural durability" of Mizner's houses; however, his extant architecture has successfully survived to the present. Although many Mizner homes have been razed, they were done so not because of deficiencies in materials or construction but mostly because the owners desired to develop the land that the buildings occupied. His houses have fared as well as any in the face of the numerous tropical storms that have ravaged the Atlantic coast of Florida since the 1920s. Perhaps the most remarkable testament to the durability of his structures was The Cloister in Sea Island, Georgia. Initially unsure of the economic viability of the resort in 1928, the owners asked Mizner to build a temporary structure as economically as possible. Complying with their wishes, Mizner incongruously built a hotel of forty rooms out of wood without a concrete foundation. This "temporary" structure lasted for seventy-five years until it was demolished in 2003 in order to build a much larger resort complex. The only damage to the original building was done by termites.

Turpin Bannister's questioning the aesthetics of Mizner's architecture with its "gross detail" and "excessive theatricality"

Warden Residence, 1922. Remarkably, for wealthy clients seeking comfort, status, or both in 1920s Palm Beach, Mizner was the preferred architect far more often than not. His clients had worked with America's leading (and Ecole-trained) architects in the creation of cottages in Long Island, Newport, and Maine. Their embrace of Mizner's Palm Beach architecture was evidence of a deep resonance with his particular approach, which was an amalgam of personality, resourcefulness, trust, and delight.
Photograph by Craig Kuhner.

is also problematic. In a broader sense, Bannister's criticism was a reference to Academic Eclecticism and the Picturesque, architectural movements that had become outdated and disparaged at the time of the architect's death. One of the most damning things said about Mizner's architecture concerned his indiscriminate mixture of style and ornament. It was the movement toward a broader embrace of historical architectural artifact at the core of Academic Eclecticism that permitted Mizner to borrow, somewhat randomly, from many types and periods of architecture. This flexible approach of

Casa Nana, 1926. The rampant misrepresentation of Mizner's neglect of stairs, bathrooms, and windows was unfortunately abetted by Mizner himself. Among the most persistent stories was the late addition of the grand stair tower in the Rasmussen house. In fact, Mizner began with the stair tower to shield the view of the entry court.

In considering Mizner's intentions in his design, it is always important to remember his view that architecture was best when it represented changes that occurred over time. What may seem to be a collision of forms worked for Mizner as a way of transitioning from one period to another.

Photograph by Craig Kuhner.

adaptation was taught at the Ecole des Beaux Arts and had been brought to America by Richard Morris Hunt and other graduates.

The Picturesque was an organizing principle that traced its origins to the eighteenth century. Although it had ceased to resonate among architects and critics by the 1930s, it continued to be popular in general terms. As more Americans took the Grand Tour of Europe, the continent's picturesque qualities were widely captured in photographs, postcards, stereoviewers, books, and magazines and this broad exposure led to the popularization of southern Europe. With his exposure to Central America and to Mediterranean countries, Mizner had become acutely sensitive to the assemblage of all that represented the complete scene, a holistic perspective that was the foundation of his conceptual approach to architecture. Ada Louise Huxtable, the first architecture critic of the *New York Times* and a recipient of the Pulitzer Prize for Criticism, offered an assessment that counters Bannister's condemnation: "It was Mizner's sensitivity to his surroundings that distinguished his product, more than his antiquarian leanings." His architecture "looked calculatedly picturesque but never absurd."[7] Simply, Mizner's conceptual approach was aligned with the tastes and romantic notions of his clients.

A balanced evaluation of Mizner's work at the time of his death in 1933 was complicated by the onset of the Depression and especially by the growing affinity for modern architecture among American academics. The modern establishment believed that architecture should be functional and moral, a rational reflection of society's needs, an expression devoid of meaningless ornamentation. Ada Louise Huxtable noted that "Americans tend to want morality in architecture—a rational justification of building in terms of social intent and effect. The merely beautiful or artful is dismissed as beyond serious consideration. . . ."[8] In this light, many academics at the time deemed his houses impractical and stylistically outmoded and they regarded his ideas as intellectually bereft. These opinions only reverberated more strongly when considered through the lens of poverty brought on by the Depression.

While many Mizner houses were considered extravagant by critics, they must be viewed in the context of the 1920s. His clients were the most wealthy Americans, whose principal desire was to live well and to entertain graciously during the winter months. These houses provided a relaxed environment for sporting activities during the day and a more formal setting for elaborate parties during the evening. Additionally, Mizner's conceptions must be considered in their totality, unified compositions of structure and environment that were meant to be approached, entered, and experienced with the clients' desires in mind. Many of his critics have been myopic in their exclusive view of his architecture without the benefit of examining his holistic vision.

In a less intellectually inflamed period, Mizner's houses can be more evenly evaluated. Huxtable pronounced his plans "expert" and commented on "the beauty of [its] concept, spaces and execution."[9] In the end, Mizner's style of architecture was appropriately guided by various determinants: site, climate, materials, construction methods, the purpose of the building, the tastes and preferences of his clients, and the architect's imagination and inventiveness. Noting that his clients could not tolerate anything that was not expensive, Mizner built magnificent, artisanal houses intended to impress. For their conservative owners, the houses were a material confirmation of their good taste and prominent social position.

Much of the condemnation leveled at Mizner upon his death came from critics with an affinity for modern architecture. As the American intellectual world had already embraced the tenets of European modernism in artistic and literary disciplines, it was not surprising that academics and critics in the world of architecture in the 1930s would have been ill-disposed to Mizner's style that was perceived as anachronistic. The geometric simplicity of the newly popular International Style was antithetical to the curated, artisanal, and articulated approach favored by Mizner.

Despite the fact that modernism and Mizner's Mediterranean Revival style were conceptually at variance, there were in fact some similarities between the two. First, it must be acknowledged that the modernist perspective in Europe differed from country to country. The Germans and Austrians believed in *Gesamtkunstwerk*, meaning "a total work of art," a concept in which the architect is responsible for the design and execution of a building's totality, everything from the house and garden to the furnishings and everyday utensils.[10] Mizner insisted on the same oversight and responsibility in all of his projects, because he knew that only a holistic vision would ensure consistency, unity, and a satisfying effect.

Modernists, just like Mizner, were dedicated to allowing the beauty of materials to be appreciated and both also liked to use vernacular materials. When Walter Gropius left Europe to take a position at Harvard University, he built a house in the Bauhaus style for himself in nearby Lincoln using local woods, brick, and fieldstone along with the customary industrial materials. Likewise, when Addison Mizner built The Cloister in Sea Island, Georgia, he chose to use the tabby construction native to the area. Although some modernists favored machine production, there were some, like the *Wiener Werkstaette* (Vienna Workshops) in Vienna and the Parisian art deco designers of the 1920s, who revered the same high level of hand craftsmanship preferred by Mizner. There was

Paris Singer Apartment, Everglades Club, 1919. Addison Mizner's holistic approach to design is evident in this image of Paris Singer's apartment at the Everglades Club. The floor tiles, stained glass, stone window surrounds, iron candle stands, and most of the furniture was made at Mizner Industries. This vast array of products is a testament to Mizner's status as a master builder, an individual with a thorough knowledge of all of the trades required to design and build important houses.

Photograph by Frank E. Geisler reproduced by Craig Kuhner.

even commonality between Mizner and Frank Lloyd Wright in their belief that a building must be sited and designed in a manner that allows it to be compatible with the landscape. Both architects also liked interior spaces that interacted with the outdoors. While Mizner favored an antique style of architecture, he certainly shared many ideas with modern architects.

Addison Mizner was an architect of imagination and vision. It was his comprehensive understanding of Spanish and Mediterranean architecture and his capacity for reimagining its various parts into a coherent whole that established his innovative style. While Spanish houses of the fifteenth and sixteenth centuries were fortresses, intended to be unbreachable and forbidding, Mizner's houses were conceived to be open and inviting. He described his process as turning "Spanish architecture inside out, as you would a glove."[11] By planning his houses one room wide and liberally using large windows and doors that open to loggias and patios, Mizner encouraged movement from inside to outside and inside again through a different portal.

Not only did his planning facilitate spatial progression but it also served as an excellent environmental strategy, allowing any breeze to find its way through the house cooling all in its path. With this approach, he adopted the planning of palaces in Islamic Spain and its fountained courtyards and quiet pools. His houses were so appropriately suited to the lazy climate and to the habits of his clientele that he can be credited as a principal catalyst in changing the lifestyle of Palm Beach from its pre-war formality to the more relaxed and casual behavior that characterized the 1920s and beyond. The Mizner style of resort architecture defines the state today.

Building in an area without picturesque landscape, Mizner compensated by creating interest with massing and varying roof lines. These dynamic elements interacted with swaying coconut trees and with the movement of the sun to create a continuously changing play of light and shadow on surfaces. His façades were ingeniously conceived to convey movement as an antidote to the flat landscape, and his disposition of rooms maximized views and sight lines. His affinity for having reception rooms open to patios, arcaded cloisters, and gardens further enhanced ventilation and created visual interest. Vegetation, used to soften hard surfaces and to absorb heat, was exotically prevalent. Water devices not only suggested coolness but the flow of water was pleasing to the ear.

Color also played an integral part in Addison Mizner's architecture. Vivid colors, inspired by the richness of the sky and ocean, were used for the tiles that embellished interior spaces and for the ubiquitous terra cotta pots and urns. Red roof tiles, one of his defining characteristics, complemented the blue sky and the green palm trees that towered above. The softer hues used on facades muted the harsh sun and continually changed in value as the light shifted throughout the day. Ultimately, his houses were neither Spanish nor Spanish Revival; they were a synthesis of his learning and experience, a refined product of a vigorous imagination and they were appropriate to place, purpose, and time.

Mizner's houses were, not surprisingly, a reflection of his personality in that they frequently charmed and even surprised. His spaces offered a meandering procession from human to heroic scale, from indoor to outdoor rooms, all animated with color, flowers, and water devices that entertained. Mizner's architecture, with its great variety, delighted as it presented the visitor with unanticipated registers of enjoyment and discovery. Large houses can frequently be forbidding and cold; to the contrary, Mizner's houses possessed great dignity and were remarkably invested with a welcoming personality.

Addison Mizner was an architect in the truest sense. The word *architect* derives from classical Greek and means "chief builder," a concept that survives through the Renaissance as "master builder."[12] Beginning in the ancient world, the design and construction of buildings were overseen by a master builder who had risen from the artisan ranks as a result of his expertise in all facets of architecture. An authority on Spanish architecture and art, Addison Mizner also possessed a comprehensive understanding of all of the building trades that

Villa Mizner, 1924. This view from the mirador of Villa Mizner provides a western perspective featuring the Everglades Club and Lake Worth. As Addison Mizner spent his last days in his villa on Worth Avenue, he was able to look out of any window to appreciate his architectural accomplishments in Palm Beach. Seeing the Everglades Club would have recalled his fortuitous beginning with his friend Paris Singer in 1918.
Photograph by Frank E. Geisler reproduced by Craig Kuhner.

allowed him to develop his own artisans and workshops. It is remarkable that one man could accomplish what Mizner did: develop his own clientele by cultivating deep relationships; plan, design, and oversee the construction and interior design of numerous large estates simultaneously; and develop hundreds of highly skilled craftsmen who could satisfy his uncompromising standards.

To appreciate his accomplishments, one must consider that, upon his arrival in Palm Beach in 1918, there were only a few skilled craftsmen and no building supplies due to the war, there was a culture of vacationers whose activities were concentrated for the most part around two hotels, and there was only a nascent Mediterranean residential architectural style truly sympathetic to the conditions of Palm Beach. In short order, all of this changed. Such a thorough metamorphosis could only be accomplished by someone with a deep reservoir of energy, an encompassing vision, a complete understanding of his vocabulary, and a powerful imagination.

Addison Mizner can be imagined in his last days reflectively surveying the Palm Beach landscape from a high vantage point at the Villa Mizner. What he would have seen and appreciated were familiar roof lines and crenellations silhouetted against a

Playa Riente, 1923. Mizner's structures were meant to withstand time and weather. The loss of so many important houses and buildings was exclusively the result of demolition in favor of redevelopment. Playa Riente, Mizner's most majestic house, its seawall shown in the 1928 Geisler photograph, was razed in 1957.

Interestingly, for all of the investment in these houses, many were sold within a few years of their occupancy. Of the twenty-eight houses published in Florida Architecture of Addison Mizner *in 1928, one-third had changed hands before 1928 including three houses that Mizner designed for himself.*

The great loss of Mizner's portfolio to redevelopment has continued. In October 2009, a giant clawed bulldozer attacked Mizner's last-built great estate, La Ronda, in Bryn Mawr, Pennsylvania.

Photograph by Frank E. Geisler reproduced by Craig Kuhner.

dusking sky. His buildings offered a self-portrait of the society architect: They represented the refined culmination of many disciplines of art and craft; they told rich stories of Spanish history; they offered humor and surprise; they shared a memorable relationship with their owners; and they commanded attention in the Palm Beach landscape.

Perhaps these timeless structures were most accurately summarized by Addison Mizner's good friend Paris Singer: his buildings "are so subtly adapted to this state and its warm climate that, although inspired by the art of Spain and Italy, they are an order of Architecture of his own which will live in the history of American Architecture when we are gone and forgotten."[13] Addison Mizner's distinctive buildings gratify the eye today, just as they did when originally built, and they contribute greatly to the celebrated reputation of Palm Beach as one of the world's premier resort communities. This thought would give Addison Cairns Mizner a measure of pleasure.

ENDNOTES

CHAPTER ONE: "I JOSH AND I PAINT"

1. Shelley, *Adonaïs* 1821, 20.
2. Curl, *Boca Raton Resort & Club*, 64.
3. Tarbell, *Florida Architecture of Addison Mizner*, Foreword by Paris Singer, xxxix.
4. Mizner, *Many Mizners*, Introduction by Arthur Somer Roche, v–vi.
5. Seebohm, *Boca Rococo*, 257.
6. *New York Times*, "Mizner Memorial Rites," February 10, 1933, 17.
7. Briggs, *Fire in the Crucible*, 170 ("sublimated math"); Le Corbusier, *Toward a New Architecture*, 148 ("intellectual speculation").
8. Johnston, *Legendary Mizners*, 263.
9. Tindall, "Bubble in the Sun," 80.
10. Mizner, Typescript, 70.
11. Johnston, "Profile: Palm Beach Architect," *New Yorker*, November 22, 1952, 60.
12. Johnston, *Legendary Mizners*, 158.
13. Johnston, "Profile: Legend of a Sport," *New Yorker*, February 25, 1950, 39.

CHAPTER TWO: CALIFORNIA PIONEERS

1. Showalter, *Many Mizners*, 13.
2. Sullivan, *Fabulous Wilson Mizner*, 32.
3. Mizner, *Many Mizners*, 2.
4. Seebohm, *Boca Rococo*, 12.
5. Prosser, *History of the Puget Sound Country*, 534.
6. Prosser, *History of the Puget Sound Country*, 534.
7. Burton, "James Semple, Prairie Entrepreneur," 66–84.
8. Showalter, *Many Mizners*, 11.
9. Showalter, *Many Mizners*, 11.
10. Mizner, *Many Mizners*, 4.
11. Mizner, *Many Mizners*, 4.
12. Showalter, *Many Mizners*, 13.
13. Bussinger and Phelan, *Images of America: Benicia*, 57.
14. Showalter, *Many Mizners*, 13, 16.
15. Tarbell, *Ida Tarbell*, xlii.
16. Holliday, *Rush for Riches*, 98–101.
17. Drown, "Loss of the Steamer Independence," *Daily Alta California* April 2, 1853, 2.
18. *Journal of Illinois State Historical Society*, October 1914, 265.
19. Watson, Letter to Franklin Reynolds.
20. *Daily Alta California*, "Burning of the Independence," April 1, 1853, 1.
21. Seebohm, *Boca Rococo*, 18, letter to Ella Watson dated February 12, 1856.
22. Showalter, *Many Mizners*, 13, letter to Ella Watson dated January 7, 1856.
23. Hoover, Rensch, and Rensch, *Historic Spots in California*, 517.
24. Bussinger and Phelan, *Images of America: Benicia*, 105.
25. Mizner, *Many Mizners*, 1.
26. Mizner, *Many Mizners*, 2.

CHAPTER THREE: "THE GREATEST DAY OF MY LIFE"

1. Mizner, *Many Mizners*, 1.
2. Benicia Historical Museum, Benicia History: 1860s, 1870s, 1880s, 1890s.
3. Johnston, *Legendary Mizners*, 3.
4. Mizner, *Many Mizners*, 72.
5. Mizner, *Many Mizners*, 17.
6. Mizner, *Many Mizners*, 7.
7. Mizner, *Many Mizners*, 5.
8. Mizner, *Many Mizners*, 6.
9. Mizner, *Many Mizners*, 31.
10. Sullivan, *Fabulous Wilson Mizner*, 45.
11. Mizner, *Many Mizners*, 28.

12. Mizner, *Many Mizners*, 27.

13. Mizner, *Many Mizners*, 40.

14. Emmett, Clara Database for Women Artists.

15. Mizner, *Many Mizners*, 44.

16. Mizner, *Many Mizners*, 45.

17. Mizner, *Many Mizners*, 47.

18. Mizner, *Many Mizners*, 48.

19. Sullivan, *Fabulous Wilson Mizner*, 66.

20. Mizner, *Many Mizners*, 56.

21. Chapman, "Mission of Lansing Bond Mizner to Central America," 385–401.

22. Chapman, "Mission of Lansing Bond Mizner to Central America," 399.

23. Mizner, *Many Mizners*, 57.

24. Berglund, *Making San Francisco American*, 40.

25. Carnegie, *Round the World*, 12.

26. Berglund, *Making San Francisco American*, 6 (pop. under 1,000); Issel and Cherny, *San Francisco 1865–1932*, 24 (pop. of approx 300,000).

27. Dienkelspiel, *Towers of Gold*, 139.

28. Small, *Complete Works of Oscar Wilde*, Volume 3, *The Picture of Dorian Gray*, 156 (quote at beginning of Chapter 19).

29. Drabelle, *Mile-High Fever*, 132.

30. Drabelle, *Mile-High Fever*, 138.

31. Mizner, *Many Mizners*, 61.

32. Curl, *Mizner's Florida*, 4.

33. Mizner, *Many Mizners*, 62.

34. Mizner, *Many Mizners*, 63.

35. Tarbell, *Florida Architecture of Addison Mizner*, xlv.

36. Seebohm, *Boca Rococo*, 48.

37. Curl, *Mizner's Florida*, 9.

38. Orr, *Addison Mizner: Architect of Dreams and Realities*, 9.

39. Mizner, *Many Mizners*, 64.

40. Seebohm, *Boca Rococo*, 51.

CHAPTER FOUR: PATH TO ARCHITECTURE

1. Longstreth, *On the Edge of the World*, 13.

2. Floyd, "Inspiration and Synthesis," in Meister, *H.H. Richardson*, 4.

3. Floyd, "Inspiration and Synthesis," in Meister, *H.H. Richardson*, 4.

4. Floyd, "Inspiration and Synthesis," in Meister, *H.H. Richardson*, 4.

5. Floyd, "Inspiration and Synthesis," in Meister, *H.H. Richardson*, 7.

6. Van Rensselaer, "Development of American Homes," *Forum*, January 1892, 675, in Longstreth, *On the Edge of the World*, 17.

7. Longstreth, *On the Edge of the World*, 17–18.

8. Scully, "Shingle Style," in Longstreth, *On the Edge of the World*, 18.

9. Van Rensselaer, "Henry Hobson Richardson and His Works," in Longstreth, *On the Edge of the World*, 19.

10. Longstreth, *On the Edge of the World*, 24.

11. Longstreth, *On the Edge of the World*, 80.

12. Longstreth, *On the Edge of the World*, 81.

13. Longstreth, *On the Edge of the World*, 55.

14. Longstreth, *On the Edge of the World*, 82–83.

15. Parry, "Arthur Page Brown," *Encyclopedia of San Francisco*.

16. Longstreth, *On the Edge of the World*, 55.

17. Kirker, *California's Architectural Frontier*, 118.

18. Kirker, *California's Architectural Frontier*, 115.

19. Kirker, *California's Architectural Frontier*, 122.

20. Kirker, *California's Architectural Frontier*, 122.

21. Kirker, *California's Architectural Frontier*, 122.

22. Longstreth, *On the Edge of the World*, 51.

23. Longstreth, *On the Edge of the World*, 51.

24. Longstreth, *On the Edge of the World*, 53–55.

25. Longstreth, *On the Edge of the World*, 54.

26. Drabelle, *Great American Railroad War*, 192.

27. Starr, *America and the California Dream*.

28. Orr-Cahall, "An Identification and Discussion," 18.
29. Orr-Cahall, "An Identification and Discussion," 19.
30. Orr, *Addison Mizner: Architect of Dreams and Realities*, 11.
31. Seebohm, *Boca Rococo*, 88.
32. Mizner, *Many Mizners*, 84.
33. Mizner, *Many Mizners*, 84.
34. Mizner, *Many Mizners*, 84.

CHAPTER FIVE: MINER, PAINTER, WRITER, FIGHTER

1. Mizner, *Many Mizners*, 89.
2. Levi, *Boom and Bust*, 5.
3. Levi, *Boom and Bust*, 20 (35,000); Mizner, *Many Mizners*, 119 (1,500).
4. Mizner, *Many Mizners*, 108.
5. Mizner, *Many Mizners*, 101.
6. Mizner, *Many Mizners*, 120.
7. Johnston, *Legendary Mizners*, 128.
8. Mizner, *Many Mizners*, 136.
9. Mizner, *Many Mizners*, 116.
10. Mizner, *Many Mizners*, 142.
11. Mizner, *Many Mizners*, 148.
12. Mizner, *Many Mizners*, 148.
13. Mizner, *Many Mizners*, 153.
14. Levi, *Boom and Bust*, 80.
15. Levi, *Boom and Bust*, 80.
16. Levi, *Boom and Bust*, 120.
17. Mizner, *Many Mizners*, 172.
18. Johnston, *Legendary Mizners*, 99.
19. Johnston, *Legendary Mizners*, 70 (both quotes).
20. Johnston, *Legendary Mizners*, 158.
21. Johnston, *Legendary Mizners*, 10.
22. Mizner, *Many Mizners*, 178.
23. Mizner, *Many Mizners*, 178.
24. Mizner, *Many Mizners*, 182.
25. Mizner, *Many Mizners*, 185.

26. Mizner, *Many Mizners*, 199.
27. Mizner, *Many Mizners*, 199.
28. Mizner, *Many Mizners*, 204.
29. Mizner, *Many Mizners*, 205.
30. Mizner, *Many Mizners*, 207.
31. Mizner, *Many Mizners*, 212.
32. Mizner, *Many Mizners*, 213.
33. Mizner, *Many Mizners*, 213.
34. Mizner, *Many Mizners*, 213.
35. Mizner, *Many Mizners*, 214.
36. Mizner, *Many Mizners*, 217.
37. Seebohm, *Boca Rococo*, 95.
38. Mizner, *Many Mizners*, 217.
39. Mizner, *Many Mizners*, 222.
40. Mizner, *Many Mizners*, 223.
41. Mizner, *Many Mizners*, 224.
42. Curl, 4.

CHAPTER SIX: EXTRAVAGANCE AND DISPLAY

1. Tuchman, *Proud Tower*.
2. King, *Season of Splendor*, 3.
3. Fulton, *Reverend Mark Twain*, 28.
4. Veblen, *Theory of the Leisure Class*, 36.
5. King, *Season of Splendor*, 6.
6. King, *Season of Splendor*, 3.
7. King, *Season of Splendor*, 38.
8. King, *Season of Splendor*, 38.
9. Ridley, *Life of Edward VII*, 49.
10. Ruth Brandon, *Dollar Princesses*, 1.
11. Vanderbilt II, *Fortune's Children*, 87.
12. King, *Season of Splendor*, 58–59; also Vanderbilt II, *Fortune's Children*, 89.
13. Vanderbilt II, *Fortune's Children*, 102–3.
14. King, *Season of Splendor*, 62; also Vanderbilt II, *Fortune's Children*, 112–13.

15. Vanderbilt II, *Fortune's Children*, 89.

16. Vanderbilt II, *Fortune's Children*, 149.

CHAPTER SEVEN: "FRIENDS IN HIGH PLACES"

1. Chandler, *Four Thousand Years of Urban Growth*, 492.

2. Vanderbilt II, *Fortune's Children*, 264.

3. Beer, *Mauve Decade*, 90.

4. King, *Season of Splendor*, 79.

5. Mizner, *Many Mizners*, 235.

6. King, *Season of Splendor*, 79.

7. Amory, *Last Resorts*, 214.

8. Mizner, *Many Mizners*, 256.

9. Mizner, *Many Mizners*, 257.

10. Mizner, *Many Mizners*, 244.

11. Mizner, *Many Mizners*, 252.

12. King, *Season of Splendor*, 85.

13. Wharton, *Age of Innocence*, 3.

14. Mizner, *Many Mizners*, 245.

15. Mizner, *Many Mizners*, 246.

16. Mizner, *Many Mizners*, 253.

17. Mizner, *Many Mizners*, 253.

18. Starr, *Inventing the Dream*, 189.

19. White and White, *Stanford White Architect*, 191–93.

20. Mizner, *Many Mizners*, 244.

21. Mizner, *Many Mizners*, 253.

22. Mizner, *Many Mizners*, 235.

23. Mizner, *Many Mizners*, 247.

24. Mizner, *Many Mizners*, 252.

25. Mizner, *Many Mizners*, 263 ("old wooden Flagler hotels"); Johnston, *Legendary Mizners*, 49 ("hotel culture").

26. Mizner, *Many Mizners*, 237.

27. Trager, *New York Chronology*, 302.

28. Johnston, *Legendary Mizners*, 107.

29. Sullivan, *Fabulous Wilson Mizner*, 176.

30. Sullivan, *Fabulous Wilson Mizner*, 183.

31. Burke, *Rogue's Progress*, 90.

32. Mizner, *Many Mizners*, 269.

33. Mizner, *Many Mizners*, 274.

34. Burke, *Rogue's Progress*, 81.

35. Mizner, *Many Mizners*, 266.

36. Beck and Williams, *California*, 332.

37. Mizner, *Many Mizners*, 278.

CHAPTER EIGHT: AMBITION AND ARCHITECTURE

1. Murphy, "Eyeing the Unreal Estate of Gatsby Esq.," *New York Times*, September 30, 2010, 1.

2. Smith, *Early History of the Long Island Railroad*, 4.

3. "Old Cow Bay Manor House," *Architectural Record*, 1917, 259–66.

4. Curl, *Mizner's Florida*, 19.

5. Mizner, *Many Mizners*, 285.

6. Baker, MacKay, and Traynor, *Long Island Country Houses and Their Architects*, 292.

7. *Long Island Country House*, 117.

8. Johnston, *Legendary Mizners*, 19.

9. Johnston, "Profile: Palm Beach Architect," *New Yorker*, November 22, 1952, 91; November 29, 1952, 72.

10. Curl, *Mizner's Florida*, 18.

11. Olendorf, Olendorf, and Tolf, *Addison Mizner, Architect to the Affluent*, 14.

12. Johnston, *Legendary Mizners*, 112.

13. Curl, *Mizner's Florida*, 25.

14. Seebohm, *Boca Rococo*, 136 ("gardens planted helter-skelter").

15. Curl, *Mizner's Florida*, 22.

16. Floyd, "Inspiration and Synthesis," in Meister, *H.H. Richardson*, 48.

17. Curl, *Mizner's Florida*, 23.

18. Curl, *Mizner's Florida*, 207.

19. Maxwell, *R. S. V. P.*, 107.

20. Lee, *Marie Dressler*, 119.

21. Johnston, *Legendary Mizners*, 121.
22. Johnston, *Legendary Mizners*, 193 ("telling lies"); Johnston, "Profile: Palm Beach Architect," *New Yorker*, November 29, 1952, 74 ("night key").
23. Johnston, *Legendary Mizners*, 196.
24. Mizner, *Many Mizners*, 301.
25. Showalter, *Many Mizners*, 33, 41.
26. Larson, *Dead Wake*, 403 (1,965 total passengers), 300 (1,195 total deaths, 123 Americans).
27. Mizner, Typescript, 2.
28. Johnston, "Profile: Palm Beach Architect," *New Yorker* November 22, 1952, 93.
29. *New York Times*, "War Bazaar Ready for Opening Tonight," June 3, 1916.
30. Maxwell, *R. S. V. P.*, 137–38.
31. Mizner, Typescript, 16.

CHAPTER NINE: THE PERFECT SETTING

1. Rockoff, "Until It's Over, Over There."
2. Maddison, *Contours of the World Economy*, 379, table A.4.
3. Johnston, "Profile: Palm Beach Architect," *New Yorker*, November 29, 1952, 83.
4. Wharton, *Italian Villas and Their Gardens*, 231–50, Chapter 8, "Villas of Venezia."
5. DeLamar, Letter to Alva Johnston, 7.
6. Bonhams, Sale Catalogue, Rolls Royce.
7. Kurth, *Isadora*, 249.
8. Dean, *Human-Powered Home*, 19 (1.35 mill in 1903); Singer Sewing Company, singerco.com/company/history.html.
9. Hiler, "Once Tallest Standing," *New York Times*, June 17, 2013.
10. Kurth, *Isadora*, 73.
11. Kurth, *Isadora*, 250.
12. Kurth, *Isadora*, 251; Wilson, 146.
13. Johnston, "Profile: Palm Beach Architect," *New Yorker*, November 29, 1952, 46.

14. Johnston, "Profile: Palm Beach Architect," *New Yorker*, November 29, 1952, 46.
15. Duncan, *My Life*, 202.
16. Kurth, *Isadora*, 254.
17. Kurth, *Isadora*, 256–57.
18. Wilson, "Paris Singer: A Life Portrait: Part I," 143.
19. DeLamar, letter, 10.
20. "Pioneer Reminisces," *Palm Beach Life*, March 15, 1932, 22–23, in Research Atlantica, Inc., "Town of Palm Beach, Florida, 2010 Historic Sites Survey."
21. Geer, *The Lake Worth Historian*, in Research Atlantica, Inc., "Town of Palm Beach, Florida, 2010 Historic Sites Survey."
22. Oldfather, "Elisha Newton Dimick," 11–15, in Research Atlantica, Inc., "Town of Palm Beach, Florida, 2010 Historic Sites Survey."
23. Palm Beach Yacht Club, History, www.palmbeachyachtclub/history.
24. R. K. Brown, "Days of Early Settlement on Lake Recalled," January 15, 1937.
25. "Sea Gull Cottage Groundbreaking," Preservation Foundation of Palm Beach, November 18, 2007.
26. Oldfather, "Elisha Newton Dimick," 24–28, in Research Atlantica, Inc., "Town of Palm Beach, Florida, 2010 Historic Sites Survey."
27. "First Real Estate Boom," *Tropical Sun*, March 19, 1937, in Research Atlantica, Inc., "Town of Palm Beach, Florida, 2010 Historic Sites Survey."
28. Oldfather, "Elisha Newton Dimick," 45, in Research Atlantica, Inc., "Town of Palm Beach, Florida, 2010 Historic Sites Survey."
29. Oldfather, "Elisha Newton Dimick," 45, in Research Atlantica, Inc., "Town of Palm Beach, Florida, 2010 Historic Sites Survey."
30. Oldfather, "Elisha Newton Dimick," 45, in Research Atlantica, Inc., "Town of Palm Beach, Florida, 2010 Historic Sites Survey."

31. Oldfather, "Elisha Newton Dimick," 69, in Research
Atlantica, Inc., "Town of Palm Beach, Florida, 2010 Historic
Sites Survey."
32. Oldfather, "Elisha Newton Dimick," 71–77, in Research
Atlantica, Inc., "Town of Palm Beach, Florida, 2010 Historic
Sites Survey."
33. Amory, *Last Resorts*, 339.
34. *Palm Beach Daily News*, February 2, 1901, 8; also see AM 9.
35. Curl, *Mizner's Florida*, 39.
36. Bingham-Blossom House, www.loc.gov/pictures/item/
fl0173/.
37. Aslet, *American Country House*, 222.
38. Augustus Mayhew, "Design Providence," in New York Social
Diary, February 22, 2016.
39. Curl, "Introduction to the Dover Edition," in Tarbell, *Florida
Architecture of Addison Mizner*, xii.
40. Amory, *Last Resorts*, 347.
41. Amory, *Last Resorts*, 349.
42. Alex Waugh, Autobiographical typescript, Chapter 2, 10.
43. Amory, *Last Resorts*, 349.
44. Johnston, *Legendary Mizners*, 48.
45. Mizner, Typescript, 20–21.
46. Ida Tarbell, *Florida Architecture of Addison Mizner*, xxxvii.
47. Mizner, Typescript, 18.
48. Mizner, Typescript, 19.
49. Mizner, Typescript, 24.
50. Mizner, Typescript, 24.
51. Mizner, Typescript, 27.

CHAPTER TEN: A MOORISH TOWER

1. Augustus Mayhew, "Remaking History," Palm Beach Social
Diary, November 1, 2013 (from an article in *Palm Beach Post*,
April 25, 1918: "Paris Singer will build ten villas and turn
them over to the government.").
2. Mizner, Typescript, 27.
3. Mizner, Typescript, 30.
4. *Palm Beach Post*, "Singer to Build Ten Villas," April 25, 1918.
5. Mizner, Typescript, 35.
6. Murphy, "Castles in Spain," *Palm Beach Post*, May 26, 1923,
16.
7. Murphy, "Castles in Spain," *Palm Beach Post*, May 26, 1923,
16.
8. Padwee, tilesinnewyork.blogspot.com.
9. Curl, *Mizner's Florida*, 42.
10. *Palm Beach Post*, "Singer May Go to California," August 3,
1918.
11. Mayhew, "Remaking History," Palm Beach Social Diary,
November 1, 2013.
12. Wilma Spencer, "Did You Know That Mrs. Byrd E. White?"
13. *Palm Beach Post*, "Palatial Homes for Shell-Shocked
Convalescent Soldiers, " December 22, 1918.
14. *Palm Beach Post*, "Palatial Homes for Shell-Shocked
Convalescent Soldiers," December 22, 1918.
15. Curl, *Mizner's Florida*, 44.
16. Curl, *Mizner's Florida*, 45.
17. Amory, *Last Resorts*, 401.
18. Curl, *Mizner's Florida*, 49–50.

CHAPTER ELEVEN: SOCIETY ARCHITECT

1. Johnston, *Legendary Mizners*, 28.
2. *Tropical Sun*, February 21, 1919, 8.
3. Wector, *Saga of American Society*, 143.
4. Young, *Memorial History of the City of Philadelphia*, 66.
5. Burt, *Perennial Philadelphians*, 523.
6. Burt, *Perennial Philadelphians*, 514.
7. Burt, *Perennial Philadelphians*, 3.
8. Birmingham, *Grandes Dames*, 30.
9. Birmingham, *Grandes Dames*, 25.
10. Birmingham, *Grandes Dames*, 32.
11. Birmingham, *Grandes Dames*, 36.
12. Birmingham, *Grandes Dames*, 36.
13. Mizner, Typescript, 45–46.

14. *Palm Beach Post*, January 27, 1920, March 31, 1923, in Curl, *Mizner's Florida*.

15. *Palm Beach Daily News*, February 15, 1926, February 27, 1925, in Curl, *Mizner's Florida*.

16. Mayhew, "House of Munn," New York Social Diary, November 24, 2006.

17. Curl, "Tony Biddle and the New Palm Beach" (unpublished report), 2.

18. Curl, "Tony Biddle and the New Palm Beach" (unpublished report), 1.

19. Lawson, "New University to Be Built," *New York Times*, February 24, 1924.

20. Lawson, "New University to Be Built," *New York Times*, February 24, 1924.

21. Curl, *Mizner's Florida*, 79.

22. Curl, *Mizner's Florida*, 89.

23. Seebohm, *Boca Rococo*, 207.

24. Seebohm, *Boca Rococo*, 207.

25. Curl, *Mizner's Florida*, 93.

26. DeLamar, Handwritten letter to Heller, 1 (see Waugh notes).

27. Singer, Foreword in Tarbell, *Florida Architecture of Addison Mizner*, xxxii.

28. Mizner, Typescript, 74.

29. *Spokane Spokesman-Review*, "Restless Peggy Caught by Love at Last," September 12, 1925, 17.

30. Mizner, Typescript, 86.

31. Mizner, Typescript, 87.

32. Mizner, Typescript, 87.

33. Curl, *Mizner's Florida*, 104.

34. Singer, Foreword in Tarbell, *Florida Architecture of Addison Mizner*, xxxii.

35. Waugh, Autobiographical typescript, Chapter 4, 4.

36. Waugh, Autobiographical typescript, Chapter 4, 4.

37. Burke, *Rogue's Progress*, 215.

38. Mizner, Typescript, 64.

39. Mizner, Typescript, 64.

40. Mizner, Typescript, 67.

41. Waugh, Autobiographical typescript, Chapter 4, 8.

42. Waugh, Autobiographical typescript, Chapter 4, 5.

43. Mizner, Typescript, 83.

44. Amory, *Last Resorts*, 376.

45. Mizner, Typescript, 49.

46. Mizner, Typescript, 49.

47. Mizner, Typescript, 49.

48. Johnston, *Legendary Mizners*, 35.

49. Brown, Interview, 1992.

50. DeLamar, Handwritten letter to Heller, 10.

51. DeLamar, Letter to Alva Johnston, 15.

52. Seebohm, *Boca Rococo*, ref. to *Palm Beach Post*, August 8, 1918, 161, fn 1.

53. Brown, Interview, 1992.

54. DeLamar, Handwritten letter to the *Miami Herald* (never mailed).

55. Waugh, Autobiographical typescript, Chapter 7, 16.

56. *Palm Beach Post*, "Million Dollar Moving Picture Company Being Formed by Local Men," October 29, 1922, 1.

57. DeLamar, Handwritten letter to Heller, 2.

58. Curl, *Mizner's Florida*, 77.

59. Waugh, Autobiographical typescript, Chapter 6, 13.

60. Waugh, Autobiographical typescript, Chapter 4, 10.

61. *San Francisco Call*, "The Rich Duke to Marry the Poor Girl," June 22, 1913, 4.

62. Waugh, Autobiographical typescript, Chapter 7, 14.

CHAPTER TWELVE: AN ENTREPRENEUR

1. Waugh, "Mizner Industries," Typescript, 5.

2. Hoyt, "The Housing Shortage," 67–73.

3. Johnston, *Legendary Mizners*, 7.

4. Olendorf, Olendorf, and Tolf, *Addison Mizner, Architect to the Affluent*, 72.

5. Orr-Cahall, "An Identification and Discussion," 91.

6. Waugh, "Mizner Industries," typescript, 2.

7. Mizner, Typescript, 55.

8. Spanish River Papers, February 1982, n.p. (4), article by Donald Curl.

9. Spanish River Papers, February 1982, n.p., article by Donald Curl.

10. Spanish River Papers, February 1982, n.p. (4–5), article by Donald Curl.

11. Spanish River Papers, February 1982, n.p. (5), article by Donald Curl.

12. Waugh, "Mizner Industries," typescript, 5–6.

13. Mizner, Typescript, 59.

14. Mizner, Typescript, 55.

15. Waugh, "Mizner Industries," typescript, 6.

16. Orr-Cahall, "An Identification and Discussion," 90, fn 21 ("fleecy cloud").

17. Waugh, "Mizner Industries," typescript, 6.

18. Orr, *Addison Mizner: Architect of Dreams and Realities*, 56, fn 14.

19. Spanish River Papers, 9, reprint of *Palm Beach Weekly News*, December 13, 1918.

20. Waugh, "Mizner Industries," typescript, Chapter 7, 14.

21. Mizner, Typescript, 121.

22. Seiden, "The Mizner Touch," 46.

23. Orr-Cahall, "An Identification and Discussion," 83, fn 13.

24. Spanish River Papers, reprint of "New Mizner Industries Planned," from *Palm Beach Post*, April 4, 1929, n.p. (17).

25. Spanish River Papers, n.p. (17).

26. Curl, *Mizner's Florida*, 59.

27. Spanish River Papers, February 1982, n.p. (20).

28. Spanish River Papers, February 1982, n.p. (20).

CHAPTER THIRTEEN: THE GREATEST RESORT IN THE WORLD

1. Levy, *Herbert Croly of the New Republic*, 101.

2. Coolidge, "Address to the American Society of Newspaper Editors, Washington, D.C.," January 17, 1925.

3. Literary Digest, "Columbia, the Land of the Multi-Millionaire," April 16, 1927, 10.

4. Tebeau, *History of Florida*, 377.

5. Tindall, "Bubble in the Sun," 79.

6. Tindall, "Bubble in the Sun," 82.

7. Nijman, *Miami: Mistress of the Americas*, 72.

8. Tebeau, *History of Florida*, 384.

9. Allen, *Only Yesterday*, 235; Galbraith, *The Great Crash*, 10.

10. Allen, *Only Yesterday*, 240.

11. Curl, *Mizner's Florida*, 137; also see, Chapter 5, fn 7.

12. Tindall, "The Bubble in the Sun," 76.

13. *New York Times*, "Miami and The Story of Its Remarkable Growth," March 15, 1925.

14. Allen, *Only Yesterday*, 238.

15. Curl, *Mizner's Florida*, 138.

16. Curl, *Boca Raton Resort & Club*, 15.

17. Curl, *Mizner's Florida*, 140.

18. Seebohm, *Boca Rococo*, 212–13.

19. Orr-Cahall, Mizner ad, 1926, in "An Identification and Discussion," 62.

20. Curl, Mizner ad in *Boca Raton Resort & Club*, 38.

21. *Palm Beach Post*, August 4, 1925.

22. Spanish River Papers, February 1974, n.p.

23. Curl, *Boca Raton Resort & Club*, 15.

24. Vickers, "Addison Mizner: Promoter in Paradise," 383.

25. Gillis, Mizner ad, in *Boomtime Boca*, 53.

26. Curl, *Boca Raton Resort & Club*, 22.

27. Curl, *Boca Raton Resort & Club*, 22.

28. Vickers, "Addison Mizner: Promoter in Paradise," 388.

29. Curl, *Mizner's Florida*, 140–41.

30. Orr, *Addison Mizner: Architect of Dreams and Realities*, 43.

31. Mizner Development Corporation Sales Brochure, 1925, 31.

32. DeLamar, Letter to Alva Johnston, 31.

33. Allvine, "Press Agent Who Is Paid $1,000 a Week," *Photoplay*, August 1923, 52.

34. Reichenbach, *Phantom Fame*, 2.

35. Olendorf, Olendorf, and Tolf, *Addison Mizner, Architect to the Affluent*, 136.

36. *New York Times*, "Tumulty Refutes Kidnapping Fake," July 31, 1920, 5.

37. Johnston, *Legendary Mizners*, 212.

38. Johnston, *Legendary Mizners*, 221.

39. *Palm Beach Post*, "Marie Dressler Tells World," October 26, 1925.

40. *Palm Beach Post*, "Marie Dressler Tells World," October 26, 1925.

41. Allen, *Only Yesterday*, 242.

42. Curl, *Mizner's Florida*, 154.

43. *Palm Beach Post*, "Mizners Offer U.S. Use of Their Planes," October 5, 1925.

44. McElvaine, *Great Depression*, 42.

45. Tebeau, *History of Florida*, 387.

46. Vickers, "Addison Mizner: Promoter in Paradise," 401.

47. Curl, *Mizner's Florida*, 154.

48. Seebohm, *Boca Rococo*, 220.

49. Curl, *Mizner's Florida*, 145.

50. Johnston, *Legendary Mizners*, 40; *Palm Beach Post*, Mizner ad, May 14, 1926, 7.

51. *Palm Beach Post*, Mizner ad, September 15, 1925, 20.

52. *Palm Beach Post*, Mizner ad, September 30, 1925; also BR, 26.

53. Gillis, *Boomtime Boca*, Mizner ad, 1925, 34.

54. Curl, *Boca Raton Resort & Club*, 19 (Mizner ad).

55. *Palm Beach Post*, Mizner ad, September 12, 1925.

56. *Palm Beach Post*, Mizner ad, September 30, 1925.

57. Johnston, "Profile: Palm Beach Architect," New Yorker, December 6, 1952, 48.

58. Curl, *Boca Raton Resort & Club*, 35 (Mizner ad).

59. Curl, *Boca Raton Resort & Club*, 28–30.

60. Spanish River Papers, February 1974.

61. Curl, *Boca Raton Resort & Club*, 38.

62. Curl, *Boca Raton Resort & Club*, 31.

63. Tarbell, *Florida Architecture of Addison Mizner*, xxxiv.

64. Curl, *Mizner's Florida*, 158.

65. Curl, *Boca Raton Resort & Club*, 40.

66. Curl, *Boca Raton Resort & Club*, 40.

67. Susan Gillis, *Boomtime Boca*, 55 (Mizner ad).

68. Curl, *Boca Raton Resort & Club*, 42.

69. Curl, *Boca Raton Resort & Club*, 42.

70. Vickers, *Panic in Paradise*, 171–75.

71. Vickers, "Addison Mizner: Promoter in Paradise," 403–4.

72. Vickers, "Addison Mizner: Promoter in Paradise," 405.

73. Vickers, "Addison Mizner: Promoter in Paradise," 405.

74. Vickers, "Addison Mizner: Promoter in Paradise," 394.

75. Vickers, "Addison Mizner: Promoter in Paradise," 387.

76. DeLamar, Letter to Alva Johnston, 14.

77. Alva Johnston, "Profile: Palm Beach Architect," *New Yorker*, December 13, 1952, 44.

78. DeLamar, Unpublished letter to the *Miami Herald*, n.d.

79. Blake and Gibney, "Deadliest, Costliest, and Most Intense United States Tropical Cyclones," 7 (lives), 11 (cost).

80. Sheffield, "Stark Memories of Storms Gone By," *Boca Raton News*, June 28, 1981, 4.

81. Tindall, "Bubble in the Sun," 111.

82. Nicholson, letter to Salida Investment Co., December 4, 1926.

83. Curl, *Mizner's Florida*, 164.

CHAPTER FOURTEEN: REBIRTH AND RECOGNITION

1. Orr-Cahall, "An Identification and Discussion," 27.

2. Hallam, "Riverside Remembered," n.p.

3. Curl, *Mizner's Florida*, 167.

4. Showalter, *Many Mizners*, 52.

5. Wilson Mizner, Letter to "Arthur" (Somers Roche), August 19, 1926.

6. Curl, *Boca Raton Resort & Club*, 43–44.

7. Seebohm, *Boca Rococo*, 234.

8. Maxwell, *R. S. V. P.*, 188–89.

9. DeLamar, Introduction to Tarbell, *Florida Architecture of Addison Mizner*, xv.

10. Curl, Introduction to Tarbell, *Florida Architecture of Addison Mizner*, xv.

11. DeLamar, Introduction to Tarbell, *Florida Architecture of Addison Mizner*, xiv.

12. DeLamar, Introduction to Tarbell, *Florida Architecture of Addison Mizner*, xi.

13. Seebohm, *Boca Rococo*, 238.

14. Curl, *Mizner's Florida*, 174.

15. Allen and Cardoso, "Mizner Mansion to Be Razed," *Sun Sentinel*, April 26, 2001.

16. Allen and Cardoso, "Mizner Mansion to Be Razed," *Sun Sentinel*, April 26, 2001.

17. Curl, *Mizner's Florida*, 186.

18. Jones III, "Addison Mizner in Sea Island," interview, January 23, 2016.

19. Foerderer Family Papers, Collection 31021.

20. Orr-Cahall, "An Identification and Discussion," 85.

21. Tebeau, *History of Florida*, 388.

22. Nelander, "Palm Beach Has Long History of Weathering Hurricanes," *Palm Beach Daily News*, May 31, 2011.

23. Seebohm, *Boca Rococo*, 244.

24. Brown, Interview, 1992.

25. DeLamar, Letter to Alva Johnston, 47.

26. DeLamar, Letter to Alva Johnson, 1.

27. DeLamar, Letter to Alva Johnston, 40.

28. Mayhew, "Unforgettable Palm Beach," *Palm Beach Daily News*, Feb. 21, 2011.

29. Mockler, *Maurice Fatio: Palm Beach Architect*, 236.

30. Curl, *Mizner's Florida*, 191.

31. Crane, "Casa Coe da Sol," *St. Petersburg Independent*, April 9, 1982, Section D.

32. *New York Times*, January 2, 1932, Social section, 8.

33. *Palm Beach Times*, January 31, 1929; *Palm Beach Post*, March 17, 1929.

34. Curl, *Mizner's Florida*, 200.

35. Mizner, Typescript, 1.

36. Mizner, Typescript, 121.

37. Seebohm, *Boca Rococo*, 250

38. Seebohm, *Boca Rococo*, 250.

39. Johnston, *Legendary Mizners*, 111.

40. Burke, *Rogue's Progress*, 262.

41. Burke, *Rogue's Progress*, 264.

42. Burke, *Rogue's Progress*, 268.

43. Burke, *Rogue's Progress*, 262, 268.

44. Burke, *Rogue's Progress*, 257.

45. Burke, *Rogue's Progress*, 259.

46. Seebohm, *Boca Rococo*, 252.

47. Johnston, *Legendary Mizners*, 303.

48. Seebohm, *Boca Rococo*, 254.

49. Seebohm, *Boca Rococo*, 253.

CHAPTER FIFTEEN: MASTER BUILDER

1. Seebohm, *Boca Rococo*, 127.

2. Waugh, Alex. Autobiography typescript, Chapter 5, 2.

3. Curl, Donald. *Boca Raton*, 43.

4. Curl, *Mizner's Florida*. 201.

5. Mizner, Cynic's Calendar for 1904, entry for August 1904, n.p., 1903.

6. Starr, *Dictionary of American Biography*, Vol XXI, Suppl. one. "Mizner" entry by Bannister, 558–560.

7. Huxtable, "Architecture View: Palm Beach." March 20, 1977. *New York Times*.

8. Huxtable, "Architecture View: Palm Beach."

9. Huxtable, "Architecture View: Palm Beach."

10. Childers, *The Oxford English Dictionary*, 282.

11. Holley, "A Creator of Castles in Spain," *The Hollywood Magazine*, September 1925, 34.

12. Onions, *The Oxford Dictionary of English Etymology*, 47–48.

13. Singer, Paris, foreword to Tarbell, *Florida Architecture of Addison Mizner*, xxxi.

BIBLIOGRAPHY

BOOKS

Allen, Frederick Lewis. *Only Yesterday: An Informal History of the 1920s*. New York: Harper and Brothers, 1931.

Amory, Cleveland. *The Last Resorts*. New York: Harper and Brothers, 1948.

Aslet, Clive. *The American Country House*. New Haven: Yale University Press, 1990.

Baker, Anthony, Robert B. MacKay, and Carol A. Traynor, eds. *Long Island Country Houses and Their Architects, 1860–1940*. New York: W. W. Norton & Company, 1997.

Beck, Warren A., and David A. Williams. *California: A History of the Golden State*. Garden City, NY: Doubleday & Company, Inc., 1972.

Beebe, Lucius. *The Big Spenders: The Epic Story of the Rich Rich, the Grandees of America and the Magnificoes, and How They Spent Their Fortunes*. Mount Jackson, VA: Axios Press, 1966.

Beer, Thomas. *The Mauve Decade: American Life at the End of the Nineteenth Century*. New York: Carroll & Graf Publishers, Inc., 1926.

Berglund, Barbara. *Making San Francisco American: Cultural Frontiers in the Urban American West, 1846–1906*. Lawrence: University Press of Kansas, 2007.

Birmingham, Stephen. *California Rich*. New York: Simon & Schuster, 1980.

Birmingham, Stephen. *Grandes Dames*. New York: Simon & Schuster, 1982.

Birmingham, Stephen. *The Right People: A Portrait of the American Social Establishment*. Boston: Little, Brown and Co., 1968.

Bonhams. Sale Catalogue: *Important Collectors' Motor Cars, Collectors' Motorcycles and Fine Automobilia*. Lot 604: THE OLDEST KNOWN SURVIVING ROLLS-ROYCE IN THE WORLD, THE 1904 PARIS SALON AND 1905 OLYMPIA MOTOR EXHIBITION DISPLAY CAR, 1904 ROLLS-ROYCE 10HP TWO SEATER. Auction on December 3, 2007. London. Accessed May 15, 2016. https://www.bonhams.com/auctions/15348/lot/604/.

Brandon, Ruth. *A Capitalist Romance: Singer and the Sewing Machine*. Philadelphia: J. B. Lippincott Co., 1977.

Brandon, Ruth. *The Dollar Princesses: Sagas of Upward Nobility, 1870–1914*. New York: Knopf, 1980.

Briggs, John. *Fire in the Crucible: Understanding the Process of Creative Genius*. Grand Rapids, MI: Phanes Press, November 2000.

Burke, John. *Rogue's Progress*. New York: G. P. Putnam's Sons, 1975.

Burt, Nathaniel. *First Families: The Making of an American Aristocracy*. Boston: Little, Brown and Company, 1970.

Burt, Nathaniel. *The Perennial Philadelphians: The Anatomy of an American Aristocracy*. Philadelphia: University of Pennsylvania Press, 1999.

"Bussinger, Julia, and Beverly Phelan. *Images of America: Benicia*. Charleston, SC: Arcadia Publishing, 2004.

Calhoun, Charles W., ed. *The Gilded Age: Perspectives on the Origins of Modern America*. Lanham, MD: Rowman & Littlefield Publishers, Inc., 2007.

Carnegie, Andrew. *Round the World*. New York: Charles Scribner's Sons, 1884.

Chandler, Tertius. *Four Thousand Years of Urban Growth: An Historical Census*. Lewiston, NY: The Edwin Mellen Press, 1987.

Childers, Ian, ed. *The Oxford English Dictionary*, 3rd Edition. London: Oxford University Press, 2004.

Croly, Herbert. *The Promise of American Life*. New York: Cosimo, 2005 (originally 1909).

Curl, Donald W. and The Boca Raton Historical Society. *The Boca Raton Resort & Club: Mizner's Inn*. Charleston, SC: The History Press, 2008.

Curl, Donald W. "Introduction to the Dover Edition." In Tarbell, Ida, *The Florida Architecture of Addison Mizner*. New York: Dover Publications, 1996.

Curl, Donald W. *Mizner's Florida: American Resort Architecture*. Cambridge, MA: MIT Press, 1984.

Davis, Deborah. *Gilded: How Newport Became America's Richest Resort*. Hoboken, NJ: John Wiley & Sons, Inc., 2009.

Dean, Tamara. *The Human-Powered Home: Choosing Muscles Over Motors*. Gabriola Island, BC: New Society Publishers, 2008.

Dienkelspiel, Frances. *Towers of Gold: How One Jewish Immigrant Named Isaias Hellman Created California*. New York: St. Martin's Press, 2008.

Drabelle, Dennis. *The Great American Railroad War: How Ambrose Bierce and Frank Norris Took On the Notorious Central Pacific Railroad*. New York: St. Martin's Press, 2012.

Drabelle, Dennis. *Mile-High Fever: Silver Mines, Boom Towns and High Living on the Comstock Lode*. New York: St. Martin's Press, 2009.

Duncan, Isadora. *My Life*. New York: Liveright Publishing Corporation, 2013 (originally 1927).

Fiori, Pamela. *In the Spirit of Palm Beach*. New York: Assouline, 2012.

Floyd, Margaret Henderson, "Inspiration and Synthesis in Richardson's Paine House." In Meister, Maureen, ed. *H.H. Richardson, The Architect, His Peers and Their Era*, Cambridge, MA and London, England: MIT Press, 1999.

Fulton, Joe B. *The Reverend Mark Twain: Theological Burlesque, Form, and Content*. Columbus: Ohio State University Press, 2005.

Galbraith, John Kenneth. *The Great Crash: 1929*. Boston: Houghton Mifflin Company, 1954.

Gay, Peter. *Modernism: The Lure of Heresy: From Baudelaire to Beckett and Beyond*. New York: W. W. Norton & Company, 2008.

Gillis, Susan and the Boca Raton Historical Society. *Boomtime Boca: Boca Raton in the 1920s*. Charleston, SC: Arcadia Publishing, 2007.

Hayward, Helena, ed. *World Furniture: An Illustrated History from Earliest Times*. New York: Crescent Books, 1965.

Herford, Oliver, Ethel Watts Mumford, and Addison Mizner. *The Cynic's Calendar of Revised Wisdom*. 7 editions. San Francisco: Paul Elder and Co., 1903–1917.

Hoffstott, Barbara. *Landmark Architecture of Palm Beach*. Lanham, MD: Rowman & Littlefield, 2015.

Holliday, J. S. *Rush for Riches: Gold Fever and the Making of California*. Berkeley: University of California Press, 1999.

Hoover, Mildred Brooke, Hero Eugene Rensch, and Ethel Grace Rensch, *Historic Spots in California*, 3rd edition. Revised by William N. Abeloe. Stanford, CA: Stanford University Press, 1966.

Howard, Hugh. *Architecture's Odd Couple*. New York: Bloomsbury Press, 2016.

Issel, William, and Robert W. Cherny. *San Francisco 1865–1932*. Berkeley: University of California Press, 1986.

James, Edward T., ed., Janet Wilson James, assoc. ed., and Paul S. Boyer, asst. ed. *Notable American Women: A Biographical Dictionary*. Volume I, A–F. Cambridge, MA: Belknap Press, 1971.

James, Edward T., ed., Janet Wilson James, assoc. ed., and Paul S. Boyer, asst. ed. *Notable American Women: A Biographical Dictionary*. Volume III, P–Z. Cambridge, MA: Belknap Press, 1971.

Johnston, Alva. *The Legendary Mizners*. New York: Farrar, Straus and Young, 1953.

Kaplan, Justin. *When the Astors Owned New York: Bluebloods and Grand Hotels in a Gilded Age*. New York: Plume, 2006.

King, Greg. *A Season of Splendor: The Court of Mrs. Astor in Gilded Age New York*. Hoboken, NJ: John Wiley & Sons, Inc., 2009.

Kirker, Harold. *California's Architectural Frontier*. Santa Barbara, CA and Salt Lake City: Peregine Smith, Inc., 1973.

Kurth, Peter. *Isadora: A Sensational Life*. Boston: Little, Brown and Company, 2001.

Larson, Erik. *Dead Wake: The Last Crossing of the Lusitania*. New York: Crown Publishers, 2015.

Le Corbusier. *Toward a New Architecture*. Trans. by Frederick Etchells for the 13th French edition. New York: Dover Publications, Inc., 1986.

Lee, Betty. *Marie Dressler: The Unlikeliest Star*. Lexington: University Press of Kentucky, 1997.

Levi, Stephen C. *Boom and Bust in the Alaska Goldfields*. Westport, CT: Praeger Publishers, 2008.

Levy, David W. *Herbert Croly of the New Republic: The Life and Thought of an American Progressive*. Princeton, NJ: Princeton University Press, 2014.

The Long Island Country House, 1870–1930. Water Mill, NY: Parrish Art Museum, 1988.

Longstreth, Richard. *On the Edge of the World: Four Architects in San Francisco at the Turn of the Century*. New York: The Architectural History Foundation and Cambridge, MA and London, England: MIT Press, 1983.

Loos, Anita. *A Girl Like I*. New York: Viking Press, 1966.

Maddison, Angus. *Contours of the World Economy, 1–2030 AD: Essays in Macro-Economic History*. Oxford: Oxford University Press, 2007.

Marconi, Richard A., and Debi Murray with the Historical Society of Palm Beach County. *Palm Beach*. Charleston, SC: Arcadia Publishing, 2009.

Martin, Harold H. *This Happy Isle: The Story of Sea Island and the Cloister*. Sea Island, GA: The Sea Island Co., 1978.

Maxwell, Elsa. *R. S. V. P.: Elsa Maxwell's Own Story*. Boston: Little, Brown and Company, 1954.

Mayhew, Augustus. *Lost in Wonderland: Reflections on Palm Beach*. West Palm Beach, FL: Palm Beach Editorial Services, 2012.

Mayhew, Augustus. *Palm Beach: A Greater Grandeur*. Palm Beach, FL: East Side Press, 2016.

McElvaine, Robert S. *The Great Depression: America, 1929–1941*. New York: Times Books, 1984.

McIver, Stuart B. *Yesterday's Palm Beach: Including Palm Beach County*. Miami: E. A. Seemann Publishing, Inc., 1976.

Mizner, Addison. *Cynic's Calendar* for 1904, entry for August 1904, pub. 1903.

Mizner, Addison. *The Many Mizners*. New York: Sears Publishing Co., 1932.

Mockler, Kim. *Maurice Fatio: Palm Beach Architect*. New York: Acanthus Press, 2010.

Nijman, Jan. *Miami: Mistress of the Americas*. Philadelphia: University of Pennsylvania Press, 2011.

Olendorf, Donna, William Olendorf, and Robert Tolf. *Addison Mizner, Architect to the Affluent: A Sketchbook Raisonne of His Work*. Ft. Lauderdale, FL: Gale Graphics, 1983.

Onions, C. T., ed., with the assistance of G. W. S. Friedrichsen and R. W. Burchfield. *The Oxford Dictionary of English Etymology*. London: Oxford University Press, 1969 (originally Oxford: Clarendon House Press, 1966).

Orr, Christina. *Addison Mizner: Architect of Dreams and Realities (1872–1933)*. Palm Beach: Norton Gallery of Art, 1977.

Prosser, William Farr. *A History of the Puget Sound Country, Its Resources, Its Commerce and Its People*. Chicago: Lewis Publishing Company, 1903, retrieved online March 23, 2016 at https://books.google.com.

Reichenbach, Harry, as told to David Freedman. *Phantom Fame*. New York: Simon & Schuster, 1931.

Ridley, Jane Bertie. *A Life of Edward VII*. London: Chatto & Windus, 2012.

Roberts, Kenneth L. *Florida*. Boca Raton: Mizner Development Corporation, 1926.

Rockoff, Hugh. *Until It's Over, Over There: The U.S. Economy in World War I* (June 2004). NBER Working Paper No. w10580, available at SSRN: http://ssrn.com/abstract=559230, viewed on July 17, 2015.

Rubica, Jose Claret. *Encyclopedia of Spanish Period Furniture Designs*. New York: Sterling Publishing Co., Inc., 1984.

Rybczynski, Witold, and Laurie Olin. *Vizcaya: An American Villa and Its Makers*. Penn Studies in Landscape Architecture. Philadelphia: University of Pennsylvania Press, 2006.

Scully, Vincent. *The Shingle Style*. New Haven: Yale University Press, 1955.

Seebohm, Caroline. *Boca Rococo: How Addison Mizner Invented Florida's Gold Coast*. New York: Clarkson Potter Publishers, 2001.

Shelley, Percy Bysshe. *Adonaïs 1821*. Oxford: Woodstock Books, 1992.

Showalter, J. Camille. *The Many Mizners: California Clan Extraordinary*. Oakland, CA: The Oakland Museum, 1978.

Shlaes, Amity. *Coolidge*. New York: HarperCollins, 2013.

Small, Ian, gen. ed. *The Complete Works of Oscar Wilde, Volume 3. The Picture of Dorian Gray: The 1890 and 1891 Texts*. Joseph Bristow, ed. Oxford: Oxford University Press, 2005.

Smith, Mildred H. *Early History of the Long Island Railroad, 1834–1900*. Uniondale, NY: Salisbury Printers, 1959.

Starr, Harris E., ed. *Dictionary of American Biography*. Vol XXI, Supplement 1. "Mizner" entry by Turpin C. Bannister.

Starr, Kevin, *America and the California Dream*. New York: Oxford University Press, 1973. Google Books: https://books.google.com/books?id=V9brMMe5PtIC&printsec=copyright&source=gbs_pub_info_r#v=onepage&q&f=false, accessed January 17, 2017.

Starr, Kevin. *Inventing the Dream: California through the Progressive Era*. New York: Oxford University Press, 1985.

Sullivan, Edward Dean. *The Fabulous Wilson Mizner*. New York: The Henkle Co., 1935.

Tarbell, Ida. *Florida Architecture of Addison Mizner*. Foreword by Paris Singer. New York: William Helburn, 1928.

Tebeau, Charlton. *A History of Florida*. Coral Gables, FL: University of Miami Press, 1971.

Trager, James. *The New York Chronology: The Ultimate Compendium of Events, People, and Anecdotes from the Dutch to the Present*. New York: Harper Resource, 2003.

Tuchman, Barbara W. *The Proud Tower: A Portrait of the World Before the War, 1890–1914*. New York: Random House Publishing Group, 2014 (Kindle edition).

Twain, Mark, and Charles Dudley Warner. *The Gilded Age*. New York: Quill Pen Classics, 2008.

Vanderbilt II, Arthur. *Fortune's Children: The Fall of the House of Vanderbilt*. New York: William Morrow, 1989.

Van Rensselaer, Mariana Griswold. *Henry Hobson Richardson and His Works*. Boston: Houghton Mifflin, 1888.

Veblen, Thorstein. *The Theory of the Leisure Class*. New York: Random House, 1934.

Vickers, Raymond B. *Panic in Paradise: Florida's Banking Crash of 1926*. Tuscaloosa: University of Alabama Press, 1994.

Wecter, Dixon. *The Saga of American Society: A Record of Social Aspiration*. New York: Charles Scribner's Sons, 1937.

Wharton, Edith. *The Age of Innocence*. New York: Penguin Books, 1996.

Wharton, Edith. *Italian Villas and Their Gardens*. Illus. by Maxfield Parrish. New York: The Century Company, 1905.

White, Samuel G., and Elizabeth White. *Stanford White Architect*. New York: Rizzoli, 2008.

Young, John Russell, ed. *Memorial History of the City of Philadelphia: From Its First Settlement to the Year 1895*. Volume II, Special and Biographical, George Overcash Seilhamer. New York: New York History Company, 1898.

PERIODICALS

Allvine, Gendon. "The Press Agent Who Is Paid $1,000 a Week." *Photoplay*, August 1923.

Blake, Eric S., and Ethan J. Gibney. "The Deadliest, Costliest, and Most Intense United States Tropical Cyclones from 1851 to 2010 (and other frequently requested hurricane facts)" (PDF). United States National Oceanic and Atmospheric Administration Technical Memorandum, August 2011, National Hurricane Center, accessed September 4, 2015, http://nhc.noaa.gov/news.

Boyd, John Taylor, Jr. "The Florida House: Mr. Addison Mizner Recounts the Birth of the New Florida Architecture at Palm Beach in an Interview." *Arts and Decoration* 32 (January 1930): 37–40, 80, 102.

Burton, William L. "James Semple, Prairie Entrepreneur." *Illinois Historical Journal* 80 (Summer 1987): 66–84.

Chapman, Mary Patricia. "The Mission of Lansing Bond Mizner to Central America." *The Historian* 19 (August 1957): 385–401, accessed April 18, 2016, https://www.deepdyve.com/lp/wiley/the-mission-of-lansing-bond-mizner-to-central-america-.

Coolidge, Calvin. "Address to the American Society of Newspaper Editors, Washington, D.C.," January 17, 1925. Gerhard Peters and John T. Woolley, The American Presidency Project, accessed September 22, 2015, www.presidency.ucsb.edu/ws/?pid=24180.

Holley, Lillian Harlow. "A Creator of Castles in Spain." *The Hollywood Magazine*, September 1925, Vol. 1, no. 11.

Hoyt, Homer. "The Housing Shortage and the Supply of Building Materials." *Annals of the American Academy of Political and Social Science* 89, Prices (May 1920), 67–73, www.jstor.org/stable/1014207.

Johnston, Alva. "Profile: The Legend of a Sport." *New Yorker*, 5 installments: February 25, 1950, 39–67; July 22, 1950, 30–45; July 29, 1950, 26–41; December 23, 1950, 28–39; December 30, 1950, 26–41.

Johnston, Alva. "Profile: The Palm Beach Architect." *New Yorker*, 4 installments: November 22, 1952, 46–48+, November 29, 1952, 46–48+, December 6, 1952, 48–50+, December 13, 1952, 42–46+.

Journal of Illinois State Historical Society, October 1914, 265, accessed February 20, 2016, https://archive.org/stream/journalishs07illiuoft#page/265/mode/1up.

Literary Digest. "Columbia, the Land of the Multi-Millionaire" (PDF). April 16, 1927, accessed September 15, 2015, www.unz.org/Pub/LiteraryDigest/?Period=1927_04.

"The Old Cow Bay Manor House." *Architectural Record* 41 (March 1917): 259–66.

Patterson, Curtis. "A Shelf of New Books: Addison Mizner and Florida." *International Studio* XC, August 1928, 73–74.

Price, Matlack. "'Mediterranean' Architecture in Florida." *Architectural Forum* 44 (January 1926): 33–40.

Spanish River Papers, February 1974, Vol. II, no. 1. Boca Raton Historical Society, reprint of "Mizner Gives Big Material Order for Boca Raton," *Miami Herald*, February 21, 1926, accessed April 23, 2016, www.bocahistory.org/_files/span_river/SRP%20Feb%201974.pdf.

Spanish River Papers, February 1974, Vol. II, no. 1. Boca Raton Historical Society, "The Cloister Inn Is Opened," accessed April 23, 2016, www.bocahistory.org/_files/span_river/SRP%20Feb%201974.pdf.

Spanish River Papers, February 1976, Vol. IV, no. 2. Boca Raton Historical Society, "Building of Boca Raton Town Hall," accessed January 18, 2016, www.bocahistory.org/_files/span_river/SRP%20Feb%201976.pdf.

Spanish River Papers, February 1977, Vol. V, no. 2. Boca Raton Historical Society, "Boca Raton's 'Old Floresta,'" accessed July 17, 2015, www.bocahistory.org/_files/span_river/SRP%20Feb%201977.pdf.

Spanish River Papers, October 1978, Vol. VII, no. 1. Boca Raton Historical Society, "The Architecture of Addison Mizner," www.bocahistory.org/_files/span_river/SRP%20Oct%201978.pdf.

Spanish River Papers, February 1982, Vol. X, no. 2. Boca Raton Historical Society, "Mizner Industries," accessed October 14, 1915, www.bocahistory.org/_files/span_river/SRP%20Feb%201982.pdf.

Spanish River Papers, Fall 1982, Vol. XI, no. 1. Boca Raton Historical Society, "Addison Mizner's Ritz Carlton Cloister Opens," accessed November 14, 2015, www.bocahistory.org/_files/span_river/SRP%20Fall%201982.pdf.

Spanish River Papers, Fall/Winter 1983/1984, Vol. XII, no. 1 & 2. Boca Raton Historical Society, "The Mizner Development Corporation's Administration Buildings," accessed November 15, 2015, www.bocahistory.org/_files/span_river/SRP%20Fall%20Winter%201983-1984.pdf.

Tindall, George B. "The Bubble in the Sun." *American Heritage* 16 (August 1965): 76–83.

Van Rensselaer, Mariana Griswold. "The Development of American Homes." *Forum*, January 1892, 675.

Vickers, Raymond. "Addison Mizner: Promoter in Paradise." *Florida Historical Quarterly*, Vol. LXXV, no. 4, Spring 1997: 403–4.

Wilson, John R. A. "Paris Singer: A Life Portrait: Part I: The Oldway Years (1867–1914)." *Torquay Natural History Society's Transactions and Proceedings*, 1997.

Wilson, John R. A. "Paris Singer: A Life Portrait: Part II: The Palm Beach Era (1915–1932)." *Torquay Natural History Society's Transactions and Proceedings*, 1998.

NEWSPAPERS

Allen, C. Ron and Tara Cardoso, "Mizner Mansion to Be Razed, Co-Owner Says." *Sun Sentinel*, April 26, 2001, accessed December 10, 2016, http://articles.sun-sentinel.com/2001-04-26/news/0104260267_1_palm-beach-county-mansion-addison-mizner.

Crane, Jeanette, "Casa Coe da Sol: Magnificent Mizner Mansion." *St. Petersburg Independent*, April 9, 1982, Section D.

Daily Alta California. "Burning of the Independence, Names of the Dead." Vol. 4, no. 90, April 1, 1853, 1, retrieved April 5, 2016 through California Digital Newspaper Collection, http://cdnc.ucr.edu/cgi-bin.

Drown, Ezra. "Loss of the Steamer Independence." *Daily Alta California*, Vol. 4, no. 91, April 2, 1853, 2, retrieved through California Digital Newspaper Collection on March 23, 2016, http://cdnc.ucr.edu/cgi-bin.

Hiler, Katie. "Once Tallest Standing, Then the Tallest to Come Down." *New York Times*, June 17, 2013, Science section, 1.

Huxtable, Ada Louise. "Architecture View: Palm Beach." *New York Times*, March 20, 1977, accessed January 14, 2017, www.nytimes.com/1977/03/20/archives/architecture-view-the-maverick-who-created-palm-beach-architecture.html?_r=0.

Keyes, Emilie. "Song, Poetry and Flowers Build Intangible Memorial to Mizner." *Palm Beach News*, February 6, 1933.

Lawson, Mrs. "New University to Be Built by Duke Family at Durham, N. C., to Be Designed by Addison Mizner." *New York Times*, February 24, 1924.

Mayhew, Augustus. "Unforgettable Palm Beach: Island Endured Great Depression Largely Unscathed." *Palm Beach Daily News*, February 21, 2011, accessed November 11, 2015, https://www.palmbeachdailynews.com/news/news/unforgettable-palmbeach/nMCps/.

Murphy, Janet. "Castles in Spain Are Drab Huts Beside Palm Beach, Lightbown Says." *Palm Beach Post*, May 26, 1923.

Murphy, Mary Jo. "Eyeing the Unreal Estate of Gatsby Esq." *New York Times*, September 30, 2010, New York / Region section, 1.

Nelander, John. "Palm Beach Has Long History of Weathering Hurricanes." *Palm Beach Daily News*, May 31, 2011, accessed November 10, 2015, https://www.palmbeachdailynews.com/news/news/palm-beach-has-long-history-of-weathering-hurricane.

New York Herald Tribune. "Restraint in Design," an interview with Mies van der Rohe. June 28, 1959, 18.

New York Times. "Miami and the Story of Its Remarkable Growth: An Interview with George E. Merrick." March 15, 1925, accessed October 12, 2015, http://merrick.library.miami.edu/cdm/ref/collection/pamphlets/id/1095.

New York Times. "Mizner Memorial Rites." February 10, 1933.

New York Times. Social section. January 2, 1932, 8.

New York Times. "Tumulty Refutes Kidnapping Fake." July 31, 1920, 5.

New York Times. "War Bazaar Ready for Opening Tonight." June 3, 1916, accessed March 23, 2017, www.nytimes.com/movie/reviewres=9D07E2D7163BE633A25750C0A9609C946796D6CF.

Owens, Mitchell, "Mansion Bobs Up and Moves In." *New York Times*, February 15, 2001, accessed on 18 October 2016, www

.nytimes.com/2001/02/15/garden/mansion-bobs-up-and-moves-in.html.

Palm Beach Daily News, February 2, 1901, article part of Mizner Archives at Historical Society of Palm Beach County.

Palm Beach Daily News, February 15, 1926, in Curl, *Mizner's Florida*, 211.

Palm Beach Daily News, February 10, 1933, article part of Mizner Archives at Historical Society of Palm Beach County.

Palm Beach News. "Friends Meet to Do Honor to Memory of Mizner." February 10, 1933.

Palm Beach Post. January 27, 1920, March 31, 1923. In Curl, *Mizner's Florida*, 211.

Palm Beach Post. August 4, 1925, found in notes of Donald Curl, Boca Raton Historical Society.

Palm Beach Post. March 17, 1929.

Palm Beach Post. "Marie Dressler Tells World She Is in Love with Florida." October 26, 1925.

Palm Beach Post. "Million Dollar Moving Picture Company Being Formed by Local Men." October 29, 1922, 1.

Palm Beach Post. Mizner ad, September 12, 1925.

Palm Beach Post. Mizner ad, September 15, 1925, 20.

Palm Beach Post. Mizner ad, September 30, 1925.

Palm Beach Post. Mizner ad, May 14, 1926, 7.

Palm Beach Post. "Mizners Offer U.S. Use of Their Planes." October 5, 1925.

Palm Beach Post. "Palatial Homes for Shell-shocked Convalescent Soldiers Built By Singer Nearing Completion." December 22, 1918.

Palm Beach Post. "Singer May Go to California; Wants No Trouble with Labor." August 3, 1918.

Palm Beach Post. "Singer to Build Ten Villas in Palm Beach and Turn Them Over to Government to End of War." April 25, 1918.

Palm Beach Times. January 31, 1929.

San Francisco Call. "The Rich Duke to Marry the Poor Girl." Vol. 114, no. 22, June 22, 1913, 4, accessed July 22, 2016, https://cdnc.ucr.edu/cgi-bin/cdnc?a=d&d=SFC19130622.2.133.5.

Sheffield, Skip. "Stark Memories of Storms Gone By." *Boca Raton News*, June 28, 1981.

Spokane Spokesman-Review. "Restless Peggy Caught by Love at Last." September 12, 1925, 17, accessed July 24, 2016, https://newspapers.lib.utah.edu/details?id=6551445.

Tropical Sun, February 21, 1919, Historical Society of Palm Beach County.

UNPUBLISHED

Benicia Historical Museum. Benicia History: 1860s, 1870s, 1880s, 1890s. Accessed September 21, 1915, http://beniciahistoricalmuseum.org/1860s-1870s-1880s-1890s/.

Bingham-Blossom House, 1250 South Ocean Boulevard, Palm Beach, Palm Beach County, FL. Library of Congress. Accessed January 5, 2017, www.loc.gov/pictures/item/fl0173/, Historic American Buildings Survey, Engineering Record, Landscapes Survey.

Brown, Ozie Belle. Interview. Historical Society of Palm Beach County, 1992.

Brown, R. K. "Days of Early Settlement on Lake Recalled." January 15, 1937. On file at Historical Society of Palm Beach County.

Curl, Donald W. "Tony Biddle and the New Palm Beach" (unpublished report). Property of Historical Society of Palm Beach County, n.d.

DeLamar, Alice. Handwritten letter to Franklin Heller. January 10, 1967. Historical Society of Palm Beach County.

DeLamar, Alice. Letter to Alva Johnston. March 14, 1948. Historical Society of Palm Beach County.

DeLamar, Alice. Unpublished letter to the *Miami Herald* (never mailed), n.d. Historical Society of Palm Beach County.

Eckel, Fred. "Addison Mizner as an Architect." Telephone interviews by James F. Caughman, April 18, 2017 and May 2, 2017.

"The First Real Estate Boom Here Started in the Spring of 1893," *Tropical Sun*, March 19, 1937. In Research Atlantica, Inc., "Town of Palm Beach, Florida, 2010 Historic Sites Survey—Prepared for The Town of Palm Beach Florida, 2010," The Growth and Development of the Town of Palm Beach—A Chronological Overview, 4–19.

Foerderer Family Papers, Collection 3102. The Historical Society of Pennsylvania, 1881–ca. 1997. Processed by Cary Majewicz, April 2008. Accessed February 2, 2016, http://hsp.org/sites/default/files/legacy_files/migrated/findingaid3102foerderer.pdf.

Geer, Marian Dimick, *The Lake Worth Historian*, Palm Beach, 1896. In Research Atlantica, Inc., "Town of Palm Beach, Florida, 2010 Historic Sites Survey—Prepared for The Town of Palm Beach Florida, 2010," The Growth and Development of the Town of Palm Beach—A Chronological Overview, 4–19.

Hallam, George. "Riverside Remembered." Drummond Press, 1976, Jacksonville (FL) in "Riverside Baptist Church," Jean Grimsley, www.jaxhistory.org/riverside_baptist_church/, accessed March 2017.

Jones III, A. W. "Bill," "Addison Mizner in Sea Island." Interview by James F. Caughman at Sea Island, Georgia. January 23, 2016.

Mayhew, Augustus. "Design Providence: Horace Trumbauer—Alfred Browning Parker—Addison Mizner." Article in New York Social Diary, February 22, 2016, accessed December 20, 2016, www.newyorksocialdiary.com/social-history/2016/design-providence-horace-trumbauer-alfred-browning-parker-addison-mizner.

Mayhew, Augustus C. "The House of Munn: The Palm Beach Story." New York Social Diary, November 24, 2006, accessed July 20, 2016, www.newyorksocialdiary.com/legacy/socialdiary/2006/11_24_06/socialdiary11_24_06.php.

Mayhew, Augustus. "Remaking History: Paris Singer & the Everglades Club, 1918–1932." Palm Beach Social Diary, November 1, 2013 (from an article in the *Palm Beach Post* of September 7, 1918), accessed October 25, 2016, www.newyorksocialdiary.com/social-history/2013/palm-beach-social-diary.

Mizner, Addison. Architect's Library. Mizner Collection, The Society of the Four Arts, Palm Beach, Florida.

Mizner, Addison. Autobiographical typescript (1933). The Historical Society of Palm Beach County.

Mizner, Addison. Design Scrapbooks, 1905–1932. Mizner Collection, The Society of the Four Arts, Palm Beach, Florida.

Mizner Development Corporation Advertisements. Meisner Collection, Historical Society of Boca Raton.

Mizner Development Corporation Sales Brochure. 1925. Boca Raton Historical Society.

Mizner, Wilson. Letter to "Arthur" (Somers Roche), August 19, 1926. Historical Society of Palm Beach County.

Murphy, Janet, Murphy-Stillings, LLC, Designation Report for 127 Dunbar Road, Palm Beach, January 16, 2013 for the Landmarks Preservation Commission, Palm Beach, Florida.

Nicholson, James R. Letter to Salida Investment Co., December 4, 1926. Historical Society of Palm Beach County.

Oldfather, Susan J. "Elisha Newton Dimick and His Influence on the Development of Palm Beach." Boca Raton, FL: Florida Atlantic University, Thesis, 1989, 11–15. In Research Atlantica, Inc., "Town of Palm Beach, Florida, 2010 Historic Sites Survey—Prepared for The Town of Palm Beach Florida, 2010," The Growth and Development of the Town of Palm Beach—A Chronological Overview, 4–19.

Orr-Cahall, Anona Christina. "An Identification and Discussion of the Architecture and Decorative Arts of Addison Mizner (1872–1933)." 2 volumes. PhD Diss., Yale University, 1979.

Padwee, Michael, tilesinnewyork.blogspot.com, accessed December 1, 2016.

Palm Beach Yacht Club. History. www.palmbeachyachtclub/history, accessed June 2016.

Parry, David, "Arthur Page Brown." *Encyclopedia of San Francisco.* The San Francisco Museum and Historical Society. Entry from www.classicSFproperties.com accessed on January 23, 2017.

"Pioneer Reminisces." *Palm Beach Life*, Palm Beach, Florida, March 15, 1932, 22–23. In Research Atlantica, Inc., "Town of Palm Beach, Florida, 2010 Historic Sites Survey—Prepared for The Town of Palm Beach Florida, 2010," The Growth and Development of the Town of Palm Beach—A Chronological Overview, 4–19.

Prospectus of Mizner Industries, Inc. Typewritten manuscript, no date (circa 1928). Historical Society of Palm Beach County.

Rand, Ellen Emmet; Clara Database for Women Artists. Accessed September 24, 2015, http://clara.nmwa.org/index.php?g=entity_detail&entity_id=6875.

"Sea Gull Cottage Groundbreaking," Preservation Foundation of Palm Beach, Palm Beach, Florida, November 18, 2007, accessed January 23, 2017, www.palmbeachpreservation.org/index.cfm?fuseaction=news.one&content_id=41&x=2906550.

Seiden, Steven Arnold. "The Mizner Touch." Senior thesis, Yale University, 1958.

Singer Sewing Company, singerco.com/company/history.html, accessed June 4, 2015.

Spencer, Wilma. "Did You Know That Mrs. Byrd E. White (then Mrs. George W. Jonas) of 129 Sea Spray Avenue Named the Everglades?" Palm Beach newspaper article included in the Mizner Archives at the Historical Society of Palm Beach County.

Watson, Mary Reynolds. Letter to Franklin Reynolds (copy). Historical Society of Palm Beach County.

Waugh, Alex. "The Mizner Industries." January 1963, typescript, Historical Society of Palm Beach County.

Waugh, Alex. Autobiographical typescript, 1976. Historical Society of Palm Beach County.

INDEX

A

Abele, Julian F., 181

"Addison Mizner: Promoter in Paradise"
(Vickers), 263

Addison Mizner Inc., 233

Addison Station. *See* Boca Raton (FL)

Age of Innocence, The (Wharton), 92

Alaska, gold in, 63, 64, 66

Albert Edward, Prince of Wales, 81–82

Alcazar Hotel, 51

Alda, Frances, 198

Alexander, Kenneth D., house of, 301–2

Alexandre, Jerome, 109–10

Alfonso, King, 213

Allom, Sir Charles, 170

Amado, 150, 166, 176, 177

America
  building materials in, 1919, 222
  City Beautiful movement in, *14,*
    242–43, *246*
  country houses in, 87
  in early 1900s, 79, 126
  Gilded Age in, 82, 90
  importance of Philadelphia in, 167–68
  interest in Japanese architecture, 107
  1920s in, 162, 240
  19th century architecture in, 47–49, 50–51
  war with Mexico, 20–21

Angeli, Achille, 195, 291

Angeli, Federico, 195

Antigua Shops, 233

Architectural News, 54, 55, 56

See also Polk, Willis J.

architecture, 13
  Academic Eclecticism in, 315, 316
  Colonial Revival, 53, 55
  education in, 47–48
  Hispanic Revival Style, 314
  International Style, 317
  Italianate style, 128
  Mission Revival, 10, 53, 54, 55
  Picturesque principle in, 316
  Shingle Style, 50, 53, 58
  in 19th century America, 47–49, 50–51
  See also Mediterranean Revival
    architecture; Mizner, Addison

Arden, Elizabeth, 12, *245,* 246

Armitage, Pauline, 274

Armstrong, Paul, 121

Armstrong, William Lilburn, *122*

Aspasia, Princess, 300

Asquith, Henry Herbert, 124

Astor, Mrs. Caroline Webster Schermerhorn,
  12, 25, 80, 81, 85
  death of, 91

Astor, William Backhouse, Jr., 81

Atkinson, Florence, 215, 217, 291, 305

Atwood, Charles, 53, 55

Audita, 150

B

Baird, Jack, 75, 290

Balfour, Arthur, 124

Bankhead, Tallulah, 303

Bannister, Turpin C., 314, 315, 316

Bardo Palace, 153

Barillas Bercian, Gen. Manuel, 61

Barnes, Djuna, 120

Barrios, Algeria, 61

Barrymore, John, 304

Barthelmess, Richard, 253

Bates, Joan, 132, 143

Baxter, Oliver, 101

Baxter Homestead. *See* "Old Bay Manor
  House"

Beacon Towers, 87, 118

Beale, Phelan, 123

Beaux Arts Fashion Building &
  Promenade, 140

Beer, Thomas, 90

Belcourt, 87

Belmont, Mrs. Alva, 91, 116, 301, 305
  operetta by, 120

Belmont, Oliver Hazard Perry, 86

Berenson, Bernard, 277

Berlin, Irving, 12, 253, 262, 293, 301
  and Mizner Development Corp., *245,* 246

Betts, John, 101

Biddle, Anthony J. Drexel, Jr., 169, 177, *178,*
  179–80

Biddle, Edward, 169

Biddle, Edward, III, 179

Bierce, Ambrose, 59

Bigler, Gov. John, 22

Biltmore Hotel. *See* Merrick, George E.

Bingham, Charles W., 138, *139,* 140

Bingham, Frances. *See* Bolton, Frances Bingham

Bingham, Sen. William, 167

Birmingham, Stephen, 169

Blaine, Sec. of State James, 35, 36

Blossom, Henry, 205

Blue Heron, The, 272

Blythedunes, 140

Boca Raton Club, The, 275, 279

Boca Raton (FL), 239

    Mizner's plan for, 14–15, 242, 245–59

    See also Cloister Inn, The

Bolton, Chester C., 140–41

Bolton, Frances Bingham, 140–41

Bond, Shadrack, 19

Bourn, William B., 57–58

Box Hill, 94

Boyer, Isabelle, 131

Bradley, Edward R., 135, 141, 275, 288

Bradley, John R., 135, 275

Breakers, The, 128

Brelsford, Edmund, 133

Brelsford, John Hale, 133

Brian, Donald, 91

Brookholt, 87

Brown, A. Page, 44, 46, 52–53, 54, 95

    and Polk, 56

Brown, Mrs. Stephen, 105

Brown, Ozie, 214, 289

Brown, Stephen, 105, 118, 132

Brown Derby (restaurant), 303–4

Brown & Wilcox Co., 141

Bryan, William Jennings, 241

Buchanan, Pres. James, 81

Burden, I. Townsend, Jr., 114, 116, 117

Burgess, Gillette, 59

Burnham, Daniel, 42, 46, 55, 243, *246*

Burnham & Root (architecture firm), 52, 53

Burt, Nathaniel, 167

C

Cagney, James, 303

Cairns, Dr. Caldwell, 19

Cairns, Mary Stevenson, 19

California

    architectural styles in, 314

    Benicia, 24, 25–26, 29

    See also San Francisco (CA)

Camino Real. *See* Boca Raton (FL)

Camp, Alexander, 294

Carlisle, Jay F., 158

Carnegie, Andrew, 37, 133

    and Phipps, 186–87

Carrère & Hastings (architects), 51, 53, 86, 104, 136

    and Whitehall, 138, 140

Carstairs, Daniel H., 177

Carstairs (mansion), 196, 197, 198

Casa Apava, 141, 154

Casa Bendita, 150, 151, 165, 166, 186–89, 285

Casa Coe da Sol, 295–99, 300

Casa de Leoni, 165, 177, 184–85, 186

Casa Florencia, 201, 202–3

Casa Maria Marrone, *213*

Casa Nana, 316

Casa Serena, 275–76

Castillo del Rey, 249

Castle Mizner, 250, 251

    See also Boca Raton (FL)

Cathedral of St. Mary of Burgos, *194*, 195

Cedars, The. *See* Cockran, William Bourke

Central Equities Corp., 263, 265

Chalfin, Paul, *165*

    villa by, *126*, 127, 128, 129

Chapin, Roy D., 281

Chaplin, Charlie, 303

Chapman, F. Burnham, 170

Chase, Eleanor, 217

Chase, Horace Blanchard, 217, 240, 274, 277, 289, 293, 308

    marriage of, 30, *31*, 32

Chase, Minnie Mizner, 56, 100, 240

Chase, William Merritt, 34

Chase, Ysabel, 240, 293

Château de Maison-sur-Seine, 104

Chateau Myscene, 102, 103

Chemla, Jacob, 153, 154

Chemla Pottery, 152–53

Chicago World's Fair. *See* World's Columbian Exposition, 1893

Churchill, Lady Randolph, 107

Churchill, Lord Randolph, 82

Churchill, Winston, 101, 107

Claflin, Arthur B., house of, 7, 310

Clarke, Charles J., 134, 135

Cloister at Sea Island, The, 282, 315, 318

Cloister Inn, The, 249, 258–61, 266, 267, 279, 282

    grand opening of, *264*

    sale of, 275

Coburn, Forrest A., 138

Cockran, William Bourke, 101, 107

Coconut Grove House, 134

Coffin, Howard, 281–82

Colebrooke, Lady Alexandra, 123–24

Concha Marina, *206*, 207–8, 209

Conkling, Donald Herbert, 264

Consolidated Virginia Silver Mine, 37
Coolidge, Pres. Calvin, 240, 282
Coral Gables (FL). *See* Merrick, George E.
Cosden, Eleanor, *191,* 195–96, 200
   relationship with Mizner, 193, 199, 283
Cosden, Joshua, 193–94
   mansion of, 194–96
Cragin, C. I., 133
Crocker, Charles, 53
Crocker, Mary Ann, 53
Crocker Bank building. *See* Brown, A. Page
Croly, Herbert, 240
Cromwell, Eva Roberts. *See* Stotesbury, Eva
Cromwell, Louise, 175
Cromwell, Oliver, 168
Crosley, Stella, 265
Curl, Donald, 39, 77, 105, 158, 218, 237, 267
   on Spanish Village, 262
Cynic's Calendar, The (Mizner & Mumford),
   71, 72

D

Davidova, Lucia, *277*
Davis, Alexander Jackson, 128
Davis, Richard Harding, 39
Dawes, Charles, 263
Dawes, Rufus, 263
Dawson City (AK), 64
Deep Purple, The (Mizner & Armstrong), 121
Deering, Charles, 128, 129
Deering, James, *126,* 128, 129, 163, *165*
   See also Villa Vizcaya
DeLamar, Alice, 215, 217, 240, 251, 264–65,
   276–78
   on Mizner's personal life, 290, 291
Delmas, Delphin, 39

Delmas, Paul, 39
de Young, Michael, 52
Dieterich, Albert, 286, *287*
Dieterich, Alfred E., 114, 115
Dieterich, Charles F., 114
Dietsch, Percival, 203
Dillman, Hugh, 294
Dimick, E. N., 133, 134, 135, 136
   fountain honoring, *289*
Dimick, Frank, 132, 133
Dixie Highway. *See* Fisher, Carl
Dodge, Mrs. Horace, 196
Dolbeer, Bertha, 74, 75, 77, 290
Dolbeer, John, 74
Dole, Sanford, 70
Donnell, E. B., 155
Doro, Marie, 120
Douglas, Robert Dun, 140
Downing, Andrew Jackson, 128
Dressler, Marie, 92, 100, 120, 253, 262
Drexel, Emilie Taylor, 178
Duchess of Richelieu. *See* Wise, Elinor
   Douglas
Duke, Angier Buchanan, 179, 180, 193
Duke, Benjamin N., 180
Duke, Cordelia Biddle, 179, 180
Duke, James Buchanan, 180, 181
Duncan, Isadora, 131, 132
du Pont, T. Coleman, 12, 177, 252, 254, 256
   and Boca Raton project, 257–58
   and Mizner Development Corp., 245, 246
Duveen, Lord Joseph, 170

E

E. F. Hutton Brokerage Office, 236
Eagle's Nest, The, 105

Eames, Emma, 105
Earman, Joe, 155, 214
Ecole des Beaux Arts, 47, 49, 316
Edbrooke, Willoughby J., *56*
Edgerton, Giles, 261
Edward, Prince of Wales, 81, *82,* 200
El Mirasol, 9, 10, 150, 151, 165–66, 168,
   170–76
El Sarimento, 178, 179, 180
El Solano, 207, *273*
Emmet, Ellen, 34
Everglades Rod and Gun Club, 9, 145,
   147–58, 151, 176, 259, 272, 309
   and Casa Leoni, 185
   growth of, 210
   members of, 158–60
   on pets, 273
   photos of, 152, 154, 160, 161, 213
   Singer's apartment in, 318
Excelsior (steamer), 63, 64

F

Fair, James Graham, 37–38, *89, 90,* 91, *104*
Fair, Teresa. *See* Oelrichs, Theresa Fair
Fair, Virginia. *See* Vanderbilt, Virginia Fair
Fairbanks, Douglas, Sr., 303
Fatio, Maurice, 217, 237, 273–74, 288, *289,*
   292, 294
Fielding, Viscountess, 300
Figulus, 138, 139, 154
Fish, Mrs. Stuyvesant (Mamie), 91, 92
Fisher, Carl, 244, 248
   and Dixie Highway, 240–41
Fitzgerald, F. Scott, 101
Flagler, Henry Morrison, 51, 128, 133, 159
   fountain honoring, 289

home of, 140
hotels designed by, *1*, 51, 142
Palm Beach development by, 97, 135,
   136–38
Florida
  in 1919, 222
  growth in, 240–42, 243–44
  1928 hurricane in, 287–88
  real estate bubble in, 14, 256
  Spanish colonial history of, 51
  See also Boca Raton (FL); Palm Beach (FL)
Florida Architecture of Addison Mizner, The
   (Tarbell), 276–77, 281
Florida Embassy Club, 288
Flynn, William J., 249
Foerderer, Percival, 283
Ford, John, 106
Frankl, Paul, 298–99

G
Garfield, Abram, 141
Gedney, Jerome, house of, 184, 279–81
Geer, Albert, 133
Geiger, August, 140
Geisler, Frank, 278
Geisler, Lester, 288
Geist, Clarence, 158, 246, 275, 279
George, David Lloyd, 124
Gilded Age. *See* New York City (NY)
Gillies, Rev. Andrew, 99
Girandolle, Jerry, 291
Goad, Aileen, 60
Goad, Frank, 96
Goad, Genevieve, 60, 68, 69
Goelet, Mary, 83
Golfstream Golf Club, 196, 199

Grace, Michael P., 140
Grant, Ulysses S., 25
Greber, Jacques, 170
Green, Lewis Henry, 136
Greenway, Ned, 38, 69–70
Griffin, Marion Mahony, 143
Gropius, Walter, 318
Guest, Amy Phipps, 140
Guest, Frederick, 140
Gwin, Mary Belle, 60

H
Hamilton, F. F., 52
Hammon, H. F., 133
Harbor Hill, 104
Harris, John F., 278
Harrison, Pres. Benjamin, 21, 33
Hastings, Daniel, 28, 51, 53
Heamaw, 140, 150, 154, 166, 187
Hearst, William Randolph, 52
Hillwood, 112
Histed, Ernest W., 207
Histed, Walter, *134*
Hitchcock. Raymond, 106
Hobart, Ella, 60
Hoffman, F. Burrall, 140
  and Villa Vizcaya, *126*, 127, 128, 129, *165*
Hollins, Harry Bowly, 293
Hollins, Kim Mizner, 302
Hollins, Marion, 293
Hollins, McKim, 293
Hollins, Ysabel Chase, 302
Hooker, Joseph, 25
Hotel Ponce de Leon, 136
Hotel Rand, 106
Howard, George Bronson, 121

Hull, Lytle, 258
Hunt, Richard Morris, 55, 86, 97, 104,
   243, 316
  at Ecole des Beaux Arts, 47, 85
  and Marble House, 87, 88
  and Petit Chateau, *118*
  and White City, 42
Hunt, William Morris, 87
Hutchings, Robert, 101
Hutton, Edward F., 158, 273, 294
  and Prime house, *110*, 111–12
Huxtable, Ada Louise, 316, 317

I
Idle Hour, 87
Iglesia de la Vera Cruz, 270
Independence, sinking of, 23–24
Irving, Washington, 101

J
James, Henry, 34
Japanese Homes and Their Surroundings (Morse),
  49, 107
Jenkins, Frederick John, *123*
Jenney, William L., 243
Jerome, Jennie, 82, 107
Jerome, Leonard, 82
Johnston, Alva, 131, 203, 223, 265, 291
Jonas, Mrs. George W., 156
Jones, A. W., 282, 283
Jones, Clarence, 205, 207, *273*

K
Kenan, Mary Lily, 137, 138
Kern, Jerome, 92, 198, 301
Kimball, Fiske, 170

Kingsley, Willey Lyon, 183–84
Kirker, Harold, 54
Koehne, William, 143
Koehne, Zila, 143
Kurth, Peter, 131

L
La Bellucia, 165, 182, 183, 184, 279, 280
La Bienvenida, 286–87
Lainhart, George, 138, *139*, 141
Lake Boca Raton. *See* Boca Raton (FL)
Lanehart, Will, 133
Lang, Albert, 295
Lark, The (periodical), 56, 58–59
La Ronda, *194*, 224, 283–86, *321*
Las Manos (factory), 233
Lawes, Lewis E., 303
Leary, Timothy, 115
Le Corbusier (architect), 13
Legendary Mizners, The (Johnston), 291
Legg, Jerome B., 55
Leslie, Shane, 107
Lightbown, Charles, 150
Lightbown, Cooper, 141, 150–51, 156, 165
    See also Everglades Rod and Gun Club
Liliuokalani, Queen, 70, 71
Lincoln, Abraham, 19, 20
Livermore, Jesse, 258
Longfellow, A. W., 50
Longfellow, Henry, 101
Long Island (NY), popularity of, 101
Longstreth, Richard, 47, 50, 51, 55
Loos, Anita, 217, 304
Los Incas, 140, 150, 154, 166
Louis Philippe I, 167
Louwana, 166, 176, 177

Lusitania, sinking of, 122

M
MacArthur, Douglas, 174
Mackay, Clarence, 104–5
Mackay, John William, 104
MacMullan, Katherine, 169, 170
Major, Howard, 273
Manoir d'Ango, 49, 50, 58
Mansart, Francois, 104
Mansart, Jules Hardouin, 95
Many Mizners, The (Mizner), 122, 300, 301
Mar-a-Lago, 150, 273
Marble House, 87, 88, 97
Martin, Andrew, 42, 68
Martin, Florence Brokaw. *See* Satterwhite,
    Florence
Martin, James E., 201, 202
Martin, John W., 254
Martin, Peter, 42, 91
Maugham, Syrie, 124, 295
Mauve Decade, The (Beer), 90
Maxwell, Elsa, 120, 124, 276
May, Edward Harrison, painting by, 130
Maybeck, Bernard, 51–52, 53
McAllister, Julian, 25
McAllister, Matthew Hall, 25
McAllister, Ward, 25, 81
McCormick, Mrs. Cyrus, 52
McCormick, Robert R., 133
McKay, Katherine Duer, 104–5
McKim, Charles, 50
    See also McKim, Mead & White
McKim, Mead & White, 48–49, 50, 51, 53,
    86, 243
    and Long Island mansions, 104

Pennsylvania Station, *92*, 93
    See also White, Stanford
Mediterranean Revival architecture, 10,
    128, 231, 247, 318
    materials for, 222
    in Palm Beach, 140, 163
Melinda and Her Sisters (Belmont), 120
Merrick, George E., 243
Metcalfe, Mortimer Dickerson, 223
Miami Beach, development of, 244
Mills, Darius Ogden, 52
Mission Dolores, 55
Mission Revival architecture. See
    architecture
Mitchell, Col. Billy, 254
Mizner, Addison
    in 1927, 274, 275–77
    in 1930–1931, 294–95
    address to Women's Club, 163
    and Alaskan gold mine, 63–67
    Alexander's commission, 301–2
    Alexandre's house, 109–10
    architectural philosophy and legacy of,
        9–11, 146–47, 312–22
    arrives in Palm Beach, 125, 126, 138
    autobiography of, 300–301
    and Barrios, 61–62
    Belmont's project, 118
    Boca Raton project, 14, 239, 242, 245–67,
        311–12
    brother's house, 216
    Browns' house, 118–20
    Casa Bendita and Warden Residence,
        186–90, 192–93
    in Central America, 34–35, 36–37
    Coffin's hotel project, 281–82

commissions, 1921–24, 177, 178, 179
construction of El Mirasol, 168, 171, 172–76
creation of Woodite, 234–35
critics of, 14–15
deaths of parents, 44, 121–22
and DeLamar, 276–77, 278
designs Everglades Club, 140, 147–58, 159, 160, 163
develops Mizner Mile, 244–45
Dieterich's and Burden's houses, 114–16, 117, 286–87
Duke commission, 180–81
education of, 39–42
and Fair's daughters, 38, 39
family and early life of, 5–6, 11, 19–26, 27–32
financial problems of, 292–93
Florida Embassy Club, 288
Foerderer's commission, 283–86
friendships of, 203–5
Gedney's house, 278–81
and Greenway, 69–70
in Guatemala, 75–77, 314
Gulfstream Golf Club design, 196, 198
in Hawaii, South Pacific, Australia, 70–73
health problems of, 289–90, 293–94, 304–5
homes of, 198, 207–13
as host, 198–200
Hotel Rand project of, 106
impact of Chicago World's Fair, 1893, 42, 43, 44, 45, 46
Jones' house, 282–83
journals of, 60

La Bellucia and Casa Leoni, 182, 183, 184–86
and Lady Colebrooke, 123–24
leg injuries of, 32–33, 123, 309–11
on Long Island, 101, 103–5, 106–7, 108–9
and Martin's project, 68–69
and Maxwell, 276
Mediterranean Revival villas by, 161–62
Memorial Fountain & Plaza, 288, 289, *306*
memorial service for, 1–2, 4, 13
memory of, 8–9
New Year's Day parties of, 299–300
in New York City, 79, 87, 89–92, 95–96, 96–97
and other architects, 273–74
Parker's house, 112–14
personal and professional habits of, 214–15, 217–20, 290–92
personality of, 4–5, 12–14, 15–16, 162, 307–8, 309, 311
pet monkey of, 273, 274, 307
Playa Riente, 189, 191, 192, 193–96
and Polk, 8, *54*, 56, 57, 58, 59, 60, 243
Prime's house, 110–12
projects, 1919–24, 163, 165–67
relationships with elites, 12
relationship with Dolbeer, 74–75, 77
relationship with Jones, 205, 207
relationship with Singer, 126, 129, 215, 307–8, 310
relationship with Wilson, 16–17, 68, 99, 100, 215, 217, 308–9
Riverside Baptist Church project, 269–72
and San Francisco earthquake, 100
and Satterwhite's house, 201–3
and Singer's bungalow, 142–44

in Spain and China, 45–46
and Thayer, 200–201
trip to California, 302–3
trip with Oelrich, 96
Villa Vizcaya, 128, 129, 163
and White, 92, 94
Williams' commission, 295–99, 300
See also Mizner Industries; Mizner Development Corp.; Villa Mizner
Mizner, Charles, 19
Mizner, Edgar, 30, 97, 308
in Alaska, 63, 64
in Central America, 33
photos of, 27, 36
and Tessie Fair, 38
Mizner, Ella Watson, 22–24, 25, 26, 27, 36
children of, 28–29, 30, 31, 308–9
death of, 121–22
and San Francisco earthquake, 100
Mizner, Henry, 27, 30, 42, 240, 308
Mizner, Henry Caldwell, 19
Mizner, Lansing, 20–22, 36, 100
Addison's respect for, 31–32
children of, 308–9
death of, 44
envoy to Central America, 33, 35–36
home of in Benicia, 27–28
Mizner, Lansing, Jr., 27, 30, 308
Mizner, Lansing Bond, 19, 21, 27
marriage of, 24, 26
Mizner, Lawrence, 19, 20
Mizner, Mary Isabella, 27, 31, 32, 36
marriage of, 30, 32, 308
Mizner, Murray, 30
Mizner, Rev. Henry, 262
Mizner, William, 27, 30, 42

in Alaska, 63, 64, 66, 67
and San Francisco earthquake, 100
Mizner, Wilson, 16–17, 28, 120–21, 215,
    308–9
  in Alaska, 63, 64
  and Armitage, 274–75
  and Boca Raton development, 249–50,
    250–51, 252, 258, 265
  in Central America, 33, 35
  and Duke project, 181, 183
  early life of, 29, 30, 31, 39–40
  financial problems of, 293
  in Hollywood, 303–4, 305
  home of, 216, 217
  and Hotel Rand, 106
  marriage of, 97, 99–100
  and Mizner Mile, 244
  in New York, 96, 106
  in Palm Beach, 217, 239
  relationship with Addison, 68, 215, 217,
    308–9
  and Yerkes, 205
Mizner Development Corp., 245, 250, *252*,
    258, 279
  ads by, 257
  bankruptcy of, 263–64, 265, 267, 275
  in Boca Raton, 239
  El Distrito de Boca Raton (real estate parcel),
    261–62
  offer to postal service, 254, *255*
  See also Boca Raton, development of
Mizner Industries, 221, 224–38, 245, *292*
  bankruptcy of, 302
Monson, Sarah Cowen, 107, 108
Moore, Alexander P., 260
Moore, Edward S., 208, 210

Morgan, Jim, 280, 281
Morgan, Ranney, 280, 281
Morse, Edward S., 49, 107
Mosque of Kairouan, 153
Mueller, Jose, 236
Mumford, Ethel Watts, 70–71
Mundy, Harold Hastings, 140
Munn, Charles A., Jr., 176–77
  house of, 166
Munn, Gurnee, 176–77
  house of, 166
Munn, Louise, 177, 195, 205
Munn, Mary Louise, 177

N

Nesbit, Evelyn, 94
New York City (NY)
  architecture in, 48–49
  Gilded Age in, 79–83, 90
Nicholson, James R., 265
Nome (AK), 66
Norris, Frank, 59
Novelty Works, 154

O

Oelrichs, Hermann, 38, *89*, 90
Oelrichs, Theresa Fair, 38–39, 89, 90–91,
    92, 104, 105
  house of, 94–95
  trip with Mizner, 32, 96
"Old Bay Manor House," 101
Old Floresta, 262
  See also Boca Raton, development of
Olmsted, Frederick Law, 51
Olson, Addison Mizner, 65
Only Law, The (Mizner & Howard), 121

*On the Edge of the World: Four Architects in
    San Francisco at the Turn of the Century*
    (Longstreth), 48
Orr-Cahall, Christina, 42, 287, 314

P

Paget, Alexandra Harriet. *See* Colebrooke,
    Lady Alexandra
Palais, Chateaux, Hotels, et Maisons de France
    (Sauvageot), 105
Palladio, Andrea, 128
Palm Beach Daily News, 137
Palm Beach (FL), 17, 79, 97, 160, 321–22
  in 1919, 222
  in 1930, 292
  after WWI, 157
  Bath and Tennis Club, 150, 179
  Bradley's Beach Club, 141–42
  Floral Park, 135–36
  1928 hurricane in, 287–88
  Jungle Road, 134
  Mediterranean Revival influence in, 140
  Memorial Fountain & Plaza, 288, 289, *306*
  Philadelphians in, 167–68
  popularity of, 126, 128, 157
  in 1920s, 162
  settlement and development of, 132–40
  St. Edward's Church in, 223
  See also Everglades Rod and Gun Club
Palm Beach Inn. *See* Royal Poinciana Hotel
Palm Beach National Bank, 264
Palm Beach Yacht Club (PBYC), 133, 135
Parker, John Alley, house of, 112–13, 114
Patio de las Escuelas Menores, 155
Patio del Palacio de la Salinas, 46
Paul, Mary Astor, 177

Pennsylvania Station, *92*, 93
Petit Chateau, 84, 85–86
Petronis, Edith, 295–96, 299
Petronis, Henry, 299
Phipps, Anne, 139
Phipps, Henry, 133, 139–40, 186–87
Phipps, Henry C., 140, 176
Phipps, John S., 140, *166*, 186, 187
Phipps, Mrs. Henry Carnegie, 140
Pierre, Prince of Monaco, 276
Piper, Lilias, 219
Pissis, Albert, 52
Playa Riente, 165, 189, 192, 193, 194–96,
    285–86, 321
  floor plan of, 191
  and Lightbown, 151
Polk, W. W., 55
Polk, Willis J., 53–59, 313
  and Bourn's house, 57–58
  and City Beautiful movement, 242, *246*
  employs Mizner, 8, 10, 46, 52
Ponce de Leon Hotel, 51–52
Pope, John Russell, 104
Porter, Bruce, 59
Porter, Cole, 106
Post, C. W., *110*
Post, George B., 243
Post, Marjorie Merriweather, *110*, 112,
    273, 294
Potter, Dr. R. B., 138
Potter, George, 141
Prathers, Dyoll, 150
Prime, William A., house of, 110–12
Pulitzer, Joseph, 141

R
Rand, Ellen. *See* Emmet, Ellen
Raschen, Henry, painting by, 31
Raynor, Seth, 158
Reichenbach, Harry, 252–53, 256–57, 265
Reyna Barrios, José Maria, 61–62
Reynolds, Sir Joshua, 23
Richardson, Henry Hobson, 49–50, 51, 55,
    56, 107
  architecture style of, 53
  and Ecole des Beaux Arts, 47
Ritz Carlton Cloister Inn. *See* Cloister Inn
Ritz-Carlton Hotel, 258
Riverside Baptist Church, 269–72
Robert Rossman Co., The, 153
Roberts, Kenneth, 241
Roberts, Mary Fanton, 145, 146, 225
Robinson, Dwight, 262
Robinson, Edward G., 303
Roche, Arthur Somers, 12
Roosevelt, Pres. Franklin D., 34
Root, John W., 243
Rosecliff, 91, 92, 94–95
Ross, Donald J., 249
Ross, Gary, 280, 281
Roy, Jack, 291
Royal Poinciana Hotel, 95, 128, 135, 136,
    137, 142
  photos of, 98, *99*, 138, 142
Runyon, Damon, 17

S
Saint Sergius church, 270
Salm, Countess Millicent, 262
San Francisco (CA)
  architecture in 1890s, 52, 53
  earthquake in, 100
  growth of, 24–25, 37
  Hallidie Building in, 58
San Vitale (church), 269, 270
Satterwhite, Dr. Preston Pope, 202, 203
Satterwhite, Florence, 201, 202–3
Sauvageot, Claude, 105
Schweinfurth, Albert, 53
Scully, Vincent, 50
Sea Gull Cottage, 133–34
Seebohm, Carolyn, 41
Semple, James, 20, 21
Semple, Robert Baylor, 21
Sert, Jose Maria, 195
Shepley, Rutan & Coolidge (architects), 51
Shingle Style (architecture), 50, 53, 58
Showalter, Camille, 122
Silver Kings. *See* Fair, James Graham
Simonson, Byron, 288, 298
Simonson, Mrs. Byron, 295–96
Sin Cuidado, 208, 210
Singer, Isaac, *125*, 129, 130–31
Singer, Isabelle-Blanche, 131
Singer, Mortimer, 131
Singer, Paris, 12, 125, 128, 129–30, 131–32,
    158, 162, 203, 310
  apartment of, 152, 153, 318
  and The Blue Heron, 272
  bungalow of, 143–44
  death of, 302
  and Everglades Club, 145, 147, 148, 156,
    157, 160, 161, 309
  in Florida real estate, 244
  and golf club, 158
  and Lady Colebrooke, *123*, 124
  and Mizner Development Corp., 246

on Mizner's buildings, 322
and Mizner's factory, 225
moves to France, 292
in Palm Beach, 138, 142
relationship with Mizner, 126, 129, 215, 276, 307–8, 310
visit to Villa Vizcaya, 163
See also Via Parigi
Singer, Winaretta, 131
Singer Manufacturing Co. *See* Singer, Isaac
Sloane, George, 209
Sloane, Isabel Dodge, 209
Smith, Alfred E., 107
Smith, George Washington, 286, *287*
Society of California Pioneers, 19
Somborn, Herbert, 303
South Florida, 222
skilled labor in, 8
See also Florida
Spain, architecture of, 45–46
Spanish Village, 262
See also Boca Raton, development of
St. Mary's of the Pacific (school), 29
Stanford, Leland, 51
Starr, Kevin, 57
Steinert, Oscar J., 295
Stickley, Gustav, 153
Stotesbury, Edward T., 9, 168, 170, 179, 185, 203
house of, 10, 166
Stotesbury, Eva, 9, 168–70, 171, 176, 179, *191*, 203, 205
house of, 10, 166
at Mizner's memorial service, 2
party for, 217
Sullivan, Louis, 42

T
Talbott, Harold, 282
Talbott, Katherine, 282, 283
Tarbell, Ida, 260–61, 277–78
Thaw, Harry, 94
Thayer, Margaret, 195, 199, 200, 290
relationship with Addison, 282–83
Thomas, Leonard, 177, 184–85
Thomas, Ralph, 108
Thomas, Rev. Nathaniel Seymour, 2, 4
Tindall, George B., 15
Touchstone Convalescent's Club, *145*, 146, 147, 156
See also Everglades Rod and Gun Club
Treanor, William, 274
Trumbauer, Horace, 9, 139, 170, 172, 181, 294
Tunisian Products, Inc., 154
Twain, Mark, 80

U
University of Salamanca, 11, 147
Urban, Joseph, *178*, 273

V
Vallejo, Mariano, 21
Van Brunt, Henry, 55
Van Buren, Pres. Martin, 20
Vanderbilt, Alva Erskine Smith, 83, 85, 86–87
Vanderbilt, Com. Cornelius, 23, 83, 91
Vanderbilt, Consuelo, 83
Vanderbilt, Cornelius, II, 138
Vanderbilt, Harold, 207, 245, 288, *289*
Vanderbilt, Virginia Fair, 90, 91, 104, 105, 249

house of, 97
Vanderbilt, William Henry, 83
Vanderbilt, William K., 83, 91, 245
house of, 83, 84, 85, 86
Vanderbilt, William K., II, 12, *90*, 91
house of, 97
Long Island mansion of, 105
Van Rensselaer, Mariana Griswold, 50
Veblen, Thorstein, 80–81
Via Mizner, *177*, 209, 210, 211, 212–13, 214
mixed-use development of, 165, 167
Via Parigi, 165, 167, *177*, 210, 212, 214
Vickers. Raymond B., 263
Villa Artemis, 140, 150, 151, 154
Villa Flora, 13, 234
Villa Mizner, 165, 177, 198, 209, 212, 213, 250
living room of, 2, 3
view from, 320
See also Mizner, Addison
Villa Rezzonico Borella, 128
Villa Vizcaya, *126*, 127, 128, 143, 154, 163, 164, 165
Villa Zila. *See* Griffin, Marion Mahony
Volk, John, 273
Vought, Harry, 262

W
Wanamaker, John, 220
Wanamaker, Marie Louise. *See* Munn, Mary Louise
Wanamaker, Mary Brown, 177
Wanamaker, Rodman, 12, 177, 220, 245, 246
Warburton, Barclay H., 177, *213*, 292
Warden, William Gray, 189–90, 196

Warden, William Gray, II, 177
Warden Residence, 150, 165, 188, 190,
    192–93, 226
  staircase and ceiling decoration, 189
Ware, William Robert, 47, 56
Warner, Jack, 303
Warren, Whitney, 105
Watson, Asa, *24*
Watson, Ella. *See* Mizner, Ella Watson
Watson, John, 23, 24
  portrait of, 22
Watson, Mary Reynolds, 23, 24, 29
Waugh, Alex, 19, 203, 274, 293, 308
  antiques business of, 218
  on Mizner, 231
  on Mizner's car, 215
  working for Mizner, 222, 224
Wave, The, 56–57
Wector, Dixon, 167
Wells, Joseph, 49

Wharton, Edith, 92, 128
White, Archibald S., 106
White, Stanford, 44, 46, 50–51, 55, 58,
    260, 312
  and Harbor Hill, 104
  houses by, 91
  and Manoir d'Ange, *49*
  and Mizner, 92, 94
  Newport Casino, 50
  and Rosecliff, 95
"White City." *See* World's Columbian
    Exposition, 1893
Whitehall, 140
Whitemarsh Hall, 170
  See also Stotesbury, Eva
Widener, Joseph, 273, 292
Wilde, Oscar, 37
Wilgus, William J., portrait by, 22
William Gray Warden, 165
Williams, William J., 295

Wise, Elinor Douglas, 219
Wood, Ruby Ross, 219–20
Woodite. *See* Mizner Industries
World's Columbian Exposition, 1893, 42, 43,
    44, 46, 53, 243
  and City Beautiful Movement, 14, 242,
    243, *246*
Worth, Charles Frederick, 85, *86*
Wright, Frank Lloyd, 13, 143, 299, 312, 319
Wyeth, Marion Sims, 158, 272–73, 288

Y
Yerkes, Charles, 97, 99, *181*, 205
Yerkes, Myra, 97, 99, 100, *181*, 205
Yznaga, Consuelo, 82, 83, 85

Z
Ziegfeld, Flo, 177

ACKNOWLEDGMENTS

We endeavor to recognize the many individuals, groups, and institutions, present and long absent, that have supported our understanding and appreciation of Addison Cairns Mizner, a man of many interlocking circles of friends, family, clients, employees, craftsmen, and builders.

Examining the life and work of Addison Mizner has been a highly entertaining and rewarding experience, but also one that presented challenges. The houses designed by Mizner have been either razed or, with few exceptions, altered to such a degree that the extant structure obscures the architect's original intent. Happily, there is sufficient scholarship and significant archives to permit an assessment of the architect's concepts and construction as well as an appreciation of his rich personal associations.

The record of Mizner's life and times has been mined extensively and the published writing about him has been deeply valuable to our appreciation of his personal vision and growth, his professional contribution, and his many deep relationships in New York and Palm Beach. The 1928 *Florida Architecture of Addison Mizner* by Frank E. Geisler and Ida Tarbell, produced by Mizner's close friend Alice DeLamar, remains the most complete visual record of Mizner's South Florida work between 1919 and 1928.

From his death in 1933, Mizner's reputation suffered until new interest in the architect and his work was found in the mid-1970s. In 1977, an exhibition was organized by the Norton Gallery of Art and sponsored by Norton, the Society of the Four Arts, the Henry Morrison Flagler Museum, and the Historical Society of Palm Beach County. The catalog, with text by Christina Orr, is represented as the "first contemporary publication on the architect, Addison Mizner."

Many of the photographs in this catalog and so many other books on Mizner are by Craig Kuhner, the excellent architect and architectural photographer who joined to produce our book. Craig is a consummate professional and brilliant photographer whose collection of Mizner architectural images is without parallel. Having captured, from 1977 to 1983, so many homes before their demolition or modification beyond recognition, Craig's photographs are particularly valuable in assessing Mizner's design ideas.

J. Camille Showalter's Oakland Museum exhibition and catalog, *The Many Mizners: California Clan Extraordinary*, which ran from November 7, 1978, to February 5, 1979, sought to describe more fully the Mizner family history and its relationship to the underpinnings of Mizner's interests and architectural origins.

For the Oakland exhibition, Christina Orr-Cahall's catalog essay, "Addison—From Scrambled Eggs to Red Tile

Roofs" was taken from her excellent 1979 Yale dissertation on Mizner. Orr-Cahall's dissertation explicated the academic origins of Mizner's work by tying specific organization, plans, and details to images from Mizner's library, scrapbooks, and places with which he would have been familiar from his extensive travels.

Donald W. Curl's *Mizner's Florida: American Resort Architecture*, published in 1984, is a valuable academic approach to Mizner's professional growth as an architect, and his *The Boca Raton Resort & Club: Mizner's Inn*, written in 2008 in collaboration with the Boca Raton Historical Society, offers a thorough treatment of the architect's involvement in Boca Raton. Caroline Seebohm's *Boca Rococo* is a comprehensive and charming account of Mizner's life and work. Our beaten copies of these books are ample testimony to the value we drew from these authors.

A 2014 house party focused on architecture, hosted by Barbara and Wesley Price, was the impetus for a deeper examination of Mizner's life, and Martha Perkins's suggestion that we write a new book about Mizner was followed by years of research, dialogue, and writing. Our abiding curiosity about the architect was also enriched by several individuals who were unhesitatingly unselfish with their time and always willing to share their knowledge.

Betse Gori at the Society of the Four Arts was very generous with her time and provided ready access to the Mizner Collection and particularly to the original Mizner scrapbooks, which were, by far, the most illuminating gateway to the working of Mizner's architectural impressions and original thought about antiquity and its uses and applications.

Debi Murray and Nick Golubov at the Historical Society of Palm Beach County have been both highly resourceful advisors and encyclopedic sources of specific knowledge about Mizner and Palm Beach. Both have been patient with naïve questions and unrelenting in fulfilling copious requests for archives, plans, and images. Each should know how important they have been to our research, writing, and understanding. We appreciate Debi's critical review of transcript portions.

Susan Gillis of the Boca Raton Historical Society and Museum has been an enthusiastic supporter of our research and writing. She and Bonnie Dearborn have provided excellent tours of Mizner's extant architecture in Boca Raton and have supported our understanding of the original 1925 real estate development goals and original plan. Also, the museum's collection and documentation of Mizner Industries artifacts were critical to our appreciation of the architect's entrepreneurial strength and to appreciating the magnitude of Mizner's manufacturing and distribution enterprises. Mizner Industries proved to be a resource for architects and builders alike and enabled the deep-rooted architecture of Mediterranean Revival to dominate South Florida for generations.

We also benefitted from the extensive understanding of Mizner and his architecture from Fred Eckel, the partner and research contributor of Donald Curl. Bill Jones III, the grandson of the developer of The Cloister at Sea Island, happily shared reminiscences of his grandparents and their association with Mizner. Janet Murphy's historical knowledge of Cooper Lightbown and his insufficiently heralded role in building so many of the houses and institutions that define Palm Beach contributed to a clearer picture of the roles and responsibilities of Palm Beach builders from 1912 to 1928. For the provision of many records, articles, and heretofore unseen photographs of Casa Coe da Sol's construction, we thank Amy and Laurie Petronis, daughters of Edith and Henry Petronis, who bought a worn Casa Coe da Sol in the early 1960s and restored it to its original intent, complete with furnishings.

We would like to thank Amanda Skier of the Preservation Society of Palm Beach, Anna Bunting of the Oakland Museum of California, and Beverly Phelan of the Benicia History Museum for the support of their organizations and access to archives. Also, our persistent interest in the social and architectural history of Palm Beach was continually informed by the books and articles of Augustus Mayhew.

For the many architectural drawings in our book, we thank Chase R. Cothran and for tours of West Palm Beach neighborhoods made extensively with products of Mizner Industries, we thank Kelly Shoaf.

Of course, this book would not have been possible without the wise guidance of Gene Brissie, our editor, and the enthusiastic patronage of Jed Lyons, our publisher.

Writing a book on Addison Mizner provided an unforeseen gift to the authors. On our quest, we consistently encountered individuals who appreciated Addison Mizner as an inimitable personality and remarkable architect who enriched so many with his humanity and creativity. The shared anecdotes and laughs temporarily brought the great man back to life, and the analysis and discussion of his work provided endless gratification. We hope that some of this joy and pleasure shines through in the book.